Heidegger in the Literary World

New Heidegger Research

Series Editors: Gregory Fried, Professor of Philosophy, Boston College, USA and Richard Polt, Professor of Philosophy, Xavier University, USA

The *New Heidegger Research* series promotes informed and critical dialogue that breaks new philosophical ground by taking into account the full range of Heidegger's thought, as well as the enduring questions raised by his work.

Titles in the Series:
After Heidegger?
Edited by Gregory Fried and Richard Polt
Correspondence 1949–1975
By Martin Heidegger and Ernst Jünger – Translated by Timothy Quinn
Existential Medicine
Edited by Kevin Aho
Heidegger and Jewish Thought
Edited by Micha Brumlik and Elad Lapidot
Heidegger and the Environment
Casey Rentmeester
Heidegger and the Global Age
Edited by Antonio Cerella and Louiza Odysseos
Heidegger Becoming Phenomenological: Preferring Dilthey to Husserl, 1916–25
Robert C. Scharff
Heidegger in Russia and Eastern Europe
Edited by Jeff Love
Heidegger's Gods: An Ecofeminist Perspective
Susanne Claxton
Making Sense of Heidegger
Thomas Sheehan
Proto-Phenomenology and the Nature of Language
Lawrence J. Hatab
Heidegger in the Islamicate World
Edited by Kata Moser, Urs Gösken and Josh Michael Hayes
Time and Trauma: Thinking Through Heidegger in the Thirties
Richard Polt
Contexts of Suffering: A Heideggerian Approach to Psychopathology
Kevin Aho
Heidegger's Phenomenology of Perception: An Introduction, Volume I
David Kleinberg-Levin
Confronting Heidegger: A Critical Dialogue on Politics and Philosophy
Edited by Gregory Fried
Proto-Phenomenology, Language Acquisition, Orality and Literacy: Dwelling in Speech II
Lawrence J. Hatab

Transcending Reason: Heidegger on Rationality
Edited by Matthew Burch and Irene McMullin
The Fate of Phenomenology: Heidegger's Legacy
William McNeill
Agency, Freedom, and Responsibility in the Early Heidegger
Hans Pedersen
Heidegger's Phenomenology of Perception: Learning to See and Hear Hermeneutically, Volume II
David Kleinberg-Levin
Towards a Polemical Ethics: Between Heidegger and Plato
Gregory Fried
Thought Poems: A Translation of Heidegger's Verse
By Martin Heidegger – Translated by Eoghan Walls
Correspondence: 1919–1973
By Martin Heidegger and Karl Löwith – Translated by J. Goesser Assaiante and S. Montgomery Ewegen
Heidegger and the Holy
Edited by Richard Capobianco
Heidegger in the Literary World
Edited by Florian Grosser and Nassima Sahraoui

Heidegger in the Literary World

Variations on Poetic Thinking

Edited by
Florian Grosser and Nassima Sahraoui

ROWMAN & LITTLEFIELD
Lanham • Boulder • New York • London

Published by Rowman & Littlefield
An imprint of The Rowman & Littlefield Publishing Group, Inc.
4501 Forbes Boulevard, Suite 200, Lanham, Maryland 20706
www.rowman.com

86-90 Paul Street, London EC2A 4NE

Selection and editorial matter © by Florian Grosser and Nassima Sahraoui 2021.

Copyright in individual chapters is held by the respective chapter authors.

All rights reserved. No part of this book may be reproduced in any form or by any electronic or mechanical means, including information storage and retrieval systems, without written permission from the publisher, except by a reviewer who may quote passages in a review.

British Library Cataloguing in Publication Information Available

Library of Congress Cataloging-in-Publication Data available

ISBN 978-1-5381-6255-2 (cloth)
ISBN 978-1-5381-6257-6 (pbk.)
ISBN 978-1-5381-6256-9 (electronic)

Contents

Variations on a Theme of "Poetic Thinking": An Introduction   ix
Florian Grosser and Nassima Sahraoui

PART I: IN-BETWEEN PHILOSOPHY AND LITERATURE   1

Text, Exegesis and Salvation   3

1   Heidegger and the Critics   5
     Julia A. Ireland

2   Heidegger as Introduction to Talmud   21
     Elad Lapidot

3   Reactionary Nostalgia: Badiou, Heidegger and the Poets   37
     Luca Di Blasi

4   In the Outhouse of Being: What Satires Tell Us about Heidegger's Philosophy   47
     Dieter Thomä

Displacing the House of Being   65

5   "Beth – That Is the House": Paul Celan's Hebrew Dwelling   67
     Simone Stirner

6   Meridians of Truth: From Heidegger's Geography of Being to Celan's Topology of Language   81
     Nassima Sahraoui

7   Handke's Doubt: *Slow Homecoming* in Conversation with Heidegger   103
     Florian Grosser

PART II: LITERARY RECEPTION POLITICS BETWEEN EAST AND WEST — 123

Hölderlin and the Poetics of the States — 125

8 "The Right to Be": Stevens and Heidegger on Thinking and Poetising — 127
Frederick Dolan

9 "Victory Is an Illusion of Philosophers and Fools": Heidegger, Faulkner and the Ruination of the Proper — 141
Benjamin Brewer

10 "The Gods Are Never Quite Forgotten": John Ashbery's Heidegger — 157
Luke Carson

11 Heidegger's Mistress? Meditations on *Dasein* in David Markson's *Wittgenstein's Mistress* — 169
Tim Personn

Crossing the Boundaries of the Other: History, Time and Silence — 183

12 The Impossible Death of Julia de Burgos: Reading "¡Dádme mi número!" at the Limits of *Dasein* — 185
Ronald Mendoza-de Jesús

13 Lezama Lima and the Resurrection of the Image (An Ontological Enigma) — 205
Mauricio González

14 The Boundary of Ontological Time and its Crossing: Shūzō Kuki's Analysis of Japanese Poetry as an Unrealised Dialogue with Heidegger — 229
Yohei Kageyama

15 Heidegger and Russian Revolutionary Nonsense — 241
Jeff Love

Bibliography — 255

Index — 273

About the Contributors — 283

Variations on a Theme of "Poetic Thinking"
An Introduction
Florian Grosser and Nassima Sahraoui

It is one of the few uncontested notions in the vast, notoriously charged field of Heidegger research that the trajectory of Heidegger's intellectual development is marked by a turn towards "poetic thinking". Whether this turn is situated after *Being and Time*, understood as a response to his ill-fated political engagement in support of the Nazi movement, or associated with his post-war writings, commentators both affirmative and critical of Heidegger's shift from philosophy to poetics agree that it is the foil on which crucial tenets of his later thought are formulated as they relate to art and its transformative capacities or to reconceiving "world" in terms of the "fourfold". Whether "poetic", *dichterisch* is read in the narrow sense and tied to Heidegger's reflections on specific poets or interpreted more broadly as shorthand for the "essencing" of the truth happening that is art, this distinct reorientation is seen as a culmination point of Heidegger's programmatic "destruction of metaphysics". The wide consensus concerning the occurrence and significance of this poetic substitution among Heidegger scholars – a consensus that cuts across disciplinary and ideological, as well as philological and philosophical differences – has brought about remarkable structural similarities in the manner in which Heidegger's "poetic thinking" is approached. With very few exceptions, studies on the subject concur in assuming that either certain texts written by Heidegger himself or certain texts designated by him as manifestations of such an alternative, post-metaphysical mode of thought are the privileged sites in which it unfolds.[1] It is on the basis of this assumption that achievements and limitations of "late Heidegger" are analysed or that the (in-)adequacy of his interpretations and appropriations of the works of poets – most notably, of Friedrich Hölderlin – is examined.

This volume takes a different path: whilst heeding Heidegger's commitment to the idea that poetising thought allows for new forms of being in language, for disclosing experiences and naming phenomena anew, and for transforming interpersonal, communal configurations, it questions, displaces and deconstructs the very same. Hence, this volume inverts the standard approach in Heidegger research: rather than placing Heidegger's own understanding and expression of "poetic thinking" at the centre, rather than taking its lead entirely from his idiosyncratic version thereof, the volume explores variations on a theme of "poetic thinking" that have been proposed by poets and writers themselves. Their works reveal differing degrees of affinities and differences with, or even rejections of the Heideggerian notion and framework.

Thus, the fifteen contributions assembled here do not primarily focus on the way in which Heidegger draws on poetry from Pindar to Novalis, Georg Trakl and Paul Celan and on literature from Fyodor Dostoevsky to Knut Hamsun, Ernst Jünger and Rainer Maria Rilke in his own poetico-philosophical endeavours. Instead, the essays pay particular attention to the differing artistic repertoires in which poets and writers have worked in light of, have worked with, worked against or worked through these endeavours, in which they have taken up, modified or disallowed certain pertinent motifs, questions and problems. This inversion as to the point of departure – an inversion in emphasis from "Heidegger" to "the poets" – opens up a number of novel and productive perspectives.

First, it gives access to a unique, yet rarely appreciated strand within the reception history of Heidegger's thought since the middle of the 20th century. Unlike the discourses and "controversies" – often amplified to "scandals" in the mediatised public – on Heidegger in academic philosophy, the impact of his work on disciplines such as psychology, or its dissemination in popular culture,[2] the manifold ways in which poets, novelists and playwrights have addressed Heideggerian concepts and concerns remain largely outside the scope of how this history is narrated. This is all the more surprising as the list of writers who, at one point or another in their lives, have engaged with Heidegger's oeuvre includes prominent names, John Ashbery and Samuel Beckett among them,[3] and even five Nobel Prize laureates: Thomas Mann, Saul Bellow, Günter Grass, Elfriede Jelinek and Peter Handke; and as, since the middle of the past century, many more literary movements – from the American "Beat Generation" to the "New People" (*Neue Leute*) in Germany – and individual authors – for instance, Cormac McCarthy in his "border trilogy" or Benjamin Kunkel in *Indecision* – have drawn on or responded to fragments of Heideggerian thought in their explorations of "Being-in-the-world" under contemporary conditions.[4] Granted, not all encounters by writers with Heidegger's thought have left cognisable literary marks: one would be hard-pressed to find traces of Max Frisch's sympathetic review of the 1936 lecture "The Origin of the Work of Art" Heidegger gave in Zurich in his novels and plays – or to argue that Ingeborg Bachmann's poems, libretti, short stories and novels reflect the lasting influence of her dissertation on "The Critical Reception of Martin Heidegger's Existential Philosophy".[5] Yet, there is an abundance of material, scattered not only across different literary genres and styles, movements and periods, but also spread across the globe, that invites the tracing and charting of this unique line of Heidegger reception. It is this material, it is the practice of (re-)reading, of (re-)appropriation, deconstruction, inversion, disfiguration and critique employed by writers who have come into contact with Heidegger's thinking, poetic and otherwise, that our collected volume exhibits: its focus is on the ways in which Heidegger's reflections on language, text and interpretation, on being at home and experiencing the foreign, or on late-modern disorientation and nihilism have served as the background against which literary projects have formulated and performatively realised diverse versions of "poetic thinking".

Second, and in addition to analyses of individual poetic and literary works that are directly related to Heideggerian themes, the proposed shift in approach and emphasis allows for a reappraisal of literary-philosophical constellations that, albeit independent of any immediate influence, are nonetheless indicative of certain parallels in content or of certain resonances in "mood". Whether such constellations unfold around explorations into the origin of language in silence, into the "groundlessness" of existence or into the dialectics of "danger" and "salvation". of immanence and transcendence in the technological age, they often bridge considerable distances in space and time as well as in cultural context and political orientation: as demonstrated by some of the essays included in this volume, Heidegger becomes legible in unforeseen ways once his thinking is brought into conversation with the Talmudic tradition, with experiments in poetry at the time of the Russian Revolution, or with mid-20th-century Latin American literature. Becoming aware of affinities as well as productive dissimilarities and tensions outside and beyond the scope of German- and English-language literatures makes possible recontextualisations that, in contesting and "deprovincialising" well-established interpretive habits, shed new light on Heidegger's work.

Finally, investigating the specific case of "the poets and Heidegger" points beyond itself since it invites a more general reassessment of the relation between literature and philosophy. Among other things, the various forms in which elements of Heideggerian thought get appropriated, transformed and rejected by writers or reflected in vague, often broken mirror images in their works, constitute renegotiations concerning the question what philosophical "access rights" to literary texts – and vice versa – entail. Attesting to the agency and resistance of poetry and literature with respect to philosophy, the contributions in this collected volume challenge the notion that poems, novels and plays serve as freely available material to be seized and deployed at the sovereign discretion of philosophers, predetermined to illustrate their arguments, to advance their programmes, to render accessible *logos* through *mythos*. Besides tracing such renegotiations, the contributions also question the very gesture – one that Heidegger is not immune to – with which philosophers declare selected writers and works to possess relevance; a gesture which, to draw on Arthur Danto's critical comparison, in the absence of comprehensive literary-historical expertise and non-idiosyncratic criteria is reminiscent of the royal act of conferring knighthood.[6] In examining how writers have approached and processed a philosopher's text, they thus probe the possibilities of a literary hermeneutics that is more tentative, experimental and playful – of what Jacques Derrida calls "an ethics or politics of reading" in which interpretations are "modest",[7] are suggestions at the beginning of a conversation open to interruption and critique rather than instructions that lay claim to authoritatively unlocking a text's hidden meaning or to determining its "historical" weight. An ethical interest also comes to light in some of the essays in this collection that consider implications of the narrative logic inherent to literary and philosophical writing, respectively: unconcerned with meeting the formal demands of generality, linearity and systematicity, the poems and novels perceptively and imaginatively capture unique lived, situated experiences, in particular of suffering, injustice and violence.

In bringing together these perspectives, the volume unveils the immense creativity that crystallises in poetic and literary responses to, in traces and disseminations of Heidegger's thinking. In its interdisciplinary and intercultural approach, it questions the predominant vocabularies of science, of (the) capital, culture and, not least, of the colonial and finally points to new ways to critically intervene in current philosophical and literary debates.

The individual contributions are organised in two parts. All essays included in the first part address major philosophical and literary concepts, such as being-towards-death, existence and dwelling, geographies of home and, not least, language, text and exegesis. Layer by layer, they unearth the dialectic structures of the strange realm *Between Philosophy and Literature*, and also between poetry and politics, narration and phenomenality of the world. This "in-between" might be seen as an abyss; first and foremost, however, it is a potential source for developing another, a more critical line of thought. Taking its point of departure from poetic and literary deconstructions of Heidegger's thinking in the "States" and traversing the boundaries, borders, thresholds and pathologies of the so-called Western hemisphere, the essays of the second part of the volume discuss *Literary Reception Politics Between East and West*. They question time, limits and death, as well as the politics of dialogue and silence, the ruins of *Dasein*, and finally revolution.

TEXT, EXEGESIS, SATIRE

All four essays in the opening section depart from a meta-philosophical and meta-philological question: how are texts and their exegeses related to historical, intellectual and editorial context? The authors approach this challenging question by contextualising the political and metaphysical role of poetry and literature *in* Heidegger as well as the implications *of* his destructive readings of poetic and literary texts from four different relational angles: a critical editorial history of Heidegger's reading of Hölderlin's *Wie wenn am Feiertage . . . /As when on a holiday . . .*; a political cross-reading of Heidegger's "poeticised" thinking and the Talmud; an examination of Heidegger's turn to a "God [that] can save us" in *and* against Alain Badiou's interpretation of that God being the "God of the poets"; and a contraposition between the history of satirical approaches to Heidegger on the one hand and, on the other, the relation of Heidegger's own work to the comical through its counterpart, the sublime.

What is the "poet's vocation" in this fiercely disputed field *in-between* text and interpretation, Julia A. Ireland asks in her contribution. She departs from Heidegger's unpublished correspondence with Eduard Lachmann on Hölderlin's hymn *As when on a holiday* . . . to explore this paradoxical realm. Ireland reflects on this paradox through Hölderlin's presentation of the notion of danger in his reception of the divine as well as on Heidegger's inclusion of a variant referring to Semele's ashes – a Greek goddess mentioned in the poem. In the course of her analysis, she unveils the unique, but also controversial character of Heidegger's Hölderlin reception. She finally argues that danger establishes a historicity of reading that distinguishes Heidegger from his critics.

The interplay between historicity and textual exegeses is the point of departure of Elad Lapidot's contribution. Lapidot focuses on one of the oldest and most venerable of all text corpuses, the Talmud, and opposes it with the Western philosophical tradition, which not only seldomly mentions the Talmud, but is convoyed by an inherent anti-Semitism. Heidegger, following this tradition, never directly referred to the Talmud and where he indirectly does so (as in the *Black Notebooks*), it is in terms of the strongly negative, anti-Semitically charged stereotypes of "the" Jewish. At the same time, Heidegger deconstructs the very same philosophical tradition for its insistence on the metaphysical *logos* – a critical movement that has been identified by recent scholarship as a central feature of rabbinic literature. The historical setting notwithstanding, Lapidot therefore points out surprising moments of contact between Heideggerian and Talmudic text and text theory, finally suggesting a comparative grammato-political theory.

Whilst Heidegger's destruction of metaphysics has shaken the very foundations of the Western philosophical tradition, his famous late proclamation that "only a god can save us" is undeniably one of his most peculiar and contested statements. Luca Di Blasi approaches this statement through a specific exegetical reading: that of French philosopher Alain Badiou who argues that Heidegger referred to a *different* God, namely the "God of the poets". In his contribution, Di Blasi critically discusses Badiou's interpretation of the "God of the poets" and illustrates how the latter, at the same time, takes up and rejects the traditional notion of poetry. Di Blasi furthermore shows how Badiou's reading of the "God of the poets" leads him to a critique of melancholic or even nostalgic depictions of the world, which, in turn, culminates in a critical discussion of Heidegger's work. The essay unfolds how Badious critical undertaking is itself already undermined by certain anachronistic and nostalgic tendencies. Between text and its exegesis, Di Blasi identifies Badiou's reading as traversed by an almost ahistorical unworldliness.

With Dieter Thomä's contribution, this section takes a turn from God, the holy text and editorial exegeses towards satire. Like many philosophers before him, Heidegger was the object of satire for numerous literary writers among his contemporaries. Identifying aspects and qualities inherent to his work that invite satirical reactions, Thomä draws a panoramic image of some of the most prominent representatives of the literary subgenre of Heidegger satire. Satire, he shows, is a powerful tool to uncover and better grasp certain aspects of Heidegger's philosophy. However, to adequately understand why Heidegger's thought lends itself to ridicule, it is necessary to focus on the counter-concept: the sublime. It is because Heidegger's attempts to think the sublime remain inapt, Thomä argues, that they easily tilt over towards and, ultimately, collapse into the ridiculous. In revealing the close ties between these two counter-notions, he also indicates how, *in-between* satirical exegesis and philosophical sublimity, a narrow gate is opened up for the disclosing power of satire.

DISPLACING THE HOUSE OF BEING

Throughout Heidegger's oeuvre, the reader is confronted with a multitude of references to and thoughts about housing, houses, dwelling and the Earth that have their climax in the famous saying in his 1946–1947 *Letter on Humanism*: "Language is the house of being. In its home human beings dwell. Those who think and those who create with words are the guardians of this home".[8] All of these references bear witness to the overarching philosophical quest to respond to the question where, what and how the site, place or abode of *(Da-)*

Sein actually is. The three contributions in this section approach this search from the perspective of 20th- and 21st-century lyricists and novelists, whose works critically re-examine the "house of Being" and challenge its relation to language, experience, perception, truth, topology and, not least, to the politics of Heidegger's *Hütte*, his hut, itself.

The window of the *Hütte* lies at the centre of Simone Stirner's contribution. She stages an encounter between Martin Heidegger and Paul Celan through the latter's poem *Hüttenfenster (Tabernacle Window)*. Although the poem was written well before their short meeting in the Black Forest, it becomes apparent that it initiates a demanding conversation with the Heideggerian concept of language as well as with his notions of dwelling and, especially, with the notion of language as the "house of Being". Stirner elucidates the connections and correlations between "house" and the Hebrew letter *beth* (and word *bayit*). Working through images in *Hüttenfenster* that are resonant of Heidegger's thought, her essay illustrates how Celan's poetry unfolds theoretical propositions that exceed Heidegger's position from within the very moments in which their language overlaps. Challenging Heidegger from within, Stirner concludes, finally leads to a poetic critique of Heidegger in poetic language itself and opens up perspectives towards another form of dwelling.

In his famous Büchner award speech in 1960, *The Meridian*, Celan discusses the possibility of what he calls "topological research". Nassima Sahraoui takes this as the point of departure for her theoretical encounter between Celan and Heidegger. She juxtaposes Heidegger's geographical, terrestrial and ground-rooted approach to Being with Celan's topological and meridional experience of the world. In her contribution, she deconstructs Heideggerian notions such as light (*Licht*), clearing (*Lichtung*), sheltering and dwelling by referring to both key terms of the Western philosophical tradition – "word" (*logos*), "truth" (*alētheia*) and "site" (*topos*) – *and* to the mythological narrations – from *Isis and Osiris* to *Odin* – that lie at their heart. Sahraoui concludes her essay with a reading of Celan's impressive poem *Todtnauberg*, written right after the poet visited Heidegger in his *Hütte*, in which he seems to not only criticise Heidegger for his silence over his involvement in the National Socialist Behemoth, but also theoretically opposes his geography of Being and, thus, gives insight into a potentially other form of perceiving and experiencing the world.

A literary re-appropriation that combines poetic critique and theoretical opposition with moments of affirmative reception is the aggregate of Austrian novelist Peter Handke's encounter with Heidegger. Florian Grosser explores Handke's novel *Slow Homecoming* in its proximity as well as distance to Heidegger's thought. In Heidegger's binary distinction between poetic and literary writing, Handke finds a source *ex negativo* for his engagement with the philosopher. Grosser's reading revolves around the focal point in the virtual conversation between poet and thinker: the concept of "home", and with it, the cluster of dwelling, belonging and origin, of self and other, own and foreign which finally leads to the ethico-political question of returning home. Beyond Heidegger's diagnosis of late modernity's ontological homelessness, so Grosser's conclusion, Handke's re-reading of Heidegger's late thinking on space leads him towards a new, transitory and playful understanding of (co-)existing in a "home".

HÖLDERLIN AND THE POETICS OF THE STATES

Heidegger's work has been widely discussed among poets, writers and literary critics in the United States.[9] This section provides an exemplary and, at the same time, detailed insight into four poetic approaches to Heidegger, in Wallace Stevens, William Faulkner, John Ashbery and David Markson. Although departing from different literary perspectives, these authors all search for their own creative voice at the interface of theoretical investigations into the relation between poetry and thinking on the one hand, the actual practice of writing on the other. Questions of phenomenology, *aesthesis* and apprehension hence merge in this section with linguistic and historic expressions and experiences of the star-spangled world of the States, in which Heidegger's Hölderlin takes a crucial role.

In his later work, Wallace Stevens arrives at Heidegger's thinking through his reading of Hölderlin, as Frederick Dolan shows in his contribution. Dolan traces the differences and similarities between both authors who, as he expounds, likewise interpret poetry as a revelation of reality: where Heidegger includes poetics into his philosophical thought, Stevens lets philosophy enter into his poems which are driven by a deep engagement with metaphysics and God. Herein lies the clearest point of contact and, simultaneously, of divergence between Heidegger and Stevens: whereas Heidegger deconstructs metaphysics whilst still awaiting a God, Stevens, in a Nietzschean ellipsis via God's death, reaches the point where the Heideggerian awaiting turns into an active and authentic process of creating powerful fiction.

Leaving behind the problem of how to dwell poetically beyond the divine and Heidegger, the section turns to the constellatory interdependence of destiny, remembrance and historic memory. Heidegger's Hölderlin and his notion of time lie at the core of Benjamin Brewer's essay on William Faulkner's virtual dialogue with Heidegger. Rather than tracing correlations between both authors, Brewer focuses on the fundamental incompatibility of Faulkner's fiction with Heidegger's thinking of temporality. A close reading of crucial passages from Faulkner's famous Southern epos *Absalom, Absalom!*

shows that it is not Heidegger's thinking of time and history – and hence of the destiny of "the people" – that takes effect in the novel; on the contrary, it is the way in which Faulkner's accelerates the spiral of remembrance and destiny to the extreme that challenges the Heideggerian conception and, thus, allows for another understanding of past, present and future.

With Luke Carson's essay on the poet John Ashbery, this section includes the third contribution that recalls Heidegger's Hölderlin. The first experience of Heidegger's Hölderlin, Carson argues, marks a watershed in Ashbery's creative work: from that moment on, a phenomenological perspective on the world enters and shapes his poetic oeuvre. Even years later, in Ashbery's return to Hölderlin, the memories of the first encounter with Heidegger resonate in his stanzas. Taken together, the twists and turns between initial encounter via Hölderlin, the memory of Heidegger's Hölderlin, and, finally, Ashbery's own "homecoming" to the German poet, constitute a voyage into an open space in which the difference between departure and return has vanished.

In the final contribution to this section, Tim Personn discusses Heidegger's impact on the novelist David Markson. In his interpretation of Markson's novel *Wittgenstein's Mistress* – and, especially, of its solipsistic protagonist Kate – Personn identifies significant traces of Heidegger's thought. Departing from Heidegger's criticism of the dualism between mind and world, he shows how a contemporary novelist intervenes in the philosophical debate over scepticism by dramatising Heidegger's notion of the primacy of Being. This line of literary enquiry amplifies the importance of Heidegger's account of "readiness-to-hand" which counters the rationalist model of subjectivity that leads the novel's heroine into solipsism and depression. On the other hand, Personn's essay reads the literary form of *Wittgenstein's Mistress* as the site of an imagined dialogue between Heidegger and Ludwig Wittgenstein, demonstrating that Markson's ironic aesthetics is a response to Heidegger's style of philosophising. Drawing on the work of selected "New Wittgensteinians", Personn presents irony as a way of throwing into relief Heideggerian themes after successful Wittgensteinian "therapy" and, thus, renews the question of philosophy's inheritability in and as literature.

CROSSING THE BOUNDARIES OF THE OTHER: HISTORY, TIME AND SILENCE

With the final section of this volume, the reader crosses the barriers of Western and, especially, Eurocentric geographies of Being. The first two essays provide a lucid discussion of two Caribbean authors, the Puerto Rican poet and political activist Julia de Burgos (1914–1953), and the influential

Cuban poet and writer José Lezama Lima (1910–1976), respectively; the third essay in this section perceives the world of poetry through the lens of the Japanese philosopher Shūzō Kuki (1888–1941); it is followed by the last contribution to this volume in which surprising affinities between poets Alexei Kruchenykh (1886–1968) and Velimir Khlebnikov (1885–1922), both representatives of Russian Futurism, and Heidegger are brought to light.

Ronald Mendoza-de Jesús starts from the question why certain Heideggerian notions such as "event", "language" and "death" return across the humanities today. The actuality of these notions originates in contemporary debates on what being human means: discussions about the Anthropocene on the one hand, the so-called post-humanist turn on the other. In referring to Giorgio Agamben's and Sylvia Wynter's endeavours to respond to these questions beyond the boundaries of metaphysics, Mendoza-de Jesús, in the first part of his essay, holds that their attempts still rely on Heidegger's logocentrism of *Da-sein*. The second part of his contribution is devoted to the enigmatic Puerto Rican poet Julia de Burgos. Rather than focussing on her already widely explored biography, he discusses the notions of "survival", "death" and "language" in her posthumously published poetry volume *The Sea and You*. Subsequently, de Burgos's poem *¡Dadme mi número!* is presented as offering another understanding of the relation between mortality and language, one that is grounded in "exappropriation" and the infinity of death – an infinity that precedes Heidegger's thinking of the ipseitological finitude of *Dasein* whilst, at the same time, also longing for it. Mendoza-de Jesús points to this *aporia* of humanness which clarifies rather than solves the question of what it means to be human today.

It remains uncertain in how far the Cuban poet and writer José Lezama Lima knew the writings of Heidegger. What is certain, though, is that Heideggerian motifs have reached Latin America's intelligentsia through widespread translations into Spanish during the 20th century. In his contribution, Maurico González traces some unexpected echoes of Heidegger's thoughts and motifs in the works of Lezama Lima. Rather than discussing direct influences of the philosopher on Lezama Lima, González directs us towards the *confluencias*, the confluences and intertwinements of ideas that are at work in the poems, novels and essays of this outstanding literary figure. Lezama Lima's "tropology" of the "image" – read in a constellatory setting with Walter Benjamin and Maurice Blanchot, among others – forces us to rethink and displace the understanding of time, space, finality and the ethical. Once brought to contemporary discourses, González concludes, this tropology bears the potential to write another history of the geopolitical situation of our world.

An unrealised dialogue on poetry between the Japanese philosopher Shūzō Kuki and Heidegger is the focal point of Yohei Kageyama's contribution.

In elucidating, with Kuki, how poetic practice at once constructs and crosses boundaries between "Eastern and Western" experiences of time, he sketches a genealogy of East Asian literary receptions of Heidegger. Kageyama reconstructs Kuki's reflections on "eternal presence" and on the reprise of "recurrent time" in Japanese poetry – especially in rhyme where it finds expression in an attunement to phonetic similarities that transcend the boundaries of any particular language or culture. In the final section of his chapter, he shows how a dialogue with Heidegger's thinking on the relation between East and West, mediated by Kuki's philosophical thinking, has shaped the literary imagination in Japan where it resonates in the works of writers such as Kobo Abe and Yukio Mishima.

Jeff Love's essay departs from the observation that Martin Heidegger's attitude to language – and, in particular, to grammar – evinces a marked affinity to that of the most radical Russian poets of the early 20th century. His chapter explores that affinity by examining two basic Heideggerian claims about language – that it originates in silence and that it cannot be reduced to a grammatical interpretation – in the context of the poetic experiments of two leading futurist poets, Alexei Kruchenykh and Velimir Khlebnikov. Whilst there is no question of influence since Heidegger became well known only after the futurists had ceased to play any role in the Soviet literary scene, he much like the poets who shaped Russian Futurism sought a revolution in language that could return to the beginning of all language. Love's considerations conclude with a brief enquiry concerning the question how the apparently converging attitudes to language and the more than passing similarities in linguistic experimentation between Heidegger and these poets inform profoundly opposed political orientations.

***

With this volume, we are tracing a limited number of the manifold possible poetical engagements with Heidegger. The assembled variations on a theme of "poetic thinking" have been put into dialogue within the four sections for the sake of a thematic order. But variations, of course, allow for different rhythms of reading, and it is up to the reader to compose them anew in response to the many other entanglements, the harmonies, resonances and dissonances that emerge when the essays in this volume are juxtaposed.

The idea for this collection of essays originates in a seminar entitled *The Poets and Heidegger* that was held at the American Comparative Literature Association's annual meeting at the University of California in Los Angeles in 2018. Whereas some of the essays in this volume were presented as talks in the seminar, others were added at later stages. We would like to cordially thank all authors for their willingness to be part of this experimental undertaking to poetically rethink Heidegger's thought and for their commitment to rendering previously unexplored dwelling spaces of "poetic thinking" accessible. We are particularly thankful to Gregory Fried and Richard Polt, editors of the series *New Heidegger Research*, for the openness, optimism and sound advice with which they have generously supported this project from the beginning. Furthermore, we are thankful to Frankie Mace and Scarlet Furness at *Rowman & Littlefield International* who have provided guidance and assistance in all organisational and editorial matters. Finally, we would like to express our thanks to the two anonymous reviewers whose careful reading and productive criticism have helped to refine this volume.

Florian Grosser, Nassima Sahraoui
San Francisco and Frankfurt, April 2021

NOTES

1. See, for instance, Véronique M. Fóti, *Heidegger and the Poets: Poēsis/Sophia/Technē* (New York: Humanity Books, 1992). For one such exception, see *Heidegger und die Literatur*, ed. Günter Figal/Ulrich Raulff (Frankfurt: Klostermann, 2012). The collection contains several essays that address how selected writers have read and interpreted Heidegger.

2. See Martin Woessner, *Heidegger in America* (Cambridge et al.: Cambridge University Press, 2011). Recent examples of such a popular dissemination include Hubert Dreyfus and Sean Dorrance Kelly's *All Things Shining: Reading the Western Classics to Find Meaning in a Secular Age* (New York et al.: Free Press, 2011) which maps literary works from Homer to David Foster Wallace onto Heidegger's epochal "history of being"; and the chapters on Heidegger as a proto-existentialist thinker in Sarah Bakewell's *At the Existentialist Café: Freedom, Being, and Apricot Cocktails* (New York: Other Press, 2016).

3. See Rodney Sharkey, "Beaufret, Beckett, and Heidegger: The Question(s) of Influence", in *Samuel Beckett Today/Aujourd'hui* 22 (2010): 409–22.

4. For examinations of these strands of reception, see Josh Michael Hayes, "Being-at-Home: Gary Snyder and the Poetics of Place", in *The Philosophy of the Beats*, ed. Sharin N. Elkholy (Lexington: University of Kentucky Press, 2012), 47–61; Christian Metz, "Unausgesprochen bleibt das Gedicht nur bei Heidegger", in *Frankfurter Allgemeine Zeitung* N. 88, April 13 (2017): 12; the chapter "The Hermit's and the Priest's Injustices: Reading Cormac McCarthy's *The Crossing* with Heidegger and Anaximander" in Robert Mugerauer's *Responding to Loss: Heideggerian Reflections on Literature, Architecture, and Film* (New York: Fordham University Press, 2015), 1–45; and the chapter "*Dasein* and *das Man*" in Woessner, *Heidegger in America*, 160–79.

5. See Max Frisch, "Vom Ursprung der Kunst: Vortrag von Martin Heidegger", in *Tagesanzeiger* N. 21, January 25 (1936) and Ingeborg Bachmann, *Die kritische Aufnahme der Existentialphilosophie Martin Heideggers*, ed. Robert Pichl (Munich: Piper, 1985).

6. See Arthur Danto, "Wakeful Dreams", in *What Art Is* (New Haven/London: Yale University Press, 2013), 1–52, here 33.

7. Jacques Derrida, *Sovereignties in Question: The Poetics of Paul Celan*, ed. Thomas Dutoit/Outi Pasanen (New York: Fordham University Press, 2005), 166.

8. Martin Heidegger, "Letter on 'Humanism'", in *Pathmarks*, ed. and trans. William McNeill (Cambridge: Cambridge University Press, 2006), 239.

9. See Krystof Ziarek, "The Reception of Heidegger's Thought in American Literary Criticism", in *Diacritics* 19 (1989): 124–26.

Part I

IN-BETWEEN PHILOSOPHY AND LITERATURE

TEXT, EXEGESIS AND SALVATION

Chapter 1

Heidegger and the Critics

Julia A. Ireland

When Eduard Lachmann writes Heidegger on 2 February 1938,[1] it is with a specific question about Hölderlin's fragmentary hymn *As when on a holiday* . . ., namely whether the "it" in the phrase "it singes not [*versengt es nicht*]" refers to "the eternal heart" that Norbert von Hellingrath reads as the poem's concluding line.[2] Though Heidegger had offered his first lecture course on Hölderlin during the Winter Semester of 1934–1935 in what was a highly esoteric and national style, Lachmann approached him on the basis of his 1936 Rome talk *Hölderlin and the Essence of Poetry*. That talk, together with the far more challenging *Wie wenn am Feiertage* . . . (1939) the correspondence prompted him to write, have played a disproportionate role in an excoriating critical response to Heidegger's Hölderlin reception begun in 1941 with Max Kommerell's pilgrimage to Todtnauberg.[3] This response has gone on to include Paul de Man (*Les exégèses de Hölderlin par Martin Heidegger*, 1954), Walter Muschg (*Die Zerstörung der deutschen Literatur*, 1956), Peter Szondi (*Der andere Pfeil: Zur Entstehungsgeschichte des hymnischen Spätstils*, 1962), Theodor Adorno (*Parataxis: Zur späten Lyrik Hölderlins*, 1963), as well as a host of others who have adopted the positions of these critics as authoritative.

Lachmann was the unusual combination of lawyer and Hölderlin enthusiast, combining a philological pedantry with a legalistic interest in the letter of Hölderlin's text. He had undertaken to reconstruct not just Hellingrath's 1910 edition of *As when on a holiday* . . ., which Hellingrath decisively positioned as Hölderlin's first hymn in his 1924 *Hölderlins Sämtliche Werke*. He sought to supply the critical argument missing from both Hellingrath and Franz Zinkernagel's radically different versions of the poem's final strophe – whence the letter to Heidegger. For where Hellingrath appended variant readings and a prose sketch of the hymn's possible conclusion in notes,

Zinkernagel's 1922 *Kritisch-historische Ausgabe* added a full further strophe, whose blank spaces and multiple ellipses revealed the hymn's fragmentary status. Heidegger required students to purchase both editions, and indicates familiarity with the manuscript in the 1934–1935 *Hölderlin's Hymns "Germania" and "The Rhine"* lecture course (GA39: 61/57).

Despite the similarity between the two versions, Zinkernagel's supplementary volume justifying his editorial decisions was never published. Lachmann's resulting article, *Hölderlins erste Hymne* (1939), which was clearly influenced by the correspondence, is as much a vindication of Hellingrath's version of the poem as it is an argument for its positioning as Hölderlin's first hymn. Confronted with a practice of revision that he claims suggests "simultaneity" (*Gleichzeitigkeit*) rather than finality, Lachmann's critical innovation was to publish a photographic reproduction of the hymn's deeply overwritten final page. That page includes a prose sketch of the poem's possible conclusion embedded within a draft of *Midpoint of Life* (the connection is essential for Szondi), as well as the rarely commented on fragment *In the Forest*,[4] whose characterisation of language as "that most dangerous of goods [*der Güter Gefährlichstes*]" informs Heidegger's reading of the hymn's presentation of the poet's vocation. Lachmann cites Heidegger's interpretation of the fragment at the conclusion of his article[5] – Heidegger's concern was not to reconstruct how the hymn might have ended, but how "danger" illuminates what William Fitzgerald has analysed as the "poet's predicament"[6] – and Lachmann's reference is the sole, if indirect, acknowledgement of the correspondence.

Lachmann's decision to photographically reproduce Hölderlin's manuscript forced the hermeneutical paradox operative in Hellingrath and Zinkernagel's efforts to establish the hymn's 'text', at the same time it reduced *As when on a holiday* . . . to a material artefact at once over- and underdetermined. (Lachmann's February 2 letter seeks to restrict Heidegger to a sheerly "grammatical" interpretation of the "it", eschewing any wider commentary as he himself "spins out" a succession of questions that demonstrate the impossibility of that demand.) While ink and handwriting analysis have established when Hölderlin added variants, and stylometrics have identified patterns of word usage with the aim of reconstructing authorial intent, these scientifically philological techniques treat the poem as though it were something objectively present, what Heidegger terms a *Lesestück*. In the attempt as per Szondi to show why "the hymn remained unfinished",[7] editors and critics alike have filled in what Hölderlin meant to say in often byzantine constructions of the hymn's 'true' text – an effort supported by a thoroughly dubious reliance on Hegel. However, the understanding of the hymn as materially incomplete generates a fictive objective text that then metaphysically grounds and legitimates the *Wissenschaftlichkeit* of these same techniques by *effacing them as interpretive*. The paradox Lachmann's photographic reproduction exposed does not concern the decidability of what Hölderlin meant to say, but rather concerns the temporally asymmetric while reciprocally constitutive relation between text and interpretation intrinsic to reading itself as an event of reception. As Heidegger writes in a line from *Wie wenn am Feiertage* . . . cited as evidence of unabashed interpretive violence,

> The text [of the hymn] which shall here serve as the basis for the present lecture, and which has been repeatedly checked against the original manuscripts [these would have been the manuscript photographs and partial transcriptions supplied to him by Lachmann in 1938], rests upon the following attempt at an interpretation. (GA4: 74/51)

William Arctander O'Brien makes this same point in his seminal discussion of Heidegger and Szondi's approaches to the hymn's manuscript when he states: "[*As when on a holiday*. . .] provokes on a most material level the vicious hermeneutic of the priority of editing and interpretation over one another: the one cannot be undertaken without the other having been already performed".[8]

Heidegger was not averse to vicious hermeneutic circles as the occasion to render explicit ontological assumptions, here assumptions about the essence of language in relation to precisely Hölderlin's poetry. In answer to a 1953 letter by doctoral candidate Detlev Lüders singling out the above line – Lüders confesses, "I do not understand how a text can be based upon its interpretation; a text, I think, is something definitely established in its literal wording [*ist etwas im Wortlaut Feststehendes*]" – Heidegger replies, "*Is there a text in itself?* [Gibt es einen Text an sich?]" (GA4: 206–207/236–237). Is there a "literal", or even "grammatical", text that 'exists' somewhere independently as the objective ground for interpretation? Or is the 'text' dependent on the act of reading in the historicity of *its* presuppositions, which in *As when on a holiday* . . . includes fundamentally different interpretations of the relation between reception and completion taken up in Hölderlin's self-figuration of the poet in the hymn's final complete strophe?

Playing off de Man, who reduces Heidegger's "exegeses" to a caricature of sense-certainty duped by the objective text, this makes establishing *As when on a holiday* . . . into an allegory of the historicity of reading in relation to certain problems posed by *Hölderlinrezeption*. What is more, it does so at two politically loaded moments: the first inaugurated by Hellingrath and the national and sacrificial aims that converged in his Hölderlin edition and 1917 death at Verdun, and the second authorised by critics' moralising response to Heidegger's Hölderlin reception as a post-war referendum on his Nazism. (And the irony here is that Heidegger explicitly rejects the Nazi "biologistic" interpretation of Hölderlin on the same metaphysical grounds that he rejects *Literaturwissenschaft*, that is, on the failure to understand language.) In a deeply conflicted article, Karsten Harries finds in Heidegger's "eli[sion]" of *As when on a holiday*['s] . . . 'final' strophe confirmation of a pride the "root of all evil" – a judgement that 'fixes' Hölderlin's text in order to hold Heidegger to account for an authoritarian reading taken as evidence of fascism.[9] In addition to being factually insupportable, in failing to engage the hermeneutical paradox posed by Hölderlin's manuscript, such interpretations evade being placed into a genuinely critical reflexivity about the relation between language and text. Lachmann's question about the "it" invites understanding critique not in terms of the 'givenness' of the literal text as objective ground, but in its interpretive enactment as the limit of reading as reception.

I take up this claim in an analysis of the poet's vocation, using Heidegger's exchange with Lachmann to elucidate the hymn's text in *Wie wenn am Feiertage* . . . . With the exception of O'Brien, Heidegger's critics have failed to notice that his departure from the Hellingrath edition – most importantly his inclusion of the variant referring to Semele's incineration in strophe 6, "And ashes mortally struck gave birth to [*Und Asche tödtlich getroffne gebahr,*]" (l. 52) – constitutes a unique edition of the hymn. As the correspondence shows, Heidegger interprets the line, "And hence it is without danger now/The sons of the Earth drink heavenly fire", that begins strophe 7 to signal a shift in temporality that implicates the hymn's completion *within* the poet's reception by the "people" or *Volk*. As such, "danger" orients the mortal finitude of the hymn's reception and first becomes readable only against the remainder of Semele's ashes. Embedded within my analysis are the ways critics' various misreadings of *Wie wenn am Feiertage* . . . expose presuppositions about an objective text. Szondi and O'Brien after him mistake Heidegger's reference to Semele as a *Gegenbeispiel* (counter-example) rather than a structural *Gegenspiel* (counter-play), and de Man's privileging of a Hegelian conception of immediacy misinterprets the relation between "danger" and "innocence" that threatens the poet's reception with a "mediacy" (*Mittelbarkeit*) that is the source of the hymn's reduction to a *Text an sich. All* Heidegger's critics sanitise Hölderlin's reference to the people as intrinsic to his vocation, as well as the manuscript's draft of *German Song* with which *Wie wenn am Feiertage* . . . concludes, in order to make isolated claims about Hölderlin's reception of the divine and a definition of the hymnic derived exclusively from the prose draft. Though none of these critics could have been aware of the way the correspondence with Lachmann informed the philological detail of *Wie wenn am Feiertage* . . ., these misreadings point to how their claims to legitimacy against Heidegger's interpretive violence rest upon a fictional objective text they are compelled to presuppose but can just as little ground.

When Heidegger replies to Lachmann on 12 March 1938, he answers with a definitive "Indeed" (*Allerdings.*): the "it" grammatically refers to the heart. But the question becomes "which heart" – the "pure heart" of the poets, whose "innocent hands" "grasp [*fassen*]/the Father's ray" in the concluding line of strophe 7, or "the eternal heart" that has since become Hellingrath's most contested variant? Heidegger answers that the "it" refers to the poets' heart but takes issue with Lachmann that "the eternal heart" refers to the Earth, claiming it refers to "Nature", which he writes in *Wie wenn am Feiertage* . . . "thoroughly attunes the entire poem *up to its very last word* [emphasis mine]" (GA4: 52/75). Grammatically establishing which heart the "it" refers to – and whether to include the "eternal" – thus introduces an *irreducible* moment of interpretation into the hymn's literal text.

The incursion of interpretation at exactly the juncture in which Hölderlin makes self-reflexive reference to the poet has had two critical implications. First, it has determined what editors have regarded as the hymn's conclusion as they have sought to constitute a 'readable' (rather than objective) edition of the poem, where 'readable' implies the exclusion of possible variants. Second, in implicating Hölderlin's own reception of the divine within the interpretation of the poets' "grasping", it has determined the definition of the hymnic from out of what editors establish as the poem's conclusion; the understanding of the "*Hymnische*" has consistently determined what is and can be read as the hymn's text. Hellingrath's original decision to include the "eternal" was central to Lachmann's thesis that the hymn is a "unity" (rather than a fragment) in its twofold poetising of "the purity [of the poet]", which protects him from destruction by "divine fire", and the "superhuman occurrence" of Hölderlin's "awakening of divinely beautiful Nature".[10] Lachmann's interpretive reconstruction retrospectively substantiated Hellingrath's positioning of *As when on a holiday* . . . as Hölderlin's first hymn, at the same time it formally required the inclusion of the "eternal" as the hymn's ending. (Heidegger's interpretation of "the holy" [*das Heilige*] likewise requires the "eternal", whose priority embraces Hölderlin's reception of the divine without being reducible to it, and similarly informs his definition of the hymnic.) By contrast, the exclusion of the "eternal" in the Beißner edition subsequently taken up by critics shifts interpretation away from the hymn's poetising of the poet and Nature towards the prose draft as the hymn is understood to fragment against the "purity" of the poet's reception with the irruption of Hölderlin's subjective "I". Szondi reads in this irruption the re-assertion of the elegiac voice, which in turn prevents the hymn's completion in its undoing of the hymnic.[11]

Yet in each case, grammatically determining the "it" presupposes a reading of Semele, whose divine blasting reconfigures what, until strophe 6, had been the hymn's presentation of the "successful" (*glükt*) reception of divine immediacy (l. 49). Where Beißner's exclusion of the "eternal" invites Szondi and O'Brien's quite different conflations of Hölderlin's "grasping" with Semele's presumption, for Heidegger Semele's sudden emergence from out of the manuscript's translation of the opening of Euripides' *Bacchae* introduces neither an "example" nor "counter-example" on the model of a traditional Pindaric. Instead, Semele functions as a structural counter-play, a *Gegenspiel*, that plays Hölderlin's calling on the poets "to grasp/the Father's ray" *against* "the sons of the Earth['s]" reception without danger. Heidegger's characterisation of Semele as a *Gegenspiel* takes up the first in a series of numbered points that comprise his July 15 reply to Lachmann. As he elaborates, the "And hence [*Und daher*]" that begins strophe 7 is the "pivot" (*Drehpunkt*) at which point he and Lachmann diverge in their reading of the poet's reception. (Heidegger's reply suggests that Lachmann interprets the poets' similarity to Dionysus in terms of their both being "sons of the Earth", which mistakes the specifically mortal nature of the poet's finitude as a "between" [*Zwischen*] in relation to language.) In gesturing towards a reception "without danger [*ohne Gefahr*]", strophe 7 re-reads Semele's unmediated exposure to the God by way of a dangerous but un-endangering mediation that undoes the event of divine reception. In *Wie wenn am Feiertage*['s] . . . most misconstrued claim, the poet is "threatened" (*droht*) by a mediation that runs counter to the "mediacy" of the holy, which Heidegger understands to issue from "immediacy itself" in summoning Hölderlin to his vocation ("And what I saw, may the holy be my word", l. 20). Semele is introduced not as a mythic counter-example, a *Gegenbeispiel* to the hymn's presentation of Nature, but instead functions as a caesura who, like Tireisias in Hölderlin's *Remarks*, announces a counter-rhythmic interruption who temporally suspends the hymn's configuration of immediacy and mediation over the question of Hölderlin's reception of the divine and the status of the hymn as text.

Situated between the fatality of Semele's too immediate reception and the un-endangered mortality of "the sons of the Earth['s]" too mediate one, Hölderlin directly calls on the poets in a strophe that is universally interpreted by critics as his mature expression of the poet's vocation and transition to the hymnic mode. I have included Beißner's version of line 52 in brackets to show how it informs reading the "And hence" as an anachronistic conclusion rather than a *Drehpunkt* that re-reads the poets' "grasping" by way of Semele's ashes and in relation to the hymn's own reception:

That quickly struck, for a long time 45
Known to the infinite, it quakes
With recollection, and kindled by the holy ray,
Its fruit born in love, the work of gods and men,
The song, so that it may bear witness to both, succeeds.
So, as poets say, when she desired to see 50
The God, visible, his lightning flash fell on Semele's house
And ashes mortally struck gave birth to [And divinely struck gave birth to]
The fruit of the thunderstorm, holy Bacchus.

And hence the sons of the earth now
Drink heavenly fire without danger. 55
Yet us it behooves, beneath God's thunderstorms,
You poets! to stand with bared heads,
To grasp the Father's ray, itself, with our own hands
And to the people shrouded in the song
To pass on the heavenly gift. 60
For only if we are pure in heart,
Like children, are our hands without guilt.

To fill in the background of Heidegger's reply to Lachmann, I want to briefly review his partial citation of strophe 7 in the *Germania and The Rhine* course's discussion of the "linguistic character" (*Sprachcharakter*) of poetry. Heidegger's description of Hölderlin as *the poet of the poet* is fundamental to the distinction he draws between poetry and poem, *Dichtung* and *das Gedicht*, where the latter *necessarily* includes the possibility of being read as "a piece of text merely lying present-at-hand" (GA39: 19/21). Heidegger excerpted his discussion of language as *Hölderlin and the Essence of Poetry*, inverting the order of his interpretations of *As when on a holiday* ... and *In the Forest*,[12] and Lachmann was clearly able to discern the peculiar way that Heidegger's understanding of the poet's vocation derived from a reading of *As when on a holiday*['s] ... final manuscript page. However, the result of this re-ordering also served to obscure the way that Heidegger initially conceived the "dangerousness of language" *from out* of the problem introduced by the poet's predicament, whose reading presupposes the variant referring to Semele's ashes that Heidegger went on to add in 1939. And in this respect, the hymn's text does indeed rest upon its interpretation.

When Heidegger turns to *As when on a holiday* ... in the *Germania and The Rhine* course, it is to challenge the psychologistic and Nazi interpretations of poetry as the causally deterministic "expression of lived experience" (*Erlebnisausdruck*). As he comments to Lachmann, the name "Hölderlin" designates the situation of the poet as a "between" whose relation to language is the articulation of the gap between two non-identical configurations of mortality: not divine, as attested to by Semele's ashes, but also not a "son of the Earth". Where critics reinstall a substantivised conception of Hölderlin's personhood in their reading of the prose draft's "I", Heidegger understands the tension expressed in Hölderlin's imperative "to grasp the Father's ray" in terms of the disclosive event of language enacted in the poem's reception as hymn. In playing off and against "the sons of the Earth", the impersonal formulation, "Yet it behooves us/ You poets! [*Doch uns gebührt es/Ihr Dichter!*]", together with the direct address of the apostrophe, calls the poets to what is fitting, interpolating them into their vocation while at the same time bringing Hölderlin into his own; in calling on the poets, Hölderlin thus shows himself to risk the divine in a "grasping" mediatively "veiled/in song [*ins Lied/gehüllt*]" and extended to the people. For Heidegger, the danger that threatens the poet is thus not an abstractly metaphysical conception of immediacy but an unprotectedness before language that strophe 7 reveals to be an intrinsic condition of receptivity itself, one that is intimately bound to Hölderlin's later assertion of the poets' "innocence" ("*schuldlos unsere Hände*", l. 62). The opposite of a substantivised "I", this unprotectedness renders Hölderlin the site of a radical "exposure", or *Ausgesetzheit* (*Hölderlin and the Essence of Poetry* describes the poet as "the one cast out [*ein Hinausgeworfener*]" [GA4: 47/64]), whose reception of the divine requires an absence of protection, since protection is first arrived at only through the mediation *of* language in an ambiguously double-sense. On the one side, the poet's "grasping" mediates language, which is to say, it "captures" (*fangt*) the disclosive event of language *in language*, founding it in the "word" as this is enacted through the poem's reception as text. Yet at the same time, Hölderlin's self-reflexivity reveals this reception to in fact be a mediation whose "veiling" or "shrouding" (*hüllen*) discloses danger precisely *through* the protection from danger, sustaining the poet's risking exposure as an intrinsic dimension of the poem's language.

In reading strophe 7, Heidegger thus stresses the significance of the poets' "bared heads", which he characterises as the "most extreme outside of a naked exposure to the thunderstorms" (GA39: 31/30). While this nakedness recalls Semele's "desire" (*begehren*) to see the God "in person", or "visible" (*sichtbar*) – an affinity that Hölderlin underscores with the "it itself, with our own hands" in which the absence of protection is made inseparable from presumption – Heidegger reads the "Father's ray" in conjunction with the line from the poem *Rousseau*, "and beckonings [*Winke*] are/from time immemorial the language of the gods". (This line is itself a hintingly intertextual reference to Heraclitus' Fragment 93 on the Delphic oracle, which Heidegger writes "neither makes directly manifest nor simply altogether conceals [*verhüllt*]" [GA39: 127–128/114].) As this connection suggests, Heidegger conceives the poet's exposure as exposure to the disclosive event of language *as such*, which he expresses in directly Semelean terms as "the danger of the supreme proximity to the gods and thereby to being annihilated by their excessive character" (GA39: 63/59).

In contrast to the onto-theological conception of the divine, Heidegger emphasises that "the gods simply beckon insofar as they *are*", a claim that connects the event structure of language to divine revelation (GA39: 32/31). The "singeing" (*versengt*) concentration of divine presence taken up in the hymn's repeated references to the "holy ray" and the "Father's ray" is here understood not as a permanent *Anwesenheit* that the poets "grasp" and that de Man misleadingly renders with "Parousia" in his *Exegeses*. Instead, it is the revelation from out of darkness of the event of disclosure, whose sudden flash – the *ekaphaines* of Heidegger's *Augenblick* – inaugurates the spatio-temporal relations of nearness and remoteness that allow the possibility of the gods' approach. Reminiscent of Nietzsche's analysis in the *Genealogy* that "lightening is its flash", the poet does not "grasp" divine immediacy as an object, rather he is exposed to divine excess through the disclosive event enacted in the hymn's reception as language. To the extent Heidegger is concerned with the hymn's conclusion in *Wie wenn am Feiertage* (the correspondence with Lachmann indicates that he was "uninformed" about the debate over the poem's ending), it is to connect the hymn's incompleteness to the manuscript's "overflow" (*Überfluß*) of words (GA4: 75/97). The hymn does not fragment but "spills" (*quillt*), revealing the divine excess that is the well-spring of the poet's creativity as the gush of language exceeds the poet's capacity to give it form.

Heidegger makes the connection between the poets' exposure as exposure to the disclosive event of language in its characterisation as an "originary unveiling itself", where this formulation implies a transitivity that is the rejection of the metaphysically dualistic conception of language as the previous disclosure of sign and signified. In identifying language as the "supreme danger" (*höchste Gefahr*), Heidegger re-reads the risk operative in the poet's "grasping" against the "sons of the Earth['s]" reception "without danger" as an itself intrinsic dimension of language. As he writes in directly connecting *As when on a holiday* to *In the Forest*,

> It is presumably no accident that immediately preceding it [the elegy "Midpoint of Life"] there stands the poem "As when on a holiday . . ". (cf. Ger. 30/Eng. 29). It is in this context that the word concerning language – that it is "that most dangerous of goods" – occurs. In language, the Dasein of the human being attains, or better, has from it very ground the supreme danger. For in language, the human being ventures [*sich wagt*] farthest: With language as such he first ventures forth into being. In language, there occurs the revelation of beings – not just the post facto expression of what is already unveiled but the originary unveiling itself – yet for this very reason, a veiling also, together with its preeminent derivative, *semblance*. [*In der Sprache geschieht die Offenbarung*

des Seienden, nicht erst ein nackdrücklicher Ausdruck des Enthüllten, sondern die ursprüngliche Enthullung selbst, aber eben deshalb auch die Verhüllung und deren vorherrschende Abart, der Schein]. (GA39: 61–62/57)

While I will address how this "originary unveiling" implies the modification of language into an objective presence that collapses the hymn into the literal text – and this "derivation" situates the different possibilities of reading – the transitivity of the poet's "venture" makes clear that there is no threat outside of language but only *through* it, or, more accurately, *as* it. Where Szondi, Fitzgerald and O'Brien focus exclusively on the presumption inherent in the poet's "grasping" read in conjunction with the prose draft, Heidegger locates the predicament of the poet in strophe 7's revelation of the hymn's enactment as a "veiling" whose originariness necessarily includes the possibility of the hymn's own undoing as an exposure; Semele's "desire" is not the conceptual equivalent of the poet's "grasping" but locates the poet's predicament with respect to the ambivalent eventfulness of Hölderlin's unveiling the hymn as a veiling. As a result, the poet is threatened less by the metaphysical impossibility of mediating immediacy interpreted by de Man in reductively Hegelian terms than by an excess intrinsic within the hymn's *mediation*, whose self-endangering more broadly locates the problem of reception.

The locus of this self-endangering resides in the way that the poet's grasping reifies the event of language – Heidegger importantly uses the word "*verwahren*" (to preserve) in *Hölderlin and the Essence of Poetry* (GA4: 37/55) – for the sake of its specifically mortal transmission to the people. The hymn's mediation as at once a protection and a preserving makes clear that the 'subjective' disposition of the poets' "heart" is oriented by the irreducible ambiguity of their "hands", which introduces a finite temporality into the hymn's enactment of divine reception. Heidegger is the sole commentator to make this point: the "hand" that reaches out "to grasp the Father's ray" is the same hand extended in "offering" (*Gaabe*) to the people – a receiving as 'giving' that implicates a still further reception within the poet's reception. This decisively transforms the interpretation of the "And hence", which Beißner's edition of strophe 6 sets up reading in an interpretively anachronistic manner. In 'pivoting' between Semele and "the sons of the Earth", Hölderlin calls on the poets in specifically Semelean terms in order to *re-assert* the danger that inheres in the poet's mediation of language against the possibility of a reception "without danger". In a point that Heidegger stresses to Lachmann, Hölderlin's imperative "to grasp" shifts the temporality of the hymn to the future tense, suspending the question of Hölderlin's reception in a manner that leaves it open. Thus, rather than drawing a conclusion that confirms Hölderlin's "successful" mediation, the "And hence" discloses a new and more dangerous danger, one that requires the remainder of Semele's ashes to orient the problem of danger *per se* with respect to the finitude of the hymn's mediation.

This returns to Heidegger's analysis of the derivation of language into semblance. In what he describes as its "playful corrupted essence [*spielerisches Unwesen*]", the veiling intrinsic in "originary unveiling itself" modifies the disclosive event of language and so precipitates its "decline" (*Verfall*) into objective presence: poetry dissimulates itself into "prose" (*Prosa*), dissimulates itself into "idle talk" (*Gerede*), dissimulates itself into the text as literary artefact. What is at stake in each case is not the distinction between 'genres' but the self-endangering of language through the disclosive event of language (GA39: 64/60). The notion of excess announced in Semele's blasting thus encompasses the tension between an annihilating proximity and the veiling of veiling that proves to be the properly unmasterable aspect of disclosure in implicating the historical finitude of the human – namely, the poet's dependency on the people's reception of the poet – within the essence of language.

Given Heidegger's terminology here, which links "idle talk" to the "decline" (*Verfall*) of language, it is instructive to go back to his analysis of the modification of the "hermeneutical as" into assertion in §44 of *Being and Time*. In that analysis, Heidegger returns to his initial definition of "discourse" (*Rede*) as *apophansis* (*logos* as *Rede* becomes *Sprache* as *Gespräch* in the context of Hölderlin), which is comprised of two moments: a "being-toward" that Heidegger defines as an "uncovering" (*Entdecken*) and "primary discovering", and the "preserving" (*bewahren*) of what is uncovered. The latter is expressed as the relation between that discovering and what is discovered, and constitutes what discourse is "about". The decline of *apophansis* into idle talk takes place in the diremption of the "towards" and the "about" as language's preserving of the relation between the two is itself taken up as something ready-to-hand. As Heidegger puts it in *Being and Time*, "the relation itself now acquires the character of presence-at-hand by getting switched over [*umschaltet*] to a relationship between things which are present-at-hand" (SZ: 224/267). Like the derivation of originary unveiling, this "switching over" transforms the ontological status of what is preserved through the previous disclosure of the "about", foreclosing the necessity of a primary discovering. As a result, discourse (or the relationship to 'the text') becomes citational, at the same time it still harbours an originary disclosivity that conserves the future advent of language precisely by concealing it; this is how danger "saves". This structure is evident not only in Heidegger's critique of Nazi *Hölderlinrezeption*, whose stitching together of selected passages on the *Volk* and "destiny" (*Schicksal*) rendered Heidegger's own dialogue with Hölderlin a site of privileged linguistic contestation, but in his assertion that the decline of poetry into idle talk is the basis for the "scientific" (*wissenschaftlich*) conception of language. For Heidegger, the decline of poetry into an objective text, as well as the literary critical approach to reading that follows from it, situates the hermeneutical paradox that Lachmann's photographic reproduction first forced into view: the self-endangering of language allows the hymn to be read as something present-at-hand – scientific philology substitutes for an exposure to danger that implicates reading as an event of reception – at the same time it is only from out of the disclosive structure of that reception that "there is", *es gibt*, a hymn.

Hölderlin's self-reflexivity shows the way through this hermeneutical paradox by revealing the predicament of the poet's reception to be an intrinsic aspect of the disclosive event of language. In his first ever etymology of the word *Dichten*, Heidegger traces the German back to the Greek *deiknumi*, which he defines as "*a telling in the manner of a making manifest that points* [ein Sagen in der Art des weisenden Offenbarmachens]" (GA39: 31/30). As this complex interweaving of disclosive modalities suggests, such "telling" sustains the apophantic dimension of language as poetry's "pointing", which is at once self-revelatory *and* referential: Hölderlin's calling on the poets "to grasp" gestures "towards" what the hymn both presents and enacts as Hölderlin's own reception of the divine – the revelation of Nature and the holy as what the hymn is "about" – suspending that "towards" in holding open the question of his own reception of the divine. In other words, Hölderlin's self-reflexivity is self-disclosive in relation to the event of the hymn's disclosure, whose future tense is situated between the danger of an excessive immediacy (Semele) and an excessive mediation ("the sons of the Earth"), neither of whom completes the event of reception. In this regard, Hölderlin's "poetising of the poet" carries through on the counter-play introduced by Semele's ashes as itself orienting the danger of reception. Heidegger understands Hölderlin's 'pointing-calling on' the poets to "co-respond" (*ent-spricht*) to the gods' presencing as a "hinting further" (*Weiterwinken*) where the *ent*- in the *ent-sprechen* gestures towards Hölderlin's making manifest of the event of manifestation through which the gods 'speak' and are themselves revealed in Hölderlin's unveiling of the hymn's veiling. This "hinting further" makes Hölderlin a figure of language, a "sign" (*Zeichen*) whose reading implicates the danger of the poet's reception *within* the hymn's enactment of language; absent such exposure to danger, the hymn's reception *as language* remains incomplete.

While de Man, Szondi and Adorno have all criticised Heidegger for his denial of *As when on a holiday*['s] . . . open-endedness – and this is taken to be the expression of an authoritarian style of reading whose denial of a plurality of interpretations is evidenced in his 'suppression' of the prose draft – Hölderlin's self-disclosive calling on the poets introduces a temporality of reception that makes the hymn's completion dependent not on the establishment of its text but on the people's reception of Hölderlin's reception. This temporality is expressed in Hölderlin's characterisation of the hymn as an "offering" whose gifting itself implicates a further reception that completes the hymn's event of language. At the same time, however, the enactment of this reception also first constitutes the people as a people through which Hölderlin is established as poet. The hymn's status as text is thus not limited to the decidability of how, for example, the "it" is grammatically interpreted, but is internal to the disclosive event of language, which inaugurates a historicity of reading through the act of reception. At stake is the paradoxical relation between the text's ontological ambiguity and the hymn's inexhaustibility, whose preserving of the event of language situates two different possibilities of reading: the "without danger" of literary criticism's objective text, and the finitude operative in the event of reception as constitutive of a historical community through the poet. To return to Heidegger's question to Lüders, "Is there a text in itself?", the "in itself" preempts the need for an always future reception itself implicated within the disclosive event of language. It imposes terms on the hymn's "offering" that ironically replicate Semele's presumption in the desire for an "in itself" that refuses the finitude of reception – refuses the reciprocally constitutive relation between text and interpretation – at the cost of the hymn.

The asymmetry operative in the temporality of reception as futural transforms the question of what it means for *As when on a holiday . . .* to be complete, which cannot be found in either Lachmann's photographic reproduction of the manuscript or in the critical edifice of Beißner's *Stuttgarter Ausgabe*. This temporal asymmetry encompasses the 110-year interval between Hölderlin's composition of *As when on a holiday . . .* and Hellingrath's initial edition of the poem in 1910, which for the first time made the hymn materially available. However, 'materially available' does not mean that the hymn was 'received,' which requires learning to read the poet as a figure of language. Where Semele was annihilated by her reception of the divine, Hölderlin was "sacrificed" (*geöpfert*) first in the failure to be a reception, whose exposure of the historical limits of reading in turn served as a critique of the possibility of poetry in the absence of the gods. Yet the publication of the Hellingrath and Zinkernagel editions also did not mean that Hölderlin finally became readable. Heidegger understood this to be an indictment not of Hölderlin's editors but of the Germans; *As when on a holiday . . .* remains incomplete not because it is 'unfinished' but because it has not been received. This leads to a final question. Critics' charges of interpretive violence and an authoritarian style rest upon an objective text that disavows the finitude of reading in its historicity as an event of reception. Where is the danger?

APPENDIX A

Daß schnellbetroffen sie, Unendlichem
Bekannt seit langer Zeit, von Erinnerung
Erbebt, und ihr, von heilgem Strahl entzündet.
Die Frucht in Liebe geboren, der Götter und Menschen Werk
Der Gesang, damit er beiden zeuge, glückt.
So fiel, wie Dichter sagen, da sie sichtbar
Den Gott zu sehen begehrte, sein Blitz auf Semeles Haus
Und die Göttlichgetroffne gebahr,
Die Frucht des Gewitters, den heilgen Bacchus.

Und daher trinken himmlisches Feuer jezt
Die Erdensöhne ohne Gefahr.
Doch uns gebührt es, unter Gottes Gewittern,
Ihr Dichter! mit entblösstem Haupte zu stehen.
Des Vaters Stral, ihn selbst mit eigner Hand
Zu fassen und dem Volk ins Lied
Gehüllt die himmlische Gaabe zu reichen,
Denn sind nur reinen Herzens
Wie Kinder, wir, schuldlos unsere Hände.

Des Vaters Stral, der reine, versengt es nicht
Und tieferschüttert, die Leiden des Stärkeren
Mitleidend, bleibt in den hochherstürzenden Stürmen
Des Gottes, wenn er nahet, das Herz doch fest.

Doch weh mir wenn von

Weh mir!

Und sag ich gleich,

Ich sei genaht, die Himmlischen zu schauen,
Sie selbst, sie werfen mich tief unter die Lebenden
Den falschen Priester, ins Dunkel, dass ich
Das warnende Lied den Gelehrigen singe.
Dort

NOTES

1. Heidegger's correspondence with Eduard Lachmann consists of four letters included in the Heidegger *Nachlaß* housed at the Deutsches Literaturarchiv (DLA 75.7393,3). Joachim W. Storck's chapter, "'Zwiesprache von Dichten und Denken': Hölderlin bei Martin Heidegger und Max Kommerell", contextualises the correspondence and partially cites Heidegger's 12 March 1938 letter. (See *Klassiker in finsteren Zeiten 1933–1945*, Vol I, ed. Bernhard Zeller [Marbach: Dt. Schillergesellschaft, 1983], 352–7.) The first two-page letter from Lachmann is dated 2 February 1938. Heidegger's three-page reply is dated 12 March 1938, and is followed by a subsequent seven-page letter dated 15 July 1938; the latter is the most philosophically rich and makes reference to Lachmann's inclusion of Hölderlin's "complete manuscript" as part of the exchange. At its close Heidegger confirms that he destroyed – at Lachmann's request – a draft of what was to become the influential article. "Hölderlins erste Hymne", published in 1939 in the *Deutsche Vierteljahresschrift für Literaturwissenschaft und Geistesgeschichte*, 17 (1939): 221–251. A final two-page letter, dated 4 September 1938, praises Lachmann for his presumably final version of the article, and continues to challenge him on several interpretive points, e.g., the "solitariness" (*Einsamkeit*) of the poet.

2. I will refer to Hölderlin's poem with the English translation of its title, *As when on a holiday . . .*, and Heidegger's lecture by the same name with the German *Wie wenn am Feiertage . . .* See pages 10-11 of this article for the English translation of Heidegger's unique edition of strophes 6 and 7 of the hymn; Heidegger's version of the complete poem can be found in GA4: 49–50/68–73. Appendix A cites in German Beißner's edition of these same strophes, and appends a prose draft of the hymn's possible conclusion as a fragmentary final strophe.

GA4 editor Friedrich Wilhelm von Hermann notes that Heidegger delivered *Wie wenn am Feiertage . . .* as a talk in 1939, and again in 1940, before it was published by Max Niemeyer Verlag in 1941. The lecture was unusually important to Heidegger. On 20 October 1941, he appeals to the Rector of Freiburg University for support after publication was denied by Niemeyer due to a paper shortage. He refers to the lecture as part of a series of *Kriegsvorträge* or "war-time talks" – one that "had to be repeated" – and grounds his appeal on its popularity and the value of "making [it] available to students at the front" ("174. Publication blocked", GA16: 360).

3. Heidegger sent Kommerell a copy of *Wie wenn am Feiertage . . .* after Kommerell's August 1941 visit to Heidegger's hut. See Max Kommerell, *Max Kommerell Briefe und Aufzeichnungen 1919–1944*, ed. Inge Jens (Olten und Freiburg im Breisgau: Walter Verlag, 1967), 384–390; 396–405.

4. For analysis of this fragment, see Hans-Jost Frey's "Hölderlin's Marginalization of Language", in *The Solid Letter: Readings of Friedrich Hölderlin*, ed. A. Fioretos (Palo Alto: Stanford University Press, 2000), 356–374.

5. Lachmann, "Hölderlins erste Hymne", 251.

6. See the chapter, "The Poetry of Reception", in William Fitzgerald, *Agonistic Poetry: The Pindaric Mode in Pindar, Horace, Hölderlin, and the English Ode* (Berkeley: University of California Press, 1987), 19–47.

7. Peter Szondi, "The Other Arrow: On the Genesis of the Late Hymnic Style", in *On Textual Understanding and Other Essays*, trans. Harvey Mendelsohn (Minneapolis: University of Minnesota Press, 1986), 36.

8. William Arctander O'Brien, "Getting blasted: Hölderlin's 'Wie Wenn am Feiertage ...,'" in MLN vol. 94, no. 3 (April 1979): 569. This article has benefitted tremendously from O'Brien's nuanced analyses.

9. Karsten Harries, "The Root of All Evil: Lessons of an Epigram", *International Journal of Philosophical Studies* 1, no. 1 (1993): 18.

10. Lachmann, "Hölderlins erste Hymne", 221–2.

11. Szondi, "The Other Arrow", 41.

12. Heidegger analyses *As when on a holiday . . .* in §4, "On the Essence of Poetry", which also includes the discussion of Hölderlin's January 1799 letter to his mother characterising poetry as the "most innocent of all occupations" (*unschuldigste aller Geschäffte*) that begins *Hölderlin and the Essence of Poetry*. The subsequent *Leitworte* that comprise the latter talk are almost all taken from §7, "The Linguistic Character of Poetry".

Chapter 2

Heidegger as Introduction to Talmud

Elad Lapidot

This chapter seeks to consider Heidegger's work as a contemporary introduction to Talmudic literature.[1] "Talmud" or "Talmudic literature", also known as "rabbinic literature", means here, in the broadest sense, the tradition that is based on a corpus of texts known as the Talmud,[2] whose most canonic version is believed to have been redacted in Babylonia around the 7th century CE, and which is currently still active and developing.[3] The proposition that Heidegger may be considered as an introduction to Talmud is at first sight odd and even scandalous: it raises both, a question and an exclamation mark. It is odd because Heidegger, like virtually all Western philosophers, never mentioned the Talmud. It is scandalous because, if any indirect reference may be found in Heidegger's work to the Talmud, it is in his references to the Jewish. It is indeed first and foremost as Jewish that the Talmud's existence is registered in contemporary knowledge. However, as has become public since 2014 with the *Black Notebooks*, Heidegger's notes concerning the Jewish, written in the time of the Holocaust, were strongly negative and anti-Semitic. Accordingly, if Heidegger's work provides any perspective on the Talmud, it should be rather situated in the tradition of anti-Semitic introductions to the Talmud.[4]

Without denying both facts, Heidegger's ignorance of Talmud and his anti-Semitism, both unexceptional in the history of modern philosophy, this chapter nonetheless seeks to make the claim that Heidegger's thought, unlike modern philosophy before him, opened, within contemporary thought, an access to, or a path towards Talmudic literature, an introduction of sorts. This claim not only dismisses neither the oddity nor the scandal, neither the question nor the exclamation, but it sets out from them. Heidegger, like virtually the entire tradition of philosophy, ignored Talmud; however, more than any other modern philosopher it was Heidegger who sought for thought beyond philosophy, for "another" thought. Heidegger's thought was embedded in the discourse, world and time, in the *being* of Nazi anti-Semitism, and so of the Holocaust. But it is also Heidegger who, more than any other modern philosopher, portrayed the encounter with philosophy's Other and so with the otherness of the West, not as a peaceful academic exchange, but as end of world. It is in Heidegger's thought, as it was deployed in the immediate proximity to the end of world that were WWII and the Holocaust, which this chapter points at an introductory door to Talmud.

THE JEWISH-CHRISTIAN JEW OF BIBLE

The site at which this apocalyptic event of encounter or introduction of contemporary thought to Talmud takes place, or in which a space is opened for such a place to be taken, is *the Jewish*. The Jewish is the site, figure or configuration through which the Talmud has obtained some kind of presence in Western thought, and in Heidegger, be that a presence of absence, a trace. The Jewish has been and still is a very unstable and ambivalent site. In the case of Heidegger, long before the appearance of the *Black Notebooks*, Emmanuel Levinas, for instance, could portray Heideggerian thought as the contemporary epitome of Western philosophy of Being, of Greek origin, to be contrasted with a Jewish – and Talmudic – wisdom of the Other.[5] In 1990, simultaneous with the wide debate following Victor Farías' book on Heidegger's involvement in National Socialism, albeit in pronounced detachment from this debate and from any *political* question, Marlène Zarader, against Levinas, revalorised Heidegger's own quest for otherness, that is, for a non-Greek, "other" way of thinking. Zarader's provocative claim was that Heidegger's portrayal of this non-Greek thought – centred on language, memory, faithfulness and prophetic poetry – not only sounded Jewish, but was in fact indebted to the "Hebraic heritage". Zarader identified this heritage with the *Hebrew Bible* and the – Jewish – tradition of its Hebrew exegesis, from early Midrash to medieval Kabbalah.[6]

This was prior to the *Black Notebooks*, on the background of a virtually total silence of Heidegger on the Jewish. The explicit anti-Judaism found in the published *Black Notebooks* could be asserted now as evidence against Zarader's thesis, even though she was well aware that the Jewishness she identified in Heidegger's thought was and would be never acknowledged but only *denied* by Heidegger himself. This denial, a self-denial, was actually a central element in Zarader's analysis. Nonetheless, the actual debate that has unfolded regarding Heidegger's anti-Semitism did not so much refute Zarader's claim of Heideggerian Jewishness, as it exposed the ambivalence of its epistemo-political meaning, which Zarader carefully avoided discussing. To state it briefly, already in the context of the debate on Heidegger's National Socialism, and now also in the context of the debate on Heidegger's anti-Semitism, various scholars have indicated, in a more or less direct and explicit way, that both Heidegger's National Socialism and anti-Semitism arise from a political metaphysics or even theology, which is very Old Testamentary and so indeed Hebraic-Jewish. John Caputo, for instance, in 2000, before the publication of the *Black Notebooks*, pointed at the "Jewish *Urquell*" of the "murderous twin myth of the people of God and of the people of being", both myths of "the originary language, the originary people, the original land", arising from "the narratives of the Jews and their God in the Tanach".[7] And in 2015, writing on the *Black Notebooks*, Françoise Dastur was reminded of the "Old Testament", where, inherent to "Jewish self-conscience", appeared notions of "blood" and "soil", rooted in "the principle of separation, founded on the biblical doctrine of election", which, she added, "a universal religion doesn't acknowledge".[8]

According to this kind of reading, not only are there Jewish elements in Heidegger's thought, it is precisely in this unavowed Jewishness that Heidegger was still too connected to the intellectual and political heritage of the West, including nationalism and anti-Judaism. If there is indeed a promise of radical "other thinking" in Heidegger, it would have to be as much non-Greek as non-Jewish. In fact, also in Zarader's reading, "the Hebraic" – as the unavowed source of Heidegger's other, non-Greek thinking – is not brought to light through Heidegger's work as radically other, as lying *beyond* the West, but, on the contrary, as the "unthought" *origin* of the West. Zarader's reproach to Heidegger is to have radically *effaced* the West's Hebraic origin by attributing it to the – pre-philosophical, pre-Socratic – Greek. Indeed, it is a deeply Western "Jewish" that Zarader renders visible through Heidegger, a deeply familiar Jewishness, which requires no "specific erudition in the domain of Jewish Studies", since it is a rather evident, obvious Jewishness, which "marked our culture".[9] Zarader follows Ricoeur and is in agreement with Caputo and Dastur when she identifies the textual source and paradigm of this Western Jewishness, this "Hebraic heritage", in the Hebrew Bible. It is the heritage of biblical literature, of literature as Bible. I suggest that this Biblical, Hebraic, Western Jewishness is the Christian Jewishness, the *Judeo*-Christian. It is the "Jewish" as it has been seen and constructed by the Christian and post-Christian West, traditionally as the *negative* origin, from which the West emerges by an act of *Aufhebung*, sublation. Arguably, it is essentially this very same act that Caputo and Dastur perform in the Heideggerian corpus.

Identifying in "the Jewish", as a site of textual presence in Heidegger, an access to Talmudic literature as radical otherness, otherness to Heideggerian, philosophical and Western text and politics, would therefore require identifying in Heidegger an act or position of opposition to "the Jewish" as Christian, as Biblical; an act or position of opposition, which would not however itself be Christian and Biblical (New Testament instead of Old). I suggest that such a position – or preliminary elements thereof – may be found in Heidegger's opposition to National Socialism. My claim is therefore that it was not so much from Heidegger's pro-Nazi as from his anti-Nazi position that his anti-Semitism arose.

HEIDEGGER'S ANTI-NAZI ANTI-JUDAISM

Heidegger claimed to have developed his opposition to National Socialism, during the Nazi era, after his *Rektorat* period, in his work on Nietzsche and Hölderlin. I will focus on the Hölderlin lectures, which concentrate less on polemics with Western tradition of philosophy and metaphysics, and more on a positive attempt to indicate its otherness, which would be *eo ipso* other to National Socialism. The Hölderlin lectures are in particular pertinent for the present context, since the otherness of thought is marked and analysed there paradigmatically as otherness of language, discourse or text. The radical other of philosophical thought is thinking as *Dichtung*, poetry. This site of poeto-political opposition to National Socialism is also a site, so my claim, of Heidegger's critique against the Jewish-Christian, against the Jewish as Bible.

The basic figure around which Heidegger's discourse is built, the figure that bears the name Hölderlin, is the *Dichter*, the poet. The *Dichter* is the founder, who lays the ground for human existence, for being and dwelling in the world. The *dichterische*, poetic foundation of human dwelling is *worthafte Stiftung*, "verbal foundation", an act of words, a linguistic operation – *the* foundational operation of language. The *Dichter* is therefore not exactly poet, not engaged in *poiesis*, in "making" or "producing". Heidegger more precisely explains the verb *dichten* as akin to the Latin verb *dicere*, "to say", and Greek *dokein*, "to show": *Dichtung*, foundational language, is "Sagen in der Art des *weisenden Offenbarmachung*" (GA 39: 30). I translate:[10] "saying in the manner of indicative revelation", namely making something manifest by pointing at it. The basic operation of *Dichten* is indicating, which is paradigmatically done in language through *naming*.

This "wordly foundation" of the world by the *Dichter* may be deemed as profoundly theological – and biblical. The speech act of *dichten*, as Heidegger reads in Hölderlin, is inherently related to the "gods". It responds to the gods, it names the gods. In *Dichtung*, Heidegger says, "gods come into word and world appear" (GA 4: 40). *Dichterich wohnen,* "to dwell poetically" means "standing in the presence of the gods" (GA 4: 42). *Dichtung*, and so

Stiftung, "foundation", arises from the union, the wedding of gods with men. Hölderlin's poems that Heidegger focuses on are his *Hymnen*, namely, he explains, "praise of the gods" (GA 53, 1), Psalms. It should be noted, as a first sign of distance from Jewish-Christian theology, that Heidegger, with Hölderlin, speaks of *gods*, not of God. The plural does not signify rejection of monotheism in favour of polytheism, but rather signifies a *distance* from theological certainty.

The second main feature to highlight in Heidegger's conception of the *dichterische* theological foundation is its *political* nature. "Gods", he says in 1935, "are always gods of the people (*Volk*)" (GA 39: 170). This explosive word, *Volk*, must be handled with care. Heidegger's *Volk* does not arise from race, but from history. *Volk* is collective human existence not as abstract "human race", but under historical conditions, in the course of *Geschichte*, namely a collective that is specific, temporal and diverse: generated and corresponding to a shared lot, a *Geschick*. *Volk* is a *geschichtliche*[s] *Menschentum*, a "historical mankind" (GA 4: 106). This means that, as Heidegger says, "*Dichtung* is the *Ursprache* of a people" (GA 39: 74), "poetry is the original language of a people". The *Dichter*'s gods are the people's gods, and so are his words. Accordingly, the *dichterische*, poetic dwelling is the dwelling of a people, it is a *polis*.

One may therefore say that what Heidegger offered his students during the Nazi time in his Hölderlin lectures is a political theology, which is not dogmatic but *poetic*, less New and more Old Testamentary, more prophetic and "Hebraic", a Jewish kind of Bible. I recall of Caputo's claim, whereby Heidegger's support of Nazism was a turn to Jewish myth. Nevertheless, what Heidegger claimed to have formulated in these lectures is rather his opposition to National Socialism, and he explicitly addressed this opposition against Jewish-Christian prophetic political theology. We could therefore say that, at least structurally, Heidegger's Hölderlin purports to offer an *internal* break or distinction within biblical or scriptural theo-logo-politics.

Let us begin with Heidegger's basic understanding of politics: of the *polis*, and of what it means to found and inhabit it. In Heidegger's lectures on Hölderlin's poem "The Ister" of 1942 he elucidates politics indeed in contrast to National Socialism. The essence of *polis*, he says, is not the modern State, as unquestionable, *fraglos*, as the absolute and totalitarian apparatus of domination technology. Rather, *polis* is the *site*, *Stätte*, of "human historical dwelling in the midst of beings" (GA 53: 101). *Polis* is the site of the *Volk*: homeland, *Heimat*, which is, I recall, dwelling in the nearness of the gods. Politics thus means acquiring *Heimat*, "*Heimischwerden*, coming to be at home in the midst of beings" (GA 53: 101).

However, a basic thrust of Heidegger's Hölderlin readings is that *Heimischwerden* in the midst of beings, of *Seiendes*, requires a more fundamental detachment and *distance* from beings, what he calls relation to or understanding of or truth of Being, *Sein*, which accordingly features man as profoundly *unheimlich* – uncanny – and *unheimisch* – "homelandless". As a site of *becoming heimisch*, the *polis* is more fundamentally the site of the *Unheimische*: not "State", but the site of homelessness and questionability, *das Fragwürdige*. *Dichterisch* foundation of home thus implies not clinging to national identity, but, in contrast, *Unheimischwerden*, turning away from homeland and *Ausfahrt in die Fremde*, going in *exile*. The *Dichter* are not farmers but seamen.

This is the most explicit statement of political opposition that Heidegger's lectures on Hölderlin offer. In this explicitness, they no doubt challenge common understandings of nationalistic patriotism and under the Nazi regime, during wartime, they could very well have been intended, felt and heard as political critique. At the same time, however, and certainly with the great advantage of retrospect, there are many difficulties in reading this as anti-Nazi resistance. The *Fremde*, foreignness, Heidegger speaks of is very specific and very German, namely the German *Greek*, that is, "the Greek" as a constitutive figure in the constitutive texts of "the German", not the least in Hölderlin. It is in a German, not in a Greek *Dichter* that Heidegger looks for the Foreign. Accordingly, his *Ausfahrt*, "emigration", cannot but sound very allegoric, almost pure symbol for *return*, which in its turn is almost pure symbol for *staying, bleiben*, which Heidegger in fact did. Heidegger could be thus said to use the language of foreignness only allegorically or metaphorically, not *literally* enough.

Yet, there seems to be here a more fundamental difficulty in the status and state of foreignness *in language*. Heidegger himself is aware of this difficulty when he distinguishes between poetic and prophetic language, so to speak between poetry (*Dichtung*) and the (Christian-)Jewish Bible. At a certain point in his essay on Hölderlin's *Andenken* (*Remembrance*) of 1943, commenting on the *Dichter*'s "golden dreams", Heidegger describes the *dichterische* act of foundation as giving words to something unreal – a "dream" – that is however not *less* existent than the real, but more existent, because foundational to reality, something like a *vision*. The poets are the visionaries, they say not what is real, but what is *in coming*. This means that "[t]heir word is the *foretelling* [*voraussagende*] word in the strict sense of *propheteuein*. *Dichter* are 'prophetic'" (GA 4: 114). This literal kinship, however, serves Heidegger for marking a decisive *difference*. If *Dichter* are 'prophetic', he immediately explains, it is not in "the Jewish-Christian meaning of this name" (GA 4: 114). What characterises Jewish-Christian prophets, according to Heidegger, is that "[t]hey immediately foretell the God, on whom the confidence of salvation in the celestial beatitude relies" (GA 4: 114). Jewish-Christian prophecy immediately foretells, immediately *speaks of* God – its words have certainty, nearness, *Heimat*. In other words, Heidegger does not criticise here the Bible for its basic theo-logo-political concern. Zarader is right to point out that Heidegger basically shares this "Hebraic" concern. Nonetheless, precisely because of this affinity, Heidegger more fundamentally criticises the mode of relation *to* god that constitutes language as biblical prophecy, namely the mode of immediate, direct speech, the word in the immediacy of God; and perhaps: the word that *is* immediately God.

The *Dichter*'s words, in contrast, are godly, but do not speak of God or the gods. The word of the *Dichter*, Hölderlin's word, as Heidegger keeps saying, is not God, but *das Heilige, the Holy*. The Holy, Heidegger explains, is not God, but "the Time-space of the appearance of the gods" (GA 4: 114), the dimension in which something like "gods" may be encountered and so "the dwelling of historical man on this earth" (GA 4: 114) may be founded. The *Dichter* is in this sense more foundational than the prophet. This means that the *Dichter* does not dwell in the nearness and certainty of god, his words are not "powerfully sounding" (GA 4: 138) as the prophet's. His site is not the *Heimat*, but *Wanderschaft*, a wandering *Dichter*, close to the *Fremde*: not in the sense of a different place than his birth place or home, but in the sense of the place of no-place, of words that speak the absence of what they mean. Consequently, the *Dichter*'s discourse, *Dichtung*, even as it ultimately means god, that is, aims at an encounter with the godly, is not exactly a discourse of God, *theo-logos*. As Heidegger notes: "The Holy may not at all be accounted for 'theologically', because all 'Theology' already presupposes the *theos*, the God" (GA 52: 132–133). *Dichtung* is not theology, but, literally, *hierology*, discourse of holiness.

All this is highly conceptual. Heidegger's thought, however, insists on being *geschichtlich*, historical. In fact, the distinction between prophets and *Dichter*, theology and hierology, is not just conceptual, but inherently temporal. Prophecy and *Dichtung* are discourses of different *times*. Transcendentally, one might say that the *Dichter precedes* and *prepares* the Prophet, by opening the space in which the coming gods may appear. However, what Heidegger insists on is that the *Dichter* belongs to the time of the *absence* of gods, which not only precedes presence, but also follows presence. Heidegger's focus is on the *Dichter* that comes *after* the gods, namely after the gods' disappearance or departure, what Heidegger calls the *flight* of the gods, *die Flucht der Götter*. "What does Hölderlin's *Dichtung* say? Its word is: the Holy. This word speaks of the flight of the gods" (GA 4: 195).

Heidegger's Hölderlin, and so Heidegger himself, the *Denker* of the *Dichter*, belong to a historical time that Heidegger describes as a "space-time of the godlessness", of *Gott ist tot*, of holiness that is a "Holy *Night*" (GA 4: 109). In Hölderlin's words, Heidegger calls this time a *dürftige Zeit*, a "desolate time". Hölderlin is a *Dichter* in a *dürftige Zeit*. It is a time of double absence, double "no": the "no-longer" of the gods who have flown, and the "not-yet" of the gods to come. Furthermore, Hölderlin's time, *our* time, is so desolate, so *dürftig*, that the very absence of the gods is unnoticed, is an absent absence. The gods' absence becomes invisible inasmuch as the very dimension of godly appearance, *the Holy*, disappears: *Das Heile entzieht sich. Die Welt wird heil-los*,

> What is whole [das Heile] withdraws. The world is being emptied of what is whole and heals [heil-los]. As a result, not only does the holy [das Heilige] remain hidden as the track to the godhead, but even what is whole, the track to the holy, appears to be extinguished. (GA 5: 295)

What Heidegger means with this is not *secularisation*, insofar as this term means the disappearance of *God*, namely the Jewish-Christian one. On the contrary: against Christian readings of Hölderlin, Heidegger asserts that it is upon the death of Christ, that is, with the beginning of Christianity, that "the end of the day of the gods began. Evening falls [*Es wird Abend*]" (GA 5: 269). Christianity *is* the absence of gods. Christian nearness to God, knowledge and discourse of God, *Theology*, Heidegger says, "already presupposes the *theos*, the god, and with such certainty, that whenever theology arises, the god already began the *flight*" (GA 52: 132–133). Theology is the gods' absence that appears as the presence of God, the God of what Heidegger also calls "onto-theology".[11] The era of (onto-)theology, the Christian era, would thus be the time of the absent absence, the *dürftige Zeit*. The Christian era is however *eo ipso* a Jewish-Christian era, and Christian theology presupposes and regenerates the prophets of the Jewish Bible. A *Black Notebooks* entry of the mid-1940s in fact names, beyond Christian theology, *Jewish prophecy* as discourse of the desolate time. "Prophecy", Heidegger writes there, in one of his strongest anti-Jewish notes, is "forward-looking history", arising from technology, thus being "an instrument of the will to power" and – we may add – the modern, total, and also the National Socialist State (GA 97: 159).

It is thus that Heidegger's critique of National Socialism can be read as based on a critique of Biblical Judaism, insofar as it has operated, through Christianity, as an origin of the West. On this reading, the Jewish Bible is understood as an alleged nearness of the word to God, to *Heimat*, which conceals actual godlessness and *Heimatlosigkeit*, homelessness. It is crucial to insist once again that this is a critique not of what the Bible says, but of the constitutive biblical mode of saying: the immediacy of the biblical word of god, paradigmatically in the very word God. For this reason, against the Jewish Bible, Heidegger does not propose the Christian Bible, which is all the more biblical, but the words of Hölderlin, *Dichter in dürftiger Zeit*, the poet in desolate times, which reveal neither God nor gods, but their absence, and this by revealing, or unconcealing, the time-space of the godless Holy Night. This would be the hiero-political act performed by Hölderlin's *Dichtung*, foundational accordingly of a specific historical dwelling, an alternative site and *polis*, a land of the night, *Abend-land*, which will not be a State, but a *Heimat* of *Unheimischkeit*, a homeland of homelessness, whose citizens would thus have to be themselves dwellers of the *Unheimische*, unhomely: poets and thinkers, *Dichter und Denker*.

JEWS INTERRUPTED

I now wish to indicate how Heidegger's critique of the Jewish-Christian *logos*, as *logos* of presence, even as it posits the Jewish-Christian as origin of the National Socialist (in a similar way to the current critique against Heidegger), nonetheless opens a horizon for the emergence, within contemporary thought, of a different notion of the Jewish, a non-Judeo-Christian Jewishness, which in its turn, so my claim, opens access to the non-biblical Jewish, perhaps even non-Jewish Jewish, namely to the Talmud. I will indicate this horizon within the reception of Heidegger in post-war French thought, focusing on Phillipe Lacoue-Labarthe's critical reflections on the relations between politics and literature.[12]

Lacoue-Labarthe, characteristically of the post-war French reception of Heidegger, subscribes to Heidegger's basic observation and pronouncement of the end, limit or closure (*clôture*) of philosophy, meaning the hegemonic tradition of Western thought, and the ensuing intentionality towards non-philosophical otherness. A central element of Lacoue-Labarthe's argument is the rigorous insistence that the very pronouncement of the end of philosophy still takes place *within* philosophy, such that its operation can be only negative or reflective, that is, its sole object can be *philosophy*, but it cannot have an image, idea, notion or *figure* of, that is, it cannot "see" philosophy's *otherness*, the non-philosophical thought that lies beyond or after philosophy. "[S]een from here, namely from philosophy itself, this beyond, always suspected, remains undetectable (*indécelable*)".[13]

In fact, the concept of the figure stands at the centre of Lacoue-Labarthe's *general* characterisation of Western thought, which is at the same time epistemological, poetological and political. In a very condensed nutshell, Lacoue-Labarthe argued that Western thought and praxis, from Plato to National Socialism, consisted in what he called "onto-typology", that is, a mode of conceptualisation and construction of existence, of "being", which is oriented by the notion of the type – the model, paradigm, ideal, idea or figure. The idea generated by Western philosophy has been operating as the ideal for Western politics, which thus consists in the mimetic self-modelling of the collective subject in light of its ideal: politics as self-fabrication and self-fabulation – as *fiction*.[14] "The City (*la Cité*) arises from plastics, formation and information, fiction in the strict sense".[15] Western politics is a self-producing artwork. The paradigmatic paradigm for Western philosophy and politics has therefore been the paradigm that has no paradigm, a figure without a model, that is, entirely original, independent and immanent, entirely self-sustaining – absolute. The literary form of this paradigmatic figure of the West, Lacoue-Labarthe argues, has been the *myth*, whose most powerful modern deployment was the "Nazi myth".[16]

The affinity between Lacoue-Labarthe's critique of Western self-presence in myth and Heidegger's critique of Western God's presence in biblical prophecy is visible, but neither obvious nor clearly articulated by Lacoue-Labarthe. He rather highlights in Heidegger's work on Hölderlin Heidegger's falling back into Western philosophy. This fall, or *fault*, would consist, first, in Heidegger's very attempt to present a *figure* for non-philosophical thought, that is, Hölderlin's poetry. Second, on Lacoue-Labarthe's reading, the notion of *Dichtung* that Heidegger develops from Hölderlin's text conceives of poetry essentially as *myth*, as *Sage*, which consolidates the self-presence of the historical people in its historical language. Heidegger's opposed factual National Socialism, so Lacoue-Labarthe's famous claim, for the sake of the truth *underlying* National Socialism (and dissimilated by it), which is the accomplished form of Western politics of fiction as modern "national aestheticism".[17]

In the terms of my above analysis, Lacoue-Labarthe's critique could be said to expose Heidegger's Hölderlin, notwithstanding Heidegger's own critique of the prophetic *logos* of presence, as still too prophetic, too biblical, too Judeo-Christian. The *Dichter* word is still revelation, still foundation and dwelling. *Dichtung*, "indicating revelation", is still *Sage*, and the *Dichter*, if godless, is nonetheless holy, a *Halbgott*, "demigod" (GA 4: 103, 147) – divine Author. To be sure, Lacoue-Labarthe's initial analysis traces national aestheticism back rather to Plato, not the Bible. Yet, in later texts he characterises the problem in Heidegger's poeto-politics as "religiosity" and "piety",[18] and problematises Heideggerian and National Socialist national aestheticism as theo-politics of "[d]eploring 'existential' loss, calling to recommencement, hearing the 'evangelical' poem", and so of "messianic" hope for the "restoration (which is only profane with respect to Christianism) of political religion".[19] It is a small step to Caputo's critique of Heidegger's nationalism as Old Testamentary, Jewish myth.

Nonetheless, it is in this horizon that Lacoue-Labarthe, following Heidegger's quest of the *other* thought, attempts to indicate beyond or in contrast to Platonic-Biblical mythology, which other, anti-mythical, and in this sense anti-biblical Jewish figure emerges. In fact, as resistance to Western and specifically Heideggerian *figuration*, Lacoue-Labarthe explicitly avoids presenting or representing Western philosophy's otherness in any narrative, history or figure. His indication of otherness consists rather in conceptualising the negative need to "interrupt": interruption of philosophy, of myth, of the absolute subject, interruption of theo-politics, of the people, of history, of language. Interestingly, very similarly to Heidegger, it is however less through abstract conceptualisation than through the identification and analysis of a *positive* trace that Lacoue-Labarthe articulates the anti-mythical interruption of the West. Like Heidegger, he finds this trace primarily in the *Denker*'s *Dichter*, that is, in Hölderlin, as read by Walter Benjamin. It is in Benjamin's Hölderlin that Lacoue-Labarthe identifies a modern conception of poetry not as myth and figuration, but on the contrary as *disfiguration*, literalisation and "rupture of the name",[20] as "holy sobriety", such that modern poetry would manifest itself paradigmatically in prose and even more radically in literary theory and critique. The disfigurative rupture of the name is *eo ipso* interruption of poeto-politics: "the life of a pure work of art can never be the life of a people, or the life of an individual, or anything else than this pure element that we find in the *dictamen*".[21]

But there is another positive trace, another figure, that Lacoue-Labarthe's earlier text renders visible, and which vanishes in his later essays. In fact, Lacoue-Labarthe initially identified the rupture of Western myth not only in the "pure element" of poetics, be it Heidegger's philosophy, Hölderlin's *Dichtung* or Benjamin's theory, but also in "life", in an event of post-modern revelation, around which the entire debate and *topos* of Heidegger may be deemed to revolve, which Lacoue-Labarthe names "the apocalypse of Auschwitz": "In the apocalypse of Auschwitz, it is not more and not less than the West, in its essence, that revealed itself – and that, since, does not cease from revealing itself".[22] Auschwitz is the caesura, the break and interruption of history and of History, of Western figuration and myth: it interrupts all representation and *eo ipso* makes the regime or history of representation and aesthetics, that is, the West, visible. But at the same time, by the same event, the apocalypse of Auschwitz, by its very exterminatory blaze, renders visible also the *Other* of the West, namely that which the West, by the inherent force of its mytho-political presence, as it culminated in Nazism, negated: the Jews.

God in fact died in Auschwitz – the God of the Greco-Christian [in the English translation: Judaeo-Christian] West at least. And it is by no sort of chance that those who were sought to be exterminated were the witnesses, in this same West, of another origin of God who was venerated and thought of there – if it's not, maybe, another God, who remained free of the Hellenistic and Roman rendition.[23]

Beyond the Jewish-Christian, another Jewish figure appears, or, better, is *signalled* towards, because it is the paradoxical figure of disfiguration. As Lacoue-Labarthe quotes Blanchot: "the Jews incarnate [...] the rejection of the myths, the renouncement of idols, the recognition of an ethical order that manifests itself by the respect of the law".[24] Jewish aniconism, a biblical *topos*, emerges here as renouncement of figuration itself – renouncement or resistance to the figure, the idea, image and form. This is a rejection of the myth that does not transcend any discourse of God, people and language. On the contrary, it consists precisely in their disfiguration: the imageless god has a formless people, "an unformed, unaesthetic 'people'",[25] whose text generates no work, no *oeuvre*, or rather the *désoeuvre*, the no work, the no-Bible.

TALMUD UNTHOUGHT

This non-Jewish-Christian Jewish, signalled by a French reworking of Heidegger's indication towards a non-philosophical, *other* mode of thinking, marks a contemporary access, so the claim of this chapter, to Talmud. In conclusion, I can only provide a few concise indications of how this signal was and may be concretely understood, and to what extent it may give access to Talmud. As already noted, Lacoue-Labarthe himself, in his later texts, follows this signal towards Walter Benjamin and the essence of "modern literature" as *prose*. Closer to Jewish textual tradition, the same modern category of literature may guide and has guided, within literary theory, a revision or re-reading of the Old Testament, which could be characterised as anti-mythical, prosaic and disfigurative, that is, suspending and interrupting the text's immediate power of indication, of representation – and incarnation. Already Erich Auerbach noted how, in contrast to the Homeric gods, God in the Bible "is not comprehensible in his presence, as is Zeus; it is always only 'something' of him that appears, he always extends into depths".[26] A reading of the Hebrew Bible in the mode of non-presence was recently proposed by Michael Fagenblat, critiquing Heidegger's German through Gershom Scholem's Jewish Hölderlin.[27]

Taking a step further from the Bible, contemporary thought conjured the non-Judeo-Christian Jewish in the figure of post-Biblical *rabbinic* literature.

In 1982, Sarah Handelman identified the emergence of elements from "rabbinic hermeneutics" in contemporary literary theory, such as Freud, Lacan, Derrida and Harold Bloom, noting among other things a "debt to the thought of Heidegger".[28] Handelman characterised rabbinic hermeneutics with the term "Slayers of Moses", namely through an anti-prophetic, anti-Bible disposition, while nonetheless, similarly to Zarader, maintaining the Bible as the central point of reference, such that the paradigmatic rabbinic text and genre is presented as *midrash*, that is, classic rabbinic biblical exegesis, as well as later, medieval rabbinic exegesis in *kabbalah* literature.[29]

It would in fact be an illuminating exercise to show how the biblical paradigm has been configuring and regulating the various discourses through which "the Jewish" and even the non-Christian Jewish, that is, the rabbinic, appeared for modern and contemporary knowledge, science and thought. The "biblical paradigm" does not only or not exactly refer to the specific textual corpus of the Old Testament; rather it refers to this corpus inasmuch as it has been constructed, represented and developed as the prototype for the *biblios*, the Book, and so as the paradigmatic *logos* of theo-poeto-political presence. The most critical places to observe and examine the workings of this biblical paradigm in the contemporary epistemological construction of "the Jewish" are the academic and philosophical studies of Talmud. The Talmudic text in fact is not based on the biblical text, is not biblical exegesis. The references that are made to the biblical text in the Talmud, in the form of occasional quotes, sometimes of just one word, do not portray a book, but something like an archive of discrete acts of signification, of textual and verbal fragments. In fact, the Talmud is to a constitutive extent generated by a non- or anti-biblical paradigm, which – to use Lacoue-Labarthe's terminology – "interrupts" the basic signifying function of the text, of the name, of the *Sage*, of "indicative revelation".

Accordingly, it is a question to be discussed elsewhere, whether the biblical paradigm is still operative in current projects such as Daniel Boyarin's and Sergey Dolgopolski's,[30] which have gone the furthest in critically exploring the potential significance of the Talmud to contemporary thought, inasmuch as these projects continue to access Talmud through the basic category of *literature*. It seems that the emergence of Talmud in contemporary thought, as at least one potential *Other* to Western Greco-Judeo-Christian thought, would have to activate just as fundamentally this operative and performative mode of language that is *law*, considering the strongly normative or practical element of the Talmudic discourse. The formulation of this set of questions, and thus this chapter, could be deemed as a preparation and introduction to a reading of the most manifest locus where Talmud emerges in directly post-Heideggerian thought (with all the complexities of this *post* – a complex of reception, continuation, critique and opposition): the Talmudic readings of Emmanuel Levinas.[31]

NOTES

1. A version of this chapter was included in Elad Lapidot, *Jews Out of the Question: A Critique of Anti-Anti-Semitism* (Albany: SUNY Press, 2020), which deals more broadly with ambiguities and problems in the theoretical response to anti-Semitism in post-Holocaust philosophy.
2. I follow Sergey Dolgopolski in differentiating between "the Talmud" as a textual corpus (like "the Bible" or "the Odyssey") and "Talmud" as a system of thought, a discourse or an episteme (like "Philosophy", "Modern Historiography", etc.); see Sergey Dolgopolski, *Other Others. The Political After the Talmud* (New York: Fordham University Press, 2018).
3. For a recent accessible exposition, see Barry Wimpfheimer, *The Talmud: A Biography* (Princeton/Oxford: Princeton University Press, 2018).
4. There is in fact a motif of "exposing" the Talmud as the secret, anti-Christian and later anti-non-Jews book of the Jews, which has operated as a constitutive act of modern anti-Judaism and later anti-Semitism. The history and development of this motif can be traced, in German literature, from Johann Andreas Eisenmenger's *Entdecktes Judentum* ("Judaism Revealed") of 1700, exposing Jews' contempt of Christianity as stated in their "own books", "so far completely or partly unknown among the Christians", to the 1893 edition (Dresden, Otto Brander), which present itself as "literal translation of the most important passages of the Talmud and other Hebrew-rabbinic literature, to a large extent still completely unknown to the Christians", passing through August Rohling, *Der Talmudjude* (Münster: Adolph Russells Verlag, 1871), and featuring in works such as Fritsch's *Anti-Semiten-Katechismus* (12ff.).
5. See for instance Emmanuel Levinas, *Totalité et Infini: Essai sur l'extériorité* (Paris: Kluwer Academic, 1991 [1961]), translated by Alphonso Lingis as *Totality and Infinity. An Essay on Exteriority* (The Hague/Boston/London: Martinus Nijhoff Publishers, 1979), where on the first page Levinas writes, clearly with Heidegger in mind: "We do not need obscure fragments of Heraclitus to prove that being reveals itself as war to philosophical thought" (11). On the nonetheless much more complex relation of Levinas' to Heidegger's philosophy, see Michael Fagenblat, "Levinas and Heidegger: The Elemental Confrontation", in Michael L. Morgan (ed.), *The Oxford Handbook of Levinas* (Oxford: Oxford University Press, 2019), 103–133.
6. Marlène Zarader, *La Dette impensée. Heidegger et l'héritage hébraïque* (Paris: Seuil, 1990), translated by Bettina Bergo as *The Unthought Debt: Heidegger and the Hebraic Heritage* (Stanford, CA: Stanford University Press, 2006).
7. John Caputo, "People of God, People of Being: The Theological Presuppositions of Heidegger's Path of Thought", in James E. Falconer and Mark A. Wrathall (eds.) *Appropriating Heidegger* (Cambridge: Cambridge University Press, 2000), 88, 90–96.
8. Dastur, "Y a-t-il une 'essence' de l'antisémitisme?", in Peter Trawny and Andrew J. Mitchell (eds.), *Heidegger, die Juden, noch einmal* (Frankfurt a. M.: Vittorio Klostermann, 2015), 75–96; p. 79, 87 and p. 88, note 30. To demonstrate the

relevance of these notions for 20th century Jews, Dastur refers to Franz Rosenzweig's understanding of the Jewish people as a "blood community", p. 87, note 29.

9. Zarader, *La Dette*, 31.

10. All the translations in this chapter are mine.

11. On "ontotheology", see the recently published article of Iain Thomson, "Technology, Ontotheology", in Aaron James Wendland et al. (eds.), *Heidegger on Technology* (New York: Taylor & Francis, 2018), 174–193; see also Laurence Paul Hemming, "Heidegger's God", in Hubert Dreyfus and Mark Wrathall (eds.), *Heidegger Reexamined. Vol. 3: Art, Poetry, Technology* (New York and London: Routledge, 2002), 249–294; for a broader recent discussion, see the various contributions in Mårten Björk and Jayne Svenungsson (eds.), *Heidegger's Black Notebooks and the Future of Theology* (Switzerland: Palgrave Macmillan, 2017).

12. Philippe Lacoue-Labarthe, *La Fiction du politique. Heidegger, l'art et la politique* (Paris: Christian Bourgois Editeur, 1998 [1987]), translated by Chris Turner as *Heidegger, Art and Politics. The Fiction of the Political* (Oxford: Blackwell, 1990); idem, Philippe Lacoue-Labarthe, *Heidegger. La politique du poème* (Paris: Galilée, 2002), translated by Jeff Fort as *Heidegger and the Politics of Poetry* (Urbana and Chicago: University of Illinois Press, 2007). Unless otherwise indicated, the translations below are mine.

13. Lacoue-Labarthe, *La Fiction*, 16.

14. Cf. Jean-Luc Nancy's critique of the conception of the community as *œuvre*, in *La communauté désoeuvrée* (Paris: Christian Bourgois Editeur, 1986, 1990), to which Lacoue-Labarthe explicitly refers and subscribes, see idem, *La Fiction*, 111.

15. Lacoue-Labarthe, *La Fiction*, 102.

16. Lacoue-Labarthe, *La Fiction*, 134–139; cf. Phillipe Lacoue-Labarthe and Jean-Luc Nancy, *Le mythe nazi* (La Tour d'Aigues: Editions de l'Aube, 1991); Jean-Luc Nancy, "Le mythe interrompu" (1984), in idem, *La communauté*, 110–174).

17. Lacoue-Labarthe, *La Fiction*, 83.

18. Lacoue-Labarthe, *Heidegger*, 40–41.

19. Lacoue-Labarthe, *Heidegger*, 174.

20. Lacoue-Labarthe, *Heidegger*, 110.

21. Lacoue-Labarthe, *Heidegger*, 104.

22. Lacoue-Labarthe, *La Fiction*, 59.

23. Lacoue-Labarthe, *La Fiction*, 62.

24. Lacoue-Labarthe, *La Fiction*, 138.

25. Lacoue-Labarthe, *La Fiction*, 139.

26. Erich Auerbrach, *Mimesis. Dargestellte Wirklichkeit in der abendländischen Literatur* (Bern: Francke, 1994 [1946]), translated by Willard Trask as *Mimesis: The Representation of Reality in Western Literature* (Princeton: Princeton University Press, 2003).

27. Michael Fagenblat, "On Dwelling Prophetically: On Heidegger and Jewish Political Theology", in Elad Lapidot and Micha Brumlik (eds.), *Heidegger and Jewish Thought: Difficult Others* (London/New York: Rowman & Littlefield, 2017), 245–268.

28. Sarah Handelman, *The Slayers of Moses. The Emergence of Rabbinic Interpretation in Modern Literary Theory* (Albany: SUNY Press, 1982), 16.

29. On Heidegger and Kabbalah, see the extensive work of Elliot Wolfson, for instance in *Language, Eros, and Being: Kabbalistic Hermeneutics and the Poetic Imagination* (New York: Fordham University Press, 2005); idem, *Alef, Mem, Tau: Kabbalistic Musings on Time, Truth, and Death* (University of California Press, 2006); idem, *Giving Beyond the Gift: Apophasis and Overcoming Theomania* (New York: Fordham University Press, 2014); idem, *The Duplicity of Philosophy's Shadow: Heidegger, Nazism, and the Jewish Other* (New York: Columbia University Press, 2018). Forthcoming: idem, *Heidegger and Kabbalah. Hidden Gnosis and the Path of Poiēsis* (Bloomington: Indiana University Press, 2019).

30. See for instance Daniel Boyarin, *Socrates & the Fat Rabbis* (Chicago/London: The University of Chicago Press, 2009), idem, *A Traveling Homeland: The Babylonian Talmud as Diaspora* (Philadelphia: University of Pennsylvania Press, 2015); Sergey Dolgopolski, *What Is Talmud? The Art of Disagreement* (New York: Fordham University Press, 2009), idem, *Other Others. The Political After the Talmud* (New York: Fordham University Press, 2018).

31. The importance of Levinas' Talmudic readings for the question of Talmud in contemporary thought is too great to allow giving it any appropriate place in the framework of this short chapter, other than as marking the future of the investigation that this chapter initiates. For a recent introduction to this topic, see Ethan Kleinberg, "Levinas as a Reader of Jewish Texts: The Talmudic Commentaries", in Morgan, *Handbook of Levinas*, 300–317.

Chapter 3

Reactionary Nostalgia

Badiou, Heidegger, and the Poets

Luca Di Blasi

In an interview for the German weekly journal *DER SPIEGEL* that Martin Heidegger gave in 1966 and that was published after his death in 1976, he famously declared that "only a god can save us".[1] This statement might have appeared puzzling, given that Heidegger had broken with the Christian and likewise destructed the metaphysical God of the Western philosophical tradition. The riddle is solved, however, if one assumes that Heidegger spoke of a *different* God. According to Alain Badiou, this God is the "God of poets".

In the following text, I will examine Badiou's notion of this "God of poets" and try to show that he not only uses it in order to designate *and* abandon a specific notion of poetry that, according to him, has prevailed for more than 150 years. He also uses this "God" in order to formulate a criticism of a "melancholic" or "nostalgic" reference to the world in general and such an (alleged) reference by Martin Heidegger in particular. The goal of this chapter is to provide an understanding of the poets and Heidegger by critically considering Badiou's understanding of the figure of the "God of poets".

GOD OF POETS

Badiou introduces the figure of the "God of poets" in the prologue "God is Dead" of his book *Briefings on Existence* from 1998.[2] Being the last God, after the God of religion and the God of the philosophers, one might say that it is the youngest God – and it is the God with the shortest lifetime. However, "shortest lifetime", does not seem to be accurate. In difference to both, the Biblical God, who *was*, according to Badiou, once a *living* God and could therefore die,[3] and the metaphysical God, "[who] has already died or has been dead from the beginning"[4], this "God of poets" has remained in a state between life and death from its very beginning:

> About this God, we can say that it is neither dead nor alive and it cannot be deconstructed as a tired, saturated, or sedimented concept. The central poetic expression concerning it is as follows: this God has withdrawn and left the world as prey to idleness. The question of the poem is thus that of the retreat of the gods.[5]

Moreover, introduced as a "creation of Romanticism and distinctly of the poet Hölderlin",[6] the reader gets to know *ab initio* that this "God" neither is a creator, nor exists beyond mortal beings; rather the "God of poets" is created by humans, and hence, it is not or not only a God but it could equally be designated as an idol.

The special ontological status of the God of poets between life and death leads to a specific relation between men and God: this relation is neither of the "order of mourning",[7] which, according to Badiou, characterises nowadays the relation between men and the dead God of religions nor is it of the "order of critique"[8] like the philosophical relation to a metaphysical God. Instead, it is a *nostalgic* relationship that *melancholically* envisages "a chance to re-enchant the word through the gods' improbable return".[9]

At this point, Heidegger's god that can save us comes into play, since his destruction of metaphysics as well as his acceptance of the death of the Christian God upholds the chance for the God of the poem.[10] In contrast, Badiou argues for an atheism that challenges this "God of poets":

> I call *contemporary atheism* what breaks with this disposition. It is about no longer entrusting the nostalgic God of the return with the joint balance consisting of the death of the living God and the deconstruction of the metaphysical God. All in all, it is about finishing up with promises.[11]

Here, a central objective of Badiou's text becomes clear. In continuation of anti-religious atheism as well as of the destruction of metaphysics and the metaphysical God, Badiou applies the atheist gesture of *breaking* or *finishing up* with the last of the Gods, the nostalgic God of the return, the God of poets.[12] Instead of subordinating themselves to this "nostalgic God" and continuing to be the melancholic guardians of finitude, today's poets should rather conquer their own atheism and, in the words of Badiou, "destroy the powers of natural language, nostalgic phraseology, posturing of the promise, or prophetic destination to the Open".[13] And he continues:

The poem has only to be devoted to the enchantment of what the world is capable of – as it is. It has only to discern the infinite 'surrection' of invisible possibilities up to the impossible itself. [. . .] As for the God of poetry, the poem must cleanse language from within by slicing off the agency of loss and return. That is because we have lost nothing[,] and nothing returns.[14]

Here the notion of infinity is important. Badiou's thoughts about poetry are conceptually based on his assumption that Georg Cantor broke with a traditional connection between infinity and the One (and hence with the *mono*theistic God)[15] in favour of the notion of manifoldness. Instead of adhering to loss and nostalgia, poets should evoke the true infinity of possibilities.

INTERRUPTION OF THE POEM AND THE TEMPTATION OF A RETURN

Badiou's break with the "God of poets" can be better understood if we consider an earlier text from 1989 with the programmatic title *Manifesto for Philosophy*,[16] which was written shortly after *Being and Event*.[17] Like in his later prologue "God is Dead", the French philosopher points to an end of the "God of poets". He does so in referring to the so-called age of the poets,[18] an age that stretches from Hölderlin to Celan, in which poetry "traced in the oriented representations of History a disorienting diagonal".[19]

The central operation of the poet of this age is "his 'method' of disobjectication"[20] of the "destitution of the category of object",[21] which – given the correlation between subject and object – also means: of the subject. As Badiou points out:

> Poetry is then on essentially *disobjectifying*. This in no way signifies that sense is handed over to the subject, or the subjective. On the contrary, for what poetry is acutely conscious of is the 'bond' organized by the sutures between 'object', or objectivity, and 'subject'.[22]

Already in this earlier text, Badiou relates his discourse on poetry particularly to Heidegger. According to him, the force of Heidegger's project essentially consists in the fact that he has "*crossed the strictly philosophical critique* of *objectivity with its poetic destitution*"[23] and, thus, reached the point at which it is "possible to hand philosophy over to poetry".[24] But while, according to Badiou, it was true that there was an "age of poets",[25] this age is now completed and the time has come to "de-suture philosophy from its poetic condition" and to formulate a "fundamental criticism of Heidegger".[26]

This criticism concerns a specific "point of falsification":[27] Heidegger's identification of the destitution of objectivity with the destitution of science. According to Badiou, Heidegger "'constructs' the antinomy of the matheme and the poem *in such a way as to make it coincide with the opposition of knowledge and truth, or the subject/object couple and Being*".[28]

In order to understand this point better, one should take a look at Badiou's first main work *Being and Event*, in which he had already formulated his basic disagreement with Heidegger:

> For Heidegger, the poetico-natural orientation, which lets-be presentation as non-veiling, is the authentic origin. The mathematico-ideal orientation, which subtracts presence and promotes evidence, is the metaphysical closure, the first step of the forgetting. What I propose is not an overturning but another disposition of these two orientations. (. . .) The Greeks did not invent the poem. Rather, they interrupted the poem with the matheme.[29]

"Matheme" was adopted by Badiou from Lacan and further developed into a central concept of his own thought. Samo Tomšič defined it as a "tool of formalisation able to push the limits of linguistic enunciation" that "establishes philosophy's polemical positioning in the discursive field, helping it to delimit itself from sophistic discourse by thinking the real of being beyond its symbolic interplays".[30] The "matheme" hence interrupts the poem, and thereby helps philosophy – mainly Parmenides and Plato – to untie the "thought of being from its poetic enchainment to natural appearing".[31] After (and through) this interruption, the poem "nevertheless never ceased" but rather became a "temptation of a return", a temptation that "Heidegger believed to be a nostalgia and a loss, whereas it is merely the permanent play induced in thought by the unrelenting novelty of the matheme".[32]

Unfortunately, Badiou does not seem to provide here any reason for why a "temptation of a return", originating from an event in Greek antiquity, would become effective only 2300 years later with the birth of the "God of poets". And it is even less clear why this temptation should have lasted, as Badiou claims, only until Celan. Even if one might assume that there is a correspondence between the processes of intensified and accelerating modernisation, transformations, and, in consequence, losses that facilitated a "nostalgia" and, accordingly, an "age of poets", it is difficult to see why the consciousness of loss could have been completed at the end of the 1960s. Shouldn't we rather say that exactly around 1970, a new *ecological* consciousness, a new understanding of the fragility *and finitude* of the Earth, of the devastations of modern industrialisation, awoke? And is this not one important reason for why Heidegger, with his early criticism of technology and modern nihilism, became an important voice for postmodernity, and after the alleged end of the "age of poets"?

POETRY AND EARTH

Heidegger's rediscovery of Hölderlin at the end of the 1920s[33] was closely related to the introduction of a new "concept" or theme in his thought, that of *earth*. This term designates a counter-concept to "world" and hence indicates the opposite of what "world" means for Heidegger: a self-opening openness.[34] "Earth", moreover, is closely related to poetry. According to Heidegger, in poetry (and in art in general) both self-opening and self-closing-off are present. As Hans-Georg Gadamer aptly puts it:

> A work of art does not 'mean' something or function as a sign that refers to a meaning; rather, it presents itself in its own Being, so that the beholder must tarry by it. It is so very much present itself that the ingredients out of which it is composed – stone, color, tone, word – only come into a real existence of their own within the work of art itself. [. . .] But what comes forth in this way in the work is precisely its being closed-off and closing-itself-off – what Heidegger calls the Being of the earth. The earth, in truth, is not stuff, but that out of which everything comes forth and into which everything disappears.[35]

This is why Heidegger can relate art to truth. As is well known, after what is usually referred to as his *Kehre*, his turn, Heidegger preferred for 'truth' the Greek term *alētheia*, since this term entails the dimension of *lethe*, of concealing and forgetting, and articulates the very tension of being. For this reason, the relation to loss, which is certainly relevant in Heidegger's thought, is not adequately described with the notion "melancholic".[36] The loss *belongs* to being and its history, since being is always characterised not only by its appearance, but also by its withdrawal.

The problem of an occidental, and especially modern, understanding of truth, therefore, is not that it has forgotten or "lost" *something*, but that it has forgotten the "loss", the dimension of withdrawal, of "earth". *Seinsvergessenheit,* 'forgetfulness of Being' is, in this sense, also 'forgetfulness of earth'.[37] In contrast, art and in particular poetry are able to preserve the conflictual tension (*Streit*) between clearing and concealing, earth and world, and to found a truth that, according to Heidegger, was excluded during the occidental history of philosophy, (symbolically represented by Plato's exclusion of the artists from the ideal state). And this is the conceptual ground for why, according to Heidegger, Hölderlin is capable of founding or *instituting* (*stiften*) a new beginning. (The name Hölderlin is, of course, associated with a complex and controversial *political* dimension of Heidegger's notion of poetry, that cannot be pursued further at this point.)[38]

In order to understand why Badiou would put the end of an allegedly nostalgic age of poets (and linked to that of Heidegger) in the very moment when the limits and finitude of the Earth appeared, we should take a closer look at Badiou's occupation with Heidegger and poetry. While in *Being and Event* Badiou claims he would "willingly admit that absolutely originary thought occurs in poetics and in the letting-be of appearing",[39] already the use of the term "admit" might awake some doubts about Badiou's commitment. And in fact, in his *Manifesto for Philosophy*, published only one year later, he speaks of a "'*method*' of disobjectivation" and as "central *operation* (. . .) of a poet from the Age of Poets",[40] as mentioned above. Instead of the Heideggerian "letting-be of appearing",[41] Badiou reestablishes, at least implicitly, exactly that category of subjectivity that Heidegger tried to overcome by his understanding of 'letting-be of appearing'.

REACTIONARY MODERNITY

In chapter five of his *Manifesto for Philosophy,* shortly before he announces the end of the age of the poets, Badiou turns to the question of nihilism.[42] The aim of this chapter is to defend science and technology from an allegedly *nostalgic* accusation of nihilism. In doing so, however, I would claim that Badiou reveals the deeply nostalgic and even reactionary character of his own notion of the "God of poets".

In this chapter, Badiou, once again, relates Heidegger to nostalgia. He criticises Heidegger's "denunciation of technological nihilism".[43] Any relation between "technology's planetary reign" and "nihilism" could not be accepted and Heidegger's texts on this point "do not in any way avoid this pomposity", rather his elaborations were "ridiculous".[44] Especially when Heidegger would speak of "Earth's devastation", this "reactionary nostalgia" – which would be nothing but a "feudal socialism"[45] – became clear. Badiou's strong engagement in his defence of technology is reflected in the high degree of polemics, which reaches its culmination point when he states that Hitler "certainly" is the "most complete emblem" of the "nostalgic speculations" of "feudal socialism".[46]

It is exactly at this culmination point where it becomes impossible to overlook a certain reactionary nostalgia in Badiou's own anachronistic and belated praise of technology. This is shown in an exemplary way in the following quote:

> Just look at planetary exploration, energy through thermos-nuclear fusion, flying machines for everyone, three-dimensional images. . . We must indeed say: 'Gentlemen Technicians, one more effort if you are truly working towards the planetary reign of technology!' Not enough technology, technology that is still very rudimentary–that is the real situation.[47]

Really? Hundred and fifty years after the discovery of the second law of thermodynamics and fifteen years after the Club of Rome report *The Limits to Growth*, Badiou seems to still use the terminology of early modernists or techno-utopians around 1900, just as if he had never heard of the limits of earth and serious ecological problems. It is no wonder, then, that in his nostalgia for the earth-forgetting of modernity, the Earth does not play any role, that in his resistance against "finitude" (but at the same time his obsession with the finitude of Gods of all sorts), he cannot accept the finitude of the Earth. Even ten years later, in *God is Dead*, Badiou hardly ever mentions the Earth, and where he does so, he emphasises its infinity by calling us "inhabitants of the Earth's infinite sojourn",[48] "séjour infini de la Terre".[49]

As late as 2009, Badiou demonstrated a complete lack of comprehension for ecological questions when he pompously announced that he was "not afraid to affirm" that "ecology is the new opium of the people" ("Je ne crains pas de l'affirmer: l'écologie, c'est le nouvel opium du people").[50] Only a few years later, a denial of any possible finitude of Earth and a nostalgia for modernity and technology pop up everywhere in reactionary populisms, a reactionary Earth-forgetting that openly denies or downplays the ecological crisis, the human factor of climate change, and its serious threats for humanity's future on Earth—even though or because the limits of growth and the finitude of countless species and eco-systems, has become indisputable. In this time, Heidegger's thought and the poetic discovery of the Earth, still seem contemporary and relevant. For all his unquestionable merits, however, Badiou's nostalgia for toxic modernity, instead, has little to teach us.

Against this background, we can also try to give an interpretation of Badiou's notion of the nostalgic "God of poets" by focusing on the peculiar coincidence between the end of the age of poets and the appearance of the limits of the Earth. By denouncing nostalgia and the melancholic guardians of finitude, by even denouncing the talk of "Earth's devastation" as reactionary, exactly in the very moment when the dimensions of the devastation of the Earth became visible, it is difficult not to speak of a reactionary attempt to defend modernity at the moment its limits have become obvious.

NOTES

1. Martin Heidegger, *Reden und andere Zeugnisse eines Lebensweges*, GA 16 (Frankfurt a. M.: Vittorio Klostermann, 2000), 671.
2. Alain Badiou, *Briefings on Existence. A Short Treatise on Transitory Ontology*, transl. by Norman Mndarasz (Albany: State University of New York Press, 2006), 28.
3. "If 'God is dead' is asserted, it is because the God spoken of was alive and belonged to the dimension of life" (Badiou, *Briefings on Existence*, 22).
4. Badiou, *Briefings on Existence*, 25.
5. Badiou, *Briefings on Existence*, 28.
6. Badiou, *Briefings on Existence*, 28.
7. Badiou, *Briefings on Existence*, 28.
8. Badiou, *Briefings on Existence*, 28.
9. Badiou, *Briefings on Existence*, 28.
10. Badiou, *Briefings on Existence*, 29.
11. Badiou, *Briefings on Existence*, 29.
12. By relating the "God of poets" to Heidegger, Badiou breaks with a postmodernity or poststructuralism that was mainly influenced by Heidegger. Around the same time, Slavoj Žižek likewise argued for atheism in order to reject both: the, at the time, new label of the *post-secular*, and what he understood as an endless agony of the vanishing God in influential positions of postmodernism and poststructuralism. See Luca Di Blasi, "Less than Nihilism", in *Nihilism and the State of Israel: New Critical Perspectives*, ed. Nitzan Lebovic and Roy Ben Shai (London et al.: Bloomsbury Academic, 2014), 35–49.
13. Badiou, *Briefings on Existence*, 29.
14. Badiou, *Briefings on Existence*, 29; 31.
15. Badiou, *Briefings on Existence*, 22.
16. Alain Badiou, *Manifesto for Philosophy*, transl. by Norman Mndarasz (Albany: State University or New York Press, 1999), 72.
17. Alain Badiou, *Being and Event*, transl. by Oliver Feltham (New York: Continuum, 2005).
18. Badiou, *Manifesto for Philosophy*, 69.
19. Badiou, *Manifesto for Philosophy*, 71.
20. Badiou, *Manifesto for Philosophy*, 76.
21. Badiou, *Manifesto for Philosophy*, 72.
22. Badiou, *Manifesto for Philosophy*, 72.
23. Badiou, *Manifesto for Philosophy*, 73 (italics in original).
24. Badiou, *Manifesto for Philosophy*, 74.
25. Badiou, *Manifesto for Philosophy*, 74.
26. Badiou, *Manifesto for Philosophy*, 74.
27. Badiou, *Manifesto for Philosophy*, 74.
28. Badiou, *Manifesto for Philosophy*, 74 (italics in original).
29. Badiou, *Being and Event*, 125f.

30. Samo Tomšič, "Matheme", in *The Badiou Dictionary*, ed. by Steven Corcoran (Edinburgh: Edinburgh University Press, 2015), 196–99, here 196.
31. Badiou, *Being and Event*, 126.
32. Badiou, *Being and Event*, 126.
33. Cf. Martin Heidegger, *Das Ereignis* (GA 71) (Frankfurt a. M.: Vittorio Klostermann, 2009), 89.
34. "World and earth are essentially different and yet never separated from one another. World is grounded on earth, and earth rises up through world. But the relation between world and earth never atrophies into the empty unity of opposites unconcerned with one another. In its resting upon earth the world strives to surmount it. As the self-opening it will tolerate nothing closed. As the sheltering and concealing, however, earth tends always to draw the world into itself and to keep it there". Martin Heidegger, "The Origin of the Work of Art", in *Off the Beaten Track*, ed. by Julian Young and Kenneth Haynes, 1–56, here 26.
35. Hans-Georg Gadamer, *Heidegger's Ways* (Albany: State University of New York Press, 1994), 104.
36. Similarly, attributing Hölderlin to "romanticism", as Badiou does, is, of course, a flagrant relapse into an early misunderstanding of Hölderlin that was already overcome as of the second half of the 19th century. But this misunderstanding is closely related to Badiou's distorting reduction of Hölderlin's and Heidegger's understanding of Gods and God to a conservative, melancholic hope for a "return", a distortion which, curiously, is quite similar to the common Christian misunderstanding of Heidegger as return to paganism.
37. An analogous critique was recently formulated by Giorgio Agamben. See "Gaia e Ctonia", in: *Quodlibet*, 28th December 2020. https://www.quodlibet.it/giorgio-agamben-gaia-e-ctonia [access on 5th April 2021].
38. Philippe Lacoue-Labarthe's profound investigation on this topic can be found in his book *Heidegger and the Politics of Poetry* (Urbana: University of Illinois Press, 2007).
39. Badiou, *Being and Event*, 125.
40. Badiou, *Manifesto for Philosophy*, 76 (emphasis added).
41. Badiou, *Being and Event*, 126.
42. Badiou, *Manifesto for Philosophy*, 53–59.
43. Badiou, *Manifesto for Philosophy*, 56.
44. Badiou, *Manifesto for Philosophy*, 53.
45. Badiou, *Manifesto for Philosophy*, 53.
46. Badiou, *Manifesto for Philosophy*, 57.
47. Badiou, *Manifesto for Philosophy*, 54.
48. Badiou, *Briefings on Existence*, 31.
49. Alain Badiou, *Court traité d'ontologie transitoire* (Paris: Éditions du Seuil, 1998), 23.
50. Alain Badiou, "L'hypothèse communiste – interview d'Alain Badiou par Pierre Gaultier". *Newsnet.fr*, August 7, 2009. http://newsnet.fr/29896 [access on 25th April, 2020].

Chapter 4

In the Outhouse of Being

What Satires Tell Us about Heidegger's Philosophy

Dieter Thomä

Philosophers have gained the attention of comedians and satirists ever since Socrates appeared in Aristophanes' plays. Yet no one was more frequently satirised than Martin Heidegger. This does not mean that Heidegger and the representatives of satire and comedy were kindred spirits. It is safe to assume that Heidegger was not particularly keen on being mocked or slated. As opposed to some of his colleagues, including Socrates himself, he was not fond of using elements of comedy in his own work. It may well be that the importance of being earnest so palpable in his writings has goaded some of Heidegger's readers to go against the grain and make fun of his philosophical pathos.

In any case, the special treatment Heidegger receives is a compliment of a kind and hints at a peculiar feature of his philosophy proper. Satire does not stay on the level of malevolent mischief but has its own revealing or disclosing power. Heidegger scholars have largely neglected the comical commentators engaging with his texts, even though two of his lovers, four Nobel-prize winners and other luminaries are among them.[1] Even critics who take issue with his political and philosophical missteps may be at odds with mockery, as it does not do justice to the problems at stake.

My aim in this chapter is twofold. In the first section, I will present a panorama of the most important authors satirising Heidegger. This overview will be followed by general aesthetic considerations. In the second section, I will argue that the discussion of the "comical" remains incomplete without addressing its counterpart, namely the "sublime". As it turns out, Heidegger's disproportionate exposure to satire can be explained by his own peculiar reference not to the comical but to the sublime. While my paper will discuss some more or less entertaining material at the beginning, it will turn to serious questions at the end. It could be said that the two sections are inspired by different muses: the first by Thalia, the second by Melpomene.[2]

SATIRISING HEIDEGGER: A SHORT HISTORY

The panorama presented in this section is organised chronologically and gathers material from Thomas Mann, Hannah Arendt, Margot of Sachsen-Meiningen, Mary Flannery O'Connor, Gabriel Marcel, Oskar Maria Graf, Günter Grass, Saul Bellow, Jerzy Kosinski, Carl Schmitt, Thomas Bernhard, Elfriede Jelinek, and Arnold Stadler.

An early offhand example for satirising Heidegger is given by a novelist whose talent for caricaturing philosophers remains inconspicuous compared to his other achievements. This talent comes to the fore most prominently in his *Magic Mountain*, where one of the main characters, Leo Naphta, is loosely based on Georg Lukács. It is unfortunate that Thomas Mann (1875–1955) never alludes to Heidegger in his literary writings, as his letter sent to Paul Tillich in 1944 raises expectations. Mann writes, "Heidegger – I have, from the beginning, never liked that Nazi", and plays with one of Heidegger's neologisms, *Jemeinigkeit* or "mineness". Mann suggests that someone speaking with a Berlin accent would say *jemein* when meaning *gemein*, that is, "mean". This play of words can be reproduced in English in a makeshift manner by pronouncing "mineness" like "meanness". Here is a translation of Mann's entire tirade: "Mineness! Should something like that not be punishable? I initially meant to hear a Berliner saying something like 'mean'. And that is actually to the point. [. . .] Schopenhauer would have given a mouthful to this high-brow botcher and criminal desecrator of language".[3] Heidegger meets the dismay and disdain of a writer who cherishes the wealth of a given language and regards the creation of neologisms as an act of linguistic and non-linguistic violence.

Hannah Arendt's (1906–1975) writings on Heidegger largely lack satirical or comical potential, except for a short piece written in 1953 titled *Heidegger the Fox*. In this portrait, which takes on the form of an old-fashioned fable, Arendt tells the story of a hapless fox, who, after many distressing experiences of being caught in traps, misreading a "trap" for a "non-trap", and losing his fur, retreats from the world. From then on, he lives in a burrow, a self-made trap, from which he will never be able to escape anymore. Arendt contends that Heidegger praises his burrow as "the most beautiful trap in the world", and succeeds in attracting others to keep his company. "Everyone except our fox could, of course, step out of it again. [. . .] But the fox who lived in the trap said proudly: 'So many are visiting me in my trap that I have become the best of all foxes'. And there is some truth in that, too. Nobody knows the nature of traps better than one who sits in a trap his whole life long".[4]

This text stems from a short period in Arendt's life when the distance between her and her former lover is comparably large. It is anteceded by her most critical essay *What Is Existential Philosophy*, and followed by growingly apologetic writings. The scenario sketched in *Heidegger the Fox* is quite spectacular: A philosopher gets entangled in his own shortcomings and turns constriction and limitation into a virtue. He becomes an expert on one room only, a room virtually co-extensive with himself. With this scenario oscillating between empowerment and entrapment, Arendt obviously alludes to Kafka's famous story *The Burrow*. While Arendt praises Heidegger's concept of the "world" in other writings, *Heidegger the Fox* depicts a thinker whose world shrinks to a narcissistic, claustrophobic universe. This hyperbolic, satirical scenario does not just lead to dismissive reactions. It can also generate benevolent reactions – and has done so in the case of Arendt herself: A cornered thinker deserves empathy, or does he not?

One of the most accomplished satires on Heidegger was published anonymously in 1954 in the form of a carnival speech. After initial rumours[5] that the text was written by Heidegger's brother, Fritz, the author could be identified as Margot, Princess of Sachsen-Meiningen (1911–1998). Heidegger had one of his many extra-marital affairs with her in 1945.[6] The text is loosely based on Heidegger's essay *The Thing*, where he muses about the "gift of the outpouring" (*Geschenk des Gusses*) vouching for the "singlefoldness" (*Einfalt*) of the world.[7] As drinking is a favourite pastime during carnival (*Fastnacht*), the author muses about the "gift of the outpouring" and plays with the numerous meanings of *Fass* (vat, barrel, cask) and *fassen* (hold, grasp, contain). These two words are directly related, as *Fass*, like *Gefäss* or vessel, has a holding capacity or *fasst* a certain amount of liquid. Alas, Margot of Sachsen-Meiningen's hilarious rhapsody on *fassen* is untranslatable.[8] She creates comical effects by cutting through Heidegger's pretension of relying on language or surrendering to language. By mimicking his linguistic operations, such as the substantivisation of verbs, the verbalisation of nouns, the uncoupling of preposition and noun, she shows that Heidegger's pretension may, in fact, conceal a zeal for artful or wilful composition. By creating a text which sounds almost Heideggerian, the Princess transforms the "glance into that which is" into a free-wheeling linguistic fantasy. The text plays with Heidegger's back and forth between disclosure and concealment by stating that "the cask remains absent in its appearance". It also refers to a famous passage from Heidegger's *Letter on Humanism*. Heidegger says, "Language is the house of being. [. . .] Human beings [. . .] are the guardians of this home".⁹ The satire reads, "The night is the cask of being. Man is the guardian of the cask".

Mary Flannery O'Connor (1925–1964) deserves credit for being the first non-German author writing a satire on Heidegger. In 1955, she publishes the short story *Good Country People*, which features a thirty-two-year-old woman with an artificial leg and a Ph.D. in philosophy. In an act of wilful self-definition, she has changed her name from Joy to Hulga, that is, from cheerfulness to what her mother regards as "glumness" and "deliberate rudeness". One day the mother, with whom she lives, picks up one of her daughter's favourite books and starts reading a passage "underlined with a blue pencil":

> Science, on the other hand, has to assert its soberness and seriousness afresh and declare that it is concerned solely with what-is. Nothing – how can it be for science anything but a horror and a phantasm? If science is right, then one thing stands firm: science wishes to know nothing of nothing. Such is after all the strictly scientific approach to Nothing. We know it by wishing to know nothing of Nothing.

These lines from Heidegger's *What Is Metaphysics?* "worked on Mrs. Hopewell like some evil incantation in gibberish. She shut the book quickly and went out of the room as if she were having a chill".[10] Hulga is not really irritated by her mother's concerns and does whatever she does with resolve and great seriousness: "Here I am – LIKE I AM", she says. "I don't have illusions. I'm one of those people who see *through* to nothing".[11]

One day, a young salesman knocks the door, tries to sell a bible to the women without much success, and earns himself an invitation for dinner – and also a date with Hulga. It is not perfectly clear why Hulga is willing to go out with him. She may just like the idea of doing something unconventional, search for "a deeper understanding of life", feel some sensual longing or fall for a fatal attraction. When they kiss, her reaction is rather cold. "Her mind" is "clear and detached and ironic anyway". Even though she prides herself of being in charge, she eventually gives in to his advances. As it turns out, the young man makes a habit out of seducing and hurting women. After some kissing and fondling, he makes fun of her, steals Hulga's wooden leg, and hits the road: "You ain't so smart. I been believing in nothing ever since I was born".[12]

Hulga bears some similarity with the author herself who also lived with her mother and was fatally ill. However, author and protagonist differ in a decisive point. The author is firmly grounded in her Catholic faith, whereas Hulga proudly defines herself as a non-believer. The comical effect results from the difference between her abstract, intellectual nihilism and other people's practical nihilism or outright cynicism. They actually believe in nothing, not even morality. Flannery O'Connor's satire is a tale of disillusionment and its discontents.

The most important French contribution to satirising Heidegger stems from philosopher and writer Gabriel Marcel (1889–1973). With Heidegger, he shares the birth year and the popular label as "existentialist philosopher". Like O'Connor's, his position is defined by Catholicism. Heidegger is anything but amused when he takes note of Marcel's satirical play *La Dimension Florestan*. In this play from 1958, Heidegger takes the stage as "Hans Walter Dolch", the author of a work titled *The Watch on Being* (*Die Wacht am Sein*) – a pun on the famous nationalist song "The Watch on the Rhine" (*Die Wacht am Rhein*). Marcel makes fun of Heidegger's tautological use of language, in particular of his line "The thing things"[13] by stating, "The pear *pears*, you have said, the apple *apples*, you have added with even more irrefutable authority".[14] That the ontology of fruits is a particularly fruitful resource for satires on Heidegger will be confirmed by Carl Schmitt. Ecologists may wonder whether exotic fruits also qualify for verbalisation. Is the pomegranate capable of pomegranating? And how does this relate to the phrase "The grenade grenades"? It is inexcusable that these questions have not been addressed by Heidegger scholars.

The author Oskar Maria Graf (1894–1967), who left Germany immediately after Hitler's rise to power and emigrated to the U.S. in 1938, comments on Martin Heidegger or, as he likes to call him, "Martl" (a Bavarian diminutive of his first name) in his text *Our Dialect and Existentialism* from 1961. He states, "that language exemplifies both the character and the talent of a person"[15] and expands on the experience of death and nothingness by drawing daring comparisons: "After all things have vanished, the individual human beings really stand in blind nothingness. They are exposed to it both internally and externally. Like butter in the summer sun, all those things that they could partly hold onto, melt away and evaporate. Nothing is left but bare existence, the 'shabby' care or worry about it (*Sorgerei*) and eventually the dread of death".[16]

Graf undercuts Heidegger's high-flying linguistic ambitions by playing with hyphenated words, for instance *Da-Sein* or *Ex-Sistenz*. His most intriguing contribution to this list is the word *Ab-Ort*, which aptly fits to Heidegger's extensive discussion of place, site, house, *topos*, etc. *Abort* in German means toilet, restroom or, literally, outhouse. It refers to a place or room out of the way and out of sight, which can be used for relieving oneself or defecating. Heidegger's phenomenology suffers from serious shortcomings due to its blatant neglect of the restroom or *Abort*. A scatological extension of topology is overdue. Graf hints at the fact that excrements become "the absent" (*das Abwesende*) and exemplify decomposition, *Verwesung*, which literally means a loss of essence (*Wesen*). "People might assume that something rather repulsive occurs [*west*] in there" – that is, in the *Abort*. "Yet from Martl's point of view, this is certainly not the case". As a matter of fact, Heidegger himself talks about *Verwesung* in his essay on Trakl.[17] The potential of a scatological theory of "essence" is considerable. Firstly, it could explore the connection between the person "who is apart" (*der Abgeschiedene*)[18] and the process of excretion (*Ausscheidung*). Secondly, such a theory could expand on Graf's considerations on *Stuhlgang*, that is, "bowel movement".[19] The notions of *Gang*, path and movement play a central role in Heidegger's late remarks on time and space.

The author of the most significant satire on Heidegger is arguably Nobel laureate Günter Grass (1927–2015). In his novel *Dog Years* from 1963, Grass uses Heideggerian language for illustrating experiences in the Second World War. One of the figures depicted in the novel is a sergeant who either does not talk at all or speaks like Heidegger and plots "the advent of the still unuttered essence of unconcealment". He serves as a major inspiration to his underlings, who frame their military routine by stating, "After all, the essence of being-there is its existence", and realise that "the word 'existence' and its collaterals" meet virtually "all requirements: 'Would you exist me a cigarette? Who feels like existing a movie with me? Shut your trap or I'll exist you one.' To go on sick call was to plug for a sack existence". In war times, life gets simple and basic: You do nothing but existing. In analogy to Sartre's misreading of Being, Grass emphasises its physical dimension. One of the most graphic examples for disillusioned facticity is the description of how prospective parents bury a foetus after a miscarriage:

> Ah, are we ourselves ever, is mine ever, now under the leaves, in the ground, not deeply frozen; for higher than reality is potentiality; here manifested: what primarily and ordinarily does not show itself, what is hidden but at the same time is an essential part of what does primarily and ordinarily show itself [. . .]. The baby [. . .]. There only toward death, which means: tossed in layers, with a few leaves and hollow beechnuts on top [. . .], fieldstone on it. Grounding in the ground. [. . .] The nihilating Nothing. Lousy luck. Come-to-be in errancy.

Grass also uses Heidegger's cumbersome language for describing the banality and brutality of war and for caricaturing the bureaucratic jargon of the National Socialists. The lack of humanity corresponds to the Führer's affectionate relationship to his dog and to the desperate search for it when it gets lost:

The original manifestness of the Führerdog is attuned to distantiality. [. . .] The Führerdog attuned to distantiality is acknowledged as the Nothing. [. . .] The Nothing is coming-to-be between enemy armour and our own spearheads. [. . .] The Nothing is running on four legs [. . .]. The Nothing attuned to distantiality discloses dread in every sector of the front. Dread is-there. [. . .] Never must the Reichcapital in its locus-wholeness be infirmed by dread.

The Heideggerian sergeant does not witness the dog search anymore, as he is removed from the scene when he, "in a state of drunkenness", insults the "Führer and Chancellor in sentences marked by such locutions as: forgetful of Being, mound of bones, structure of care, Stutthof, Todtnau, and concentration camp. As they were taking him away – in broad daylight – he bawled mysteriously: 'You ontic dog! Alemannic dog! [. . .] What did you do to little Husserl? [. . .] You pre-Socratic Nazi dog!'"[20] Grass's versatile appropriation and alteration of Heidegger's language lead to an important finding: This language seems to be uncannily prone to inhumanity and brutality.

Heidegger also caught the attention of another Nobel laureate, namely Saul Bellow (1915-2005). The eponymous hero of his novel *Herzog* published in 1964 is an "important professor" facing a midlife crisis. Herzog goes back and forth between everyday concerns and catastrophes on the one hand, intellectual impromptus and impasses on the other. While going through a divorce and trying to keep himself out of asylum, Herzog reads various authors, for instance Kierkegaard, Martin Buber, and Oswald Spengler, and writes letters to luminaries, which he never actually sends off. Herzog makes fun of "the cant and rant of pipsqueaks about Inauthenticity and Forlornness", but still addresses a letter to one of the thinkers responsible for popularising these terms: "Dear Doktor Professor Heidegger, I should like to know what you mean by the expression 'the fall into the quotidian.' When did this fall occur? Where were we standing when it happened?"[21] Herzog (or Bellow) also says, "No philosopher knows what the ordinary is, has not fallen into it deeply enough".[22]

More intriguing than the familiar concern about worldless thought is Herzog's critique of the elevated stance of the thinker as such. He claims that human beings cannot possibly "fall" into the quotidian. They are always already there. This line of thought could be extended to an interesting argument against a certain indecision or ambiguity in Heidegger. On the one hand, Heidegger states that "Dasein has, in the first instance, [. . .] fallen into the 'world'".[23] Like Bellow, he seems to mean that the human being is in the midst of things and already immersed in everyday life. On the other hand, the very idea of "falling" only makes sense when there is a certain drop height, that is, when a person has a position above the ground. This leads to the conclusion that Heidegger's notion of "falling" is self-defeating: It presupposes an elevated stance anteceding "falling", while, at the same time, pretending that the "falling" has already occurred.

In a sideline to the argument on everydayness, Herzog also discusses the opposition between the American way of life, a "hedonistic world in which happiness is set up on a mechanical model", and the "ingenious German models" developed by "existentialists who tell you how good dread is for you, how it saves you from distraction and gives you your freedom and makes you authentic. God is no more. But Death is. That's their story".[24] In a bold move, Herzog dismisses all those models and seeks to overcome the alternative between petty hedonism and pathetic dread, between Americanism and German-ness. It may well be that a phrase characterising Herzog fits to Heidegger even better: "Herzog had a weakness for grandeur, and even bogus grandeur".[25]

Jerzy Kosinski (1933–1991) publishes a comic novel in 1970, whose title already sounds Heideggerian: *Being There*. A movie based on a screenplay by Kosinski and featuring Peter Sellars as main protagonist receives an Academy Award, a number of Oscar nominations and other honours in 1979. Kosinski cautions against an all-too philosophical reading of his novel, and rightly so. A commentary on Heidegger it is not. Yet neither the title of the novel nor its working title *Dasein* are coincidental. In one of his rare explanations of his choice of words, Kosinski states that *Dasein* is "a philosophical term, difficult to translate, which could mean the state in which one *is* and *is not* at the same time".[26]

This description of *Dasein* as being oneself and not being oneself, as being a self, and being anybody or nobody, applies to the novel's and the film's protagonist in an intriguing fashion. Chance the gardener or Chauncey Gardiner is a feeble-minded man who has spent his whole life with gardening and watching TV. When he gets kicked out of his quarters after the death of his master, a rich couple saves him and takes his simplicity for wisdom. His imperturbable consistency, a fruit of a complete lack of imagination, earns him the recognition of insecure, wavering observers. Thus, they mistake his gardening tips as the groundwork for an economic theory of growth cycles. By holding fast to his role, Chance himself becomes a role model for others and even a possible presidential candidate. "You have the great gift . . . of being natural, and that, my dear man, is a rare talent, and the true mark of a leader".[27]

The plot of Kosinski's *Being There* playfully challenges certain features of Heidegger's philosophy: the constriction of perspectives, the nostalgia for what Gustave Flaubert calls a simple heart, an overkill of hermeneutics (the gardener's favourite sentence is "I understand"). In the novel, the difference

between everydayness and authenticity collapses: Whatever the hero says or does is meaningless and significant at the same time.

Beside Hannah Arendt and Margot of Sachsen-Meiningen, Carl Schmitt (1888–1985) is the only one on this list of satirists, who met Heidegger in person. Their exchange dates back to the time when both the infamous legal scholar and the philosopher supported the Nazi regime. Schmitt's satirical contribution, which remains as marginal and fragmentary as Thomas Mann's, stems from the period shortly after Heidegger's death. A notebook discovered in the Schmitt archives contains clippings from Heidegger's interview with the magazine *Der Spiegel* conducted in 1966 and published posthumously in 1976. Schmitt's comment on the clippings reads as follows:

ceaseless juicer of words [*Wort-Entsafter*],
however and nonetheless
– at least –
no Nobel laureate
and not even an Oslo candidate.

Driven by envy and disdain at the same time, Schmitt witnesses Heidegger's popularity and derides his linguistic capacities. He finds that juice extractors only work "with soft fruits and vegetables, not with stone-fruits, such as cherries and plums".[28] By using the metaphor of stone fruits, Schmitt means to say that Heidegger is utterly unable to deal with hard questions. Like Gabriel Marcel's (see above), Carl Schmitt's fructological observations have not been brought to bear in academic research.

In his novel *Old Masters* from 1985, Thomas Bernhard (1931–1989) takes on Heidegger as well as Adalbert Stifter, who firmly belonged to Heidegger's literary canon. Bernhard's attack on this "ridiculous Nazi philistine in plus-fours" totals more than ten pages in the original. Here is a lengthy extract:

Heidegger was a kitschy brain, [. . .] who was *always merely comical*, just as *petit-bourgeois* as Stifter, just as disastrously megalomanic, a feeble thinker from the Alpine foothills [. . .]. He was through and through an unspiritual person, devoid of all fantasy, devoid of all sensibility, a genuine German philosophical ruminant [. . .]. True, the Heidegger cow has become thinner but the Heidegger cow is still being milked. [. . .] Heidegger was a philosophical market crier who only brought stolen goods to the market, everything of Heidegger's is second-hand, he was and is the prototype of the *re*-thinker, who lacked everything, but truly everything, for independent thinking. [. . .] Heidegger has so reduced everything great that it has become

Germancompatible, you understand: *Germancompatible* [*deutschmöglich*] [. . .]. Surely it is no accident [. . .] that Heidegger [. . .] has always been popular, and is still popular, mainly with those tense women [. . .]. Heidegger is *the women's philosopher* [. . .]. Everything about Heidegger has always been repulsive to me, not only the night-cap on his head and his homespun winter long-johns above the stove which he himself had lit at Todtnauberg [. . .]. When I think that even super-intelligent people have been taken in by Heidegger and that even one of my best women friends wrote a dissertation about Heidegger, and moreover wrote that dissertation *quite seriously*, I feel sick to this day [. . .]. The people who made pilgrimages to Heidegger were mainly those who confused philosophy with culinary science, who regarded philosophy as something fried and roasted and cooked, which is entirely in line with German taste. Heidegger used to hold court at Todtnauberg and at all times would allow himself to be admired on his philosophical Black Forest plinth like a sacred cow. Even a famous and much-feared North German publisher of periodicals kneeled before him devotionally and open-mouthed.[29]

Several points addressed by Bernhard are noteworthy. The fact that he regards Heidegger as a "comical" thinker will become important in the second section of this paper. According to Bernhard, this comical, devaluating effect is generated by pretentious provinciality and the reduction of far-reaching questions to German-ness. He constructs a strict opposition between originality and Heidegger's cow-like rumination. Bernhard also comments on two major contemporary figures, namely Ingeborg Bachmann, who wrote her dissertation on Heidegger as early as 1949, and Rudolf Augstein, the editor of the weekly *Der Spiegel*, whose interview with Heidegger already upset Carl Schmitt. Like Paul Celan, her lover in the period when she writes the dissertation, Bachmann cannot help but to take Heidegger seriously. Yet this does not prevent her from criticising him and from stating that his theoretical language falls short of properly rendering the experiences, which it intends to express.[30] Like Bernhard, Bachmann could have concluded that a discrepancy between high ambition and lacklustre performance has a comical effect.

Thomas Bernhard was not right on all counts. There are exceptions to his rather misogynic rule that Heidegger was a "women's philosopher". The most famous is the fourth Nobel laureate in the series of Heidegger satirists, namely Elfriede Jelinek (*1946). In her play *Totenauberg* from 1991, she heavily relies on the Black Forest cliché, like Grass and Bernhard before her. By altering Todtnauberg, the location of Heidegger's famous hut, to

Totenauberg, Jelinek draws a line from the name of the village to the dead of the 20th century. Extremely compelling is her idea of introducing Heidegger as *Herrchen des Seins*.[31] The word *Herrchen*, formally the diminutive of "master", is intriguing for several reasons. As it is exclusively used for dog owners in German, Heidegger appears as a rather narrow-minded figure obsessed with "Being" like many dog owners are with their pets, who may still behave in an unruly manner. This *Herrchen* aptly complements the Heideggerian dog making its appearance in Grass's *Dog Years*. Moreover, Jelinek's nickname runs against Heidegger's self-proclaimed willingness to be mastered or guided by this very "Being". Like Thomas Mann, Margot of Sachsen-Meiningen and others, she questions the credibility of Heidegger's devout rhetoric.

In *Totenauberg*, Jelinek is particularly interested in the dynamic and confrontation between Heidegger and Hannah Arendt and experiments with a vocabulary sounding like Heideggerianism gone wild. The "old man" says, for example:

> In the vast autumn night, the river whooshes. Stating oneself [*sich selbst zu sagen*] is enough, anytime soon one will encounter oneself. It is as simple as that. [. . .] Great things only emerge in the homeland, by virtue of the fact that it belongs to us and to nobody else. The strangers disturb us in our exhilaration about everything [. . .]. We are there, settle down and forget everything else. We are innocent when we come up to the hut, cleansed by the washing bay of nature. [. . .] Sweet nothingness! Firing pins out of cream on the temples. [. . .] And yet: [. . .] Do you hear the footsteps? Once we stomped around in alien beings like in a barrel filled with grapes, until the red juice began to run beneath the soles. [. . .] This is over and never happened.

The "woman" alias Hannah Arendt ironically congratulates Heidegger for being "lucky" enough that "others had to experience death for you!"[32] Jelinek portrays Heidegger as a self-absorbed thinker immunising himself to political charges and assuming a state of purity. Being authentic appears as a fundamentalist exercise.

The renowned novelist Arnold Stadler (*1954) was born in Messkirch like Heidegger himself. In difference to Graf, Grass, Bernhard, Jelinek and others, his attitude towards his hometown and the country of his origin is rather generous and affectionate. Unlike Thomas Bernhard, he venerates both Stifter and Heidegger.[33] This does not prevent him from decorating his Heidegger portrait with some caricatural lines. The philosopher makes an appearance in *My Dog, My Pig, My Life* from 1994. In this novel, a philosopher named Heidegger meets his cousin and namesake, a cattle dealer. He gives him the assignment of collecting the "oldest words" used by his customers in the countryside. As soon as the philosopher will receive these words, he will use them for a task of world-historical dimensions. The criteria for such words are simple: "The older, the more venerable; the less comprehensible, the more valuable". Heidegger's highest hopes rest on "two stable maids", whom he regards as "holy:" "From them, the philosopher hoped to receive the word that will save the whole world".[34] In Stadler's scenario, it is not the poets who assume the role of saviours, but simple minds from the day before yesterday.

THE COMICAL AND THE SUBLIME IN HEIDEGGER'S THOUGHT

It would be tempting to identify features and topics that all those different satires described in the previous section have in common. Instead of pursuing this task, I will raise a more fundamental question: Why does Heidegger's philosophy evoke satirical responses in such frequency? Do his texts have an oblique, inherent quality conducive to unintended puns?

In order to answer this question, I start with a definition of satire in general. Around 1800s, the underrated German novelist and aesthetic thinker Jean Paul defined satire as a subcategory of the "comical" specifically marked by an antipathy or distaste (*Unwille*) for its object.[35] The main reason for Heidegger creating such antipathy is obviously his political behaviour, which I will leave aside here.[36] Jean Paul also says that the comical cannot be properly understood without addressing its counterpart or "archenemy", namely the "sublime". Whereas the comical belittles its object and makes it appear laughable or ridiculous (*lächerlich*), the sublime elevates or enlarges its object.[37] This means that these two procedures use the same technique, just in different directions. Like a field glass which, when turned around, has an inverted effect, the rise to sublimity can be reverted to a hard landing in ridiculousness. This is confirmed by Napoleon's proverbial comment after the deplorable retreat of his troops from Moscow: "Du sublime au ridicule il n'y a qu'un pas".[38]

It is futile to search for a direct relation between satire and Heidegger's texts as they are imbued with seriousness and lack comical qualities. In the light of the close connection between the comical and the sublime, I can explore that relation in an indirect manner, namely via the sublime. I will try to show that Heidegger does approach the sublime – yet in a strange manner. This distorted approach then has an inverse effect in the sense that it results in Heidegger's downfall into the comical. As will be shown, this very dynamic is the reason for the astounding satirical potential of his texts.

I cannot expand on the theory of the sublime as developed by Burke, Kant and some postmodern thinkers like Lyotard. Suffice it to say that Kant observes a discrepancy between overpowering, overwhelming events – e.g., "hurricanes" or "war" – on the one hand, "our power" as humans "call[ed] forth" by them and our "capacity for resistance" on the other hand.[39] In Kant, this independent stance is secured by human rationality. The discrepancy between an external event and human experience then becomes the starting point for the postmodern fascination with the sublime. In Lyotard, for instance, it becomes a centrepiece for the argument that subject and object, reason and reality are incommensurable.

It is noteworthy that Lyotard takes this incommensurability as an opportunity to liberate the modes of representation. When adequate representation is out of reach, humans can conduct experiments, in which objects appear bigger or smaller than they are. This change of scale follows the exact logic of sublime magnification or comical belittlement. This is why Lyotard also sees the opportunity for "ontology" to become "satirical".[40] He states that the postmodern difference between "thought" and its "Other" takes its inspiration from an "essential motif of Heidegger's thinking".[41]

These brief reminders of the theory of the sublime provide a small yet stable basis for asking the question of whether and how Heidegger addresses the sublime. It is safe to say that he does not use the above-mentioned discrepancy for enforcing rational self-preservation (like Kant). Nor does Heidegger use it for encouraging postmodern playfulness. Discrepancy may not be to Heidegger's liking altogether, as he aims at re-establishing an original relation between self and world, humans and things: "We are the be-thinged, the conditioned ones".[42]

Yet Heidegger does not stay away from the sublime altogether. In 1933, he says, "questioning means: exposing oneself to the sublimity of things and their laws; it means: not closing oneself off to the terror of the untamed and to the confusion of darkness".[43] That this reference to the sublime has an anti-Kantian twist comes to the fore when Heidegger establishes a conjunction between "exposedness, transportedness, tradition, and mandate".[44] Whereas Kant insists on the difference between an external event and human self-assertion, Heidegger links self-assertion to a mandate directly derived from such an event. After 1933, Heidegger revokes the idea of actively appropriating an overpowering dynamic and smoothens his powerful, wilful rhetoric. Yet he continues to adhere to sublimity in the sense that he orients his thought towards a concealed destiny reigned by "mystery", "danger", and "lightning".[45] He also claims that his thinking is uniquely qualified for exploring this dimension.

This reveals the basic flaw of Heidegger's overt or oblique references to the sublime. Heidegger appeals to it and abuses it at the same time. He does not just try "to present the fact that there is an unpresentable",[46] but offers what music lovers dream of: an exclusive backstage pass granting entrance to a hidden chamber. A steadfast attempt to face or confront the unpresentable is not desirable for Heidegger as it would be prone to subjectivation. He does not account for the gaping abyss between overwhelming events and those who experience them. The sublime incommensurability dramatised in Kantian and postmodern aesthetics comes to an end. By taking language as an "avowal" (*Zuspruch*)[47] of Being and by becoming its designated listener, he relinquishes the tension between thinking and its "Other" central to the theory of the sublime. Heidegger claims to possess the exclusive rights for staging the play of concealment and unconcealment. He is on speaking terms with strangeness. The uncanny becomes familiar – at least to him. His texts obtain a strangely self-absorbed character. He creates a short circuit.

The humility displayed in Heidegger's obtrusive willingness to listen, to let go and give in, is disturbing and misleading. As this willingness is presented as a unique achievement, it is a barely concealed claim of greatness. Heidegger does not hesitate to regard himself as a thinker of great thoughts and of world-historical import. He pretends to be indispensable. Some readers may grant Heidegger this elevated position. Those who take issue with his self-aggrandising gesture are entitled to describe it as a misguided appropriation of sublimity: He is all-too familiar with the unfamiliar. When his high-flying ambitions collapse, disenchantment becomes palpable. This is the moment when Heidegger becomes Napoleon's successor and proves the fact that "from the sublime to the ridiculous there is but a step". No little things, only lofty things can be belittled. Loftiness triggers comical reactions when it becomes pretentious. The satirists discussed in the first section of this chapter register Heidegger's sublime overzeal and react to it by tilting the image and exploiting its inherent comic. Heidegger is right when saying, "We fall upward, to a height. Its loftiness opens up a depth"[48] – except that this depth is the low point of a text being laughed about.

Thomas Mann once asked, "Is not the best in *Zarathustra* satire?"[49] Accordingly, I am inclined to ask whether Heidegger is at his best in the satires written about him.

NOTES

1. With Peter Handke, a fifth Nobel-prize winner engages with Heidegger's thought, albeit not satirically. For Handke's take on Heidegger, compare Florian Grosser's contribution in this volume.

2. This chapter is a heavily revised and expanded compilation of two German texts: Dieter Thomä, "Heidegger in der Satire: Das Herrchen des Seins", in *Heidegger-Handbuch*, ed. Dieter Thomä (Stuttgart: Metzler, 2013, 2nd ed.), 536–39; Dieter Thomä, "Am Ab-Ort des Seins: Lächerliches und Erhabenes in Heideggers Philosophie", in *Verwindungen: Arbeit an Heidegger*, ed. Wolfgang Ullrich (Frankfurt: Fischer, 2003), 89–109, 174–77.

3. Thomas Mann, "Das Deutscheste: Thomas Mann an Paul Tillich, 13. April 1944", in *Frankfurter Allgemeine Zeitung*, June 20 (2002), 45.

4. Hannah Arendt, "Heidegger the Fox", in *Essays in Understanding 1930-1954*, ed. Jerome Kohn (New York: Harcourt Brace & Company, 1994), 361–62.

5. Luzia Braun, "Da-Da-Da-Sein: Fritz Heidegger: Holzwege zur Sprache. Quasi una Philosophia", in *Die Zeit* 22, no. 9 (1989): 58.

6. Gertrud Heidegger (ed.), *"Mein liebes Seelchen!" Briefe Martin Heideggers an seine Frau Elfride 1915-1970* (München: Piper, 2005), 216, 248, 299.

7. Martin Heidegger, "The Thing", in *Poetry, Language, Thought*, trans. Albert Hofstadter (New York: Harper & Row, 1971), 163–80, 171.

8. Here is a short extract: "Das Fassende des Fassbaren ist die Nacht. Sie fasst, indem sie übernachtet. So gefasst, nachtet das Fass in der Nacht. Was fasst? Was nachtet? [. . .] Die Nacht ist das Fass des Seins. Der Mensch ist der Wächter des Fasses. Dies ist seine Ver-Fassung. Das Fassende des Fasses aber ist die Leere. Nicht das Fass fasst die Leere und nicht die Leere das Fass, sie fügen einander wechselweise in ihr Fassbares. Im Erscheinen des Fasses als solchem aber bleibt das Fass selbst aus. Es hat sein Bleibendes in der Nacht. Die Nacht übergiesst das Fass mit seinem Bleiben. Aus dem Geschenk dieses Gusses west die Fastnacht. Es ist unfassbar". See Hans Dieter Zimmermann, *Martin und Fritz Heidegger: Philosophie und Fastnacht* (Munich: Beck, 2005), 33–34.

9. Martin Heidegger, "Letter on 'Humanism'", in *Pathmarks*, ed. William McNeill (Cambridge: Cambridge University Press, 1998), 239–76, 239.

10. Mary Flannery O'Connor, "Good Country People", in *The Complete Stories* (New York: Farrar, Straus and Giroux, 1971), 271–91, 274, 280, 277. The quotation used in this story is taken from Martin Heidegger, "What Is Metaphysics?", in *Existence and Being*, ed. Werner Brock, trans. R. F. C. Hull and Alan Crick (Chicago: Henry Regnery, 1949), 353–93, 359. See Martin Woessner, *Heidegger in America* (Cambridge: Cambridge University Press, 2011), 92–95.

11. O'Connor, "Good Country People", 274, 287.

12. O'Connor, "Good Country People", 284–85, 291.

13. Heidegger, "The Thing", 172.

14. Gabriel Marcel, *La Dimension Florestan* (Paris: Plon, 1958), 11, 32. While Gabriel Marcel muses about the apple who apples, the German rapper Thomas Pigor

takes verbalisation one step further in his song "Heidegger" from 1999 and turns Heidegger himself into a verb conveying a straightforward transitive message: "I heidegger you along the wall/ I heidegger you – so small/ I heidegger you back to the beginning". <www.youtube.com/watch?v=3goPOfcu-JI> (accessed 7/21/2019).

15. Oskar Maria Graf, "Unser Dialekt und der Existenzialismus", in *An manchen Tagen: Reden, Gedanken und Zeitbetrachtungen* (Frankfurt: Nest Verlag, 1961), 97–127, 97.

16. Graf, "Unser Dialekt und der Existentialismus", 107.

17. Martin Heidegger, "Language in the Poem", in *On the Way to Language*, trans. Peter Demetz (New York: Harper & Row, 1971), 159–98, 191.

18. Heidegger, "Language in the Poem", 172.

19. Graf, "Unser Dialekt und der Existentialismus", 112.

20. Günter Grass, *Dog Years*, trans. Ralph Manheim (London: Minerva, 1997), 324–25, 347–48, 376–77, 354.

21. Saul Bellow, *Herzog* (New York: Viking Press, 1964), 61, 64, 105, 74–75, 49.

22. Bellow, *Herzog*, 106.

23. Heidegger, *Being and Time*, 220.

24. Bellow, *Herzog*, 271.

25. Bellow, *Herzog*, 61.

26. George A. Plimpton and Rocco Landesman, "The Art of Fiction XLVI", in *Conversations with Jerzy Kosinski*, ed. Tom Teicholz (Jackson: University Press of Mississippi, 1993), 20–36, 31. I am thankful to Martin Woessner for bringing Kosinski's novel to my attention; see Woessner, *Heidegger in America*, 1–2.

27. Jerzy Kozinski, *Being There* (New York: Harcourt Brace Jovanovich, 1970), 72.

28. The notebook is archived in Hauptstaatsarchiv Düsseldorf (RW 265-20034) and quoted in Reinhard Mehring, "Heidegger und Carl Schmitt: Verschärfer und Neutralisierer des Nationalsozialismus", in *Heidegger-Handbuch*, 352–55, 354.

29. Thomas Bernhard, *Old Masters: A Comedy*, trans. Ewald Osers (London: Penguin, 2010), 75–85.

30. Ingeborg Bachmann, *Die kritische Aufnahme der Existentialphilosophie Martin Heideggers*, ed. Robert Pichl (Munich: Piper, 1985), 130. In her literary writings, Bachmann refers to Heidegger only in passing. Malina, e.g., takes the "latent anxiety" experienced by a postman more seriously than lofty speculations by philosophy professors; Ingeborg Bachmann, *Malina* (Frankfurt: Suhrkamp, 1971), 253.

31. Elfriede Jelinek, *Totenauberg* (Reinbek: Rowohlt, 1991), 83.

32. Jelinek, *Totenauberg*, 77–79.

33. Arnold Stadler, "Letzte Heiterkeit: Gehversuche auf Heideggers Feldweg", in *Erbarmen mit dem Seziermesser: Über Literatur, Menschen und Orte* (Cologne: Kiepenheuer & Witsch, 2000), 88–101, 98.

34. Arnold Stadler, *Mein Hund, meine Sau, mein Leben* (Frankfurt: Suhrkamp, 1996), 30.

35. Jean Paul, *Vorschule der Ästhetik. Werke in zwölf Bänden*, Vol. 9, ed. Norbert Miller (Munich and Vienna: Hanser, 1975), 115 (§ 29).

36. Dieter Thomä, "Groundlessness and Worldlessness: Heidegger's Anti-Semitism and Jewish Thought", in *Heidegger and Jewish Thought: Difficult Others*, eds. Elad Lapidot and Micha Brumlik (London and New York: Rowman & Littlefield, 2018), 109–34; Dieter Thomä, "The Imperative Mode of Heidegger's Thought, National Socialism, and Anti-Semitism", in *Confronting Heidegger: A Critical Dialogue on Politics and Philosophy*, eds. Gregory Fried and Richard Polt (London and New York: Rowman & Littlefield, 2019), chapter 6.

37. Jean Paul, *Vorschule der Ästhetik*, 105 (§ 26).

38. Dominique-George Frédéric de Fourt de Pradt, *Histoire de l'ambassade dans le Grand Duché de Varsovie en 1812* (Paris, 1815), 215.

39. Immanuel Kant, *Critique of the Power of Judgment*, ed. Paul Guyer, trans. Paul Guyer and Eric Matthews (Cambridge: Cambridge University Press, 2000), 144–46 (§ 28).

40. Jean-François Lyotard, "Philosophy and Painting in the Age of Their Experimentation: Contribution to an Idea of Postmodernity", trans. Mária Minich Brewer and Daniel Brewer, in *The Merleau-Ponty Aesthetics Reader: Philosophy and Painting*, ed. Galen A. Johnson (Evanston: Northwestern University Press, 1993), 323–35, 335.

41. Jean-François Lyotard, "Argumentation and Presentation: The Foundation Crisis", trans. Chris Turner, *Cultural Politics* 9/2 (2013): 117–43, 137.

42. Heidegger, "The Thing", 178–79.

43. Martin Heidegger, "Declaration of Support for Adolf Hitler and the National Socialist State (November 11, 1933)", in *The Heidegger Controversy: A Critical Reader*, ed. Richard Wolin (New York: Columbia University Press, 1991), 49–52, 51.

44. Martin Heidegger, *Logic as the Question Concerning the Essence of Language*, trans. Wanda Torres Gregory and Yvonne Unnab (Albany: SUNY Press, 2009), 129.

45. On "mystery" Martin Heidegger, *Discourse on Thinking*, trans. John M. Anderson and E. Hans Freund (New York: Harper, 1969), 56; on "danger" Martin Heidegger, "The Question Concerning Technology", in *The Question Concerning Technology and Other Essays*, trans. William Lovitt (New York and London: Garland, 1977), 3–35, 26; on "lightning" Martin Heidegger, "Logos (Heraclitus Fragment B 50)", in *Early Greek Thinking*, trans. David F. Krell and Frank A. Capuzzi (New York: Harper & Row, 1975), 59–78, 72.

46. Jean-François Lyotard, *The Inhuman: Reflections on Time*, trans. Geoffrey Bennington and Rachel Bowlby (Stanford: Stanford University Press, 1991), 101.

47. Heidegger, "The Nature of Language", in *On the Way to Language*, 57–108, 76.

48. Heidegger, "Language", in *Poetry, Language, Thought*, 187–208, 189–90.

49. Thomas Mann, *Reflections of a Nonpolitical Man*, trans. Walter D. Morris (New York: Ungar, 1987), 252.

DISPLACING THE HOUSE OF BEING

Chapter 5

"Beth – That Is the House"
Paul Celan's Hebrew Dwelling
Simone Stirner

Writing about Paul Celan and Martin Heidegger one ends up, sooner or later, at Heidegger's hut in the Black Forest, at Todtnauberg, where the two met in July of 1967. It might not have been the only encounter between them; but in the complex and difficult relationship between Celan and Heidegger, it remains a significant way station. The two meet, they walk along muddy paths and Celan signs the guestbook in Heidegger's *Schwarzwaldhütte* – a small building, which Andrew Benjamin has called a "philosophical event as much as an architectural one".[1] There is the sense that the cabin, the hut, is a reflection of Heidegger's thought. Heidegger's "rhetoric of hut life", as it transpires in *Why do I stay in the Provinces?*, *The Thinker as Poet*, and *Building, Dwelling, Thinking* implies an attunement between the structure and location of the hut and the possibility for an intensified, more acute form of "dwelling", "in rigorous contact with existence".[2] Perched on a valley slope, its foundations cut deep into the ground, conveying a sense of rootedness in the land that also links up with the fascist dimensions of his thought and life: When Celan writes the poem *Todtnauberg* shortly after his visit, chronicling moments of their shared time – the midsummer flowers they saw, the well from which Celan drank – the word *"Tod"*, "death" weighs on both the poem and the encounter.[3]

Against this background, this essay locates an encounter between the two in a different poem – and a different hut. It looks to Celan's poem *Hüttenfenster*, *Tabernacle Window* written before his meeting with Heidegger yet already at a time when Celan was reading Heidegger's writings.[4] This poem, so the argument, opens up a conversation with Heidegger's image of language as the "house of Being" as well as associated concepts and concerns – the shape and stakes of dwelling, of dwelling in language, dwelling poetically.[5] In *Hüttenfenster*, Celan enlists figures that portray language as a place of dwelling, culminating in an image, which at once renders figural and literalises Heidegger's metaphor of language as "house of Being" – through the Hebrew letter "Beth:" *"Beth, - das ist / das Haus, wo der Tisch steht mit // dem Licht und dem Licht"*. ("Beth, - that is / the house, where the table stands // with the light and the light.)"

"Beth", the second letter of the Hebrew alphabet not only derives its shape from a proto-sinaitic glyph that depicts a house; it also functions as house to the extent that the letter is thought to hold space for a divine presence. Moving from "Beth" to the Hebrew word for house, *"bayit"*, the latter indicates a particular kind of poetic dwelling: *"Bayit"* signifies "house" as well as the stanza of a poem.[6] The German declarative *"das ist das Haus"*, "that is the house" in Celan's poem hence spells out a knowledge that the Hebrew letter "Beth" already contains itself. What are we to make of this strange dwelling, this house made of language, this other hut that comes to us by way of the Hebrew language? And, with the image of language as the "house of Being" in the back of the mind, how does it bear upon our understanding of the relation between Celan and Heidegger?

The question of Heidegger's influence on Celan's thought and poetry has been discussed widely. Rochelle Tobias notes that Heidegger's "idiosyncratic vocabulary informs much of Celan's work".[7] Jean Greisch insists that Celan takes a critical distance toward Heidegger, but emphasises at the same time that the poet perceived in Heidegger's thought *"manches 'Meridianhafte,'"* something Meridian-like.[8] Anja Lemke qualifies the connection between Celan's thought and poetry and Heidegger's analysis of both language and poetry as "interrupted and critically distanced".[9] Her extensive study on Celan and Heidegger describes their dialogue as a "choking conversation" (*"würgendes Gespräch"*).[10] James K. Lyon finds different terms: He speaks directly of "appropriation" and discusses several examples of what he considers "Celan's ability to borrow words, images, or concepts he found in the thinker, to translate them into his own poetic world, and to obscure or conceal his sources".[11]

Instead of looking at the constellation of Celan and Heidegger through the lens of "influence", "poetic translation", or "appropriation", I want to develop theoretical questions from within Celan's poetic world view, working through images in *Hüttenfenster*, which seemingly overlap with Heidegger's thinking. In attending to them closely, we come to see the different thought traditions entailed within them. This reading is hence not a process of uncovering the 'obscured' Heideggerian elements in Celan. Rather, it shows how Celan's poetry unfolds theoretical propositions that exceed and challenge that of Heidegger from within the very moments in which their language overlaps. *Hüttenfenster*, in this sense, constitutes a way of both working through and working apart of Heideggerian concepts, forming a poetic critique of Heidegger in poetic language itself. If Heidegger's hut in the Black Forest speaks of a "commitment to a particular relationship between philosophy and place",[12] as Andrew Benjamin puts it, Celan's *Hüttenfenster* reveals a commitment to a particular relationship between philosophy and poetry.

The first part of this essay begins by attending to Celan's *Hüttenfenster* largely independent of Heidegger, following the peculiar ways in which the poem imagines forms of dwelling as it moves between an initial image of a "tabernacle window" to the final image of the house "Beth". The second part and third part then draw Heidegger into the conversation, considering how Celan's poem both resonates with but also works apart central aspects entailed in Heidegger's image of language as "house of Being". I end with an open reflection on the stakes of formulating such a poetic critique in poetic language. Throughout, my reading focuses on moments of encounter in a fragmentary way and in doing so hopes to open up a space for further dialogue.

WOHNEN: BETWEEN HUT AND BETH

The status of "dwelling" oscillates throughout Heidegger's writing, shifting between a philosophical concept and something that finds fulfilment in a concrete shape – such as Heidegger's own *wohnen* in his *Schwarzwaldhütte*. By way of Hölderlin's *"dichterisch wohnet der Mensch"*, "poetically man dwells", Heidegger considers dwelling as a form of poetic habitation – something that registers in the *Letter on 'Humanism'* when he writes: "Language is the house of Being. In its home man dwells. Those who think and those who create with words are the guardians of this home".[13] According to Lyon, Celan read the *Letter on 'Humanism'* in 1953 – and underlined several of the moments in which Heidegger articulates the image of language as the house of Being.[14] Ten years later, *Hüttenfenster*, in a poetic movement that heads toward "Beth", develops its own thinking of what a constellation between dwelling and language might look like. Here is the poem in its entirety:

Hüttenfenster

Das Aug, dunkel:
als Hüttenfenster. Es sammelt,
was Welt war, Welt bleibt: den Wander-

Osten, die
Schwebenden, die
Menschen-und-Juden,
das Volk-vom-Gewölk, magnetisch
ziehts, mit Herzfingern, an

Tabernacle Window

The eye, dark:
as tabernacle window. It gathers,
what was world, remains world: the
    migrant-
East, the
hovering ones, the
humans beings-and-Jews,
the people of clouds, magnetically
with heart-fingers, you

dir, Erde: du kommst, du kommst, wohnen werden wir, wohnen, etwas	it attracts, Earth: you are coming, coming, we shall dwell at last, dwell, something
– ein Atem? ein Name? –	– a breath? a name? –
geht im Verwaisten umher, tänzerisch, klobig, die Engels- schwinge, schwer von Unsichtbarem, am wundgeschundenen Fuß, kopf- lastig getrimmt vom Schwarzhagel, der auch dort fiel, in Witebsk	moves about over orphaned ground, light as a dancer, cloddish, the angel's wing, heaving with what's invisible, on the foot rubbed sore, trimmed down by the head, with the black hail that fell there too, at Vitebsk
– und sie, die ihn säten, sie schreiben ihn weg mit mimetischer Panzerfaustklaue! –,	– and those who sowed it, they write it away with a mimetic anti-tank claw!–,
geht, geht umher, sucht, sucht unten, sucht droben, fern, sucht mit dem Auge, holt Alpha Centauri herunter, Arktur, holt den Strahl hinzu, aus den Gräbern,	moves, moves about, searches, searches below, searches above, far, searches, with eyes, fetches Alpha Centauri down, and Arcturus, fetches the ray as well, from the graves,
geht zu Ghetto und Eden, pflückt das Sternbild zusammen, das er, der Mensch, zum Wohnen braucht, hier, unter Menschen,	goes to ghetto and Eden, gathers the constellation which they, humans, need for dwelling, here, among humans,

schreitet
die Buchstaben ab und der Buchstaben
   sterblich-
unsterbliche Seele,
geht zu Aleph und Jud und geht weiter,
	pacing,
	musters the letters and the
	   mortal-
	immortal soul of letters,
	goes to Aleph and Yod and goes farther,

baut ihn, den Davidsschild, läßt ihn aufflammen, einmal,	builds it, the shield of David, and lets it flare up, once,
läßt ihn erlöschen – da steht er, unsichtbar, steht bei Alpha und Aleph, bei Jud, bei den andern, bei allen: in dir,	lets it go out – there he stands, invisible, stands beside Alpha and Aleph, beside Yod and the others, beside everyone: in you,
Beth, – das ist das Haus, wo der Tisch steht mit	Beth, – that is the house where the table stands with
dem Licht und dem Licht.	the light and the light.

Between the hut, the tabernacle, and "Beth", the poem performs a movement from earth to sky to language, developing on the way a fragmentary narrative of dwelling marked by history, Jewish (language) philosophy, and biblical intertext. Let me consider some of its moments that pertain to the question of dwelling.

It begins with the title itself, *Hüttenfenster*, which recalls the German name for *Sukkot*, "*Laubhüttenfest*", a holiday which "commemorates the cloud that accompanied the ancient Israelites as they wandered for forty years in the desert",[15] a memory of temporary, nomadic dwelling, being *en route*. "*Hüttenfest*" resounds in the term *Hüttenfenster* and the memory of this holiday recurs not only in the image of the "people of clouds" but also in the following motion of "*sammeln*", gathering: "*Es sammelt, was Welt war*", "It gathers what was world". *Sukkot* is not only the holiday of the tabernacle, but also the holiday of gathering, *Chag ha-Asif*. The poem too extends a gesture of gathering, drawing together what Tobias has described as markers of Jewish life, history, and experience in the East. "*Die Schwebenden*", the "hovering ones" conjures up the term "*Luftmensch*", Theodor Herzl's notion of "*dieses schwebende Proletariat*", "this floating proletariat", as well as the floating figures of Marc Chagall – which are also evoked both through the term "*Engelsschwinge*", "angel's wing" and the name "Witebsk" in the following stanza: Chagall famously painted human and angel-like figures hovering over the Jewish landscapes of Eastern Europe, and Witebsk, a Hasidic centre in Belarus and Chagall's hometown, was often the concrete site of these images.[16] This vision of Chagall's painting also maps onto the image of the "*Volk-vom-Gewölk*", "the people of clouds".

At the same time, however, the specification of an "orphaned" territory and the brutality of the image of "black hail" retroactively transposes the vision of Chagall's floating angel figures with the image of gun fire, both images now forming a harrowing palimpsest in the poem. "*Volk-vom-Gewölk*" condenses the memory of the cloud of exile with the memory of death camps and gas, of the deportation of European Jews, the Nazi genocide, which Celan himself encapsulated in the image of the "grave in the air" in his poem *Todesfuge*, *Death Fugue*. "A breath? – a name?" moves over orphaned ground, a magnetic force draws on the earth. Something is unsettled and this unsettling echoes in the language of the poem itself as individual terms double both as memories of Jewish life and death. What is being gathered in this poem are not the ripened fruits for a feast of thanksgiving, but remainders of a lost world.

And yet, against the background of an orphaned ground, against the background of stories of exile and persecution, the poem insists, "*wohnen werden wir, wohnen*", "we shall dwell at last, dwell", and this insistence too is felt in the rhythm of its language: "we shall dwell . . . dwell, something . . .

moves . . . moves, moves about, searches, searches below, searches above, far, searches" – these repetitions, while speaking of an erring, searching movement, build up a strength and persistence that carries the poem forward. Only on two occasions, the poem uses periods. One marks the end of the first sentence: "The eye, dark: / as tabernacle window". From there, it moves on, intermittently pausing at a colon, slowed down by an interjection ("– a breath? a name? –"), but ultimately coming to rest only with the last line and second period: "Beth, - that is / the house where the table stands with / the light and the light". If the stanzas of the poem are "houses" of their own as the Hebrew language teaches us, then the houses of this poem have open doors and windows, "a breath? – a name?" moving through them.

Halfway through the poem, this movement lifts up toward the stars, searching for a constellation that "humans need for dwelling", "*das Sternbild . . . das er, der Mensch, zum Wohnen braucht*". In this motion toward the stars in search for a place of dwelling, we can hear an echo of Genesis, where God guides Abram's gaze up to the star-studded heavens, announcing his propagation and promising his inheritance of the land "from the river of Egypt to the great river, the river Euphrates".[17] Celan's poem, however, takes a different route: In its final third, the poem suddenly breaches the border between geographic site and language, as language itself becomes a space to move through. The roaming agent, that "something", which still is specified no further than "a breath? a name?" "*schreitet / die Buchstaben ab [. . .] geht zu Aleph und Jud und geht weiter*", "musters the letters [. . .] goes to Aleph and Yod and goes farther", arriving, eventually at "Beth". The site of the searching movement has turned to a landscape of letters "standing" there next to each other in a form of material presence.

Both Esther Cameron and Rochelle Tobias have read some elements of *Hüttenfenster* in relation to the Kabbalistic notion of the *Shekhinah*. Following this approach, we find in the particular figuration of the letters elements of a landscape that are passed in walking and the eventual house "Beth" resonates with the kabbalistic understanding of language. As Moshe Idel points out, for Jewish mystics "[l]etters are regarded as stones, as full-fledged entities, as components intended to build up an edifice of words to serve as a temple for God and a place of encountering Him for the mystic".[18] In the writing of Rabbi Moses Eliaqim Beriah, this sounds as follows: "And the person who approaches the [study of] Torah and prayer, ought to build a house, which is the combinations of letters, filled by illumination and perfection [and] to prepare a Tabernacle for God [. . .] to dwell there in those words of prayer".[19] But it is not only the Kabbalists that understand language to be a place of dwelling. The letter 'Beth' itself speaks to the idea of dwelling in language, connecting to the understanding of the Jewish people as 'people of the Book,' to what Vivian Liska summarises as the idea of "being spiritually rooted in the word, the book and the law, over national or geographical roots".[20] This idea of language as a spiritual home answers to a history of violent displacements and uprootings. Heinrich Heine, exiled Jew, speaks in this sense of the Book, the Torah, as *"portatives Vaterland"*, "portable homeland" – a tradition, which dates back to the aftermath of the destruction of the Second Temple.[21] *Hüttenfenster,* with its narrative that moves from orphaned ground toward a form of dwelling in language, actualises this tradition. The fact that the poem ends on the image of two candles lighting this Hebrew house – an image resonant of the Shabbat candles – further emphasises it as a Jewish home.

Picking up Lyon's terminology, we could see Celan's "Beth" – and his poem itself – as a form of translation of Heidegger's idea of dwelling poetically, or dwelling in language, a transposition of the image into a different cultural context. This, however, would brush over the fact that Celan mobilises a cultural context in which these images and concepts were available independent of Heidegger's writing on language. One would rather have to consider to what extent Heidegger himself was influenced by the thought tradition that Celan draws on. Going beyond the question of influence, the following paragraphs attend directly to the resonances between Celan and Heidegger. Focusing on different moments in which the language of Celan's poem links up with aspects of Heidegger's thought on dwelling in language, I suggest that Celan's poem forms a poetic critique of Heidegger that constitutes not a "translation into a different context" but a counterpoint to his thought.

GATHERING HISTORY

Heidegger's hut, so Otto Pöggeler, was always a "sign of identity with the homeland, a rootedness in the land that maintains itself even in the present world civilization".[22] Drawing a comparison between Celan's and Heidegger's dwelling, a common approach starts from the understanding that the difference between them runs along the line of a distinction between the "territorial" and "deterritorial", between a state of rootedness and uprootedness, between dwelling at home and dwelling in exile.[23] Heidegger's dwelling, from this perspective, is "rooted in the land" like his Black Forest hut, while Celan's dwelling is subject to moves of deterritorialisation, mobile like the tabernacle, language compensating for the lack of a homeland. But *Hüttenfenster* compels a more complex understanding of this relation. The idea of a spiritual rootedness in the word, in language is evoked, but it is not detached from and does not compensate for the memory of historical uprooting.[24] What emerges in the poem is a flickering tension between the myth of rootlessness on the one hand and histories of violent uprootedness on the other – a tension that Heidegger's poetic dwelling lacks. Writing on the latter's dialogue with Hölderlin, Kathleen Wright has emphasised that Heidegger's ideal of poetic dwelling after the war is free and independent of all "historical and political (national) connotations".[25] After idealising a specific German Dasein under Hitler, as Wright suggests, Heidegger's formulation of an a-temporal and a-historic poetic dwelling allows him to cut ties with his own past.[26] From this angle, Heidegger seems to let go of "roots", removing dwelling from historical specificity while Celan's dwelling – "deterritorial" in some respect – retains a keen memory of the very moment of being uprooted, of the historical violence of displacement, deportation, genocide. In his *Meridian*-speech, Celan emphasises that the poem – *en route* like the tabernacle – "stays mindful of its dates", *es bleibt seiner Daten eingedenk*.[27] Like the *sukkah*, that is not just myth but concrete memory of a history of exile, Celan's poem realises poetic dwelling as deeply entwined with – even rooted in – history.

There might not be a single definition of what the specific mode of being is that Heidegger calls "dwelling". Beginning with the image of language as a "house", however, there remains a sense that Heidegger's dwelling is characterised by calm and steadiness and that these same principles ultimately describe language as well. As Dieter Thomä emphasises in his discussion of this image: language remains something static, "stationary" for Heidegger.[28] The following passage from *Building, Dwelling, Thinking*, in which Heidegger is concerned with dwelling in the "fourfold", the *"Sein im Geviert"*, (a folding-together of earth, sky, mortals, and divinities into a primordial, mythic unity), provides a different image for this sense of steady dwelling:

> Mortals dwell in that they receive the sky as sky. They leave to the sun and the moon their journey, to the stars their courses, to the seasons their blessing and their inclemency; they do not turn night into day nor day into a harassed unrest.[29]

Heidegger's dwelling here appears as something that keeps everything in place, the stars are left to their course, nothing is turned upside down into "harassed unrest". Celan's *Hüttenfenster*, in comparison does just that: "[something] fetches Alpha Centauri down, and Arcturus, fetches / the ray as well, from the graves, / goes to Ghetto and Eden, gathers / the constellation which they, / humans, need for dwelling [. . .]". The stars are taken down from heaven, graves are unsettled. "Ghetto", which inscribes the historic violence of pogroms and persecution into the poem and "Eden", which invokes the biblical story of expulsion from paradise merge into a constellation of stars that has nothing of Heidegger's undisturbed dwelling in a primordial unity. In *Hüttenfenster*, dwelling is not figured as an undisturbed state of presence but tied to a movement that takes down stars, breaks open the earth.

Then again, the stationary character of Heidegger's "house" is not altogether opposed to movement either. As Thomä highlights, the image of language as "house" entails a moment of movement but one that circumscribes a return to an origin, resolving itself in a unity.[30] In the late *On the Way to Language*, Heidegger will in this sense come to speak of language as that which moves the "fourfold", the *"Geviert"*: "Saying, as the way-making movement of the world's fourfold, gathers all things up into the nearness of face-to-face encounter [. . .]".[31] Celan's poem too resolves on an image of stillness, transposing the image of the tabernacle with that of a house. And on the way there, it circumscribes an ark, starting from the tabernacle window and ending on the house with two lights, "gathering" elements. But what is gathered in the movement of Heidegger's world-relating "saying" is dehistoricised, whereas in "Hüttenfenster", the gathering movement turns to "what was world / remains world: the migrant-/ East, the / hovering ones, the / human beings-and-Jews".

In a speech given on the occasion of receiving the Literature Prize of the Free Hanseatic City of Bremen in 1958, Celan makes the following statement describing language in the aftermath of the Nazi genocide: "[I]t had to go through its own lack of answers, through terrifying silence, through the thousand darknesses of murderous speech. It went through. [. . .] Went through and could resurface, 'enriched' by it all".[32] It is this enrichment, this depth of history that is felt throughout Celan's poem and that ultimately sets his figuration of dwelling most clearly apart from Heidegger's. That, and the fact that Celan's house is *beth*, is a Hebrew house, marking it not only as a Jewish site of dwelling but introducing a linguistic multiplicity in the poem that upsets the stability of Heidegger's language-house from another angle.

A HOUSE OF MANY LANGUAGES

From the opening paragraph in which the Hebrew *Chag ha-Asif* forms a silent point of reference between the German notions of *"Hütte"* and *"sammeln"*, tabernacle and gathering, to the letters from the Greek and Hebrew alphabet, there is a felt presence of other languages in the poem that disturbs the stability of the "German-language poem". This is perhaps most striking in the term *"Davidsschild"*. Seemingly one of Celan's neologisms, the word is a direct translation of the Hebrew term *"Magen David"*, what the English renders as "Star of David". The strangeness of this term pulsates in the German poem, the breath of the Hebrew language uprooting the German language from within. This multilingualism pushes against what Amir

Eshel has described as "Heidegger's awe of the sublimity of poetry written in a single, lexically correct, and profoundly deep language".[33] Since these "profoundly deep languages" are "in Heidegger's eyes, either German or Greek",[34] Celan's poem must be doubly unsettling. It introduces not only a multiplicity of languages into the poem, but also reveals the affinity between Greek and Hebrew.[35] As the poem follows the movement of "something" along the letters Aleph, Alpha, Jud, Beth, the Greek "Alpha" appears right by the side of the Hebrew "Aleph" making visible a closeness between the Greek and the Hebrew, a mobility that is already inherent within language: Greek letters are Semitic in origin, derived from Aramaic or Hebrew.[36] Seeing the Ancient Greek culture by way of its language as intimately tied to the Hebrew language and hence to Jewish culture, upsets the stability of Heidegger's vision of a unique relation between the Greek and the German. To complicate things further, "Jud" too, the letter that doubles as a German short form for Jew, is right there, next to Aleph and Alpha.[37] As these letters stand there, visualised as monuments in a landscape, a multilingual formation followed by the vision of a flaring *"Magen David"*, the poem – at least momentarily – seems to have gone over to a moment of defence, if not a pointed attack against Heidegger. Here, within the space of the German-language poem is the Hebrew-German *"Davidsschild"* and the Greek-Hebrew *Alpha-Aleph*, all within stanzas, which – according to the Hebrew – are "houses", leading up to the Hebrew house "Beth".

Reading *Hüttenfenster*, one hears echoes of Heidegger. Between the tabernacle window and "Beth", moving between earth and sky, passing by the Greek language, searching for a place where humans might dwell, Heidegger's writings on dwelling and language as a site of dwelling appear like a silent shadow text to the poem. What emerges between them, however, is not a narrative of influence or appropriation but a dialogue that shows both an affinity between them and a tension: Celan's poem pulls on Heidegger, like a magnetic force breaking open the ground of his thinking, poetically moving toward dwelling in language and then arriving at a moment of dwelling in Hebrew.

Throughout these reflections on the figure of the hut, the house, Beth, and the specific image of language as house, I have said little about Being itself. This is not the place to start doing so, but I wonder if in thinking about "house" and "to dwell" *in* poetic language, Celan's poem achieves something that Heidegger is still looking for. Toward the end of the *Letter on 'Humanism'*, Heidegger makes the following proposition: "The talk about the house of Being is no transfer of the image 'house' to Being. But one day we will, by thinking the essence of Being in a way appropriate to its matter more readily be able to think what 'house' and 'to dwell' are".[38] If language is the "house of Being", then thinking in poetic language might be more "appropriate" to its matter. Maybe, however, this remains within the stable territory of Heidegger's thought, and thinking this not only in dialogue with Celan but through Celan's poetry would mean to dis-appropriate "house" and "to dwell", that is, to detach both from the idea of language as a something static and to experience it in unrest, in its linguistic multiplicity, susceptible to the marks of history, thus dwelling otherwise.

NOTES

1. Andrew Benjamin, "Prologue. Placing Heidegger's Hut", in *Heidegger's Hut*, by Adam Sharr (Cambridge, MA: MIT Press, 2006), 6.

2. Adam Sharr, *Heidegger's Hut* (Cambridge, MA: MIT Press, 2006), 103.

3. See also Otto Pöggeler, "Todtnauberg", in *Martin Heidegger and the Holocaust*, ed. Alan Milchman and Alan Rosenberg (New Jersey: Humanities Press, 1996), 102–12; John Felstiner, *Paul Celan: Poet, Survivor, Jew* (Yale University Press, 2001), 244–47.

4. The annotated edition of Celan's collected poetry, edited by Barbara Wiedemann notes that *Hüttenfenster* is dated March 1963 but was most likely written earlier. Paul Celan, *Die Gedichte: Kommentierte Gesamtausgabe*, ed. Barbara Wiedemann (Frankfurt/Main: Suhrkamp, 2005), 157–59; Paul Celan, *Paul Celan: Poems. A Bilingual Edition*, trans. Michael Hamburger (New York: Persea, 1980), 174–77. Among the interpretations of *Hüttenfenster*, I want to highlight in particular the following two: Rochelle Tobias, *The Discourse of Nature in the Poetry of Paul Celan* (Baltimore: Johns Hopkins University Press, 2006), 66ff; Esther Cameron, *Western Art and Jewish Presence in the Work of Paul Celan: Roots and Ramifications of the Meridian-Speech* (Lanham, MD: Lexington / Rowman & Littlefield, 2014), 134ff. Tobias whose reading extensively covers the poem's relation to the Kabbalah also turns to Heidegger, focusing in particular on the notion of community.

5. This is not the first time that the image of a house in Celan's poem is read in relation to Heidegger's notion of language as the "house of Being". A number of critics have read the poem "Mit wechselndem Schlüssel", "With a Changing Key", along these lines. I find the image in "Hüttenfenster" even more pointed – and bearing additional theoretical valence due to the fact that it comes to us by way of the Hebrew language. Anja Lemke, *Konstellation ohne Sterne. Zur Poetischen und Geschichtlichen Zäsur bei Martin Heidegger und Paul Celan* (Munich: Wilhelm Fink, 2002), 465–71; James K. Lyon, *Paul Celan and Martin Heidegger: An Unresolved Conversation, 1951–1970* (Baltimore: Johns Hopkins University Press, 2006); Jean Firges, "Sprache und Sein in der Dichtung Paul Celans", *Muttersprache* 72, no. 9 (1962): 261–69.

6. As Vered Shemtov writes: "One common way poets referred to the 'text as home' trope in Israeli literature was through the double meaning of the word *bayit* in Hebrew. Following Arabic usage, *bayit* became the most common word in Hebrew both for 'home' and for 'stanza'. In poetry, it was used to refer to the text, or more specifically, to the stanzas of the poem as a dwelling space". Vered Karti

Shemtov, "Poetry and Dwelling: From Martin Heidegger to the Songbook of the Tent Revolution in Israel", *Prooftexts* 35, no. 2–3 (Spring-Fall 2015): 272.

7. Tobias, *The Discourse of Nature in the Poetry of Paul Celan*, 73.

8. In Celan's language this amounts to perceiving the promise of an encounter and of dialogue in Heidegger's thought. His *Meridian*-speech, famously, ends on the following note "I find what connects and leads, like the poem, to an encounter. [...] I find ... a *meridian*". Paul Celan, *The Meridian. Final Version-Drafts-Materials*, trans. Pierre Joris (Stanford: Stanford University Press, 2011), 12; Paul Celan, *Der Meridian: Endfassung, Entwürfe, Materialien* (Frankfurt: Suhrkamp, 1999), 12; Jean Greisch, "Paul Celan. Das 'Befremdete Ich' und die Sprache des Seins", in *Heidegger Handbuch: Leben-Werk-Wirkung*, ed. Dieter Thomä, 2nd ed. (Stuttgart: J.B. Metzler, 2013), 523.

9. Lemke, *Konstellation*, 465.

10. Lemke, *Konstellation*, 13.

11. Chapter seven of his study is titled "More Appropriations from Heidegger". James K. Lyon, *Paul Celan and Martin Heidegger: An Unresolved Conversation, 1951–1970* (JHU Press, 2006), 68, 34.

12. Benjamin, "Prologue. Placing Heidegger's Hut", xviii.

13. Martin Heidegger, "Letter on Humanism", in *Basic Writings*, trans. Frank A. Capuzzi (San Francisco: Harper, 1993), 217.

14. Lyon, *Paul Celan and Martin Heidegger*, 32.

15. Tobias, *The Discourse of Nature in the Poetry of Paul Celan*, 69.

16. On the relation to the paintings of Chagall see Celan, *Die Gedichte*, 708, note 8; Also Tobias, *The Discourse of Nature in the Poetry of Paul Celan*, 72.

17. Genesis 15:5-21. Robert Alter, *Genesis. Translation and Commentary*, trans. Robert Alter (New York and London: W. W. Norton & Company, 1996), 64–66.

18. Moshe Idel, "Reification of Language in Jewish Mysticism", in *Mysticism and Language*, ed. Steven T. Katz (New York and Oxford: Oxford University Press, 1992), 43.

19. R. Moses Elioqim Beriah, Qohelet Moshe (Lublin, 1875), fol. 8a. Quoted in Idel, 42.

20. Vivian Liska, "'Roots against Heaven.' An Aporetic Inversion in Paul Celan", *New German Critique* 91 (Winter 2004): 44.

21. Heinrich Heine, *Sämtliche Schriften. Band IV* (Munich: dtv, 1995), 4; For an extended discussion of the trope of the "portable homeland" see Liliana Ruth Feierstein, "'Das Portative Vaterland': Das Buch als Territorium", in *Topographien der Erinnerung*, ed. Bernd Witte (Munich: Königshausen & Neumann, 2008), 216–25.

22. Pöggeler, "Todtnauberg", 104–5.

23. Others who have read Celan and Heidegger along similar lines include: Liska, "'Roots against Heaven'", 41–56; Todd Presner, *Mobile Modernity: Germans, Jews, Trains* (New York: Columbia University Press, 2007); See also Donatella Di Cesare, "Being and the Jew: Between Heidegger and Levinas", in *Heidegger and Jewish Thought. Difficult Others*, ed. Elad Lapidot and Micha Brumlik (London: Rowman & Littlefield International, 2018), 75–86. Di Cesare's reflections on the differences

between Heidegger and Levinas echo paradigms of the differences between Heidegger and Celan.

24. On the complexities of this relation in Celan see also Liska, "'Roots against Heaven'", 44.

25. Wright speaks of "Heideggers Nachkriegsideal eines dichterischen Daseins […], das von allen historischen und politischen (nationalen) Konnotationen frei und unabhängig ist". Kathleen Wright, "Gespräch mit Hölderlin II. Die Heroisierung Hölderlins um 1933", in *Heidegger Handbuch: Leben-Werk-Wirkung*, ed. Dieter Thomä, 2nd ed. (Stuttgart: J.B. Metzler, 2013), 192.

26. Wright, "Gespräch mit Hölderlin II", 193.

27. Celan, *Der Meridian*, 8; Celan, *The Meridian*, 8.

28. Dieter Thomä, "Sprache. Von der 'Bewandtnisganzheit' zum 'Haus Des Seins,'" in *Heidegger Handbuch: Leben-Werk -Wirkung*, ed. Dieter Thomä, 2nd ed. (Stuttgart: J.B. Metzler, 2013), 300.

29. Martin Heidegger, "Building, Dwelling, Thinking", in *Basic Writings*, trans. Frank A. Capuzzi (San Francisco: Harper, 1993), 352.

30. Thomä, "Sprache", 300.

31. Martin Heidegger, *On the Way to Language*, trans. Peter D. Hertz (New York et al.: Harper & Row, 1982), 108; See also Thomä, "Sprache", 300.

32. Paul Celan, "Speech on the Occasion of Receiving the Literature Prize of the Free Hanseatic City of Bremen", in *Collected Prose*, trans. Rosemarie Waldrop (Riverdale-on-Hudson, NY: The Sheep Meadow Press, 1986), 34.

33. Amir Eshel, "Paul Celan's Other: History, Poetics, and Ethics", *New German Critique*, no. 91 (Winter 2004): 69.

34. Eshel, "Paul Celan's Other", 69.

35. For more on Heidegger's turn to the Greeks see for instance Glenn W. Most, "Heidegger's Greeks", *Arion: A Journal of Humanities and the Classics* 10, no. 1 (Spring-Summer 2002): 83–98.

36. Joel Hoffman, *In the Beginning: A Short History of the Hebrew Language* (New York/London: New York University Press, 2004), 35.

37. This short form comes with its own tension. It evokes the name of Lion Feuchtwanger's novel *Jud Süß* that was later misappropriated for the purposes of an anti-Semitic Nazi-propaganda film directed by Veit Harlan under the same name.

38. Heidegger, "Letter on Humanism", 260.

Chapter 6

Meridians of Truth
From Heidegger's Geography of Being to Celan's Topology of Language
Nassima Sahraoui

TOPOLOGICAL PRÉLUDE

Martin Heidegger's *Hütte* was built on the hilly moors in the southern area of the Black Forest. The name of the village, where the hut is geographically located, contains a *-berg*, a mountain, and it contains death: *Tod-(tnau)-berg*.[1] Perhaps the magnitude of this specific geological object *Berg* is an overestimation or hyperbolisation of its actual shape, at least compared to the pompous alpine panorama that unveils itself in the eye of the viewer while taking a walk on the moor; it is a panorama that – crossing the Alps in the direction of Davos – had already been the site where the epoch-making debate between Cassirer and Heidegger took place in March 1929.[2] But the magnitude or even monstrosity of the *Berg* certainly is beyond question when it comes to the philosophical (and political) implications of this mountainous setting. What is this mountain, this hill, this *Berg*, as a *topos*? Is there perhaps a topological, topo-philo-sophical or even topo-philo-logical structure springing from this setting? "Toposforschung?" – "Topologicial research?", asks Paul Celan in his famous *Meridian* address, held on the occasion of receiving the Büchner Prize for Literature in 1960, and he immediately adds: "Gewiß!" – "Certainly! But in the light of what is still to be searched for: in a u-topian light".[3] What then is this light, this lightening, this clearing – *die Lichtung*, as Heidegger names it – of this mountainous setting? Which veiled relation "certainly" needs to be cleared, as Celan claims? What, in other words, is the topology of this veiled or concealed relation between philosophy and poetry, between *this* philosopher and *this* poet at the mountain of death, Todtnauberg?

Our bookshelves are filled with thorough and pathbreaking studies and essays about the relation between the poet Celan and the philosopher Heidegger, about the (non-)dialogue between both writers, about the "event" of the *Rektoratsrede*, the 1933 Rectoral Address, and everything that Heidegger decided to leave unsaid about his political involvement during the Nazi regime – whether this silence might be traced back to a sublime and perhaps also naïve trust in the archive and in what his complete works might possibly deliver to posterity posthumously, or to a lapse into silence in view of the horrendous traumas caused by the National-Socialist Behemoth, or to both.[4]

As I have pointed out elsewhere – in another gathering between Heidegger and an opposing figure of 20th century German intellectual life, philosopher and literary critique Walter Benjamin – it is one of the tasks of philosophy to search for entanglements of thought, especially in regions where words have been left unspoken, where voices have either chosen to remain silent or have even been violently silenced, to read between the lines of virtual debates that have never factually taken place as such, and hence to gather them in a comprehensible constellatory image.[5]

The following reading therefore approaches this relation via a detour and tries to deconstruct the geo-philo-logical implications of this Heideggerian mountainous setting in light of Celan's question on topology with regard to the philosophical notion of truth. Although Heidegger's own remarks on the notions of topology and *topos* are rare, they are crucial since they belong to his ongoing elaborations on the notion of place, *Ort*. In the collection of verses *Aus der Erfahrung des Denkens* from 1947, for instance, he writes: "Aber das denkende Dichten ist in der Wahrheit die Topologie des Seyns" (*But thinking poetry is in truth the topology of being*); it is a phrase he would refer to again more than 20 years later in his 1969 lectures in Le Thor.[6] It is also in Le Thor in the same year, that Heidegger divides his oeuvre into three periods, heading them with key concepts of his work: "SINN – WAHRHEIT – ORT (τόπος)".[7] And in the same year, *Die Kunst und der Raum* stands under an epigraph he takes from Aristotle's *Physics*, in which he first quotes the Stagirite: "It appears, however, to be something overwhelming and hard to grasp, the topos", and then immediately adds, " – that is, place-space".[8]

Celan was aware of Heidegger's search for a *topos*; he knew his oeuvre very well. In some sense, one could assume – albeit carefully – that he, who was constantly questioning and repeating the trauma of having lost forever a proper home, grasped this gesture and carried it forward more consequently than Heidegger was ever able to. To a liminal but not insignificant extent, Heidegger's terrestrial reading of place, home, truth, and language still clings to the geometrical vertical line between earth and heaven, whereas, in Celan, the very notions of verticality and measurement turn into elliptic, meridional circles of an infinite approximation to the immeasurable.

Hence, no "sparks will fly"[9] – to pick up Benjamin's wording – in the encounter between poet and philosopher, but a "serious dialogue"[10] takes place, as Celan puts it in a letter to his wife Gisèle Lestrange one day after he visited Heidegger in his *Hütte* in 1967. In what follows, I will trace Celan's critical gesture and approach this encounter from three different angles: the first section will lead us through the history of the philosophical concept of *alētheia*, the second will touch on the Heideggerian notion of language in both philosophy and poetry, and the last outlines Celan's deferral of the notion of *topos* towards the a-topological in light of Werner Hamacher's reading of the poem *Todtnauberg*. Celan's insistence on the question of topology finally points us to problematic movements of thought in Heidegger's "house of being"[11] and thus directs us towards a possible *other* thinking, and finally towards re-reading a topology of language, one that challenges the geopolitical structures of our given world.

CLEARING ALĒTHEIA

The concept of *alētheia* has a long tradition in the history of Western philosophy. It is commonly translated as truth, *Wahrheit* in German, *veritas* in Latin. Throughout the history of ideas, the concept of *alētheia* is closely linked to the notion of a gradually achievable illumination or enlightening of an allegedly concealed or veiled truth of nature (*physis*) and natural phenomena. Literally, the term *a-lētheia* means "not-hidden", as the privative alpha '*a-*' indicates either a negation or the absence of the *lēthē*, which translates as concealment, oblivion, or forgetfulness. In Greek mythology, Lethe is a river or well of the underworld from which the shades of the dead are forced to drink in order to forget their former lives on earth. The ancient Greeks moreover believed that to drink the water of the Lethe was the only way for the soul to reincarnate.

The metaphor of unveiling originates in an amalgamation of ancient Egyptian and ancient Greek cults of the goddesses Isis and Athena, whose mystical appeal was promoted through Plutarch's famous saga *On Isis and Osiris*. In his introduction to the saga, the Platonist Plutarch confirms that philosophy's proper mission is to trace the hidden truth of nature: a philosopher should therefore philosophise, that is comprehend and epistemise, the word – the *logos* – of the gods to unveil the "truth [*alētheia*] contained therein".[12] This metaphorical-philosophical mysticism famously culminates in Isis' uncanny and fascinating proclamation: "I am all that has been, and is, and shall be, and my robe no mortal has yet unveiled".[13]

It certainly is no coincidence that this obscure myth of a veiled truth saw a renaissance at the end of the 18th century in German Romanticism. Before we return to Heidegger – although, in fact, I am writing about Heidegger already – I would like to take a brief detour to Friedrich Schiller's ballad on a young man's search for truth with the title *The Veiled Image of Sais*. In September 1795, Schiller – who influenced Hölderlin, who, in turn, was admired by Heidegger and Celan alike – publishes the following verses in the monthly literary journal *Die Horen*, edited by himself and printed in Tübingen, where Hölderlin resided in his tower after his mental breakdown, a place that Celan commemorated in his poem *Tübingen, January* in 1961. Schiller, however, writes:

Now, while they thus conversed, they stood within
A lonely temple, circle-shaped, and still;
And, as the young man paused abrupt, his gaze
Upon a veiled and giant image fell:
Amazed he turned unto his guide, – "And what
Beneath the veil stands shrouded yonder?"
"Truth", – Answered the priest.
"And do I, then, for Truth
Strive, and alone? And is it now by this
Thin ceremonial robe that Truth is hid?
Wherefore?"

"That wherefore with the Goddess rests;
'Till I' – thus saith the Goddess – 'lift this veil,
May it be raised by none of mortal born!
He who with guilty and unhallowed hand
Too soon profanes the holy and forbidden, –
He,' says the Goddess" – "Well?" – 'He shall see Truth!'[14]

These stanzas of the poem impressively illustrate the far-reaching consequences of the initial mystic-philosophical scene of unveiling the truth of nature, which dwells somewhere *in-between* poetry and philosophy and influenced the entire history of Western philosophy.

Heidegger himself uses the word *lēthē* – forgetfulness or concealment – in the context of his diagnosis of the "forgetfulness of being", the *Seinsvergessenheit*, which goes hand in hand with a forgetting of truth. In his conception, to unveil the hidden sense of being – the *Sinn des Seins* – is only possible against the backdrop of the historicity of *Dasein*. According to the original sense of the meaning of the concept of *alētheia*, Heidegger consequently translates it as *Unverborgenheit*, unconcealment, and decidedly not as truth.

While in his masterwork *Being and Time* from 1927, Heidegger still believes in the accordance between the traditional philosophical notion of truth and *alētheia*, he later leaps back to its pre-philosophical meaning. In a lecture he gave in Paris in 1964 under the title *The End of Philosophy and the Task of Thinking* (*Das Ende der Philosophie und der Anfang des Denkens*), he explicitly refuses the possibility to translate *alētheia* as truth at all. Against the backdrop of this new unveiling search for the sense of being, he insists, it is impossible to further simply equate *alētheia* with truth. The impossibility stems from the fact that the philosophical tradition took truth as an unalterable presupposition and as the highest metaphysical good for any new philosophical undertaking. Hence, if one does not want to remain within the realm of metaphysics – and it is, of course, the metaphysical tradition that Heidegger strives to overcome – an inversion of philosophical truth and *alētheia* is necessary. Heidegger therefore concludes that

> die 'Αλήθεια, die Unverborgenheit im Sinne der Lichtung, [darf] nicht mehr mit Wahrheit gleichgesetzt werden. Vielmehr gewährt die 'Αλήθεια, die Unverborgenheit als Lichtung gedacht, erst die Möglichkeit von Wahrheit.

> alētheia, unconcealment in the sense of clearing, may not be equated with truth. Rather, alētheia, unconcealment thought as clearing, first grants the possibility of truth.[15]

A retrospectively added remark from 1949 to a passage from his earlier lecture *On the Essence of Truth* from 1930, furthermore explains the relation between the *Lichtung*, clearing and *alētheia*:

> Weil zu ihm lichtendes Bergen gehört, erscheint Seyn anfänglich im Licht des verbergenden Entzugs. Der Name dieser Lichtung ist ἀλήθεια.

> Because sheltering that clears [*lichtendes Bergen*] belongs to it, Beyng appears originarily in the light [*im Licht*] of concealing withdrawal. The name of this clearing [Lichtung] is ἀλήθεια.[16]

It now seems that *Lichtung* and *alētheia* coincide, and where they coincide, being is not simply "lightened" as the philosophical tradition has thought. Rather being is "cleared sheltering", *lichtendes Bergen*, as Heidegger states – the "clearing sheltering" belongs (*gehört*) to it, it is part of its ontological condition. In German, the verb '*bergen*' means 'to salvage' or 'to hide', whereas '*verbergen*' means 'to conceal' and thereby accordingly 'to protect'. Following the German original meaning, one can say that in this sense, being – during the process of unconcealment – becomes a true being, and accordingly fulfills its ontological condition; that is to say, being is only brought to *alētheia* through this paradox act of "cleared sheltering" that brings it to the place it already belonged (*gehört*) to. Remarkably, the verb *'bergen'* also echoes the geo-topological point of departure of this essay: the *Berg*, the mountain – a fateful coincidence, as I will show below.

In destructing philosophy's exclusive claim to provide the only true path of epiphany, however, Heidegger's geography of being, on the one hand, overcomes the metaphysical notion of truth. On the other hand, it preserves the idea that, from the perspective of thinking, there is something in this world – namely "being" – that deserves to be sheltered through clearing. It is only through this clearing sheltering that we can approach *alētheia* or unconcealment, and only through *alētheia* that we can disclose the world. Unconcealment is thus an indication for the disclosedness the *Erschlossenheit*, of the world. The fact that *this* disclosure of the world through "lightening" and "clearing" – in spite of all efforts Heidegger takes to *not* read these concepts metaphorically – already belongs to the *White Mythology* of Western philosophy, has been discussed by Jacques Derrida.[17]

The following section leaves the philosophical implications of Heidegger's notion of *alētheia* aside for the moment and returns to the relation between philosophy and poetry: in reading some passages of Heidegger's artwork essay that are related to the concepts of *Lichtung* and or as *alētheia*, I will demonstrate that the very relation finally strives after the concept of language as such.

A GEOGRAPHY OF POETRY AND TRUTH

Heidegger first worked on his *Der Ursprung des Kunstwerks* (*The Origin of the Work of Art*) in the years around 1931/1932, one or two years before the Nazi seizure of power in 1933, and his devastating *Rektoratsrede* on *Die Selbstbehauptung der deutschen Universität* (*The Self-Assertion of the German University*), in which he fashions himself as the intellectual leader of the political "event" of the rise of the National Socialist party. In the subsequent years he rewrote, changed and supplemented this "palimpsest" at least three times and published a draft of the 1935/1935 version of the essay in *Holzwege* in 1949/1950 as well as another version – which was based on lectures he gave in Frankfurt in 1936 – in a Reclam edition.[18] Although the last version differs from the earlier ones, the constellatory mindset found therein remains quite stable: it crystallises around the relation between the essence of the artwork and truth.[19] Notably, the key term, which occurs here for the first time in Heidegger's oeuvre, is *Erde*, earth; it is the material counterpart to the notion of *Welt*, world, that frames the experiential and semantic context of man.[20] In his essay (that I henceforth quote in the final version from 1960), however, he relates the artwork, and more specifically poetry, to truth:

> Wahrheit als die Lichtung und Verbergung des Seienden geschieht, indem sie gedichtet wird. *Alle Kunst* ist als Geschehenlassen der Ankunft der Wahrheit des Seienden als eines solchen *im Wesen Dichtung*. Das Wesen der Kunst [. . .] ist das Sich-ins-Werk-setzen der Wahrheit.

> Truth, as the clearing and concealing of that which is, happens through being poetized. *All art*, as the letting happen of the advent of the truth of beings, is as such, *in essence, poetry*. [21]

Poetry is, as Heidegger states, the essential condition for the possibility of truth in the sense of *alētheia*. But the relation between poetising and *alētheia* is not the same as the relation between thinking and *alētheia*; it *is not* the same, because thinking and poetising unfold truth in fundamentally different ways. And yet, at the same time, both thinking and poetising strive for truth in the same medium, namely language: thinking and poetising are in service of language. This directedness towards language does not imply that thinking and poetising ought to be equalised, on the contrary: as stated above, they differ fundamentally in the way this directedness manifests itself, in the way it is at work and turns to an *ergon*.[22] In the 1943 epilogue to his 1929 lecture *What is Metaphysics?* Heidegger writes:

> Weil jedoch das Gleiche nur gleich ist als das Verschiedene, das Dichten und Denken aber am reinsten sich gleichen in der Sorgsamkeit des Wortes, sind beide zugleich am weitesten in ihrem Wesen getrennt. Der Denker sagt das Sein. Der Dichter nennt das Heilige.

> Yet because that which is like is so only as difference allows, and because poetising and thinking are most purely alike in their care of the world, they are at the same time farthest separated in their essence. The thinker says the being. The poet names the holy.[23]

"Der Denker sagt das Sein. Der Dichter nennt das Heilige". – "The Thinker says being. The poet names the holy". Why is the thinker *saying* and the poet *naming*? Why is one referring to *being* and the latter to the *holy*? Why is it necessary at all to draw such a vertical line from being, from the world, to the holy and to the heavens? One might read this quote as an indication of the small branchlets of a quasi-metaphysical geography – a geography of being – that seem to vein Heidegger's movement of thought. Within this movement, the holy is not discovered intellectually – that is by the thoughts of the thinker, who grants the clearing of the *alētheia* – but through poetry – that is the *poiesis*, the making of words, of language. The *poiesis* of language coincides with the naming.[24] Poetising and thinking resemble each other insofar as both operate through the *poiesis* of language.

Language, as Heidegger points out in his artwork essay, is not merely a written or oral communication medium, and hence certainly cannot be reduced to letters and words. Language rather promotes the carrying towards the openness of being, that is to say, being is brought to *Dasein* through language. Or to put it in other words, where there is no language, there is no openness of being, and where there is no openness of being, there is no *Dasein*, and where there is no *Dasein*, no such thing as non-being or emptiness exists, for the openness of being is the condition for both, *Dasein* and nothingness. Moreover, where there is no nothingness, there is no projection (*Entwerfen*). Projection, in turn, is the condition for unconcealment and thus for *alētheia*, and, as Heidegger points out, *alētheia*, in turn, emerges "out of nothingness" (*aus dem Nichts*).[25] In another passage of the artwork essay, he completes this image of poetry as being the linguistic condition for the ontological constitution of the world in concluding:

> Das entwerfende Sagen ist Dichtung: die Sage der Welt und der Erde, die Sage vom Spielraum ihres Streites und damit von der Stätte aller Nähe und Ferne der Götter. Die Dichtung ist die Unverborgenheit des Seienden. Die jeweilige Sprache ist das Geschehnis jenes Sagens, in dem geschichtlich einem Volk seine Welt aufgeht und die Erde als das Verschlossene aufbewahrt wird. Das entwerfende Sagen ist jenes, das in der Bereitung des Sagbaren zugleich das Unsagbare als ein solches zur Welt bringt. In solchem Sagen werden einem geschichtlichen Volk die Begriffe seines Wesens, d. h. seiner Zugehörigkeit zur Welt-Geschichte vorgeprägt.

> Projective saying is poetry: the saying of world and earth, the saying of the arena of their strife and thus of the place of all nearness and remoteness of the gods. Poetry is the saying of the unconcealment of beings. Actual language at any given moment is the happening of this saying, in which a people's world historically arises for it and the earth is preserved as that which remains closed. Projective saying is saying which, in preparing the sayable, simultaneously brings the unsayable as such into the world. In such saying, the concepts of a historical people's essence, i.e., of its belonging to world history, are performed for that people.[26]

The "saying" and the "naming" – and hence poetising and thinking – now come together in the *poiesis* of language. Language thus has its site in the literal sense of the meaning as *geo-logical* point, because this site is located within our world, within our earth, and – for Heidegger – even within the people. Hence, language is the *logos* of the world. Moreover, language is immediately bound to a specific locus within our *geo-historical* context. This means that language, in Heidegger, requires a "positivist predication". This predication consists in the geological factuality of the earth and the terrestrial, in which language, according to Heidegger, is bound to the terrestrial, a ground or soil, *on* and *through* which men have a home, a site for their dwelling.

While the terrestriality of language also lies at the heart of Celan's *Meridian* address, the poet and the philosopher take different paths at this junction: on the one hand, the elliptic meridian and on the other, the measuring of *gē*, Earth.[27] Heidegger, who takes the latter path, expounds accordingly that, for a proper philosophical analysis of the interwovenness and mutual dependence of *alētheia* and poetry, of poetry and language, and thus of *alētheia* and *logos*, a -*graphy*, a *geo-graphy* in the original Greek sense of the term, that is an "earth-writing", seems necessary.

In his 1951 reading of the central verse of Hölderlin's poem *In lieblicher Bläue*, "dichterisch wohnet der Mensch" (*poetically man dwells*), which is also the title of his essay, Heidegger elaborates on the thoughts of the artwork essay. "Dichterisch, wohnet der Mensch", he quotes Hölderlin, before continuing:

'. . . dichterisch, wohnet der Mensch. . .'
sagt der Dichter. Wir hören das Wort Hölderlins deutlicher, wenn wir es in das Gedicht zurücknehmen, dem es entstammt. Zunächst hören wir nur die zwei Verszeilen, aus denen wir das Wort herausgelöst und dadurch beschnitten haben. Sie lauten:
'Voll Verdienst, doch dichterisch, wohnet
Der Mensch auf dieser Erde.'

'. . . poetically man dwells . . .'
says the poet. We hear Hölderlin's words more clearly when we take them back into the poem in which they belong. First, let us listen only to the two lines from which we have detached and thus clipped the phrase. They run:
'Full of merit, yet poetically, man
Dwells on this earth.' [28]

Man's dwelling on earth encompasses a relation to both earth *and* heaven. Therefore, Heidegger concludes: "Denn der Mensch wohnt, indem er das 'auf der Erde' und das 'unter dem Himmel' durchmißt". (*For man dwells by measuring the 'on the earth' and the 'beneath the sky'.*)[29] All of a sudden, the vertical line from earth to heaven emerges again. Since men are located *between* (*zwischen*) the earth and heaven, this *between* itself becomes the original site of dwelling. Measuring this realm between earth and heaven therefore is the initial activity of dwelling: to measure is the condition of men to exist as men at all, for it is only through taking-measure that men are able to contour the realm of the *in-between* (*Zwischen*). Measuring the *Zwischen* is more than mere *geo-metry*, writes Heidegger, since no existing metric system is adequate for reckoning the realm between earth and heaven.[30] Hence, poetry, for its part, is nothing more and nothing less than the writing of the performance of measure-taking; it is the linguistic measurement, that is the saying and naming, of the *Zwischen*. If, therefore, "the thinker says being" when he denotes the original terrestrial locus of dwelling and "the poet names the holy" in gazing towards the heaven, both merge in this linguistic interspace, this *Zwischenraum*.

In another passage of his artwork essay, poetry and language are ultimately interwoven: "Die Sprache selbst ist Dichtung im wesentlichen Sinne" (*Language is poetry in the essential sense*).[31] Language is "poetry in the essential sense", as it safekeeps the essence of poetry and the essence of poetry is nothing less than the "founding of truth:" "Das Wesen der Dichtung aber ist die Stiftung der Wahrheit" (*The essence of poetry, in turn, is the founding of truth*).[32] Read in this way, each and every poem contains *alētheia* in itself, and *alētheia*, vice versa, initially forms or shapes poetry.

Finally, truth goes hand in hand with poetry, and as such it is manifested in the work. The work itself is, in turn, immediately bound to the historicity of *Dasein* (*Geschichtlichkeit des Daseins*) and as such to a *geo-graphy*, to an "earth-writing". Heidegger's *geo-graphy* thus crystallises in a constellation that is composed of a terrestrial thinking and saying in, through, and with language – a *geo-logy* – a likewise terrestrial measuring – a *geo-urano-metry* – of the *Zwischen*, and of the quasi-metaphysical *poiesis* – the work – of naming and hence creating the world in which men dwells. A passage in the artwork essay illustrates this terrestrial setting:

> Der wahrhaft dichtende Entwurf ist die Eröffnung von Jenem, worein das Dasein als geschichtliches schon geworfen ist. Dies ist die Erde und für ein geschichtliches Volk seine Erde, der sich verschließende Grund, dem es aufruht mit all dem, was es, sich selbst noch verborgen, schon ist. Es ist aber seine Welt, die aus dem Bezug des Daseins zur Unverborgenheit des Seins waltet. Deshalb muß alles dem Menschen Mitgegebene im Entwurf aus dem verschlossenen Grund heraufgeholt und eigens auf diesen gesetzt werden. So wird er als der tragende Grund erst gegründet. Weil ein solches Holen, ist alles Schaffen ein Schöpfen (das Wasser holen aus der Quelle).

Truly poeticizing projection is the opening up of that in which existence [*Dasein*] as historical is already thrown [*geworfen*]. This is the earth and, for a historical people, its earth, the self-closing ground on which it rests together with everything that it already is, though hidden from itself. For this is also its world which prevails in virtue of the relation of existence [*Dasein*] to the unconcealment of being. For this reason, everything with which man is endowed must, in the projection, be drawn up from the closed ground and expressly set upon this ground. In this way, it is first grounded as a bearing ground. Because it is such a drawing-up, all creation is a drawing (as drawing water from a spring).[33]

Tempting semblances, analogies, and associations emerge out of this quote: a metric semblance between *(to) dwell* and *well*, for instance, as well as etymological semblances between *schöpfen* (*to create/to draw*) und *Schöpfung* (*creation*) or *schaffen* (*to accomplish/to create/to work*) and *Erschaffung* (again *creation*). In the context of this essay, however, the last, parenthetical sentence seems most important, since it draws an insightful image that elliptically leads back to the whole fateful genealogy of veiling and unveiling that has its ground in the initial mythological scene of drinking from the waters of concealment: "(das Wasser holen aus der Quelle)" – "(drawing water from a well)". But who drinks the water? And where is this well?

TODTNAUBERG

There is a well next to a hut on a hill close to the small village Todtnauberg in the Black Forest. This well is mentioned in a poem Paul Celan wrote after he visited Heidegger's hut on the 1st of August, 1967 in Frankfurt, where he was just about to meet his publisher after he had lectured at the University of Freiburg in front of several hundred listeners on July 24, 1967. "Chère Gisele", he writes to his wife, "[l]a lecture à Fribourg a été un succès exceptionnel: 1200 personnes qui m'ont écouté le souffle retenu pendant une heure, puis, m'ayant longuement applaudi" (*Dear Gisèle, [. . .] the lecture in Freiburg has been an exceptional success: 1200 people listened to me with bated breath for one hour and applauded for a long time*).[34] One of the attendants of his lecture was Martin Heidegger, with whom he had already exchanged letters and books for then 11 years, but whom he had never met in person before.

In the same letter to Gisèle Lestrange, Celan recounts that Heidegger approached him and that they visited the *Hütte* on Heidegger's invitation the next day. On their way in the car, they had a "dialogue grave, avec des paroles claires de ma part" (*serious dialogue with clear words on my part*). Celan expressed his hope that Heidegger would finally break the silence about his involvement in a regime that is responsible for the most horrendous trauma of the 20th century: "J'espère que Heidegger prendra sa plume et qu'il écrira qq pages faisant écho, avertissant aussi, alors que le nazisme remonte" (*I hope that Heidegger takes up his pen and writes some responsive, warning pages that repudiate the resurgence of Nazism*).[35] In his dedication in the guest book, Celan repeats this hope in writing: "Ins Hüttenbuch, mit dem Blick auf den Brunnenstern,/ mit einer Hoffnung auf ein kommendes Wort im Herzen" (*Into the hut-book, with the view of the well-star, with hope for a coming word in the heart*). The first three stanzas of the eight stanza-poem about this encounter named *Todtnauberg*, which I quote here in its entirety, echoes the entry in the hut-book:

Todtnauberg

Arnika, Augentrost, der
Trunk aus dem Brunnen mit dem
   Sternwürfel drauf,

in der
Hütte

die in das Buch
—wessen Namen nahms auf
vor dem meinen?—,
die in dies Buch
geschriebene Zeile von
einer Hoffnung, heute,
auf eines Denkenden
kommendes
Wort
im Herzen,

Waldwasen, uneingeebnet,
Orchis und Orchis, einzeln,

krudes, später, im Fahren,
deutlich,

der uns fährt, der Mensch,
der's mit anhört,

die halb-
beschrittenen Knüppel-
Pfade im Hochmoor,

Feuchtes,
viel.[36]

Todtnauberg

Arnica, eyebright, the
draft from the well with the
   starred die above it,

in the
hut

the line
—whose name did the book
register before mine?—,
the line inscribed
in that book about
a hope, today,
of a thinking man's
coming
word
in the heart,

woodland sward, unlevelled,
orchid and orchid, single

coarse stuff, later, clear
in passing,

he who drives us, the man,
who listens in,

the half-
trodden wretched
tracks through the high moors,

dampness,
much.

This is not the place to thoroughly explicate Celan's poem – this has been done in the best possible way by Werner Hamacher in his reading of *Todtnauberg*.[37] Hamacher reads the "hope" in the third stanza, which Celan keeps "in the heart", as an openness towards the "coming/ word"[38] rather than an anticipatory wish for what the thinker Heidegger ought to say about his engagement in the Nazi regime. The line break between *kommendes* and *Wort* supports this reading; it disrupts the linearity that pre-determines the anticipated and expected result of any correlation between these two words. "Kommendes / Wort" thus is a sequence of hesitations towards pre-determination, pre-location, or "pre-position", as Hamacher aptly puts it. An irreducible and unmeasurable open difference emerges out of the disrupting break "/".[39]

Celan's "poeticized projection" in this stanza hence ungrounds the ground, rather than "draw[ing] up from the closed ground and expressly set[ing] upon this ground", as Heidegger claims in his artwork essay.[40] Disrupted "on the way to language", *Todtnauberg* points us to the "rip which can no longer contain a topos"[41] in the traditional sense of a predetermined place (or even *Volk*[42]), but its destination has been deferred towards the unmeasurable a-topolocial *in-between* (*Zwischen*). This *Zwischen* is not a measuring instance between earth and heaven – rather, it is in this *Zwischen* where the unspoken dwells and out of which those who were denied the word potentially recover their voice.[43]

Coming back the question of the relation between poetising and thinking, between *this* poet and *this* thinker, one might note that the a-topological structure of the *(Un-)Grund* in Celan's poem inverts the hierarchy of poetry over thinking that Heidegger proclaimed in the last decades of his life. As Hamacher rightly puts it, it is not thinking that assigns poetry a proper place, but vice versa, poetry gives thinking a space; it is spacing, opening, the welling up of a non-measurable linguistic un-ground.[44] Paraphrasing it in more Heideggerian terms, the "poet is un-naming" the place – the *topos* – by inverting the hierarchy between poetry and thinking, and the two verses in the third stanza of the poem *Todtnauberg* "kommendes / Wort" illustrate paradigmatically this moment of inversion.[45]

Celan's a-topolocial poetising demands another historicisation of thinking that brings along an ethical gesture towards the silenced voices as well as the silent voices, including Heidegger's own muteness. Hence, Celan's "hope for a coming word" is not driven by a naïve wish for a vindication, justification, or explanation on Heidegger's part whatsoever – in fact, as we learn from a 1959 diary entry, he preferred Heidegger's almost unbearable silence to the hypocrisies of post-war German intelligentsia.[46] His *"dialogue grave"* with Heidegger ultimately culminates in a deconstruction of the premises and assumptions of the latter's thinking of language: it contests the "Topologie des Seyns" (*topology of beyng*) from *Aus der Erfahrung des Denkens*.[47] At the root of this contestation is not so much the question of topology *per se* but rather Heidegger's amalgamation of topology and geography of being that performs an architectonic measuring of the "house of being".

What remains is the still pressing question of topology, a question that Heidegger introduced and that Celan inversed – elliptically – towards an unmeasurable topology of language. This topology is a jump "in the heart" rather than a location, as we learn from the last verse of the third stanza as well as from Celan's *Hüttenbuch* entry. Topology here is tantamount to iterating a tiger's leap, an elliptical return, in the heart of that which certainly cannot be subsumed under the traditional notions of "saying", "naming", and "writing", not even in terms of the earth, and certainly not as "earth-writing".

In an undated and unsent fragment of a letter to Heidegger, Celan jots down a warning that any further silence would undermine a "serious will to responsibility" (*ernsten Verantwortungswillen*) of thinking and poetising.[48] After reading the second and third verse in the third stanza, "wessen Namen nahms auf/ vor dem meinen? – ", one can assume that the "will to responsibility" depends on the seriousness of the attempts to elliptically iterate this question. If there still remains something to be unveiled – to use the phrasing from Plutarch/Schiller, found in *The Veil of Isis*, quoted above – then it is the names of those responsible, "wessen Namen", and the masses of silenced voices to which the long threefold hesitation alludes: the dash, that is preceded by a question mark and followed by a comma, "? – ",. The "? – ", might be identified with the a-topos that makes a topology – *a-topology* – all the more important.

"And topological research?", we might accordingly and insistently ask with Celan at this final point of the essay. The final passage of the *Meridian* address seems to provide an outlook of how to approach this endeavour:

> I find something as immaterial as language, yet earthly, terrestrial, in the shape of a circle which, via both poles, rejoins itself and on the other way serenely crosses even the tropics: I find . . . a meridian.[49]

Heidegger's foreword to *Todtnauberg*, written in poetic form, includes an untranslatable question "Wann werden Wörter/ wieder Worte" (*When will words [Wörter]/ become sayings [Worte] again*)[50] – and, following Celan, we might conclude that "words become sayings again" when the elliptical meridional circle flows through the "kommende / Worte", when it crosses the a-topological realm of the *Zwischen* again and again. Perhaps the "drinking out of the well" (*der Trunk aus dem Brunnen*), as Celan writes, finally provides another topology, another way to rethink the relation between poetising and thinking than that of Heidegger's drawing from the well Lethe.

An old saga says that Odin, the Germanic god and tragic hero, sacrificed one eye to be allowed to drink from the fountain of truth. The saga further says that one-eyed, he would see more than with two eyes, and that he would even see behind the veiled or concealed phenomena of the world right after he had drunk the water of truth. Perhaps Odin then saw more than the others did, but his one-eyed gaze – though cautiously sheltering the house of being – ranged vertically from earth to hill, from hill to mountain, and from mountain to heaven and thereby oversaw the crossing terrestrial ellipsis of the meridian.

NOTES

Parts of this essay go back to talks written for the "Space and Violence in Philosophy and Literature" conference that took place at the Polish Academy of Sciences in 2015 and the seminar "The Poets and Heidegger" at the annual American Comparative Literature Conference at UCLA in 2018. I am especially thankful to my co-organiser and co-editor Florian Grosser as well as to Benjamin Brewer, Ilit Ferber, Adam Lipszyc, Aïcha Messina, Paweł Mościcki, Caroline Sauter, and the two anonymous reviewers for their comments on various stages of this paper.

1. Although Todtnauberg is a toponym that should not be translated, the intrinsic allusions to *Tod* and *Berg* not only leap to the eye of the bilingual reader because the word itself contains them, but also because both terms "resonate throughout Celan's work", as Pierre Joris, Celan's English translator, has aptly put it. See Pierre Joris, *Celan/Heidegger: Translation at the Mountain of Death*, http://writing.upenn.edu/epc/authors/joris/todtnauberg.html.

2. See exemplarily Peter E. Gordon's thorough study, *Continental Divide: Heidegger, Cassirer, Davos* (Cambridge, MA: Harvard University Press, 2012).

3. Paul Celan, *The Meridian: Final Version-Drafts-Materials*, translated by Pierre Joris (Stanford: Stanford University Press, 2011), 10. Celan's *Meridian* address was pathbreaking in many ways. Just how far it exceeds a general reflection on the works of Georg Büchner, the namesake of this important literary prize, has been exposed in detail in Michael G. Levine's essay "Pendant: Büchner, Celan, and the Terrible Voice of the Meridian", in ibid., *A Weak Messianic Power: Figures of Time to Come in Benjamin, Derrida, and Celan* (New York: Fordham University Press, 2014), 37–62. See also Kristina Mendicino's thorough reading of the *Meridian* address "An Other Rhetoric: Paul Celan's Meridian", in Modern Language Notes 123/3 (2011): 630–650.

4. Amongst all of these studies of highest quality, I would like to point to Werner Hamacher's essay "Wasen: On Celan's *Todtnauberg*", translated by Heidi Hart, in *The Yearbook of Comparative Literature* 57 (2011): 15–54; Anja Lemke's study *Konstellation ohne Sterne: Zur poetologischen und geschichtlichen Zäsur bei Martin Heidegger und Paul Celan* (München: Fink, 2002); Krzysztof Ziarek's article "Semiosis of Listening: The Other in Heidegger's Writings on Hölderlin

and Celan's *Meridian*", in *Research in Phenomenology* 24 (1994): 113–32; Otto Pöggeler's "Heideggers Begegnung mit Paul Celan", in *Disputatio Philosophica* 1 (1999): 38–49; and Jean Greisch's entry in the Heidegger-Handbuch "Paul Celan: Das 'befremdete Ich' und die Sprache des Seins", in *Heidegger Handbuch. Leben – Werk – Wirkung*, edited by Dieter Thomä (Stuttgart/Weimar: Metzler 2013), 523–28.

5. Nassima Sahraoui, "Martin Heidegger: Wendungen. Zur Destruktion der Destruktion der Philosophie", in *Entwendungen: Walter Benjamin und seine Quellen*, edited by Jessica Nitsche and Nadine Werner (Paderborn: Wilhelm Fink, 2019), 149–68. In fact, Heidegger and Celan only met three times: all three meetings took place during and after Celan's lectures in Freiburg on July 25, 1967, June 26, 1968, and March 26, 1970.

6. Martin Heidegger, "Aus der Erfahrung des Denkens", in ibid., *Aus der Erfahrung des Denkens: 1910-1979*, GA 13 (Frankfurt: Klostermann, 1983), 75–86, here: 84. See also Martin Heidegger, "Seminar in Le Thor 1969", in ibid., *Seminare (1951-1973)*, GA 15 (Frankfurt: Klostermann, 1986), 326–71, here: 335 (Seminar: 2nd September, 1969). An early investigation of Heidegger's notion of topology can be found in Otto Pöggeler's study *Der Denkweg Martin Heideggers* (Pfullingen: Neske, 1963); a more recent one is Jeff Malpas' *Heidegger's Topology: Being, Place, World* (Cambridge, MA/London: The MIT Press, 2006).

7. Heidegger, *Seminare*, GA 15, 344 (Lecture: September 6, 1969).

8. Martin Heidegger, "Art and Space", translated by Charles H. Seibert, in *Man and World* 6 (1973): 3–8, here: 3; "Die Kunst und der Raum", GA 13, 203–10, here: 203; See also Aristotle, *Physics*, book IV, 212 a 7.

9. In a letter to Gershom Scholem from January 20, 1930, Benjamin writes: "C'est là que je trouverai sur mon chemin Heidegger et j'attends quelque scintillement de l'entre-choc de nos deux manières, très différentes, d'envisager l'histoire;" Walter Benjamin, *Gesammelte Briefe Vol. 3*, edited by Christoph Gödde and Henri Lonitz (Frankfurt/Berlin: Suhrkamp, 2008), 502–3.

10. Letter to Gisèle Lestrange-Celan, Paris, 2.8.1967, in Paul Celan, *"etwas ganz und gar Persönliches". Briefe 1934-1970*, edited by Barbara Wiedmann (Berlin: Suhrkamp, 2019), 783.

11. Simone Stirner discusses Heidegger's famous phrase "language is the house of being", taken from his *Letter on Humanism*, in relation to Celan in her essay *"Beth – that is the House": Paul Celan's Hebrew Dwelling* in this volume.

12. Plutarch, "Isis and Osiris", in *Moralia*, vol. V (London/Cambridge: Loeb Classical Library, 1936), I, 3.

13. Plutarch, *Isis and Osiris*, I, 9 (transl. modified). Pierre Hadot's brilliant study *The Veil of Isis* provides the most thorough and elaborated insight into this mythological primal scene of the history of ideas; see Pierre Hadot, *The Veil of Isis: An Essay on the History of the Idea of Nature*, translated by Michael Chase (Cambridge, MA/London: The Belknap Press of Harvard University Press, 2006).

14. Friedrich Schiller, "The Veiled Image of Sais", in ibid. *The Poems and Ballads of Schiller*, translated by Sir Edward Bulwer Lytton (New York: Thomas Y. Crowell & Co, ca. 1880), 88–91. The German original version reads as follows: "Indem sie [the young man and the priest] einst so sprachen, standen sie / In einer

einsamen Rotonde still, / Wo ein verschleiert Bild von Riesengröße / Dem Jüngling in die Augen fiel. Verwundert / Blickt er den Führer an und spricht: 'Was ists, / Das hinter diesem Schleier sich verbirgt? ' – / 'Die Wahrheit,' ist die Antwort – 'Wie?« ruft jener, / 'Nach Wahrheit streb ich ja allein, und diese / Gerade ist es, die man mir verhüllt?' // 'Das mache mit der Gottheit aus', versetzt / Der Hierophant. 'Kein Sterblicher, sagt sie, / Rückt diesen Schleier, bis ich selbst ihn hebe. / Und wer mit ungeweihter, schuldger Hand / Den heiligen, verbotnen früher hebt, / Der, spricht die Gottheit« – 'Nun?' – 'Der *sieht* die Wahrheit;'" Friedrich Schiller, "Das verschleiert Bild zu Sais", in ibid., *Gedichte und Dramen I, Sämtliche Werke, vol. 1*, edited by Gerhard Fricke and Herbert G. Göpfert (Darmstadt: Wissenschaftliche Buchgesellschaft, 1984), 224–26, here: 224.

15. Martin Heidegger, "Das Ende der Philosophie und der Anfang des Denkens", in *Zur Sache des Denkens*, GA 14 (Frankfurt: Klostermann, 2007), 67–90, here: 86; ibid., "The End of Philosophy and the Task of thinking", translated by Joan Stambaugh, reprint in *Martin Heidegger. Basic Writings: from 'Being and Time' (1927) to 'The Task of Thinking' (1964)*, edited by David Krell (New York: Harper Collins, 1977), 427–49, here: 446.

16. Martin Heidegger, "Vom Wesen der Wahrheit, in *Wegmarken*", GA 9 (Frankfurt: Klostermann, 2004), 177–202, here: 201 (see also editorial note on p. 483); ibid., "On the Essence of Truth", in ibid., *Pathmarks*, edited by William McNeill (Cambridge: Cambridge University Press, 1998), 136–54, here: 154.

17. Jacques Derrida, "La mythologie blanche. La métaphore dans le texte philosophique", in *Marges de la philosophie* (Paris: Edition de Minuit, 1972), 247–324; ibid., "White Mythology. Metaphor in the Text of Philosophy", translated by F. C. T. Moore, in *New Literary History*, vol 6/1, "On Metaphor" (Baltimore: Johns Hopkins University Press, 1974), 5–74. On the lightening heliotropy of philosophy's search for truth, see also Hans Blumenberg, "Licht als Metapher der Wahrheit. Im Vorfeld der philosophischen Begriffsbildung", in ibid., *Ästhetische und metaphorische Schriften*, edited by Anselm Haverkamp (Frankfurt: Suhrkamp, 2008), 139–71.

18. In the introduction to the "cooperative commentary" to Heidegger's artwork essay, Espinet and Keiling provide a short and crispy history of the pathbreaking "palimpsest", as they aptly put it; see *Heideggers "Ursprung des Kunstwerks". Ein kooperativer Kommentar*, edited by David Espinet, Tobias Keiling (Frankfurt: V. Klostermann, 2011), 16–18. A close discussion can be found in Jacques Taminiaux's essay "The Origin of the Work of Art", in *Reading Heidegger. Commemorations*, edited by John Sallis (Bloomington: Indiana University Press, 1993), 392–404.

19. The detailed differences between the latest version of the essay and the earlier ones are very important: while the 1960 version focuses more on the historic dimension of the artwork itself, the earlier ones are, in their essence as well as in their tonality, rooted in the political dynamics of force, power and violence of the 1930s. This becomes apparent, perhaps most evidently, in the use of certain fateful concepts, such as *Volk*, *Ereignis*, or *Erde*. The latter lies at the heart of the deconstructive reading provided in this essay. I would like to especially thank one of the reviewers of this essay for his helpful scholarly advice concerning the differences between the various versions of the artwork essay.

20. On the notion of earth, see Michel Haar, *Le chant de la terre. Heidegger et les assises de l'histoire de l'être* (Paris: Éditions de l'Herne, 1985). A great review of Haar's great book was written by Jacques Taminiaux, "Heidegger and the Earth", in *Diacritics* 19, no. 3/4. Heidegger: Art and Politics (Autumn-Winter, 1989): 76–81. For a more recent reading of the relation between *earth* and *world*, see David Espinet, "Kunst und Natur: Der Streit von Welt und Erde", in Espinet, Keiling, *Heideggers "Ursprung des Kunstwerks*, 46–65. Espinet points out that Heidegger introduces *earth* as synonym to φύσις (*physis*; nature); here: 53–55.

21. Martin Heidegger, "Der Ursprung des Kunstwerks", in *Holzwege*, GA 5 (Frankfurt: Klostermann, 1977), 1–74, here: 59. A few lines later, he writes: "Was die Dichtung als lichtender Entwurf an Unverborgenheit auseinanderfaltet und in den Riß der Gestalt vorauswirft, ist das Offene, das sie geschehen läßt und zwar dergestalt, daß jetzt das Offene erst inmitten des Seienden dieses zum Leuchten und Klingen bringt" (Heidegger, *Ursprung*, 60); ibid., "The Origin of the Work of Art, in *Basic Writings*", 139–212, here: 197 (transl. modified). On the concept of truth in the context of the artwork essay, see Tobias Keiling, "Kunst, Werk, Wahrheit. Heideggers Wahrheitstheorie in *Der Ursprung des Kunstwerks*", in Espinet, Keiling, *Heideggers "Ursprung des Kunstwerks*, 66–94.

22. To the question what poetry initially is, Heidegger, in his lecture on Hölderlin's hymns, responds: "This word belongs to the same root as the Greek δείκνυμι. It means to show, to make something visible, to make it manifest – not just in general, but by way of a specific pointing;" in: Martin Heidegger, *Hölderlins Hymnen "Germanien" und "Der Rhein"*, GA 39, 29; ibid., *Hölderlin's Hymns "Germania" and "The Rhine"*, translated by William McNeill and Julia Ireland (Bloomington: Indiana University Press, 2014), 29. On the relation between art and poetry, see also Matthias Flatscher, "Dichtung als Wesen der Kunst?", in Espinet, Keiling, *Heideggers "Ursprung des Kunstwerks*, 110–22.

23. Martin Heidegger, "Nachwort zu: *Was ist Metaphysik?*", in *Wegmarken*, GA 9, 303–12, here: 312; ibid., *Introduction to: What is Metaphysics?*, in *Pathmarks*, 237.

24. It is very interesting that Walter Benjamin's early metaphysical treatise *Über die Sprache überhaupt und über die Sprache des Menschen* (*On Language as Such and on Language of Man*) from 1916 is concerned with the "Wesen der Sprache" (essence of language), in which *naming* is the original *poiesis* of *language as such*: "*im Namen teilt das geistige Wesen des Menschen sich Gott mit*. Der Name hat im Bereich der Sprache einzig diesen Sinn und diese unvergleichlich hohe Bedeutung: daß er das innerste Wesen der Sprache selbst ist. [...] Der Name ist aber nicht allein der letzte Ausruf, er ist auch der eigentliche Anruf der Sprache. Damit erscheint im Namen das Wesensgesetz der Sprache;" Walter Benjamin, "Über die Sprache überhaupt und über die Sprache des Menschen", in *Gesammelte Schriften II.1*, edited by Rolf Tiedemann and Hermann Schweppenhäuser (Frankfurt: Suhrkamp, 2002), 140–57, here: 144–45. Benjamin ends his reading of two poems by Hölderlin – *Dichtermut* und *Blödigkeit* – from 1914 with a quote from another poem: "Aber gäbe es ein Wort, das Verhältnis jenes inneren Lebens, aus dem das Gedicht entsprang, zum Mythos zu erfassen, so wäre es jenes Hölderlinsche [...] 'Die Sagen, die der Erde

sich entfernen, ... Sie kehren zu der Menschheit sich;'" Benjamin, "Zwei Gedichte von Friedrich Hölderlin: *Dichtermut – Blödigkeit*", *GS II.1*, 105–26, here: 126.

25. Heidegger, *Ursprung*, GA 5, 64; "Poetic projection comes from nothing in this respect, that it never takes its gift from the ordinary and traditional;" ibid., *Origin*, 200.

26. Heidegger, *Ursprung*, GA 5, 61–62; ibid., *Origin*, 198–99.

27. Already in the *The London Encyclopaedia* we can find the following fine-sounding entry about the meridian: "Great circles passing through the poles of the earth, and therefore perpendicular to the equator, are called *merididans*. The meridian passing through any particular place lies in the plane of the celestial meridian of that place. It also divides the surface of the earth into two equal portions, called the eastern and western hemispheres, in respect of that place. The meridians may be considered as indefinite in number; and all places lying directly north and south from each other are upon the same meridian. Sometimes by the meridians of a place is understood the half of a great circle, passing through that place, and extending from the one pole to the other; and the other half of the circle is called the opposite meridian;" in *The London Encyclopaedia or Universal Dictionary of Science, Art, Literature, and Practical Mechanics, comprising a Popular View of the Present State of Knowledge, Illustrated by Numerous Engravings, a General Atlas, and Appropriate Diagrams* (London: Thomas Tegg, 1829), vol. X, 73. The meridian has an ellipsoid form, just as Celan's *Meridian* address itself. Levinas hence aptly describes Celans's *Meridian* as an "elliptic, allusive text, constantly interrupting itself in order to let through, in the interruptions, his other voice, as if two or more discourses were on top of one other, with a strange coherence, not that of a dialogue, but woven in a counterpoint that constitutes – despite their immediate melodic unity – the texture of his poems;" in: Emmanuel Levinas, "Paul Celan: From Being to the Other", in *Proper Names*, translated by Michael B. Smith (Stanford: Stanford University Press, 1996), 41.

28. Martin Heidegger, "'...dichterisch wohnet der Mensch...'", in *Vorträge und Aufsätze*, GA 7 (Frankfurt: Klostermann, 2000), 189–210, here: 194; ibid., '...poetically men dwells...', in *Poetry, Language, Thought*, translated by Alfred Hofstadter (New York: Harper Collins, 2001), 209–27, here: 214. During Hölderlin's lifetime, the poem was printed only in a passage of Friedrich Wilhelm Waiblinger's philosophical novel *Phaeton*, published in 1823 supposedly with Hölderlin's approval. It was not printed in the form of a poem, but as a narration. See Friedrich Wilhelm Waiblinger, *Phaeton*, Zweiter Theil (Stuttgart: Friedrich Franck, 1823), 154. The Stuttgart edition prints the "poem" under the rubric "Zweifelhaftes;" Friedrich Hölderlin, *Sämtliche Werke (Große Stuttgarter Ausgabe)*, vol. 2 (Stuttgart: Kohlhammer 1951), 372–74.

29. Heidegger, *...dichterisch*, GA 7, 202; *...poetically*, 221 (transl. modified).

30. Heidegger, *...dichterisch*, GA 7, 199; *...poetically*, 218–19.

31. Heidegger, *Ursprung*, GA 5, 62; *Origin*, 199.

32. Heidegger, Ursprung, GA 5, 63; Origin, 199.

33. Heidegger, *Ursprung*, 63; *Origin*, 200 (transl. modified).

34. Celan, *Letter to Gisèle Lestrange-Celan, Paris, 2.8.1967*, 783 (translation mine).

35. Celan, *Letter to Gisèle Lestrange-Celan, Paris, 2.8.1967*, 783 (English translation taken from Hamacher, *Wasen*, 18–19).

36. Paul Celan, "Todtnauberg", in *Paul Celan. Die Gedichte*, edited by Barbara Wiedmann (Frankfurt: Suhrkamp, 2003), 282; ibid. "Todtnauberg", in *Paul Celan: Poems. A Bilingual Edition*, selected, translated and introduced by Michael Hamburger (New York: Persea Books, 1980), 241.

37. Werner Hamacher, "WASEN. Um Celans *Todtnauberg*", in *Das Robert Altmann Projekt. Quaderno III: "Paul Celan in Vaduz"*, edited by Norbert Haas, Vreni Haas, Hansjörg Quaderer (Vaduz: edition eupalinos, 2012), 35–84 (translated into English by Heidi Hart; see FN 4).

38. Hamacher, "Wasen. Um Celans *Todtnauberg*", 48 (Engl. 27). This stanza seems to also echo Celan's short address on the occasion of receiving the Bremen literary price in 1958: "A poem, as manifestation of language and thus essentially dialogue, can be a message in a bottle, sent out in the – not always greatly hopeful – belief that somewhere and sometimes it could wash up on land, on heartland perhaps. Poems in this sense too are underway: they are making toward something. Toward what? Toward something standing open, occupiable, perhaps toward an addressable Thou, toward an addressable reality;" (*Das Gedicht kann, da es ja eine Erscheinungsform der Sprache und damit seinem Wesen nach dialogisch ist, eine Flaschenpost sein, aufgegeben in dem – gewiß nicht immer hoffnungsstarken – Glauben, sie könnte irgendwann an Land gespült werden, an Herzland vielleicht. Gedichte sind auch in dieser Weise unterwegs: sie halten auf etwas zu. Worauf? Auf etwas Offenstehendes, Besetzbares, auf ein ansprechbares Du vielleicht, auf eine ansprechbare Wirklichkeit*). In Paul Celan, "Ansprache anlässlich der Entgegennahme des Literaturpreises der Freien Hansestadt Bremen", in *Gesammelte Werke*, vol. 3 (Frankfurt: Suhrkamp, 2000), 185–86; "Speech on the Occasion of Receiving the Literature Prize of the Free Hanseatic City of Bremen", in *Selected Poems and Prose of Paul Celan*, translated by John Felstiner (New York and London: W.W. Norton, 2001), 395–96.

39. See Hamacher, *Wasen*, 48 (Engl. 27).

40. Heidegger, *Ursprung*, 63; *Origin*, 200.

41. Hamacher, "Wasen. Um Celans *Todtnauberg*", 44 (Engl. 24). According to Hamacher, one cannot even speak of a *topology* anymore, but should instead consider a *topography*, a place-writing that does not include any essence of a *logos* (Hamacher, "Wasen. Um Celans *Todtnauberg*", 73–74).

42. Cf. Heidegger, *Ursprung*, 63; *Origin*, 200.

43. "Celan's poetry", Hamacher writes, "is not only 'on the way to language,' it is on the way to a language that has no language, toward what is in no sense a language. But it is also on the way to the muteness violently robbed the speech, from which speech has been withdrawn and withheld, toward a muteness from which speech has been cast out, and to the silence of what must speak, even if it 'chokes' on the words, of this muteness and violence;" Hamacher, "Wasen, Um Celans *Todtnauberg*", 69 (Engl. 45).

44. Hamacher, "Wasen. Um Celans *Todtnauberg*", 51 (Engl. 29).

45. Moments of inversion are a central theme in Celan's poems, as Hamacher shows in his essay "The Second of Inversion – Movements of a Figure through Celan's Poetry", in *Premises: Essays on Philosophy and Literature from Kant to Celan*, translated by Peter Fenves (Stanford: Stanford University Press, 1996), 337–88.

46. In the late 1950s, the publisher Günther Neske planned to publish a *Festschrift* for Heidegger's 70th birthday and asked Celan if he would like to contribute. Celan confirmed a contribution on the condition that Neske first send him a complete list of authors. Time passed without Neske providing the list. In 1959, Celan received a notification that he had been added to the list of contributors and that his poem was due very soon. Repelled by this kind of publication politics, Celan finally withdrew his contribution – he did not see himself in line with the authors on the list (a hesitation that is similar to the question in *Todtnauberg*: "wessen Namen nahms auf/ vor dem meinen?"). In a letter to Ingeborg Bachman from August 10, 1959, he explains his decision: after having clarified why he would not publish a poem in the festschrift on such a short notice, Celan elaborates on the political meaning of the figure "Heidegger" in the context of the post-war intellectual bourgeoisie. Interestingly, Celan prefers Heidegger's (still highly problematic) silence over the (to a certain extent still "Germanic") snobbishness of Heinrich Böll or Alfred Andersch, both members of the *Gruppe 47*, who cynically mocked Celan during his reading of the *Todesfuge* at the group meeting in 1952. Compared to the ostentatious public statements of the *Gruppe 47* members, he seems to have seen in Heidegger's silence at least a slight indication of "honesty". See: Celan, Brief an Ingeborg Bachmann, Paris, 10.8.1959, 379–80.

47. Heidegger, *Aus der Erfahrung des Denkens*, GA 13, 84; see also Hamacher, "Wasen. Um Celans *Todtnauberg*", 77.

48. See Hamacher, "Wasen. On Celans *Todtnauberg*", 79.

49. Celan, *Meridian*, 12.

50. Heidegger, "Vorwort zu *Todtnauberg*", as cited in Pöggeler, *Heideggers Begegnung*, 45 (translation mine).

Chapter 7

Handke's Doubt
Slow Homecoming *in Conversation with Heidegger*
Florian Grosser

The jacket text of the first edition of Peter Handke's 1979 *Slow Homecoming* contains a quote taken from an early enthusiastic review in *Neue Zürcher Zeitung*. In his reading of the novel, the reviewer draws heavily on Heideggerian thought and terminology. For him, the expression *wie Heidegger gesagt hätte*, 'as Heidegger would have said,' captures the gist of Handke's 'philosophical fairy tale': it is a literary adaptation of Heidegger's reflections on what it means to 'dwell' under conditions of late modernity and, in its orientation towards a return home, 'the text of a redemption story'.[1] In the following decades, the reviewer's sense that *Slow Homecoming*,[2] albeit free of explicit references to Heidegger, is informed by concerns central to the philosopher's later thinking has been confirmed. The archival work of Ulrich von Bülow has been particularly instrumental in revealing the extent to which Handke, in the process of writing the novel, was immersed in studying works of Lucretius, Spinoza, Adorno, and, especially, of Heidegger.[3]

In what follows, I want to examine the reverberations of Handke's interest in Heidegger and determine whether *Slow Homecoming*, due to a shared understanding of home or other factors, indeed qualifies as a Heideggerian novel. Rather than assessing Handke's skills as an interpreter of Heidegger or measuring him against the philosopher's standards for 'great art', the aim is to show how he, free from 'anxiety of influence', enters into conversation with selected aspects of Heidegger's later thought. Accordingly, problems of potential anthropological misreadings and subjectivist distortions or of a neglect for the dividing line drawn by Heidegger between 'literature' and 'poetics' are subordinate to the tracing of the idiosyncratic way in which Handke takes up and works through Heidegger's texts.

The examination is set out in five sections. The first section focuses on affinities between Handke's literary and Heidegger's philosophical inquiries into the question of home, into what is one's own (*eigen*) and what is foreign (*fremd*). What appears to be at the heart of such affinities is the 'law of historicity' or of 'becoming at home' (*Heimischwerden*) attained by Heidegger in his engagement with Hölderlin's poetry; a law according to which venturing out into the foreign acquires meaning to the extent that the journey elsewhere folds back onto itself. By contrast, the second part turns to moments of the novel that complicate the picture of poetico-philosophical continuity and ultimately render untenable an all too Heideggerian reading of *Slow Homecoming*. Here, particular attention is paid to Handke's doubt regarding the desirability and possibility of homecoming as a fulfilled movement. Shifting focus from the narration of *Slow Homecoming* to the accompanying poetological commentary offered in *The Lesson of Mont Sainte-Victoire*,[4] the third and fourth sections are concerned with how Handke – in conversation with Paul Cézanne's pictorial 'teachings' and Heidegger's analyses of spatiality in *Building Dwelling Thinking* – approaches what he calls 'the problem of transition' to suggest a 'peaceful' integration of *eigen* and *fremd*. Against the background of the rich textual interplay of convergences and divergences in Handke and Heidegger, the final remarks consider uncanny parallels in their attempts to transpose poetic-philosophical reflections on home to specific historical moments and political contexts.

VARIETIES OF CARE, LAWS OF RETURN

Although Handke's reception of Heidegger is neither sustained nor systematic,[5] the number of overlapping concerns is remarkable. Commentators have pointed to intersections in the intellectual-aesthetic horizons (pre-classical Greece, Goethe, Hölderlin, Novalis, or Cézanne) that orient their endeavours and similarities in their self-descriptions as outsiders who challenge the 'world pictures' of their times.[6] Most substantively, Handke and Heidegger converge in problematising language and attempting to perform it differently: rejecting reference theoretical reductions and instrumentalist conceptions of language, both strive for new linguistic forms to express phenomena ignored or neglected by predominant discourses in acts of creative 'naming' that displace the frame of what is sayable and, therefore, perceptible. They agree that such acts, in opening up what has hitherto been nameless, touch on (the) 'Nothing' – throughout *Slow Homecoming*, Handke, in his self-ascribed 'sense of possibility' (*Möglichkeitssinn*), particularly aspires to tap into silence and interval.

Whether this is a matter of influence, the attunement to overlooked, unexplored forms of experiencing language, space, and time indicates a basic proximity to Heideggerian motives and moods.

From the novel's very first word, such broad affinities become more concrete – it begins with the protagonist's name: 'Sorger', 'carer' or 'one who cares'. Sorger, a geologist stationed at a research outpost in "the Far North of the other continent"[7] who is occupied with surveying and measuring the surfaces of the foreign land, understands his work as a 'search for forms'. As his examinations of soil layers and formations yield no significant results, his doings increasingly reveal to him the inadequacy of his discipline, of the epistemic frameworks and scientific instruments it requires him to employ, in this search. Moments of satisfaction occur when Sorger is making sketches of the land and ground and, however fleetingly, is granted access to "the deeper area of vision"[8] and able to bring out rhythmic qualities that escape the scientific and everyday gaze. The passages on sketching highlight the smoothness of Sorger's practical 'immersion', its capacity to lend structure and coherence to surroundings that otherwise present themselves as disparate;[9] they thus anticipate Handke's observations on Cézanne in *The Lesson of Mont Sainte-Victoire* that present sketching and painting (*be-zeichnen* in the literal sense) as twinned with naming (*be-nennen*): whether as picture or word, they are forms of touching on the sensible world, of designating its phenomena in unprecedented ways.

Yet, the Northern landscape typically appears to Sorger as amorphous. This perception of his surroundings seeps into Sorger's inner life until he finds himself confronted with a lack of composition at the core of his own existence. As an encompassing sense of "Great Formlessness"[10] takes hold of him, 'home' becomes shorthand for everything that promises to restore plenitude and give shape. Sorger's homeward journey first takes him from the outpost to "[t]he West Coast city on its peninsula"[11] he once must have considered his home away from home but where he now runs up against his anonymity and out-of-place-ness. His voyage takes him east, to the 'Mile-High City' and to a ski resort where he hopes to reconnect with a childhood friend. As he finds the friend dead, it rapidly propels him to the 'City of Cities' which, in his mind, constitutes the threshold between the 'other continent' and his own. It is at this threshold that Sorger's "law-giving moment" (*gesetzgebender Augenblick*) occurs in which he resolves to forego his way of life as "a mere witness" and, instead, to become "responsible", to "intervene", and to contribute to a "peace-fostering form".[12] In the decision to turn around his existence, he recognises a return – not only to 'his' continent, country, or region "but to the house where I was born"[13] – as a concrete and meaningful possibility.

The options to read the narration of Sorger's homeward-bound trajectory and its 'legislative' culmination point in Heideggerian registers abound. The reflections on 'moment of vision' (*Augenblick*) in *Being and Time*, on 'insight' (*Einblick/Einblitz*) and 'event of appropriation' (*Ereignis*) in Heidegger's later thought seem to resonate in Sorger's 'deep vision' and, especially, his transformative decision which furthermore echoes with the discussion of different modes of care (*Sorge*): turned into responsibility for one's own existence and for others, authentic care supersedes deficient modes of caring openly or latently tied to 'falling'.[14] As a poetic account of genuine individuation, *Slow Homecoming* seems to come particularly close to what Heidegger, in *"Remembrance"*, presents as the 'law of becoming at home' laid down in Hölderlin's eponymous 1803 hymn. There, he insists that a poet cannot 'immediately' draw on or 'easily acquire' the 'inheritance' of his homeland, but must depart from it to truly grasp and 'remain in what is his own:' "Such remaining is present only as a learning journey, the homecoming return to the origin of what is his own".[15] Or more succinctly: "In order to appropriate [one's] proper character, [one] must pass through what is foreign to [oneself]".[16]

While providing a detailed account of Heidegger's interpretations of the relation between *Eigenes* and *Fremdes* as poetised by Hölderlin goes beyond the scope of this chapter, two intertwined principles are at their core:[17] first, nothing that is one's own can be known immediately; and, second, who one is can only be understood after having passed through the mediating element of the foreign. What is an 'aesthetic rule' in Hölderlin – the 'altercation of that which is foreign and that which is one's own' – is politicised in Heidegger's 1934–1935 lectures on the hymns *Germania* and *The Rhine* where Hölderlin is cast as 'the poet of the Germans' whose 'essential destiny' is founding the history for the German people: thanks to his unique insight into Being in 'its original law-giving', he is capable of opening up a realm of meaning in which 'historical dwelling' becomes possible for the people. Although Heidegger's reflections on own and foreign undergo constant revision,[18] an ontological-political interest in collective identity, informed by Friedrich Nietzsche's ideal of 'great creators' and by Stefan George's notion of 'Secret Germany', is inscribed in his readings of the poet since his first Hölderlin lectures.[19] A 'turn towards the homeland' (*vaterländische Umkehr*) constitutes a guiding thought that is still noticeable in the 1941-42 lecture course on Hölderlin's *Remembrance*: the constellation of identity and alterity culminates in a people's appropriation (*Aneignung*) of its 'origin' which is enabled by a confrontation with what is not original to it.

Against this foil, Handke's narration, in its arc and substance, appears to be an affirmative response to Heidegger's Hölderlinian law. Albeit transposing the law from the collective to individual level, the tale of a journey abroad that leads back to the origin seems to be a faithful rejoinder to it. Since Handke's notebooks from the period of writing *Slow Homecoming* contain approving comments on Heidegger's 'elucidations' of Hölderlin,[20] it is as if the 'law of becoming at home' provides a key that unlocks the poet's works for Handke and sanctions his own poetic law-giving in which genuine care and (or as) true self-appropriation is tied to a return home.

HOMELIKE PLACES

However, Handke cautions us against a hasty association of the two laws governing the relation of own and foreign, home and elsewhere. He does so in his radical editorial decision to eliminate all references to Heidegger from the novel's final version. Although he had planned to present Sorger as a reader of Heidegger, his notes from late 1978 express growing concerns: beyond allusions to strategic considerations that a proximity to Heidegger, due to his role in the Nazi movement, might affect the public perception of *Slow Homecoming* negatively, they explicitly refer to Heidegger's (or any other) language that, in relying on primordial words like 'power' or 'love', has been "spoiled once and for all" (*für immer verschandelt*) by becoming inextricable from the *lingua tertii imperii*.[21] Handke's "HORROR" (*GRAUEN*) at this realisation – which confronts him with the "terrible problem" (*furchtbares Problem*) of developing a narration around primordial phenomena and experiences without recourse to this vocabulary – can partially account for his editing out and replacing of Heideggerian elements.[22]

Still, Handke's doubts regarding Heidegger cannot be explained contextually alone but essentially result from his own poetic working through of questions of home and identity which places him at a considerable distance from Heidegger's law: his novelistic examination of existence abroad marks home as elusive. Falling painfully short of actual conversation, Sorger's phone calls to 'the child' and another relative make evident that no intact place of familiarity awaits him: his calls, received with "silence", "indifference", and "hostility",[23] confront him with the fact that "he was not needed".[24] Moreover, the reality of indigenous homes in 'the far North', bearing witness to a history of expropriation and suffering, renders untenable notions of autochthonous belonging – 'raised on wooden blocks', the dwellings are literally ungrounded, what piles up underneath is the detritus of modern Western civilisation. Faced with the effects of colonial violence, Sorger is also sensitised to 'noises of the past' which transmit that there is no 'peaceful household' to come home to:

Cans of milk were loaded onto a platform. A brief clinking of censers, then the screams of the wounded. The rumbling of tanks; a crashing and splintering; a moment of war. Then the stillness of peace; or was it?[25]

The awareness that "he was descended from murderers" and the anxiety to be "the faithful replica of death-cult masters"[26] prevent Sorger from identifying home with his native land. Heightened by its imagery of 'sand traps' that seek to record the shifting ground in geological experiments and of 'dispersing' strata, 'grimacing' tracts, and 'dancing' fault lines traced in Sorger's sketchings, *Slow Homecoming* persistently questions the notion that home can be substantiated and sustained in familial, historical, cultural, or political attachment, let alone rootedness in a native ground.

Neither does the novel suggest that grounding can be provided poetically. A scene that has Sorger attend a concert in the 'West Coast city' makes this particularly clear. *Pace* Heidegger's characterisation of Hölderlin's hymns as foundational for a people in creating union or instituting conversation among those who are co-original, Handke offers an alternative view of how hymns act upon an audience: in accordance with the basic meaning of *humnos*, the performing singer's hymns are shown to initiate a bond or cord between those who have "nothing in common"[27] except for being (co-)exposed to their "poetically appealing" (*poetisch zuredend*) address. Thus addressed, "the idea of a perpetual new beginning [. . .] in which he could lose himself [. . .], but at the same time find himself again"[28] emerges in Sorger who, amidst strangers, ecstatically re-recognises himself. The hymns' affective force is all the more extraordinary in that, simultaneous with inciting an acute sense of individuality, they give rise to a sense of communality between those who find themselves "body to body in the slowly moving crowd", in the "embrace" of the music.[29] That this experience of community in disunity is fleeting, that the hymns are soon drowned out by 'the scraping of shoes on the pavement' does not take away from the significance of the event: at the height of feeling alienated and adrift, Sorger has come into contact with possibilities that – without any promise of fulfilled, stable individual or collective identity – are self- as well as other-disclosing. Central motifs of this scene are repeated when accidental concurrences at an 'Earthquake Park' or on an airplane, in enabling an erotic encounter, 'perfect sympathy,' or neighbourliness, prove to be similarly (trans-)formative. Whether or not such encounters occur with strangers who are foreigners,[30] the intersubjective bonds turn out to be contingently and precariously, yet sufficiently grounded; what is more, these bonds contribute to Sorger's 'coming into his own' as they allow him to 'intervene' and, thereby, learn what is 'proper' to him when being summoned to constitute another person's "indispensable opposite".[31] As if perceiving his existential situation in 'deep vision', Sorger sees that "homelike"[32] constellations do open up "'far, far away'"[33] and, albeit in inconspicuous ways, do give form to his existence.

Certain aspects in Handke's deconstruction of home and re-description of identity stand out that prevent a reading of *Slow Homecoming* as going along with Heidegger. For one thing, it marks foreignness that matters as plural: instead of limiting the significance of encountering what is foreign to a specific constellation between collectivities (the uncontemporaneous constellation between 'the Germans' and 'the Greeks') and to specific traits of this uniquely relevant other (the Greek experience of Being, 'the fire of heaven'), Handke rejects the idea of a similarly privileged foreign. Where the narration touches on relations between collectives, cultures, and historical epochs – Europe and America, the present and the colonial and totalitarian past – it shows how they underlie Sorger's interpersonal encounters without usurping their meaning. Insisting that manifestations of *Fremdes* cannot be selected and hierarchised, the novel stresses the unpredictability of its address, of the way in which it affects *Eigenes* and "transforms [the self] into a 'receiver'"[34] as it elicits a response. For Handke, adequate responses cannot consist in the sovereign acts of "a despot or a conqueror"[35] but are ethical as they recognise that dwelling always already implies cohabitation and contemporaneity.[36] Sorger's critical 'legislative' moment thus becomes legible anew: without reflecting the redeeming of a 'destiny' (or the exercise of unbound autonomy), his law, in its central command "to be the contemporary of you contemporaries, and to be a citizen of the earth among others",[37] is the articulation of an ethical response to foreignness. In its excessive meaning and appeal, the foreign thus has an inherent status, a dignity in Handke that renders it irreducible to a latently subordinating, even instrumental understanding as a 'passage' that leads home.

It is evident that *this* law cannot have *Aneignung*, appropriation, as the realisation of ownness and selfhood for its content. Rather, the conception of a journey completed by return to a native land and reintegration into a native community is countered when self-alienation is shown to be integral to processes of identity (trans-)formation.[38] While *Slow Homecoming* primarily describes such alienation in encounters with the foreign, it is endorsed in openly normative terms in *Sainte-Victoire*: drawing on 'a sentence of the philosopher' – Spinoza, not Heidegger! – it is held that "[t]o uproot others, was the greatest of all crimes; to uproot oneself, the greatest of achievements".[39] This 'achievement' is both epistemic and ethical: in awakening the senses and, with them, the 'sense of possibility' (*Möglichkeitssinn*), it expands the field of the visible and sayable and, thus, generates an ability "to vibrate in harmony with the peaceful history of mankind".[40] Without suggesting any finality, selfhood thus understood takes shape in responding to what is incidental or accidental, in "kinship with other, unknown lives:" 'formlessness' is not overcome by returning home or belonging to a people but in becoming receptive to the "cohesion of [a] never-to-be-defined nation".[41] As Handke's poetology makes explicit, perceiving such kinship and cohesion, allowing for the 'sudden transformation' this perception inflicts,[42] and naming what is thus disclosed, is not simply a theme to be explored in his writing – it is what ultimately gives him 'the right to write' (*das Recht zu schreiben*).

These destabilisations of *Fremdes* and *Eigenes*, the pluralising revaluation of the former and the re-conception of the latter in terms of alter-identity, bring with it an understanding of their relation that departs from what is set forth in Heidegger's law. What presents itself as a dialectics of own and foreign, home and elsewhere in Heidegger – the sequence of 'improper,' 'foreign,' and 'proper,' the foreign-mediated advancement from self-alienation to self-possession[43] – gives way for a polemical harmonics in Handke: 'vibrating in harmony,' own and foreign are poeticised as distinct, yet folded into one another, characterised by simultaneous not-without-ness. While in tension, they are in agreement – 'like the bow and the lyre'. Without further exploring Handke's references to Heraclitus's fragments 50 and 51, it is in the emphasis on this unapparent relation of dynamic co-presencing and co-constituting, of *polemos* as *harmonia*, that Handke dismisses Heidegger's law. In this dismissal, Heraclitus (as well as Hölderlin to whom the notion of *hen kai pan* is especially significant in the *Systemfragment*, *Lebenslauf*, and *Hyperion*) is released from Heidegger's readings that, during the 1930s and 1940s, are not only over-determined by the reception in early German Idealism but also latently politicised.[44]

In thus alluding to the 'open community' of Hölderlin's *Der Mutter Erde* and re-drawing the contours of the Heraclitean polemic-harmonic relation, Handke does not submit Heidegger's thinking to critical standards that are external to it. Instead, his poetic account of a relational overcoming of 'formlessness' has the features of an immanent critique that discloses Heidegger's failure to bring resources of his own thinking to bear on questions of home and identity: although continuously engaging with Heraclitean *polemos*, recognising its importance for a 'destruction of metaphysics', and increasingly accentuating moments of agreement rather than tension inscribed to it, Heidegger's law falls short of conceiving home and elsewhere, own and foreign in other than oppositional terms and independent of the 'redemptive' goal of self-appropriation.[45] Handke's description of 'homelike' places and being 'among others', his law of 'vibrating in harmony' and "caring-in-common"[46] thus throw into relief traces of Heidegger's disconcerting politicisations of *polemos* within the matrix of 'the people' (*Volk*) that continue to traverse his thinking on *eigen* and *fremd* beyond the period of his activism.[47]

The rejection of the Heideggerian arc of homecoming is not solely a political but also an aesthetic matter as, for Handke, something 'decisive' is missing in Heidegger – a Dionysian element of 'the drunken', of intoxication.[48] Even before this difference in taste is made explicit, it is anticipated in the narration of Sorger's journey which, echoing Hölderlin's *Mnemosyne* and Nietzsche's *The Gay Science*, is 'unconfined' and 'wave-swayed', shaped by 'having left the land and having embarked.'[49] It is therefore fitting that Handke's counter-proposal to Heidegger's law ends without being completed: *Slow Homecoming* runs out with its protagonist *en route*, in transit.

"TOUCH HOME"

The Lesson of Mont Sainte-Victoire picks up what Handke calls the 'problem of transition'. With transitions from poetics to poetology and from protagonist to author – "I had transformed Sorger, the geologist, into myself"[50] – lending performative support to its treatment, the problem is repositioned: as the specific experience of transitional relations between home and elsewhere recedes to the background, Handke's interest widens and turns to the multiplicity of interrelated, interpenetrating 'forms' and 'things' and to the 'little world-space-massifs' that unfold around or between them.[51] Correspondingly, Handke's own return to Europe from his American journey[52] does not lead him to a native country, town, or house but to what he perceives as a paradigmatic 'massif' in this sense: the Sainte-Victoire mountain in Southern France. Assuming the viewpoints and following the sightlines of Paul Cézanne – declared in hyperbole to be "*the* teacher of mankind in the here and now"[53] – he aspires to hone his 'deep vision,' to learn how to artistically express and convey the 'unity' (*Zusammenhang*) and 'cohesion' (*Zusammenhalt*) of that which is separate.[54]

Despite such shifts, Handke's aesthetic-ontological meditations on the 'earthly' or 'real' as constituted by fundamentally 'peaceful' relationality, by apartness hemmed in by mutuality and intimacy, are continuous with the novelistic deconstruction of 'becoming at home' and possessing oneself. Here too, the notion of return unravels in an endless series of detours, approximations, and new departures: Handke's account of his hikes around and across the Sainte-Victoire that never allow for the satisfaction of a "summit feeling"[55] complements his biographical reflections on the difficulty to identify an original historical moment, geographic place, cultural or linguistic space with certainty[56] – and his insight that, in return, "the circles [. . .] grow wider and wider".[57] In this light, the set phrase 'touch home soon', repeatedly invoked in *Slow Homecoming*, takes on a new quality as it foreshadows the asymptotic movement of touching as reaching and approaching that becomes thematic.

For Handke, such touching is paradigmatically achieved in Cézanne's paintings of the Sainte-Victoire. Overcoming *mimesis* in "'constructions and harmonies parallel to nature'",[58] Cézanne's work carries the search for forms the furthest: beyond revealing the transitional constitution of 'places' and 'things', it bears witness to the way in which artistic practice is itself woven into the extensive fabric of the transitional – the colours and forms on the canvas are responses 'obligated' (*verpflichtet*) by these 'things'.[59] What finally makes Cézanne's *réalisations* unique for Handke is their inhabiting the interface between and, thereby, joining together different artistic modes and media of experience and expression. As "thing-image-script-brushstroke-dance",[60] the sketches, watercolours, and oil paintings of the Sainte-Victoire develop a 'pictorial writing' (*Bilderschrift*) that achieves 'the unheard-of' (*das Unerhörte*): it realises, that is: it grasps, works out, and performs the 'harmony' (*Einklang*) that folds what appears as fragmented into one. In their synaesthetic force – underlined by Handke's own integrating of the written word, the visual, and the auditory[61] – Cézanne's works "hold open the world to us".[62] On Handke's pictorial reading, these works come to constitute 'homelike' sites: preventing a 'loss of pictures' (*Bildverlust*), a crucial aspect of the 'vanishing' of 'everything' induced by modern science and technology, they unveil our being associated with things and places, allow for moments of being "at home in colours", and open up possibilities for the "'good self' [. . .] to find new strength".[63] In rendering, as Merleau-Ponty writes about Cézanne, "*visible* how the world *touches* us",[64] they let us touch on being at home in transmitting a sense of 'solidarity' (*Zusammenhalt*) and 'nearness' (*Nähe*) amidst the 'event of worlding' (*Weltgeschehen*).[65]

While a detailed comparison of Handke's and Heidegger's interpretations of Cézanne, let alone an examination of the constellation poetry-philosophy-painting that unfolds around them, goes beyond the scope of this chapter, suffice it to point to key moments regarding homecoming that are reiterated in *Sainte-Victoire*. For Handke, the 'lessons' to be learned from Cézanne's exemplary practice confirm that, within the wide expanse of relationality that is the 'world', it is possible to 'work oneself into a new place', perceive its 'characteristic forms', 'form ties' to it, and 'feel at home there'.[66] Moreover, his reflections on Cézanne's (as well as his own) 'peace-fostering' project uphold that works of art cannot provide foundations for collective self-understanding or unity. When art 'works' and sets up 'homelike' places, it does so in an unfixed, amendable fashion. Attuned to 'the vibration of appearances' and 'continual rebirth of existence',[67] it cannot achieve more than preliminary stabilisations – or as Merleau-Ponty, in discussing Cézanne alongside with Klee and Matisse, states: "For painters, if any remain, the world will always be yet to be painted; even if it lasts millions of years . . . it will all end without being completed".[68] Like Cézanne's pictorial thinking, Handke's poetic thinking is imbued with the sense that all *be-zeichnen*, i.e. all designating in drawing, painting, and naming, must always be done anew and otherwise. Owing to their incompleteness and their status as mere 'proposals' (*Vorschlag*),[69] artworks, for Handke, cannot be received uniformly, identified and preserved in their meaning by a collective audience: if they succeed in giving rise to communality at all, such communality arises in asynchronous, dispersed experiences of 'shock' (*Erschütterung*) or 'warmth' (*Herzlichkeit*)[70] – between "monads coexisting with [these works], or the open community of future monads".[71]

SPACES JOINED

Despite Handke's doubt concerning Heidegger's language, 'thought posturing' (*Denkgehabe*) that promises but performatively contradicts freedom and openness in 'erecting concrete bunkers',[72] and take on home and selfhood, distancing and rejection do not exhaust this poetico-philosophical constellation. Substantial parallels in their understandings of art indicate that affinities do not always result from an actual literary reception of philosophical texts: although Handke appears unfamiliar with Heidegger's writings on art (including the remarks on Cézanne) and maintains commitments to the tradition of subjectivist aesthetics Heidegger seeks to overcome,[73] his explorations of the non-composite constitution of 'world' or of compartments that access its 'plasticity',[74] revolve around motifs found at the heart of Heidegger's thinking on art. Attesting to a concern with (the) nothing, Handke's meditations on fault lines in nature and lines sketched on canvas are a case in point: what is rendered visible in Cézanne's paintings of the Sainte-Victoire is that *Nichts geschah*, is the happening of (the) nothing.[75] The proximity to Heidegger's thought *das Kunstwerk stellt nichts dar* is striking:[76] beyond a rejection of representation, art is understood as a truth-happening that 'presents (the) nothing' as a well from which 'worlds' come forth. Whether unfolding in picture or in word, genuine artistic practice thus poetises, *dichtet*, in an almost literal sense for both Handke and Heidegger: it condenses or thickens this happening and, with that, brings forth a re-configuration of the sensible world.

At least in part, such affinities are attributable to an interest in space that Handke not only accidentally shares but develops through a sustained engagement with Heidegger: while elaborating the first parts of his 'homecoming cycle', he reads *Building Dwelling Thinking* 'almost like the gospel'.[77] It is in poetically thinking through artistic and lived space as alternatives to 'empty' scientific space and the 'prohibition of space' (the second chapter in *Slow Homecoming* is titled *Raumverbot*) it imposes, that Handke's own text is most openly linked to Heidegger's. As his excerpts from Heidegger's essay show, he is particularly impressed by passages that spell out 'dwelling' in terms of humans' ability to "persist" (*durchstehen*) and "go through spaces" (*durchgehen*); an ability that is owed to their embeddedness in an unsurveyable relational expanse that has 'things' for its nodal points: a "leading of the human being to the space-granting nothing"[78] is not only achieved in artistic 'works' but also enabled by an attunement to 'things' as sites of 'thickened' meaning around which space opens up.[79] The reflections on *durchstehen*, a term underlined in Handke's notes, and *durchgehen* culminate in the insight "that we already experience [spaces] by staying constantly with near and remote locations and things", that "I am never here only, as this encapsulated body".[80]

Handke's close, affirmative reading of Heidegger on space sheds new light on *Slow Homecoming* where "the raising of localities by the joining of spaces",[81] achieved in 'building' and or, rather, *as* 'dwelling', is taken up as guiding theme. Early on in the novel, an experience of Sorger's existence abroad is mentioned in passing that runs counter to his feeling of alienation and loss, of being 'nowhere at home' and having difficulty in 'keeping himself together:'

> [. . .] with luck, in times of exhaustion, all his localities joined together, the particular, freshly conquered one with those that had gone before, and formed a dome encompassing heaven and earth, a sanctuary, which was not only private but open to others.[82]

This fleeting sensation is forcefully authenticated in a scene set on a nightly beach by the Pacific Ocean. Instead of a vague vision 'in times of exhaustion', the experience of such 'joining' (*fügen*) is now presented as a 'rediscovery of reality' in which Sorger's 'longing to return' is almost cathartically overcome: at 'Land's End', at the "threefold diving line between earth, water, and air", he sees "an antique colonnade stretch[ing] across the sea into the horizon"[83] – no longer perceived as 'a large body of water which separated him from everything', the ocean is transformed into a seam that holds together here and there. Thus, Sorger's existence reveals itself as persisting and going through (sea) space, as indissolubly connected to 'his continent' and 'his child;' the 'dome' which opens around the 'colonnade' is 'realized' as the (im-)proper, (un-)homely space he is learning to dwell in.

While the debt to Heidegger's analyses on boundary and horizon, locations releasing spaces, and the spatial being of 'mortals' is apparent, Handke maintains a 'free relation' to Heidegger's thinking even in the most far-reaching joining of literary and philosophical textual spaces: the transposition of 'joining' and 'gathering' capacities from the bridge, exemplary in Heidegger's essay, to the sea gestures towards a critique of 'geo-centrism'; what is more, Handke's rendering of 'joined spaces' widens the scope of relations that give sense and direction to existence. Beyond allowing, as Heidegger does, for the possibility of a plurality of 'regionally' (*gegendhaft*) circumscribed 'worlds' within which certain apprehensions of what it is 'to be' and forms of 'gathering' and shared belonging take shape, Handke explores the possibility of transversal connections between and simultaneous, 'caring' involvement in such 'worlds'. What lends Handke's approach the character of an independent rejoinder to Heidegger, is that the experience of 'joined' space – of 'conquering' space, a *Raumeroberung* that dispenses with *Raumverbot*[84] – is brought to bear upon the relation of home and elsewhere, own and foreign. While Heidegger's thinking on space, revolving around ontological 'homelessness' that, characteristic of Western modernity, prevents a 'dwelling' in the 'fourfold', does not return to the 'legal' framework of *Eigenes* and *Fremdes*, Handke's proposal of an integrated play-space of transitions retrieves its insights. In this retrieval or *Wiederholung* that takes up Heidegger's thought and develops further what it has left unexplored, re-descriptions of one's lived position – gathered by the sea, a member in the community of 'mariners' – and new understandings of cohabitation become possible.

"*RÉUSSIR VOTRE ISOLATION*"

The controversy surrounding Handke's political commitments and their relation to his writing, initially sparked by his 1996 essay *A Journey to the Rivers: Justice for Serbia*, gained new momentum when he received the 2019 Nobel Prize in Literature.[85] Echoing the severe criticism of Handke's support for Serbia's nationalist regime under Slobodan Milošević voiced by the likes of Salman Rushdie and Jonathan Littell over the past decades, numerous writers and commentators wondered whether Handke's continued unapologetic pro-Serbian attitude, going hand in hand with a critique of Western power politics and media with its 'scandalized lip movements' and 'carefully framed images', might have served as a welcome outlet for anti-modern tendencies inscribed in Handke's literary work from the outset; some commentators suggested that his political choice exhibits 'structural analogies' to Heidegger's involvement with Nazism.[86]

Detached from the violent ethnic conflicts on the Balkan peninsula to the point of distorting historical facts – most flagrant with respect to the Srebrenica massacre in July 1995 – Handke's *Journey to the Rivers* presents

Serbia as his *Phantasieheimat*, a last bastion that defends a 'buoyant' (*heiter*), 'original' (*ursprünglich*) and 'traditional' (*volkstümlich*) way of life against the hegemonial reach of a disenchanted West. Unmistakably, Handke's 'circles' no longer 'grow wider and wider' but constrict in the identification with a political cause and collective – as if his doubts regarding belonging have dissolved in the Danube, Save, Morava, and Drina.

While tracing the textual history and examining the ideological implications of Handke's oeuvre is a separate task, *Slow Homecoming* and *The Lesson of Mont Sainte-Victoire* give some indications how his poetising might have facilitated his political stance. On the one hand, the deconstruction of homecoming as a directed, completable trajectory that forges identity does not transport or foreshadow an identity politics of home: considering the dissolution of origins in ever-more 'prehistory', the substitution of the people by a 'never-to-be-defined nation', the descriptions of navigating alter-identity, and the vision of harmonious contemporaneity, Handke's embrace of Serbian nationalism appears to be a suspension or invalidation rather than an application of the poetic thinking laid out in his 'homecoming cycle'.

On the other hand, *Slow Homecoming* and *Sainte-Victoire* exhibit traits conducive to Handke's partisan entanglements over a decade later as both works, independent of their content, reflect an underlying attitude or methodology that is highly monological and self-referential. Built entirely on the standpoint from which he minutely scrutinises the world as it registers in his experience and stimulates interminable introspection, Handke's project of rediscovering 'areas of deeper visions' does not know any external frame of orientation and correction – even where an 'epic of peace' is put forth and altered modes of coexistence are sung of, it possesses a phantasmatic, solipsistic quality. When applied to the political realm, this solitary search for a 'naming power' must go awry – a 'transmission' that exclusively operates with 'silence,' 'signs,' and 'clues' or with aesthetic categories like 'beauty' is not only bound to be misleading but must remain insufficient where genocidal violence is at stake. But even before questions of (in-)adequate address and communication arise: Handke's haughty notion that the realities of armed conflict and forced displacement can be grasped through *Möglichkeitssinn* and *Phantasie* amounts to a self-deprivation of political judgement.

Réussir votre isolation, the slogan Handke spots on a billboard ad for 'successful' home insulation near Cézanne's studio,[87] seems to capture such tendencies that yield damaging effects when politicised: perceptive of how Heidegger runs the risk of building 'concrete bunkers' in language and thought – or, with Arendt's fox fable, "a trap as his burrow"[88] – he fails to recognise how his own 'purpose-free descriptions' and 'language pictures' are sealed off against factual accounts, rendering him immune to amendment and revision. It is with regard to the question what 'things' are sensibly nameable on the basis of a poetic thinking striving to be 'spared from the turmoil of the present'[89] that Handke's doubt runs out of breath.

NOTES

1. Martin Meyer's review *Sich einlassen* appeared in *Neue Zürcher Zeitung* on October 20, 1979.
2. *Langsame Heimkehr* (*Slow Homecoming*) is the first part of a trilogy that further includes *Die Lehre der Sainte-Victoire* (1980; *The Lesson of Mont Sainte-Victoire*) and *Kindergeschichte* (1981; *Child Story*); Handke's 1982 'dramatic poem' *Über die Dörfer* (*Walk About the Villages*) constitutes the final part of his 'homecoming cycle'. The 2009 English translation entitled *Slow Homecoming* contains the trilogy in its entirety. The following observations focus on the first and second part of Handke's cycle.
3. In addition to references to Heidegger in Handke's published works and journals, von Bülow's analysis draws on unpublished notebooks kept at the German Literature Archive Marbach. See Ulrich von Bülow, "Raum, Zeit, Sprache. Peter Handke liest Martin Heidegger", in *Peter Handke. Stationen, Orte, Positionen*, ed. Anna Kinder (Berlin/Boston: de Gruyter, 2014), 111–40.
4. In Handke's understanding, 'narration' (*Erzählung*), implies an epic quality that transcends conventions of the novel such as character, action, or plot.
5. According to von Bülow, Handke's readings of Heidegger are 'sporadic.' While he is unfamiliar with Heidegger's early thought, his writings reference "... *Poetically Man Dwells...*", *Who Is Nietzsche's Zarathustra?*, the interview with *Der Spiegel*, or the *Heraclitus Seminar*. The close reading of *Building Dwelling Thinking* in the process of writing *Slow Homecoming* is an exception.
6. On Handke's 'air of refusal' that, combined with 'archive consciousness' and the urge to 'direct the reception' of his work, creates a 'brand', see Anna Kinder, "Peter Handke als Forschungsphänomen", in *Peter Handke*, 1–11.
7. Peter Handke, *Slow Homecoming*, trans. Ralph Manheim (New York: New Review Books, 2009), 3.
8. Handke, *Homecoming*, 33.
9. See Handke, *Homecoming*, 74.
10. Handke, *Homecoming*, 8.
11. Handke, *Homecoming*, 102. The refusal to use place names (San Francisco, Alaska, Denver, New York) undergirds Handke's aspiration to name otherwise. Alternatives do not necessarily need to be invented poetically: references to nicknames, popular names, and forgotten historical names question 'official' names as much as the poet's sovereignty to name. 'Hard Luck Lake' that recalls the Gold Rush in Alaska or 'Great Unknown Brook' that invokes the 'archetypal' naming of its indigenous population are cases in point.

12. Handke, *Homecoming*, 114–15.

13. Handke, *Homecoming*, 95.

14. § 26 of *Being and Time* contrasts care that 'leaps ahead' with care that 'leaps in,' marking the former as more authentic as it transcends predefined, socially recognised frameworks of meaning and conduct. See GA 2, 163–64.

15. Martin Heidegger, "'Remembrance'", in *Elucidations of Hölderlin's Poetry*, trans. Keith Hoeller (Amherst: Humanity Books, 2000), 101–73, here 141. See GA 4, 118–19.

16. Heidegger, "'Remembrance'", 112. See GA 4, 87.

17. For a concise overview of this textual history of, see Katharina Kaiser, "Gespräch mit Hölderlin I: 'Eigenes' und 'Fremdes'", in *Heidegger-Handbuch: Leben-Werk-Wirkung*, ed. Dieter Thomä (Stuttgart: J.B. Metzler, 2013), 184–88.

18. Such revisions include the re-conception of 'destiny' (*Schicksal*) as endowed to a specific people in terms of 'sending' (*Geschick*) as addressing humans independent of national belonging and heritage.

19. At the time of lecturing on Hölderlin following his resignation as rector of Freiburg University Heidegger expressed his ambition to "remain in the invisible front of the secret spiritual Germany". Martin Heidegger, *Ponderings II-VI: Black Notebooks 1931-1938*, trans. Richard Rojcewicz (Bloomington: Indiana University Press, 2016), 114. See GA 94, 155. While distancing himself from the voluntarism of 'self-assertion' that had characterised his activist period, the question of 'who we are' and the project of ontologically grounding 'German Dasein', situated at the interface between (now poeticised) philosophy and politics, are still pursued.

20. See von Bülow, "Raum, Zeit, Sprache", 126–27.

21. See von Bülow, "Raum, Zeit, Sprache", 125; 136.

22. References to Heidegger are replaced with allusions to Lucretius and Spinoza, a choice that attests to the unabashed character of Handke's engagement with philosophical thought.

23. Handke, *Homecoming*, 108.

24. Handke, *Homecoming*, 127.

25. Handke, *Homecoming*, 98.

26. Handke, *Homecoming*, 65–6.

27. Handke, *Homecoming*, 82 (my emphasis). This figure of thought is also at the centre of Roberto Esposito's reflections on community: it is 'a no-thing-in-common' that 'brings us into relation with others in a common non-belonging'. See Roberto Esposito, *Communitas: The Origin and Destiny of Community* (Stanford: Stanford University Press, 2010), esp. 135–49.

28. Handke, *Homecoming*, 81.

29. Handke, *Homecoming*, 82.

30. For instance, the figure of the 'stranger from the same country' prevents a reductive understanding of alterity. See Handke, *Homecoming*, 110.

31. Handke, *Homecoming*, 119.

32. See Handke, *Homecoming*, 114.

33. Handke, *Homecoming*, 14.

34. Handke, *Homecoming*, 93.

35. Handke, *Homecoming*, 115.

36. For a discussion of Handke's literary ethics, see Thomas Hennig, *Intertextualität als ethische Dimension: Peter Handkes Ästhetik 'nach Auschwitz'* (Würzburg: Königshausen & Neumann, 1996), esp. 28–33 and 88–120.

37. Handke, *Homecoming*, 115.

38. This motif is central to Handke's re-reading of the archetypical Odyssean narrative: what makes Homer's Odysseus Handke's 'hero' is not his return to Ithaca but his becoming "No-Man". See Peter Handke, "The Lesson of Mont Sainte-Victoire", in *Slow Homecoming*, trans. Ralph Manheim (New York: New Review Books, 2009), 139–211, here 160. The revaluation of self-alienation also informs Handke's understanding of migration as an act of liberation from the weight of 'territory,' 'genealogy,' and 'tradition.' See Christian Luckscheiter, "Flüchtlinge in der Literatur Peter Handkes", in *Niemandsbuchten und Schutzbefohlene*, ed. Thomas Hardke et al. (Göttingen: V&R unipress, 2017), 85–95, here 92.

39. Handke, "Sainte-Victoire", 159.

40. Handke, *Homecoming*, 115.

41. Handke, "Sainte-Victoire", 175.

42. See Handke, "Sainte-Victoire", 175: "[M]y usual self became strictly No One".

43. For a critique of Heidegger's Hegelian understanding of the relation own/foreign, proper/improper as culminating in 'synthesis' and 'attainment of the proper', see Esposito, *Communitas*, 107.

44. See Kaiser, "Gespräch mit Hölderlin", 186–87. Handke thus joins the ranks of Hölderlin interpreters such as Gershom Sholem who have offered readings of the poet's understanding of what is 'national' that starkly differ from Heidegger's.

45. Terms like *Aus-einander-setzung*, *Ver-hältnis*, *Zu-stand*, *Unter-schied* or *liebender Streit* are integral to Heidegger's interpretive trajectory. Renouncing an understanding of *polemos* as 'struggle' (*Kampf*), they allow him to reconceive the relation between identity and alterity. Similarly, 'pathic' or 'abyssal' moments in Heidegger's conception of 'experience' (*Erfahrung*) or of 'self-being' (*Selbstsein*) respectively are insufficiently brought to the reflections on *eigen* and *fremd*. Such omissions make Esposito wonder "[h]ow it [is] possible for a philosopher to lose a part of his own thought?" See Esposito, *Communitas*, 97.

46. Esposito, *Communitas*, 96.

47. The lecture course *On the Essence of Truth* and the *Black Notebooks* contain such politicisations that present a one-sidedly conflictual understanding of *polemos* and repeatedly short-circuit the foreign with 'inimical' or 'worldless' Jewish existence. See GA 36/37, 91–95; GA, 95, 97; GA 96, 56; Florian Grosser, "Selbstheit, Andersheit und die Möglichkeit des elementalen Bösen: Levinas' Heidegger-Kritik im Licht der 'Schwarzen Hefte'", in *Heidegger, die Juden, noch einmal*, eds. Peter Trawny/Andrew Mitchell (Frankfurt: Klostermann, 2015), 191–214.

48. A 1986 entry in Handke's notebook reads: "*Dem Heidegger fehlt aber doch das Entscheidende: das Trunkene (mit und ohne Wein)*". See von Bülow, "Raum, Zeit, Sprache", 135.

49. Handke's screenplay for Wim Wenders' 1987 film *Wings of Desire*, which shows multiple continuities with *Slow Homecoming* and even reproduces some

passages verbatim, makes this Nietzschean moment explicit when a protagonist, member of a travelling circus, emphatically declares *Nous sommes embarqués!*.

50. Handke, "Sainte-Victoire", 191. As the geologist's gaze 'persist(s) in many of my perceptions', this transformation also gestures toward transitions between science and technology on the one hand, art on the other.

51. The rich formulation *kleines Weltraummassiv* is omitted in the English translation.

52. In 1978, Handke had travelled to the United States, visiting the locations mentioned in the novel.

53. Handke, "Sainte-Victoire", 176 (original emphasis).

54. For the importance of Cézanne for Handke's artistic self-understanding and his 'epic of peace', see Handke, "Sainte-Victoire", 147: "His [Cézanne's] reality became the form he achieved [...], [which] transmits an existence in peace. Art is concerned with nothing else".

55. Handke, "Sainte-Victoire", 172. In 1979, Handke travels to Aix-en-Provence twice.

56. Discussing his multiethnic family and native border region of Carinthia, Handke states: "I'm told that Slovenian was my first language".

57. Handke, "Sainte-Victoire", 183. Such 'widening circles' include poetic-geological expeditions to Berlin, Paris, and Salzburg – 'homelike' places, too – described toward the end of *Sainte-Victoire*. Even where a return leads to Carinthia, such circular movements persist. Handke's Nobel Lecture, an explicit rejoinder to the final part the 'homecoming cycle', seems to confirm the idea of a return home as a series of approximations: it ends without being completed, in the deserted courtyard of the birth house, in 'the neighboring villages,' or in 'roaming around'. See Peter Handke, *Nobel Lecture*. <https://www.nobelprize.org/prizes/literature/2019/handke/lecture/>.

58. Handke, "Sainte-Victoire", 178. Handke's intertextual montage repeatedly includes Cézanne's own characterisations of his work.

59. See Handke, "Sainte-Victoire", 178.

60. Handke, "Sainte-Victoire", 179.

61. See Jacob Haubenreich, "Poetry, Painting, Patchwork: Peter Handke's Intermedial Writing of 'Die Lehre der Sainte-Victoire'", *German Quarterly* 92, no. 2 (Spring 2019): 187–210. Handke's synaesthetics, his attempt to merge word and image – or, to modify Merleau-Ponty's remark on Cézanne, 'to change the world into film' – culminate in *Wings of Desire*.

62. Handke, "Sainte-Victoire", 179.

63. Handke, "Sainte-Victoire", 141, 179.

64. Maurice Merleau-Ponty, "Cézanne's Doubt", in *The Merleau-Ponty Aesthetics Reader: Philosophy and Painting*, ed. Galen A. Johnson (Evanston: Northwestern University Press, 1998), 59–75, here 70 (original emphases).

65. See Handke, "Sainte-Victoire", 177–78.

66. See Handke, *Homecoming*, 72; 110.

67. See Merleau-Ponty, "Cézanne's Doubt", 68.

68. Maurice Merleau-Ponty, "Eye and Mind", in *Merleau-Ponty Aesthetics Reader*, 121–49, here 148.
69. See Handke, "Sainte-Victoire", 175: "For, unspecified reader, who but the subject of a picture or the hero of a story ever proposed anything to you in your life?"
70. See Handke, "Sainte-Victoire", 155; 177.
71. Merleau-Ponty, "Cézanne's Doubt", 69.
72. See von Bülow, 137. *Mehr so Betonbunker als Wohnstätten* – the quote is from a 1986 interview where Handke remarks on the inaccessibility of Heidegger's thinking.
73. In contrast to Heidegger's reflections on Cézanne's art as a self-revealing "coming-to-presence" of "things" in "the pure shining of images" (see GA 81, 347 and GA 13, 223), Handke insists that *réalisation* requires moments of artistic freedom, agency, and imagination. Albeit not sovereign but affected by and receptive to the performances of forms, such moments are referred to as unique *sensations* by Cézanne, as *meine Phantasie* by Handke.
74. In his notes on Paul Klee, Heidegger uses the term *Bildsamkeit*. See Martin Heidegger, "Notizen zu Klee/Notes on Klee", trans. María del Rosario Acosta López et al., *Philosophy Today* 61, no. 1 (Winter 2017): 7–17, here 10.
75. See Handke, "Sainte-Victoire", 163.
76. See Martin Heidegger, "Vom Ursprung des Kunstwerks. Erste Ausarbeitung", *Heidegger-Studies* 5 (1989): 4; Iain Thomson, *Heidegger, Art, and Postmodernity* (Cambridge: Cambridge University Press, 2011), 94–100.
77. See von Bülow, 137.
78. Heidegger, "Notes on Klee", 11.
79. In Heidegger's 1969 *Art and Space*, dedicated to the sculptor Eduardo Chillida, 'works' and 'things' coincide in the 'clearing away' and 'releasing of places' around which 'regions' open up.
80. Heidegger, "Building Dwelling Thinking", 155; see GA 7, 159.
81. Heidegger, "Building Dwelling Thinking", 157; see GA 7, 160.
82. Handke, *Slow Homecoming*, 7.
83. Handke, *Slow Homecoming*, 98.
84. See Handke, "Sainte-Victoire", 180.
85. On behalf of PEN America, Jenniger Egan stated 'deep regret' that an author who has 'offered public succor to perpetrators of genocide' had been honored; on the occasion of receiving the German Book Prize for his novel *Herkunft*, Saša Stanišić, born in Bosnia, remarked on his 'good fortune to escape what Peter Handke fails to describe in his texts'.
86. See Bert Rebhandl, "Dichter, Denker und die Politik", in *Der Standard*, December 7 (2019).
87. See Handke, "Sainte-Victoire", 171.
88. Hannah Arendt, "Heidegger, the Fox", in *Essays in Understanding 1930-1954*, ed. Jerome Kohn (New York: Harcourt Brace & Company, 1994), 362.
89. *Durch die Erzählung verschont von den Wirren der Jetztzeit* – this programmatic aspiration of Handke's 'epic' poetics is formulated in *Wings of Desire*.

Part II

LITERARY RECEPTION POLITICS BETWEEN EAST AND WEST

HÖLDERLIN AND THE POETICS OF THE STATES

Chapter 8

"The Right to Be"

Stevens and Heidegger on Thinking and Poetising

Frederick Dolan

In the last years of his life, the American poet Wallace Stevens expressed interest in the German philosopher Martin Heidegger. Stevens was led to Heidegger by his prior interest in Friedrich Hölderlin, the poet who preoccupied Heidegger after the book *Being and Time* (1927). Frank Kermode, in an essay with the marvellous title *Dwelling Poetically in Connecticut*, discusses Stevens's efforts to acquire information about Heidegger, the results of which were ambiguous.[1] Certainly, Stevens could not have had more than a passing familiarity with Heidegger's thought, but Kermode notes pertinent similarities and differences, given their nationalities and temperaments. While the German brooded on the meaning of Being as if the fate of humanity depended on it, the American indulged in what he called, in his *Adagia*, "casual" interests such as "light or color, [and] images".[2]

Although Stevens's pursuit of Heidegger went nowhere, I like to think that he was right to wonder whether Heidegger might have something to offer him. Metaphysically speaking, both men belonged to the same epoch. Stevens, like Heidegger, was haunted by the question of how to respond to the moral and spiritual disorders of a world from which the gods had fled (or worse). Heidegger worried about technological "enframing", in which beings appear as resources continually in the process of being optimised, enhanced and rendered ever more accessible to manipulation – an approach that is also applied to human beings and which obscures our true vocation as "shepherds of Being". Stevens characterises the modern world in rather different terms – "the great things have been denied and we live in an intricacy of new and local mythologies, political, economic and poetic, which are asserted with an ever-enlarging incoherence" – but he was at one with Heidegger when it came to the "pressure on the consciousness" of a disenchanted technological society that weakens the "power of contemplation".[3]

Despairing of the spiritual state of the modern world, Heidegger concluded that "The only possibility available to us is that by *thinking and poetizing* [*Denken und Dichten*] we prepare a readiness for the appearance of a god".[4] Stevens, for his part, understood the modern world in terms of the Nietzschean "death of God", and he too was in search of a remedy. The right kind of poetry, he hoped, "may some day disclose a force capable of destroying nihilism".[5] *Mutatis mutandis*, Stevens wrestled with many of the same problems as Heidegger.

If Heidegger is the philosopher who poetises, Stevens is the poet who philosophises. When we think, Heidegger says, "Being comes to language", for "language is the house [*das Haus*] of Being" and "the thinkers and poetizers are the custodians of this dwelling [*Behausung*]".[6] More sweepingly, "All philosophical thinking ... is in itself poetic".[7] Thinking as Heidegger understands it is more imaginative than logical, and when it reflects on its language, it teases out semantic intimations that will dispose us; he hopes to recognise and name the god when it does arrive.

Stevens too speaks of poetry and thinking in the same breath. He characterised his poetic intentions in a letter to his friend, Hi Simons:

> The ordinary, everyday search of the romantic mind is rewarded perhaps rather too lightly by the satisfaction that it finds in what it calls reality. But if one happened to be playing checkers somewhere near the Maginot Line, subject to a call at any moment to do some job that might be one's last job, one would spend a good deal of time thinking in order to make the situation seem reasonable, inevitable and free from question. I suppose that, in the last analysis, my own main objective is to do that kind of thinking.[8]

Stevens's "kind of thinking" is reminiscent of the "therapeutic" philosophical investigations that Ludwig Wittgenstein hoped would put an end to questioning by dissolving problems rather than solving them. For Heidegger, on the other hand, "questioning" (as he puts it in *The Question Concerning Technology*) "is the piety of thought", and thinking is more concerned with deepening questions than with answering them. Thinking about technology, for example, is a matter of asking questions that will reveal both what technology is and what it is doing to us as beings for whom Being is an issue. Questioning, Heidegger believes, can free us from technological thinking; Stevens believes that poetic thinking can free us from questioning.

But surely, it is more plausible to oppose poetry to thinking? That depends on one's understanding of poetry. In another letter, written the year before his death to Richard Eberhart, Stevens emphasises that "poetry is not a literary activity".[9] Given his verbal inventiveness, this is a very odd proposition. Stevens after all is the poet who writes, in *The Connoisseur of Chaos*, that "the squirming facts exceed the squamous mind". He crafts exquisite paradoxes, such as the one in *Peter Quince at the Clavier* in which we learn that "Beauty is momentary in the mind– / The fitful tracing of a portal; / But in the flesh it is immortal". And in *Sunday Morning*, he concludes his meditation on what Ronald Dworkin calls "religion without God"[10] with a sublimely beautiful vision of "casual flocks of pigeons" that "make / Ambiguous undulations as they sink, / Downward to darkness, on extended wings". What is this if not literary activity?

VITAL QUESTIONS

The answer is that Stevens opposes poetry as a literary activity to poetry as "a *vital* activity".[11] Poetry, he says, as a vital activity, "should stimulate the sense of living and of being alive".[12] He goes on to align poetry with music on the grounds that both fuel life and nourish the spirit. That formula accords with his lifelong search for the experience of what he variously calls "force", "passion", "fury" and even "violence". Stevens adds to his observation that poetry is a matter of life not literature that "The good writers are the good thinkers".[13] Good thinking and good writing exhibit their values in a good life, one animated by a "rage for order".[14] Stevens's poetry organises a complex of terms involving an ordinary life, the oppressive conditions it sometimes imposes, and a poetic practice that, such conditions, employs poetic philosophising to revitalise life.

"Order" is one of Stevens's words for the state in which things are free from question, an experience that occasionally dawns spontaneously but is more commonly composed with difficulty from nonsensical, empty, pointless or otherwise painful situations. Examples of order are the "arranging, deepening, enchanting" night celebrated in *The Idea of Order at Key West*, the "sudden rightnesses" and "satisfactions" we can arrive at "in the act of finding / What will suffice" evoked in *Of Modern Poetry*, and the plain jar in Tennessee that "took dominion everywhere".[15] As his rage for order indicates, the task Stevens sets for himself is especially urgent when "traditional sanctions are disappearing".[16] As he puts it in *Sad Strains of a Gay Waltz*, "There comes a time when the waltz" – a symbol of the traditional sanctions – "Is no longer a mode of desire", so that the "epic of disbelief / Blares oftener and soon, will soon be constant".[17] What we now require, Stevens thinks, are not new beliefs to replace those that are no longer credible but rather a new *mode* of belief in which we take the products of our imagination as seriously as we took God, but without taking them literally. As he explains in a letter to Simons, "If one no longer believes in God (as truth) it is not possible merely to disbelieve; it becomes necessary to believe in something else", and "I say that one's final belief must be in a fiction. I think that the history of belief will show that it has always been in a fiction".[18] But how does one believe in a fiction? By poetising. "After one has abandoned a belief in god", Stevens writes, "poetry is that essence which takes its place as life's redemption".[19]

With the rejection of the myth of a creative god, we "pass from the created to the uncreated" and find that "modern reality is a reality of decreation".[20] In *Esthétique du Mal*,[21] Stevens apprehends, with Nietzsche, that with the death of God much else is lost – for example, a robust sense of evil:

The death of Satan was a tragedy
For the imagination. A capital
Negation destroyed him in his tenement
And, with him, many blue phenomena.

That we no longer believe in Satan may be a triumph of reason, but valuable products of the imagination ("blue phenomena") that depended on that belief died with him. The collapse of the moral order is sweeping: "The death of one god is the death of all"[22] and "Christianity is an exhausted culture".[23]

In Christianity, we are God's handiwork and are graced with a purpose: to prepare ourselves for the moment when we stand in His presence and savour the Beatific Vision. The death of the Creator would seem to leave us without purpose, but for Heidegger that is not necessarily a misfortune. He was always ambivalent about the value of understanding Being as creation or production (*poiesis*). The producer's disclosure of beings as raw materials to be shaped in accordance with a predetermined end is an overly subjective perspective that obscures a more primordial understanding of Being. For Heidegger, the idea of production must yield to a way of being-in-the-world that "lets beings be" (*Gelassenheit*). This kind of engagement eschews the "management, preservation, tending, and planning of the beings in each case sought out" and exhibits instead an "open comportment" that "frees" beings and orients us to "that still uncomprehended disclosedness and disclosure of beings".[24] We are receivers of understandings of Being, not producers of them. To see Being as an object of any kind, as a substance bearing properties, is to confuse Being with beings. Existence is what all existing things have in common, but existence is neither a thing nor the totality of all things. If only objects can be characterised, we are unable to characterise Being at all, yet we immediately understand, of course, that beings *are*. If we are to have any hope of completing "the task of thinking at the end of philosophy" and articulating the "self-concealing clearing of presence", we must rid ourselves of the notion that Being is something brought into existence in the manner of beings, whether by natural or supernatural agency.[25]

Stevens's attitude could not be more different. When he turns to the imagination for redemption after the death of God, he does so not by letting beings be but rather in order to seize on things in the world as *materia poetica* and to shape them into meaningful images.[26] For the poet, "our revelations are not the revelations of beliefs, but the precious portents of our own powers".[27] Stevens's claims for the powers of the imagination reach for the heroic. In *The Man with the Blue Guitar*, he pictures the world he would reshape as a "monster", and hopes "That I may reduce the monster to / Myself, and then may be myself / In the face of the monster".[28] In a letter, he reveals that the "monster = nature, which I desire to . . . master, subjugate, acquire complete control over and use freely for my own purpose, as poet", adding that he wants, "as a man of the imagination, to write poetry with all the power of a monster equal in strength to that of the monster about whom I write. I want man's imagination completely adequate in the face of reality".[29]

The agonistic attitude expressed in *The Man with the Blue Guitar* calls to mind the "violence" Heidegger detects in the ancient Greek understanding of the relationship between being and appearance as it is exhibited in political action, by means of which the statesman can acquire "glory", the "supreme possibility of human being".[30] In *Introduction to Metaphysics*, Heidegger describes the political as the sphere of ambiguous and misleading opinion (*doxa*). The heroic founder establishes the truth that will constitute the state, a unifying principle that is concealed in the welter of conflicting opinions held by the many. To accomplish this, he must "wrest" or "rescue" the truth from its doxastic hiding place. For Heidegger, the implication that the truth is prised, with difficulty, from a resistant medium is inimical to letting beings be, but it is an apt characterisation of how Stevens apprehends the relationship between mind and world.

Like Heidegger, Stevens's aim is to assure himself that he belongs to the world. But rather than finding this in the language of dwelling, preserving, nurturing and "staying with things", as Heidegger does in *Building Dwelling Thinking*, Stevens turns things into instruments of creative vision, becoming at home in the world by mastering it.[31] In *Effects of Analogy*, he writes of "the imagination as a power . . . to have such insights into reality as will make it possible for him to be sufficient as a poet in the very center of consciousness. This results, or should result, in a central poetry".[32] In a central poem, such as *The Man with the Blue Guitar*, the poet can be:

Two things, the two together as one,
And play of the monster and of myself,

Or better not of myself at all,
But of that as its intelligence.

Stevens acknowledges "the necessity of identifying oneself with reality in order to understand it and enjoy it", but identification is possible only by means of the creative imagination's active transformation of reality.[33] The poetic value itself, Stevens says, "is the value of the imagination", without which no insights into reality will be forthcoming and poetry would be a mere literary activity in the pejorative sense. In part, Stevens can attribute this world-defining power to the imagination because he assumes that the phenomena such as affect, perception and metaphor are as real as any other aspect of the world. Like *Dasein*, Stevens finds himself thrown into a world in which things show up to him as coloured by moods, memories, anticipations, problems and tasks. "Things seen", he says, "are things as seen".[34] The root of the poetic experience is a keen awareness of what Heidegger calls the "disclosure" (*Entbergung*) of beings. The imagination must master its moods sufficiently to register not only what is present but also its presencing, if it is to observe such disclosures of disclosure as the "way, when we climb a mountain, / Vermont throws itself together".[35]

The violence of poetic imagination is also evident in *Credences of Summer*, where the "self . . . having possessed / The object, grips it in savage scrutiny . . . [to] proclaim / The meaning of the capture".[36] As Stevens puts it in *A Collect of Philosophy*, "The poet's native sphere . . . is what he can *make* of the world".[37] The poet "captures" and "subjugates" the world by fashioning it into a language whose signs, symbols, gestures, tones and rhythms arouse in him a feeling of being at home. The result delivers an apprehension of the world as a "fully made" integrated and self-sufficient whole.[38] Stevens remarks that "The habit of probing for an integration seems to be part of the general will to order", yielding his poetic drama of anticipating, glimpsing, finding, misunderstanding, losing, remembering and reflecting on ideas of order.[39]

Thinking is essential to Stevens's poetry because with the decreation of the world, a naïve belief in fictions of the absolute is no longer possible. We cannot help but ask for and offer reasons to accept fictions. Of course, poetic thinking is not mere reasoning; the fiction we accept will be "The fiction that results from feeling".[40] Even so, as he says in *Two or Three Ideas*, the "supreme fiction", the one that renders the world meaningful, "must be abstract" – that is, it must take the form of an ordinary proposition that one may accept or reject in the course of reasoning about it. As Stevens puts it, "Underlying [the supreme fiction] is the idea that, in the various predicaments of belief, it might be possible to yield, or to try to yield, ourselves to a declared fiction".[41] To yield to a declared fiction requires both reason and passion, which combine to form an "exquisite truth": "to know that it is a fiction and that you believe in it willingly".[42]

But, what precisely is thinking? Paradoxically, thinking employs questioning as a means to freedom from questioning. "The man who asks questions", Stevens says, "seeks only to reach a point where it will no longer be necessary for him to ask questions".[43] Stevens's questioning moves in the opposite direction from Heidegger, who asks what something is in ways that promise to reveal its mode of presencing. There are always more questions to be asked, because Heidegger's kind of question does not invite a definitive answer. The final three sentences of *Being and Time* ask the "the question of Being" (*Seinsfrage*) again, as Heidegger wonders whether there is "a way which leads from primordial *time* to the meaning of *Being*".[44] Stevens, on the other hand, seeks to remove objections to a fiction and to make the case for accepting it.

THE MEANINGS OF RIGHT

A clue to Stevens's understanding of thinking is found in a curious formulation in his late poem *The Sail of Ulysses*, which speaks of an enigmatic "right to be".[45] Ulysses, "symbol of the seeker", crossing the sea at night, "read his own mind. / He said, 'As I know, I am and have / The right to be'". The thought is reformulated in Canto V: "A longer, deeper breath sustains / This eloquence of right, since knowing / And being are one: the right to know / Is equal to the right to be".

Ulysses indicates the transition from the physical courage of the warrior–hero to the intellectual courage required to face up to the loss of the traditional sanctions. Removed from places and persons that would naturally confer identity and authority (Ithaca, Penelope, Telemachus), the homeless wanderer discovers the ways of his new world and turns them to his advantage so far as his wits permit. The poem's uncharacteristic explicitness regarding the meaning of Ulysses ("Symbol of the seeker") seems intended to draw our attention to Stevens's predecessors T.S. Eliot, Ezra Pound and James Joyce, for the figure of Ulysses was central to their thinking about modernity. For them, the modern artist self-consciously takes on the burdens of exile, discovery and self-invention and aligns himself with the mythic quest.

Ulysses, speaking or rather thinking in the first person, appears to derive both his existence and his right to exist from the act of "read[ing] his own mind", in what seems to be an unmistakable allusion to Descartes's observation that even radical doubt implies the existence of a doubter, so that "I am, I exist, is necessarily true each time that I . . . mentally conceive it", including the occasions when one doubts it.[46] This Cartesian "deduction" of existence from thinking ("As I know, I am") reinforces the Modernist symbolism: Descartes, like Ulysses, deprives himself of the familiar (in his case, familiar beliefs) in order to attempt the feat of hanging his existence on a mere act of thought.

This prefatory stage-setting evidently presents Stevens's own genealogy. Like Ulysses and Descartes, he sets out from privation: the death of God requires him to compose supreme fictions of order. As we work through the poem, it transpires that "deduction" is not the right characterisation: knowledge and being are unified parts of a larger self-evident whole that is expressed immediately through the "eloquence of right": "knowing / And being are one". It is this unity ("A longer, deeper breath") that expresses or asserts ("this eloquence") its right to be.

But what kind of right, exactly, is the right to be? The critics who have explored the matter emphasise that the topic of rights was imposed on Stevens by the circumstances under which the poem originated. It was written for the Phi Beta Kappa exercises at Columbia University's politically charged centennial commencement in 1954, whose organising committee asked Stevens to address the topic of *Man's Right to Knowledge and the Free Use Thereof*.[47] Yet like so much of Stevens's late poetry, the subject of *The Sail of Ulysses* seems more spiritual than political, devoted as it is to presenting an apocalyptic vision of the speaker's breakthrough to a "final order", a "great Omnium" in which "the litter of truths becomes / A whole, the day on which the last star / Has been counted, the genealogy / Of gods and men destroyed".[48] This breakthrough is achieved thanks to a kind of grace: "Not an attainment of the will / But something illogically received".[49] The accomplishment seems personal, not political, attributed after all to a single individual, Ulysses, who is interested in persuading no one but himself.

Most critics regard the poem as a failure, and they are especially dismissive of the poem's appeal to rights. As B.J. Leggett concludes, "the word *right* stands out awkwardly . . . as a sign of Stevens' inability to fuse twentieth-century ideology with Ulysses' more primitive epistemology".[50] The word "right", however, seems "awkward" for Ulysses only if one conceives of rights as exclusively political.[51] But, while rights clearly originated in political and legal contexts, ordinary usage admits of a wider range of meaning.[52] Of special relevance is the general category of *attitudinal* rights, which includes the *affective* rights illustrated by the first example (such as the right to feel proud of an accomplishment or to feel uneasy about a proposal) as well as the *epistemic* rights described in the second example (the right to affirm or deny a belief or proposition).[53] For Wenar, the basic meaning of *right* is "conclusive reason". One's right to a belief, for example, rests on the reasons one has for holding that belief: one has just as much right to a belief as one has reason to affirm it. A broad sense of "right", that is, defines rights as *justifications*.

Once we see them as conclusive reasons that support beliefs and feelings, it becomes apparent that the concept of rights, in the sense of epistemic and affective justification, is one of Stevens's central concerns.

From a logical point of view, Stevens's reflections on belief take the form of nonmonotonic reasoning: his intellectual universe is characterised by probabilities, default assumptions, revision, and, to use the most general term, "defeasibility".[54] The fact that our intellectual commitments are vulnerable to defeaters – arguments and observations that support contrary or otherwise incompatible commitments – means that nothing is "final":

We live in a constellation
Of patches and pitches,
Not in a single world,
In things said well in music,
On the piano and in speech,

As in the page of poetry—
Thinkers without final thoughts
In an always incipient cosmos.

"Thinkers without final thoughts" rely on explanations that are merely more likely than currently available alternatives (and may therefore be incorrect) and working hypotheses whose only warrant is the current absence of evidence to the contrary (so that exceptions are always on the horizon), and they stipulate the abandonment of old beliefs in the light of new knowledge. Stevens sometimes parodies analytical or dialectical forms in order to highlight the unreliability of his method, as in *Connoisseur of Chaos*:[55]

A. A violent order is a disorder; and
B. A great disorder is an order. These
    Two things are one. (Pages of illustrations.)

One expression of defeasibility is Stevens's recognition that figures of order have life cycles. An "old order", one that is no longer credible, "is a violent one" in the sense that its inconsistency with what has since come to light inhibits free transactions between imagination and reality. It would be "pleasant as port" to understand apparently competing orders (as between old and new, for example) as complementary parts of a whole by positing a "law of inherent opposites, / Of essential unity".[56] But, our default explanation of how apparent opposites are reconciled – the Christian fiction that "the pretty contrast of life and death / Proves that these opposite things partake of one" – is unavailable: "that was the theory, when bishops' books / Resolved the world. We cannot go back to that".[57] When new discoveries render old beliefs, however appealing, incompatible with what is now thought to be true – when "the squirming facts exceed the squamous mind" – consistency demands that we abandon the old.

The demands of consistency, however, do not necessarily have to be met. Stevens is more than willing to entertain an alternative to the revision of belief: that of tolerating inconsistency rather than eliminating it. From the perspective of this mood, the "violence" of a discredited order "proves nothing. Just one more truth, one more / Element in the immense disorder of truths". Stevens not only tolerates inconsistency, he affirms it, or as he puts it: "A great disorder is an order". When disorder is sufficiently dramatic, it becomes a form of order. This kind of disorder makes up in liveliness what it lacks in authority: "Now, A / And B are not like statuary, posed / For a vista in the Louvre. They are things chalked / On the sidewalk so that the pensive man may see".[58] As Heidegger argues in *The Origin of the Work of Art*, the things housed in places such as the Louvre are not in the world in the way they once were, so that while we may admire them for their beauty, they can have no real ontological significance for us.[59] Chalk drawings on sidewalks have no such meaning either, but they can be *materia poetica* if one acquires the right to the feelings and thoughts they arouse by rendering them in a compellingly poetic form.

Why, late in his career, did Stevens need to claim the right to *be*, even if only through the figure of Ulysses? As he wrote to Hi Simons, he felt that poetry improvises fictions of order as a response to the loss of traditional "sanctions". He goes farther in *The Figure of the Youth as a Virile Poet*, asserting unequivocally that "the poet *finds a sanction for life* in poetry that satisfies the imagination".[60] Successfully creating fictions of order authorises and gives authority to the poet, allowing him to take his rightful place on the public stage even at a time when "life as we live it from day to day conceals the imagination as a social form".[61]

For the early Heidegger, the metaphysical tradition was committed to the belief that one should know what one is, as opposed to resolutely and authentically deciding who one will be. Heidegger, like Nietzsche, felt that abandoning Plato's conviction that virtue and knowledge coincide would open up new vistas for humanity. To use Heidegger's language in *Being and Time*, we would see ourselves as ontological beings, in the sense that we must face up to the issue of how to understand ourselves. The later Heidegger eschewed both Plato and the Nietzschean project of "becoming what one is".[62] Instead, man was a mortal who dwells on the earth and under the sky, awaiting a new god.[63] Stevens also sees no reason to choose between Plato and Nietzsche and affirms instead that, as supreme fictions, "knowing / And being are one".

Heidegger awaits the appearance of a god, but Stevens will not wait. The aim of making supreme fictions is not only to satisfy the rage for order but to participate in the "great things in life" and establish in the world an authentically poetic way of being.[64] A poet's right to be, in the sense of the status properly assumed by poetry in the public sphere, is not a natural right. It is earned by creating a fiction so powerful that "the sense lies still, as a man lies, / Enormous, in a completing of his truth".[65] Characterising Pindar's artistic vision, Heidegger says that "poetizing is to place into the light".[66] The poet who creates "a description that makes it a divinity"[67] achieves greatness in every bit as worthy of commemoration as Ulysses, and becomes visible in the world as the "shining appearance" that Heidegger's ancient Greeks regarded as the "supreme possibility of human being", namely "glory".[68] No wonder Stevens wrote in *The Planet on the Table* that "Ariel was glad he had written his poems".[69]

It was not important that they survive.
What mattered was that they should bear
Some lineament or character,

Some affluence, if only half-perceived,
In the poverty of their words,
Of the planet of which they were a part.

NOTES

1. See Frank Kermode, "Dwelling Poetically in Connecticut", in *Wallace Stevens: A Celebration*, edited by Robert Buttel and Frank Doggett (Princeton: Princeton University Press, 1980), 256–73. Ironically, Stevens seems to have been under the impression that Heidegger was Swiss. For other studies connecting Stevens and Heidegger see Paul Bové, *Destructive Poetics: Heidegger and Modern American Poetry* (New York: Columbia University Press, 1980) and Thomas J. Hines, *The Later Poetry of Wallace Stevens: Phenomenological Parallels to Husserl and Heidegger* (Lewisburg: Bucknell University Press, 1976). For criticisms of their approaches see James S. Leonard and Christine E. Wharton, "Wallace Stevens as Phenomenologist", *Texas Studies in Literature and Language* 26, no. 3 (Fall 1984): 331–61.

2. Wallace Stevens, "Adagia", in *Wallace Stevens: Collected Poetry and Prose*, edited by Frank Kermode and Joan Richardson (The Library of America, 1997), 901.

3. Stevens, "The Noble Rider and the Sound of Words", *Poetry and Prose*, 652, 654.

4. Martin Heidegger, "Only a God Can Save Us: The *Spiegel* Interview (1966)", in *Heidegger: The Man and the Thinker*, edited by Thomas Sheehan (Precedent Publishing, 1966), 57. My emphasis.

5. Wallace Stevens, *Letters of Wallace Stevens*, edited by Holly Stevens (Berkeley: University of California Press, 1996), 602.

6. Martin Heidegger, "Letter on Humanism", in *Pathmarks*, trans. William McNeil (Cambridge: Cambridge University Press, 2006), 239.

7. Martin Heidegger, *Nietzsche: Volumes One and Two*, trans. David Farrell Krell (New York: Harper Collins, 1991), 73.

8. Stevens, *Letters*, 346.

9. Stevens, *Letters*, 815.

10. See Ronald Dworkin, *Religion Without God* (Cambridge: Harvard University Press, 2013).

11. Stevens, *Letters*, 815. Emphasis added.

12. Stevens, "Adagia", 913.

13. Stevens, *Letters*, 815.

14. Stevens, "The Idea of Order at Key West", *Poetry and Prose*, 106.

15. Stevens, "Anecdote of the Jar", *Poetry and Prose*, 60.

16. Quoted in "Talk with Mr. Stevens", *New York Times*, October 3, 1954. See also *Letters*, 334: "Life without poetry is, in effect, life without a sanction".

17. Stevens, "Sad Strains of a Gay Waltz", *Poetry and Prose*, 100.

18. Stevens, *Letters*, 409.

19. Stevens, "Adagia", 901.

20. Stevens, "The Relations Between Poetry and Painting", *Poetry and Prose*, 750–51.

21. Stevens, "Esthétique du Mal", *Poetry and Prose*, 277.

22. Stevens, "Notes Toward a Supreme Fiction", *Poetry and Prose*, 329.

23. Stevens, "Adagia", 914.

24. Martin Heidegger, "On the Essence of Truth", in *Martin Heidegger: Basic Writings*, ed. David Farrell Krell (New York: HarperCollins, 1993), 125.

25. Martin Heidegger, "The End of Philosophy and the Task of Thinking", *Basic Writings*, 448.

26. See Stevens, "Materia Poetica", *Poetry and Prose*, 916–20.

27. Stevens, "The Relations Between Poetry and Painting", 750.

28. Stevens, "The Man with the Blue Guitar", *Poetry and Prose*, 143.

29. Stevens, *Letters*, 790.

30. Martin Heidegger, *Introduction to Metaphysics*, trans. Gregory Fried and Richard Polt (New Haven: Yale University Press, 2014), 112–17.

31. See Heidegger, "Building Dwelling Thinking", *Basic Writings*, 353.

32. Stevens, "Imagination as a Value", *Poetry and Prose*, 731.

33. Stevens, *Letters*, 464.

34. Stevens, "Adagia", 902.

35. Stevens, "July Mountain", *Poetry and Prose*, 476.

36. Stevens, "Credences of Summer", *Poetry and Prose*, 325.

37. Stevens, "A Collect of Philosophy", *Poetry and Prose*, 863. My emphasis.

38. Stevens, "A Collect of Philosophy", 864.

39. Stevens, "A Collect of Philosophy", 862.

40. Stevens, "Notes Toward a Supreme Fiction", 351.

41. Stevens, "Two or Three Ideas", *Poetry and Prose*, 842.

42. Stevens, "Adagia", 903.

43. Stevens, "Adagia", 913.
44. Martin Heidegger, *Being and Time*, trans. John Macquarrie and Edward Robinson (New York: Harper & Row, 1962), 488.
45. See Stevens, "The Sail of Ulysses", *Poetry and Prose*, 462–67. See also "Presence of an External Master of Knowledge", *Poetry and Prose*, 467–68. "Presence" is a version of "Sail" published, unlike the latter, during Stevens's lifetime in the *Times Literary Supplement*. It is much shorter than "Sail", but with respect to the most important lines for my discussion "Presence" is identical to it.
46. René Descartes, *Meditations on First Philosophy*, in *The Philosophical Writings of René Descartes*, Volume II, trans. John Cottingham (Cambridge, England: Cambridge University Press, 1984), 16.
47. See Alan Filreis, *Wallace Stevens and the Actual World* (Princeton: Princeton University Press, 1991), 263–64.
48. Stevens, "The Sail of Ulysses", 464.
49. Stevens, "The Sail of Ulysses", 464.
50. B. J. Leggett, *Late Stevens: The Final Fiction* (Baton Rouge: Louisiana State University Press, 2005), 120.
51. As Leggett seems to do. See his *Late Stevens*, 120.
52. Consider two examples compiled by Leif Wenar: (1) *Artur Boruc Had Every Right to Feel Aggrieved at Eduardo's Champions League Play-Off Antics* (headline from the *Daily Telegraph*); (2) "Externalists are people who think the epistemic merit of a belief – one's right to accept a proposition as true – does not depend upon justification. Justification is only *one* of the ways of securing a right to believe". See Wenar, Leif, "Epistemic Rights and Legal Rights", *Analysis* 63, no. 2 (2003): 142–46. Wenar is quoting Fred Dretske, "Entitlement: Epistemic Rights without Epistemic Duties?", *Philosophy and Phenomenological Research* 60, no. 3 (2000): 592. See also Jeffrey Glick, "Justification and the Right to Believe", *Philosophical Quarterly* 60, no. 240 (2010): 532–44.
53. On attitudinal rights, see T.M. Scanlon, *What We Owe to Each Other* (Cambridge, MA: Harvard University Press, 1998), 22–24. See also Wenar, "Epistemic Rights and Legal Rights".
54. On the concept of defeasibility, see John L. Pollock, "Defeasible Reasoning", *Cognitive Science* 11 (1987): 481–518.
55. Stevens, "Connoisseur of Chaos", *Poetry and Prose*, 194–95.
56. Stevens, "Connoisseur of Chaos", 194.
57. Stevens, "Connoisseur of Chaos", 194.
58. Stevens, "Connoisseur of Chaos", 195.
59. Heidegger, "The Origin of the Work of Art", *Basic Writings*, 166.
60. Stevens, "The Figure of the Youth as Virile Poet", *Poetry and Prose*, 684. My emphasis.
61. Stevens, "Imagination as a Value", *Poetry and Prose*, 732.
62. Friedrich Nietzsche, *Ecce Homo*, in *The Portable Nietzsche*, ed. and trans. Walter Kaufmann (New York: Penguin Books, 1982), 657.
63. Heidegger, "Building Dwelling Thinking", *Basic Writings*, 352.
64. Stevens, "The Noble Rider and the Sound of Words", *Poetry and Prose*, 652.

65. Stevens, "Bouquet of Roses in Sunlight", *Poetry and Prose*, 370.
66. Heidegger, *Metaphysics*, 113.
67. Stevens, "An Ordinary Evening in New Haven", *Poetry and Prose*, 405.
68. Heidegger, *Metaphysics*, 117.
69. Stevens, "The Planet on the Table", *Poetry and Prose*, 450.

Chapter 9

"Victory Is an Illusion of Philosophers and Fools"

Heidegger, Faulkner and the Ruination of the Proper

Benjamin Brewer

At stake in any encounter of philosophy and literature is not simply the "philosophical" interpretation of a piece of literature but also the relation between philosophy and literature in general. By what right do philosophers arrogate to themselves the authority of the "interpretation" of literature? What kind of conversation can or should take place between poetry and thinking?

Despite the common judgement that he simply ventriloquises his own thought by way of Hölderlin's poetry, it is worth noting that Heidegger foregrounds this question in the introductions to all three of his lecture courses on Hölderlin's hymns: "If we dare, however, to think what is poetized in Hölderlin's word, do we not then stretch poetry on the rack of concepts?" (GA 52: 5).[1] For Heidegger, the answer is "not necessarily" – he maintains that poetry calls for thinking but adds that *thinking* must learn to hear (*hören*) this call. This requires that thinking *submits* to poetic saying and makes itself ready to hear what poetry has to say rather than demand that poetry speak the language of philosophy (GA 52: 2). Elsewhere, he goes so far as to say, "beyng-historical thinking is at first and for a long time only the self-annihilating pointing towards [*selbst vernichtende Hinzeigen*] the poet" (GA 97: 5).

It is particularly ironic, then, that Jean-Paul Sartre, in the most famous "philosophical" reading of William Faulkner's novels, cites Heidegger in order to chastise Faulkner for a mistaken "metaphysics of time".[2] Sartre argues that Faulkner "decapitates time", saying that his novels unfold in a time without future, a time in which the present is nothing but a stage for the repetition of the past and in which the characters collapse under the weight of an excess of memory. Interestingly, Sartre calls upon Heidegger's authority to correct this "error":

> Consciousness cannot "be in time" other than on the condition that it is made time by the same movement by which it is made consciousness. It must, as Heidegger says, *temporalize* itself . . . The nature of consciousness implies . . . that it throws itself out before itself into the future; one cannot comprehend what it is other than by what it will be, it is determined in its actual being by its own possibilities: this is what Heidegger calls "the silent force of the possible".[3]

There are two striking ironies here, neither of which Sartre seems to be aware of. The first is that in the very novel in question, namely *The Sound and the Fury*, at the very beginning, *in the very first paragraph*, of the very chapter that serves as Sartre's primary object of analysis, the novel mocks of the idea that philosophy has any authority over debates about time. Quentin Compson, staring at his pocket watch, recalls what his father told him upon giving it to him:

> I give it to you not that you may remember time, but that you might forget it now and then for a moment and not spend all your breath trying to conquer it. Because no battle is ever won he said. They are not even fought. The field only reveals to man his own folly and despair and victory is an illusion of philosophers and fools.[4]

The second irony is that of bringing in *Heidegger* to set Faulkner's novel straight, so to speak, and it cuts to the heart of the very idea that it is philosophy's job to set literature straight at all, an assumption that undergirds Sartre's concept of criticism: "a novelistic technique always refers back to the metaphysics of the novelist. The task of the critic is to extract the latter before evaluating the former".[5] It is difficult to imagine a conception of philosophy's relation to literature more diametrically opposed to the one Heidegger puts forth in all his readings of poetry (and above all in the readings of Hölderlin).

Nevertheless, this scene of misreading does contain a crucial insight: there *is* something radically incompatible with Heidegger's thinking of memory and its relation to the future in Faulkner's fiction. Sartre's mistake – one that puts him closer to Plato than Heidegger – is to trust immediately in the authority of philosophy as the arbiter of truth, and thus to fail to consider that the "impossible" temporality of Faulkner's novels might be a *challenge* to Heidegger's thought and not an error in need of correcting. The aim of this essay is to articulate precisely that challenge. Rather than asking what Heidegger's thought can tell us about Faulkner's fiction, I want to ask what Faulkner's fiction might say about Heidegger's thought, to see what might have happened to Heidegger's *Denkweg* had it ever happened to pass through Yoknapatawpha county. More specifically, I will argue that Heidegger would have found there an uncanny and unsettling double of his own thought, one in which the relation of past and future, of origin and destiny is not the basis for the establishment of the proper but the crucifix of its ruination. If Heidegger's Hölderlinian "remembrance" (*Andenken*) is the medium for the foundation of a proper community to come, Faulkner's memory relentlessly confronts the desire for a *proper* future with its own loss.

REMEMBRANCE OF A PEOPLE TO COME

Heidegger takes care to emphasise that thinking must learn to listen to Hölderlin's poetry, because, for Heidegger, the stakes of reading Hölderlin are much higher than the interpretation of the textual production of Johann Christian Friedrich Hölderlin; the essence of poetry itself is at stake (GA 4: 33). And, to raise those stakes even higher, the question of the essence of poetry is itself not limited to a specification of "poetic" language, for it concerns the destiny of the German people, the possibility of their becoming a *people*, a *Volk* at all: "Hölderlin's poetry is for us a destiny" (GA 75: 350). Only such essential poetry "poetizes what is inceptual; it delivers what is original to its proper arrival" (GA 52: 7). At stake in the relation to this essential poetry is the possibility of a *proper future* for the German people, one that would emerge from a transformed encounter with the past; in short, his poetry holds the possibility of finding within the past not only the first (Greek) beginning or inception (*Anfang*) under whose sway the history of the West continues to unfold but *another beginning*, an *other* beginning, that would disclose the possibility of an *other* future, a future proper to the German people.

There are two important senses always at play in Heidegger's discussion of "the proper" (*das Eigene*). First, there is the sense of belonging or "ownness", in this case, of a destiny that belongs to the German people, a destiny to call their *own*. For Heidegger, this does not mean that the proper is possessed like an object or a quality but rather is grounded in a relation of co-belonging; one can only claim as properly their own that to which they give themselves over (GA97: 45). A people could only claim a destiny as their own insofar as they give themselves over to it; this is crucial insofar as it distinguishes this sense of propriety from being merely a relation of property in either in the sense of a quality or of an object that one owns. Second, "the proper" also has the sense of something authentic; "authenticity" is often used to translate the German *Eigentlichkeit* that plays such a decisive role in *Being and Time*. To speak of a "proper destiny" is to speak of a destiny which *belongs* to the

German people (and thus, to be more specific, *not* to the Greeks), one that is addressed to them in their particularity and can thus be called their "own", but it is also to speak of an *authentic* destiny, which, for Heidegger means one that is not merely the continuation of the reign of the past. At the heart of Heidegger's encounter with Hölderlin and his understanding of the relation of thinking and poetry more generally is a complicated knot of possibility and history, past and future, destiny and propriety. Heidegger's reading of Hölderlin's "Remembrance" presents remembrance (*Andenken*) or memory (*Gedächtnis*) as the medium in which such a relation of the past origin to the future destiny can be glimpsed.

More specifically, this remembrance concerns the relation of the Germans to the Greeks, and Hölderlin's understanding of this relation is of fundamental importance for Heidegger's seemingly hyperbolic claims about Hölderlin's importance. Hölderlin is far from the only German writer or thinker to see a confrontation with the Greeks and their originality as a central task of German philosophy, poetry and art, but, for Heidegger, Hölderlin's particular figuration of this relation constitutes a singular and essential insight.[6] This insight receives its most direct formulation in his famous 1801 letter to Casimir Ulrich Böhlendorf. There, Hölderlin writes, "the free use of the proper is the most difficult". Not only must a people *learn* what is proper to them as a nation or a people (*das Nationelle*), they must do so *through* a learning of what is foreign to them: "The proper however must be learned as well as the foreign, which is why the Greeks are indispensable. Only we will not imitate them directly".[7] The return to the Greeks, the task of *learning* the Greeks and their national character is not undertaken in order to become *like* them, but rather in order to glimpse for the first time, there in the foreign, what is proper to the Germans in their *difference from* the Greeks.

The structure of this intimation of the proper first and only as the reflected gleam (*Widerschein*) of the foreign constitutes the core of Heidegger's interest in Hölderlin's patriotic hymns: "the proper 'is' proper and authentic [*eigen und eigentlich*] first and only in appropriation [*Aneignung*]. This however cannot happen without the dialogue with the foreign" (GA 52: 140). The dialogue with the foreign is the condition of the appropriation that will make the proper *authentically proper*. Two things follow from this: first, the proper is not "already" proper, and thus it is not something present-at-hand that could only be "located" or "designated" in the given, either in the factual history of a people or in some "characteristic". It appears rather as a *destiny*, which is to say, a historical task, or, as Heidegger puts in a letter to his brother in which he effusively praises Hitler's "greatness as a statesman", "the secret mission of the German essence".[8] Second, this destiny is not guaranteed – it is not *fate* in the sense of what is bound to happen or the inevitable – rather it is a chance, and if it is to be successful, it must undertake a dialogue with the foreign.

Heidegger holds that Hölderlin is a destiny precisely because he is the one who has already undertaken this dialogue and offers a chance of disclosing the "secret mission" of the German people; his poetry poetises the historical destiny (*geschichtliches Geschick*) of the Germans, namely, to be the people who establish a homeland for the truth of being. Hölderlin's "essential sight [*Wesensblick*] sees the essence of Greek existence [*Dasein*] in its essential opposition [*Wesensgegensatz*] to the existence of the Germans" (GA 39: 291). In other words, the possibility of entering into a genuine conversation with Hölderlin's poetry, which is to say, learning to *hear what it has to say*, rehearses or presupposes the conversation which Hölderlin "already" had with the Greeks. It is because Hölderlin already undertook this conversation that Heidegger's conversation with Hölderlin contains something *futural*, something *destinal*. The philosopher must learn to listen to the poet because the poet has already learned to listen to the Greeks, and, in this listening, found his own voice; only in learning to listen to Hölderlin, Heidegger's argument goes, can he and the German people find their own – their proper – voice.

"Remembrance" figures this dialogue with the foreign as a sea voyage into the foreign. It begins by taking leave of the homeland and, correspondingly, figures the possibility of appropriation as the turn homewards *from out of* the foreign: "In the beginning the homeland is still sealed in itself, uncleared and unfree and thus has not yet come to itself. This coming to 'itself' requires a coming-forth from out of an other" (GA 52: 190). This turn homewards (*Heimkehr*) from out of the foreign is the structure of historical destiny for Heidegger, it is the "hidden law" of the proper, of historicity itself (GA 52: 176). This law, of course, is not a law of nature and does not make the appropriation of the proper into an inevitability; rather, it provides the "measure" (*Maß*) of the historical establishment (*Stiftung*) of the proper itself. Insofar as the establishment of the proper requires a journey into the foreign, the "hidden law" (Heidegger will call it elsewhere, referencing Adalbert Stifter, the "gentle" law [GA 97: 38]), dictates that "the sojourn in the foreign and the learning of the foreign" is undertaken "not for the sake of the foreign, but for the sake of the proper" (GA 52: 190). If there is to be a homeland properly speaking, the path of the wandering into the foreign must turn homewards and not wander indefinitely or become at home in the foreign. It is this journeying experience (*Er-fahrung*) of the foreign that constitutes the learning of the foreign that is a condition for the appropriation of the proper.

And yet, if this conversation by which one learns the foreign is a journey at sea, then it is a particularly strange one, one which not only takes places across space but also time: "The conversation is recollection [*Erinnerung*]"

(GA 52: 161); "the conversation is remembrance [*Andenken*]" (GA 52: 164). The foreignness which is to be learned is not only foreign in the sense of belonging to another "people" but also to another *time*, and in this memorial conversation, what is heard is precisely the foreignness of what has been *in its having-been*: "But what is heard is not an utterance about what is past [*Vergangenes*], but rather hearing hears what-has-been as what-has-been [*das Gewesene als das Gewesene*]" (GA 52: 160). This, then, is the dual foreignness that is to be experienced: the foreignness of the Greeks as a foreign people and also as what-has-been, as *origin*.

The role of memory here is thus irreducible, indeed it is at the very heart of the double conversation between philosophy and poetry and between the proper and the foreign. And yet, what is encountered in remembrance is neither simply past nor purely foreign: "The sea . . . gives in the foreign, to those who journey into it as a foreign land, the first thinking-ahead [*Vordenken*] on the other of the foreign. That is the proper" (GA 52: 195).[9] What the poet glimpses in the memorial experience of the foreign is the possibility of *another future*, a future which the Germans could call their *own*; what is at stake in Hölderlin is thus a kind of "remembering into the future" (GA 97: 27), a remembering that encounters in the past not only *what was* but what *might have been*, what might *still be*, if only that past can be experienced *otherwise*. In a posthumously published essay from 1939 on the hymns "Remembrance" and "Mnemosyne", Heidegger claims that the singularity of Hölderlin's poetry does not come from its strange syntax or beautiful imagery; rather, these are all the "essential consequence of that instantaneousness, in which commences [*anfängt*] a fundamental convulsion [*Erschütterung*] of all metaphysical, and thus also 'religious' *and* 'aesthetic' *and* 'political', truth of beings" (GA 75: 5). The work of remembrance is the experiencing of this trembling of the origin through which the grounding of the truth of *being* can be glimpsed as a destiny; the remembrance that must be learned through the dialogue with the poet and the Greeks is a recollection of what *might yet be*.

THE UNBEARABLE MEMORY OF WHAT MIGHT-HAVE-BEEN

If for Heidegger, the truth of memory consists in its function as the medium of the hints of what might be, in Faulkner, it functions as the medium in which the devastating loss of what *might have been* relentlessly returns: "*Or perhaps it is no lack of courage either . . . but is that true wisdom which can comprehend that there is a might-have-been which is more true than truth*".[10] Sartre is correct that Faulkner often reduces the present to little more than a stage for the repetition of the past, but he misunderstands that what returns each time is not only the reiteration of "it was" but also the loss of "it might have been". Memory here is profoundly melancholic, constantly reminding of what could have been but no longer can. There *is* a future in Faulkner, but it is never the *right* future, never a proper one, certainly never one that any character could claim as their "own". If Faulkner's characters seem crushed under the weight of the past, this is not because there is *no* future before them but rather because the future that does lie before them is not one they could appropriate as *their own* or take up as a destiny (at least not in Heidegger's sense; there is indeed a powerful sense of fate and a pervasive tendency to fatalism throughout Faulkner's work).

In Faulkner as in Heidegger, this remembrance of the future is not only related to individuals but to a "people", in this case white southerners. It is well known that Faulkner's work is, at least in part, an attempt to reckon with the long, degenerative death of the "Old South", brought about not only by its decisive defeat in the Civil War but also by the moral, political and ontological consequences of the system of American chattel slavery upon which it was founded. For Faulkner, memory is the medium not of the fulfilment of destiny or the establishment of the proper; it is sooner their very impossibility and ruin.

Nowhere does Faulkner pursue the consequences of this memory of a ruined future with more devastating tenacity than in *Absalom, Absalom!* The story presents this "high and impossible destiny"[11] not through historical narration of political, military or economic events but rather as "that turgid background of a horrible and bloody mischancing of human affairs".[12] The novel recounts the story of Thomas Sutpen and his attempt to establish a dynasty as this story is narrated both to and by Quentin Compson (the same Quentin Compson whose suicide in *The Sound and the Fury* is the main evidence for Sartre's critique of Faulknerian temporality).[13] Quentin's father and Rosa Coldfield (Thomas Sutpen's sister-in-law, later his fiancée, and still later his fiercest detractor) recount various aspects of the Sutpen story to Quentin as he prepares to begin his freshman year at Harvard. In his dorm room in Cambridge, Quentin in turn narrates, perhaps invents, and seems to relive the story with his Canadian roommate, Shreve.

Already in the first pages of the novel, however, the text rigorously and obsessively undoes the possibility that memory might be the medium for the establishment of the proper:

> The mere names [of the story] were interchangeable and almost myriad. His [Quentin's] childhood was full of them, his very body was an empty hall echoing with sonorous defeated names; *he was not a being, an entity, he was a common-wealth.* He was a barracks filled with stubborn back-looking ghosts.[14]

Elsewhere in the first pages, Quentin is presented as dividing and multiplying against himself. While he supposedly listens to Rosa Coldfield, he begins to hear two Quentins speaking to each other "in the long silence of notpeople in a notlanguage".[15] As if the reference to "notpeople" was not enough, the question of haunting and ghosts is explicit: Quentin is "still too young to deserve yet to be a ghost but nevertheless having to be one for all that, since he was born and bred in the deep South". Quentin is not only filled with ghosts, with the memories of nameless others who inhabit his body and rob him of the possibility of being a "being" at all – he is himself also a ghost, indeed, an undeserving and untimely ghost. As soon as we are introduced to him, as Hortense Spillers puts it, "it is fairly clear that [Quentin] has no text, no *word/verbe* that he could call his ownmost".[16]

There is already here the intimation of a disconcerting doubling of the structure of Hölderlinian remembrance. In Quentin's case like in Hölderlin's "Andenken", memory takes place as a conversation in which listening involves submitting to the alterity of an other, as a form of historical testimony which short-circuits the distinction between (certain) individuals and a "people", and, as we will see, as a recollection that reaches back into the past in such a way as to glimpse a possible future. In this case, however, the dialogue *undoes* the possibility of claiming that future as one's own, of a people fulfilling their destiny. Quentin's ghostliness indexes the extent to which the haunting of his life by the memories of others has left him with nothing to call his own, and Quentin's improper spectrality is itself an index of the doomed attempt of white southerners to become a *Volk*. The "backwards looking ghosts" that populate Quentin are described as

> still recovering, even forty-three years afterward [i.e. after the end of the Civil War], from the fever which had cured the disease, waking from the fever without even knowing that it had been the fever itself they had fought against and not the sickness, looking with stubborn recalcitrance backward beyond the fever and into the disease with actual regret.[17]

Already in these first few pages, as the basic poles of the story and the scene of its narration are being established, the minimal conditions for an entity that could call a destiny its "own", the minimal conditions for anything like propriety or authenticity at all, are being thoroughly displaced and undermined. One might imagine, however, that this is a problem for Quentin, but that Thomas Sutpen *does* have a destiny of his own. In order to survey the full extent of the ruination of the proper in *Absalom, Absalom!* then, a recounting of the outlines of the Sutpen saga is in order.

Thomas Sutpen – "this Faustus, this demon, this Beelzebub" – is a man possessed by the need to establish a dynasty, to realise the destiny he believes to be his by rights.[18] The primal scene at the origin of Sutpen's "indomitable desperation of undefeat" occurred when Sutpen was a boy, the son of a poor farmer who worked for a wealthy plantation owner. He was tasked one day with going to the "big house" for some unspecified errand but was turned away at the front door, "before he could even state his business", by a slave who tells him to go around back.[19] This humiliating insult to his whiteness – which follows him everywhere in what he sees as the mocking and inscrutable smiles and laughter of black slaves – confronts him with the fact that he has nothing to call his own, and that he must dedicate his entire life to establishing himself as a properly white patriarch through the founding of a respectable Southern dynasty: "He was not mad . . . he was just thinking, because he knew that something would have to be done about it; he would have to do something it in order to live with himself for the rest of life".[20]

For Sutpen, like for Hölderlin's "companions" in "Remembrance", this leads him to a journey out to sea, in this case to Haiti. There he ingratiates himself to a plantation owner by helping to put down a slave revolt, at which point the plantation owner offers his daughter, Eulalia Bon, in marriage. After Sutpen has a son with her, however, it is revealed that she is $1/8^{th}$ black, making the son $1/16^{th}$ black. Sutpen's designs on his destiny are thus foiled, and he must begin again. He attempts this new beginning in Jefferson, Mississippi where he acquires 100 square miles of land (which he christens "Sutpen's Hundred"), and, through the labour of his large group of French-speaking slaves and the services of a French-speaking architect, erects his ostentatious plantation house in a pseudo-biblical act of creation:

> Then in the long unamaze Quentin seemed to watch them [the slaves] overrun suddenly the hundred square miles of tranquil and astonished earth and drag house and formal gardens violently out of the soundless Nothing and clap them down like cards upon a table beneath the up-palm immobile and pontific, creating the Sutpen's Hundred, the *Be Sutpen's Hundred* like the old-time *Be Light*.[21]

In order to secure respectability among the local white gentry, he then marries Ellen Coldfield (older sister to Rosa Coldfield), and has two children, Henry and Judith. In addition to Henry and Judith, Sutpen fathers the allegorically named Clytemnestra (Clytie), who is half-black and lives with the family rather than with the other slaves, though she is still treated as a slave rather than a member of the family. As we will see, it is precisely this racialised distinction between proper and improper descendants, marital reproduction and rape, that will ultimately be undone by Sutpen's attempts to enforce it.

When Henry goes away to college, he becomes enthralled with an older student from New Orleans named Charles Bon, who, after two brief holiday visits to Sutpen's Hundred, becomes engaged to Judith, "as though it actually were the brother who had put the spell on the sister, seduced her to his own vicarious image which walked and breathed with Bon's letter".[22] On Christmas 1860, however, Sutpen, having journeyed down to New Orleans to investigate some undisclosed suspicion about his daughter's suitor, tells Henry that Bon already has a wife and son in New Orleans and that the wife is 1/8th black. Henry refuses to believe his father's revelation of Bon's bigamous intentions, runs off with Bon to New Orleans and renounces his inheritance, only to discover his father had told the truth. Nonetheless, Henry and Bon enlist together in the confederate army, into which Sutpen has also been commissioned as an officer. All three men survive the battlefield, but in 1865, Henry shoots Bon outside the gates of Sutpen's Hundred as he is trying to return to marry Judith: "[Henry] repudiating father and blood and home to become a follower and dependent of the rejected suitor for four years before killing him apparently for the very identical reason which four years ago he quitted home to champion".[23] Sutpen returns "from the war five years later and find[s] . . . son fled for good now with a noose behind him, daughter doomed to spinsterhood . . . Came back home and found his chances of descendants gone".[24] Sutpen's is certainly not a *Heimkehr* that establishes or appropriates much of anything.

This is, however, not the whole story. Édouard Glissant argues that Faulkner's novels circulate around a secret whose revelation is continually deferred, and *Absalom, Absalom!* is no exception.[25] In this case, it is a double secret that traverses the very identity of Charles Bon. The real threat that Bon and Judith's engagement poses to the Sutpen dynasty has nothing to do with what Bon has *done* (i.e., with the fact that he is already married) but rather with who he *is* – Bon is Sutpen's son from his first marriage in Haiti. The very identity of Charles Bon figures what Glissant calls "the two impossibilities" of Southern dynastic logic – incest and miscegenation – such that his very presence threatens the possibility of Sutpen's accomplishment of his destiny.[26] Bon is not only one of the ghosts who populates the sonorous hall of Quentin's body but is also himself a ghost, an improper remainder of the past whose persistence in the present marks the erosion of the foundation Sutpen has tried to lay for a proper future for himself and his family. Importantly, the true identity of Bon is revealed to the reader in the only chapter in which Sutpen himself narrates his own life,[27] which revolves around Sutpen retracing and recollecting his entire history to find where he has gone wrong, which miscalculation in his plan has run his future aground.[28] Sutpen's memories are conveyed to the reader only at the moment when he is trying to reckon how to recover the future he believes is rightfully his and still might be, if only he can locate and correct the "mistake" in his plan.

Bon's entry into the life of the Sutpen's thus places Sutpen in an impossible bind: in order to preserve the possibility of a future dynasty unblemished by miscegenation (and incest), he would have to admit that his lineage is already marked by it; in order to prevent the ruin of his future, Sutpen would have to acknowledge this living reminder of the fact that it is *already ruined*. When Bon appears and becomes engaged to Judith and seduces Henry, the rightful heir, such that he renounces his father's inheritance in favour of his friend's company, it is the living memory of Sutpen's previous attempt to accomplish this same destiny that threatens its current chance for accomplishment. Sutpen cannot acknowledge this past as his own because to do so would undermine his future, the destiny he believes to be his; and yet, if he does not acknowledge this past and explain to his children who Bon is, Bon will snatch the fulfilment of that destiny from his hands. Denouncing Bon's bigamy is Sutpen's attempt to navigate this delicate paradox, but it backfires when Henry runs away with Bon, renouncing his inheritance and depriving Sutpen of the most necessary element of his design, namely, a "purebred", white, male heir.

Such a renunciation, however, is hardly irrevocable, and Henry eventually does revoke it by shooting Bon at the gates of Sutpen's Hundred and preventing his marriage to Judith. And yet this merely repeats and intensifies the bind in which Sutpen himself was caught: in the very same act by which Henry assumes his role as heir to the Sutpen dynasty and identifies himself with the destiny of the name "Sutpen" by guarding it from the twin spectres of impropriety, he robs himself and his father of that very future, this time *irrevocably* excluding himself from the possibility of inheritance:

> [Sutpen] *saw son gone, vanished, more insuperable to him now than if the son were dead since now . . . his name would be different and those who call him by it strangers and whatever dragon's outcropping of Sutpen blood the son might sow on the body of whatever strange woman would therefore carry on the tradition . . . under another name and upon and among people who will never have heard the right one.*[29]

In the act by which he becomes a *proper* Sutpen, Henry expropriates the possibility of that destiny itself and robs himself even of the name "Sutpen". In this single act meant to safeguard the propriety of the Sutpen destiny, that same destiny loses its character as a *might still be* and becomes an impossible might-have-been: "*No, there had been no shot. That sound was merely the sharp and final clap-to of a door between us and all that was, all that might have been*".[30] Memory thus becomes the medium in which this impossible might-have-been returns to haunt the present, superimposing an always-already-accomplished expropriation onto any dream of appropriation.

This is perhaps nowhere more legible than in the fate which befalls Sutpen's Hundred. After Sutpen's ignominious postbellum death (a consequence of insulting the young white girl with whom he tries to refound his dynasty), it is Clytie along with Bon's descendants who inhabit the ruins. The future of Sutpen's Hundred and the mansion, the living embodiment of Sutpen's dreams of his destiny, turns out to be as a subsistence home and farmstead for his disavowed lineage rather than a plantation "Big House" for his proper heirs, and this twist of fate is prepared at each juncture of the Sutpen saga by the actions and decisions meant to defend against it. On the very last pages of the novel, Quentin's roommate Shreve, surveying Sutpen's legacy, points out that the only survivor is Jim Bond, Charles Bon's grandson: "I think that in time the Jim Bonds are going to conquer the western hemisphere. Of course it wont quite be in our time . . . But it will still be Jim Bond; and so in a few thousand years, I who regard you will also have sprung from the loins of African kings".[31] It is this future-perfect, generalised miscegenation that ultimately results from Henry and Thomas Sutpen's attempts to fulfil their destiny. The future is not absent from Faulkner, as Sartre would have it; it is simply a future that cannot be appropriated in the service of establishing the authentic selfhood of either Thomas Sutpen or the white South. "The truth of history", to quote Gregory S. Jay's pithy formulation, "turns out to be miscegenation".[32]

If Heidegger found in Hölderlin the "hidden law" of history as the establishment of the proper through a recollection of a past that never was, *Absalom, Absalom!* writes the ruination of the proper by the very actions and decisions meant to establish it. Memory no longer offers the site for the recovery of a proper future but the haunting of the improper future with the tantalising dream of a destiny whose possibility has been thoroughly undone. In Heidegger's reading of "Andenken", the hidden law marks the site of the turn homeward (*Heimkehr*), the point at which the learning of the foreign is gathered together and redirected towards the establishment of the proper, the entrance into the homeland for the first time as a *proper* homeland. In the final chapter of the novel, Quentin and Rosa Coldfield return to what is left of the Sutpen mansion where Clytie and Jim Bond now live, because Rosa is convinced that the fugitive (now seventy-year-old) Henry Sutpen is living there, having undertaken, at the end of his life on the run, a kind of pathetic, perhaps even parodic, *Heimkehr* of his own. She finds him there and returns three months later with an ambulance, but Clytie burns down the house with herself and Henry inside. Thinking of this event which he did not see but nonetheless remembers, Quentin recounts a "conversation" with Henry, though he is unable or unwilling to say whether it is a dream or a memory:

waking or sleeping it was the same and would be the same forever as long as he lived:

And you are—?
Henry Sutpen.
And you have been here—?
Four years.
And you came home—?
To die. Yes.
To die?
Yes. To die.[33]

Henry has returned home, though not in order to claim his destiny but simply to die in the ruins of what might have been his own but is now, as a result of the very actions he took to try to secure that glorious future, inhabited by the descendants he hoped to keep out of the house. Furthermore, his death is not a tragic gesture of protecting the sanctity of his legacy by taking his own life, not least because it is his black half-sister Clytie rather than Henry himself who sets the fire.[34] Instead, what remains in the end is Jim Bond, the final testament to and reminder of the impossibility of Thomas and Henry Sutpen's dream of a future to call their own. This return is thus no act of foundation at all but only the consummation of the long wandering in the foreign. It is a return home that subverts the "hidden law", consummating an expropriation rather than appropriation of the proper.

Heidegger's fondness for the oracular statement from Hölderlin's "Patmos" that "where the danger is, grows the saving power also" is well known. I have tried to show here that Faulkner tenaciously pursues this logic to the point of its undecidability, not only to the limit at which the difference between incest and miscegenation – the twin threats to the proper, the former being an improper excess of the proper, the latter the loss of its purity – converge, but even further, to the limit at which the very distinguishability between "the danger" and "saving power" begins to tremble. It is not only that Sutpen *fails* to carry out the establishment of the proper and the fulfilment of his destiny – Heidegger is careful to distinguish destiny from inevitability. Faulkner's challenge to Heidegger's thinking consists in the way the returns of the past render the very distinction between foreign and proper porous, unpredictable and even illegible. If Heidegger's thinking had submitted itself to the difficult learning and experiencing of Faulkner's uncanny poetising of memory and destiny, it would have been confronted with an ironic and difficult truth, a different form of remembrance in which memory is indeed the medium in which a proper future is intimated but only as always-already irrevocably expropriated, only as an impossible might-have-been.

NOTES

1. Citations of Heidegger are taken from the *Gesamtausgabe* and cited parenthetically by volume number. Translations are my own.
2. Jean-Paul Sartre, "A propos de «Le Bruit et la fureur»: La Temporalité chez Faulkner", in *Situations, I: Essais Critiques* (Paris: Gallimard, 1947), 73.
3. Ibid.
4. William Faulkner, *The Sound and the Fury*, in *William Faulkner: Novels 1926-1929*, ed. Joseph Blotner and Noel Polk (New York: Library of America, 2006), 935.
5. Ibid., 66.
6. For more on the uniqueness of Hölderlin's relation to the Greeks and a polemic against Heidegger's reading of the Böhlendorf letter, see Peter Szondi, "Die Überwindung des Klassizismus", in *Schriften I*, eds Jean Bollack et al. (Frankfurt am Main: Suhrkamp, 2011), 345–66.
7. Friedrich Hölderlin, *Sämtliche Werke*, eds Friedrick Beissner and Adolf Beck, vol. 6.1: *Briefe*. (Stuttgart: W. Kohlhammer, 1954), 426.
8. Martin Heidegger, "Letter to Fritz Heidegger, April 13, 1933", in *Heidegger und der Antisemitismus: Positionen im Widerstreit*, eds Walter Homolka and Arnulf Heidegger (Freiburg: Herder Verlag, 2016), 35.
9. In a longer essay, it would be necessary to interrogate more closely the specular logic of this symmetry of the "other" and "proper" in Heidegger's readings of Hölderlin; Hölderlin seems to suggest, for example, in the third draft of the *Empedokles* play, that the Egyptians are the "other" of the Greeks. See Andrzej Warminski, *Readings in Interpretation: Hölderlin, Hegel, Heidegger* (Minneapolis: Minnesota UP, 1987).
10. William Faulkner, *Absalom, Absalom!*, in *William Faulkner: Novels 1936-1940*, eds Joseph Blotner and Noel Polk (New York: Library of America, 1990), 118, emphasis in original.
11. Ibid., 98.
12. Ibid., 84.
13. Sartre, 72.
14. *Absalom, Absalom!*, 7, emphasis added.
15. Ibid., 6.
16. Hortense Spillers, "Faulkner Adds Up: Reading *Absalom, Absalom!* and *The Sound and the Fury*", in *Black White and In Color: Essays on American Literature and Culture* (Chicago: Chicago UP, 2003), 337.
17. *Absalom, Absalom!*, 9.
18. Ibid., 148.
19. Ibid., 193.
20. Ibid.
21. Ibid., 6.
22. Ibid., 89.
23. Ibid., 83.
24. Ibid., 149.

25. Édouard Glissant, *Faulkner, Mississippi*, trans. Barbara Lewis and Thomas C. Spear (New York: Strauss & Giroux, 1996), 98.

26. Ibid., 144. It is, however, important to note, as Glissant also points out, that the miscegenation weighs much heavier than the incest in this case. After Thomas Sutpen finally tells Henry who Bon is, Henry and Bon have a direct conversation in which Bon tells Henry he will have to kill him in order to stop the marriage, saying explicitly: *"So it's the miscegenation, not the incest, which you cant bear"*. *Absalom, Absalom!*, 293, emphasis in original.

27. Though not directly—like everything in the novel, this story is mediated by Quentin's recounting and reliving of it. He hears it from his father, who himself heard it from his father, who was, according to Quentin's father, the closest thing Sutpen ever had to a "friend" in Jefferson.

28. *Absalom, Absalom!*, 221.

29. Ibid., 151, emphasis in original.

30. Ibid., 131, emphasis in original.

31. *Absalom, Absalom!*, 311.

32. Gregory S. Jay, *American the Scrivener* (Ithaca: Cornell UP, 1990), 163.

33. Ibid., 306.

34. This is yet another interesting twist on a Hölderlinian motif. Hölderlin wrote an ode, fittingly titled "Stimme des Volks" ("Voice of the People"), recounting the story of Xanthos, a city which twice burned itself to the ground rather than submitting to a foreign invader: "They succumbed not in open battle / but through their own [*eigenen*] hand". Hölderlin's poem, however, is not a straightforward valorisation of this gesture of conservation of the proper even at the cost of self-destruction, and it ends with a reference to the tenuous and perilous nature of stories: "So did the children hear of it, and indeed / the sagas are good, for a memorial to the / Highest are they, yet still / one is needed to interpret the holy [sagas]". Friedrich Hölderlin, *Sämtliche Werke*, ed by Friedrich Beissner and Adolf Beck, Vol. 2.1: *Gedichte nach 1800* (Stuttgart: W. Kohlhammer 1953), 55. For a reading of this poem that emphasises the ambivalence of this final stanza, see Rainer Nägele "The Discourse of the Other: Hölderlin's Voice and the Voice of the People", *Reading After Freud: Essays on Goethe, Hölderlin, Habermas, Nietzsche, Brecht, Celan, and Freud* (New York: Columbia UP, 1987), 47–66.

Chapter 10

"The Gods Are Never Quite Forgotten"
John Ashbery's Heidegger
Luke Carson

Interviewed by David Remnick in 1980, John Ashbery describes what distinguishes his work from the confessional poetry associated with his peers:

> I am trying to discover things that I am not already conscious of. Rather than deal with experiences from my past which are already familiar to me, the excitement of writing poetry for me is to explore places that I have not already found. Heidegger says that to write a poem is to make a voyage of discovery.[1]

Ashbery may be recalling what Heidegger writes in his essay on Friedrich Hölderlin's poem *Homecoming*, which is that "to write poetry is to make a discovery".[2] In this paper, I will propose that, far from supplying him with a casual metaphor, Heidegger's observation provided Ashbery with a moment of self-recognition, and that at certain moments, Ashbery's work returns to Heidegger's elucidations of Hölderlin to articulate its "discovery" of a phenomenological site that Heidegger calls, after Hölderlin, a "guest house" for the gods.

This may seem an unlikely claim, since the colloquial and comic tendencies of Ashbery's work seem irreconcilable with Heidegger's solemnity. Nonetheless, like many poets of his generation, Ashbery does have some familiarity with the phenomenological tradition, though he never affiliates himself with philosophy as such. We can see him downplay his philosophical engagement in an invited talk on "poetical phenomenology", in which he asserts that "poetry is a kind of phenomenology", but bases his judgement on the definition he finds in Webster's dictionary: "a branch of science dealing with the descriptions and classification of phenomena".[3] But, Ashbery is more familiar with phenomenology than he lets on,[4] and he has a readily available route to Heidegger by way of his profound interest in Hölderlin, who, he has said, has been an abiding influence since Michael Hamburger's translations began appearing in the 1950s, and whose importance to him increased with Richard Sieburth's 1984 translations of the late hymns and fragments.[5] Hölderlin has a unique place in Ashbery's work that parallels Hölderlin's role for Heidegger as "the Poet", that is, the one poet who arrives at the site at which poetry envisions its full vocation and capacity. In this paper, I will present some of the evidence that Ashbery's reception of Hölderlin is at times mediated by a reading of Heidegger's several "elucidations" of Hölderlin's work. I will focus in particular on three poems from his 1994 book *Hotel Lautréamont*, which is one of several of his books distinctly marked by Hölderlin.[6] In the end – by which time the evidence of Heidegger's presence will I hope seem irrefutable after having initially seemed tendentious – I will argue that Ashbery identifies, with and after Hölderlin, the highest vocation of poetry as the "song" that heralds the presence and withdrawal of the gods. Recognising this dimension of Ashbery's reception of Hölderlin, and of the presence in his work of Heidegger, allows one a better sense of the high stakes of Ashbery's characteristic strangeness and his always startling humour.

Ashbery addresses the seriousness of his poetry in *Musica Reservata*, which takes its name from an early modern form of coterie music.[7] The question the title raises is whether Ashbery will align his poetry with such music or with something that takes itself less seriously or seeks more attention, such as the foppish flâneur in whom Ashbery personifies the very poem he has started writing: "Poems are such odd little jiggers", Ashbery writes, as he imagines this poem "looking quite / stylish . . . in his reluctance to talk to the utterly / discursive" – which would include, presumably, philosophy. "'I will belove less than feared,'" this poem-within-a-poem says in its version of a higher poetic idiom, as it "trot[s] all around the town", prompting the speaker to ask: "Were his relatives" – who might also include philosophy – "jealous of him?" The speaker of this poem seems more bemused by its behaviour and its diction than jealous, and tries to imagine a poem of "another time, on the resistant edge of night", a site seemingly beyond appearances where "things" are revealed to be "pranks" that lure desire along a "road that sped underfoot / to oases of disaster, or at least the unknown".

The last line echoes Baudelaire's *The Voyage*, in which the human image reflected in the monotonous world is "an oasis of horror in a desert of ennui" and which proposes the solution of plunging "to the depths of the Unknown to discover the *new*".[8] Implicitly contrasted with Baudelairean romanticism, the higher poem Ashbery imagines affiliates itself with the Hölderlinian pursuit of what is essential, what is not a "prank". By the end of the poem, the speaker defers to a dream in which "A group of boys / was singing my poetry" to the music of "an anonymous / fifteenth-century Burgundian anthem". The poem provides a vision of time as a journey in which "days with donkey ears and packs negotiate / the narrow canyon trail that is / as white and silent as a dream". The nameless burden of the "packs" makes progress slow and the metamorphic magic or curse that gives the days "donkey ears" contrasts unfavourably with the earlier poem as it trotted about town. But, the poem we are reading clearly aligns its aspirations with this difficult journey along the canyon trail, which we might describe, citing Heidegger on Hölderlin, as "not 'a' path, but *the* narrow, inconspicuous trail".[9] For "my poetry" to be sung to the "anonymous" music of a national (or "patriotic", to use Hölderlin's word) anthem provides an indirect vision of poetry as a form of homecoming. That a Burgundian kingdom for a moment, as in a dream, becomes the provisional figure for this homeland is something Ashbery permits, but it is not simply a "prank" to lure one into a sense of belonging only then to abandon one in an oasis of disaster or ennui. What Ashbery's poem affirms is "the mnemonics / of the ride" along the trail: they are "stirring" in that they touch, as dreams do, upon remembrance of the phenomenological site that the poem as "a voyage of discovery" discloses.

This site – and Ashbery's figure of the higher, Hölderlinian "song" that discloses it – appears at the end of the poem *Avant de Quitter ces Lieux*.[10] The "lieux" of the title are, among other things, the commonplaces or *topoi* of the literary and aesthetic tradition, one of which in this poem will serve as a phenomenological site on the poem's "voyage of discovery". According to the aria from which the title is taken (Valentin's aria in Gounod's *Faust*) "ces lieux" are "the native soil of [the] ancestors" from which Valentin is about to depart for war. The poem begins with a denouement: "it is the fifth act in someone else's life"; and though the allusion to *Faust* hints at tragedy, the poem culminates in a depiction of "the mad scene" of the first act of Meyerbeer's comic opera *Le Pardon de Ploërmel*. The temporal patterns of days, seasons and years are distended throughout the poem, but overshadowing all of them is the poem's anticipation of "the ending", which in the penultimate paragraph has been called "the truth". The site appears in the form of

> an alpine pasture, with a few goats
> and, in the distance, a hovel. It is high noon. Dinorah,
> who has lost her goat, sings the mad scene for which her life
> has been a preparation, sings it out of daylight, out of the outcropping
> of rock overhead, out of the edelweiss and cowslips.[11]

Dinorah's mad scene contains the highest song available to the poem's rendition of the climactic presentation of "truth", but there is a higher song, and it is in this context that Ashbery's poem nods towards Hölderlin: "Now it is the turn of the mountain god / but he refuses to play". The comic and the serious are intimately enfolded in this passage, and the poem asks the reader to hold them together in their difference. The seriousness of the comedy becomes apparent in the allusion to Hölderlin in the proximity of "the mountain god"; in *Homecoming*, Hölderlin's poet points upwards above the Alps, above even the light, where "God [has] his dwelling, whom beams, holy, make glad with their play. / Silent, alone he dwells, and bright his countenance shines now, / He, the aethereal one".[12] Ashbery's poem goes as high as the "alpine pasture", and under the "high noon" – what Hölderlin, as we will see, calls "the heavenly fire" – Dinorah's mad song seems to be calling for the "mountain god", rather than for her lost lover or her missing goat.

The Alps of Ashbery's poem are not only Hölderlin's, but also Heidegger's, and Ashbery may be recalling the scene of Heidegger's *The Thinker as Poet*, a collection of brief poetic–philosophical aphorisms that appeared in French translation in 1966 and in English in 1971. In Heidegger's alpine scene, there are no goats, but "the cowbells keep tinkling from / the slopes of the mountain valley / where the herds wander slowly".[13] It seems an unlikely step from Dinorah's mad scene to the Heideggerian topology of Being, but in the final verse paragraph Ashbery moves the poem into more abstract territory. "The articulations" that precede "the ending", he writes, "are merely space". But this is the "space", we can safely presume, from which "we have no place to go"; we are not able to *quitter ce lieu*, to leave this place. But it is a space "in which lives can take on a single and sparing sharpness" of the kind associated with the "destiny" of the phenomenological and existential traditions, which designates the encounter, conceived most often as tragic, of the self with the conditions necessary to its unique individuation.[14] In this space as seen from the perspective of "the ending", "there are other songs" than, for example, Dinorah's mad aria, or perhaps this poem itself; these other songs, "some too true to mention, others of little weight . . . [are] waiting silently in place". Ashbery generously provides us with a phenomenological description of the place of these silent poems: "The story falls, mountains conspire, brooks hesitate, / the storm endures".

While I do think that Ashbery's alpine scene is enough to move from Dinorah's mad scene to Hölderlin's alpine gods, I do not think it is enough for the move I have just made to Heidegger. But, the final verse paragraph does provide the leverage to ascend to Heideggerian seriousness. I cannot help but hear in Ashbery's final lines a revision of the conclusion of the final section of Heidegger's *The Thinker as Poet*: "Forests spread / Brooks plunge / Rocks persist / Mist diffuses // Meadows wait / Springs well / Winds dwell / Blessing muses".[15] The only word Ashbery's poem has in common is "brooks", but the grammar is identical, and there are several significant connections. Ashbery's brooks "hesitate" while Heidegger's "plunge"; the hesitation of Ashbery's brooks is instead the action of Heidegger's meadows, which "wait". In turn, Ashbery's "stories" assume the action of plunging in their "fall", as heroes might in a dramatic denouement. But, it is the differences that signify the most: while Heidegger's words insist on characteristic events of emergence in space and time, Ashbery's tend more towards silence, separation and distinction, as if the things of the world are remaining within themselves – conspiring, hesitating – or, like falling stories are losing their impulse of emergence and fulfilment, whether that be the uprightness of buildings or a trajectory of anticipation and expectation. "The storm endures" suggests the scale of the disorder indicated by these minimal sentences, in which things do not "gather", as Heidegger's later philosophy would have it, and establish themselves in relation to that from which they are most intimately differentiated. Compare the line from Hölderlin's *Andenken (Remembrance)*, which Heidegger echoes: "into the river / Deep falls the brook".[16] For Heidegger, in his 1942 commentary on Hölderlin's poem, these lines identify the essential course of the river to the sea: "A shallow stream . . . must descend from the mountains and hasten toward the hidden depths of the wide river, and be borne by it to its destination in the sea".[17] Ashbery's observation in this poem that "great rivers run into each other", like other echoes of Heidegger and Hölderlin, also disperses the voyage that Hölderlin and Heidegger insist upon, instead suggesting that there is disorder in their course, that the rivers fail to remain distinct and to achieve their essence, which for Heidegger is to retain and to return to their source in a homecoming that guides poets on their voyage of discovery.[18]

When Ashbery disparages the sites that come into appearance in *Avant de Quitter ces Lieux* as "merely space", we see one of the motivations for the rapid displacement of scenes and characters in his poetry; the seriousness of the poems I am discussing here is most apparent in the moments when their speakers seem to feel that "song" can only fall short of what seems to be coming into appearance. Yet, the poems remain with *ces lieux* for their phenomenological capacity, that is, their power for describing and presenting what Heidegger calls the "topology" of Being, even in the midst of the anxious and often angry comedy. Finally, I want to turn to what may be the most explicitly Heideggerian glimpse of this site in Ashbery's poetry, which appears at the end of *In My Way / On My Way*.[19] One of the primary sites made available to Heidegger by his engagements with Hölderlin's poetry is that of "the Open",[20] a figure that appears in Ashbery's poem first idiomatically and then towards the end in an allusion to Heidegger. The idiomatic use occurs in the second verse paragraph of the poem, when the speaker tells us that his effort "to wriggle free of the loose skein of people's suggestions, / chirping my name", led to his discovery that such an attempt culminates in "more death and pain at the end, / so that one is better off out of the house, sleeping in the open", where "a sullen toad sits, / steeped in self-contemplation". At the end of the poem, "the open" makes a more enigmatic appearance when the speaker has decided against sleeping outside and has returned indoors: "the little house [seems] more sensible than ever before / as a boat passes, acquiescing to / the open, the shore, the listless waves that distract us / out of prurience and melancholy, every time. Yet something waits". At this point, as the poem comes to its end, the self-contemplating toad can be heard "crooning", but the final line defers whatever discovery it seems to have been undertaking: "It's another, someone's, voyage". And we are left waiting for "something", just as "the guest register awaits signing".

What we and the speaker are waiting for at the end of the poem are "the gods", who do not always arrive when we wish, but make their presence known in their absence; not finding what it seeks, the poem complains that "composure is a gift / that sometimes gods bestow, and sometimes not". Earlier in the poem, the gods are glimpsed in a fairly explicit allusion to Hölderlin's *Homecoming*, when the speaker declares his intent to "to exult / in the stacks of cloud banks, each silently yearning for the upper ether and curving its back". The first lines of Hölderlin's *Homecoming* feature a cloud "amid the Alps" that in Douglas Scott's translation is "writing of the Joyous",[21] or in Michael Hamburger's is "composing / Portents of gladness". The translations render the German word *dichtend*;[22] in Scott's translation, Heidegger comments that "the cloud writes poetry",[23] Hölderlin's "Joy" is echoed in Ashbery's "exult[ation]", and the "ether" towards which the clouds yearn is a Hölderlinian word that appears in many poems, including, as we saw earlier, *Homecoming*, in which God is described as "the aethereal one" who "seems kindly, disposed to give life, / Generate joys, with us men", and also sends the "brooding clouds".[24]

In Ashbery's "composure", we can hear *dichtet* as translated by Hamburger's "composing", but Hölderlin here is mediated by Heidegger who, in *Remembrance* (*Andenken*), describes "the open in which gods first come as guests".[25] The "little house" to which Ashbery's speaker has returned at the end of the poem recalls Heidegger's comment that the poet desires:

to build a house for the heavenly ones who are to come as guests, approaching the place of men. For only when this third element, *the guest-house*, stands between the heavenly ones and men, is there a place of mortal preparedness for the nearness of the heavenly ones . . . The poem names this one desire: to be allowed to begin the foundation of the guest-house *in the holidays of spring*. For that, however, everything, the homelike land and the air, the hearts of mortals and the heavenly ones must be *open*, i.e., *in accordance with the spirit*.[26]

While Ashbery's poem falls short of the joyous exultation it broods upon, his speaker does affirm that he "can't help placing things in the proper light", which is the light of exultation, and that "in a way it is spiritual to be out from under these / dead packages of the air", which may be the poems of the "others" he "tr[ies] to despise". In Heidegger's elucidation of Hölderlin, the "proper light" is of course the light of Being. Continuing his commentary on the poetry-composing cloud in his essay on *Homecoming*, Heidegger writes:

What it writes, the "Joyous", is the Serene. . . . The Serene, the spatially-ordered, is alone able to house everything in its proper place . . . While the serenification makes everything clear, the Serene allots each thing to that place of existence where by its nature it belongs, so that it may stand there in the brightness of the Serene, like a still light, proportionate to its own being. That which causes joy shines forth to the homecoming poet.[27]

Ashbery's poem too has its homecoming poets: they "too came out to see the sea / and having done so, returned / to selfish buildings enclosed by walls". They have followed the path of Hölderlin's poets in *Homecoming*, who, if we are to follow Heidegger's elucidations, have returned home from their voyage into foreign worlds. In *Andenken*, Heidegger describes what is required for a poet to achieve "homecoming" as the "voyage" from home into "the experience of the fire of heaven in the foreign land".[28] In Hölderlin's poem, the northeast wind "promises to mariners" a "good voyage" and "a fiery spirit",[29] and, Heidegger writes: "poets must first be *mariners* whose voyage, favored by the northeast wind, keeps the right direction towards the land of the heavenly fire".[30] For Hölderlin, who described what Heidegger calls "the law" of homecoming in a well known letter of 1805, the "heavenly fire" of "the Greeks" is the necessary complement to what is "proper" to Germans, which is "clarity of presentation", described by Heidegger as "the ability to grasp, the designing of projects, the erections of frameworks and enclosures, the construction of boundaries and divisions, dividing and classifying".[31]

However, what is proper to the Germans (or more broadly, for Hölderlin, to the West) "does not become authentically their own as long as this ability to grasp is not tested by the need to grasp the ungraspable and, in the face of the incomprehensible itself, to bring them into the proper 'disposition'".[32] Exposing themselves to "the shock of being struck by this fire", Heidegger elaborates, poets "will be compelled to appropriate and to need and use their own proper character".[33]

In My Way / On My Way begins with hints that such a journey is taking or has taken place. "We like it here as the trial begins", Ashbery writes, and "the warming trend, more air" suggests that the climate resembles Hölderlin's "foreign"; Ashbery's "prefecture garden" humorously suggests a voyage to the East that is not to Greece, but to somewhere stereotypically Japanese. But as hospitable as the speaker finds this place to be, he has no illusions about some other place he is aware of, specified simply as a threatening *"there"*:

> would we like it as much *there*? No, for we only like what we already
> know, which is familiar. Anything different
> is to be our ruin, as who stands
> on pillars and pediments of the city,
> judging us mournfully.

"On pillars and pediments of the city", we can imagine, are the founders of the *polis*, who are discussed by Heidegger in his commentary on the exposure to the "heavenly fire":

> By passing through what is foreign to them, the cool capacity to collect oneself, [the Greeks] first come into possession of their proper element. Only the rigor of such collecting in poetry, thinking, and art enables them to encounter the gods in their luminous presence. That is their founding and building of the [*polis*], as the essential place of history, which is determined by the holy.[34]

Ashbery's relation to the Heideggerian and Hölderlian text is clearly one of humility and recognition as well as humour; this is particularly evident at the end of the second verse paragraph when the motif of the "heavenly fire" of the sun appears. Awaiting the "verdict" of the trial, having "chang[ed] / to more comfortable clothing" because of the "warming trend" of his journey into the foreign, the speaker declares a troubled self-recognition in the other: when "the alarm bell sounded", he recalls – with alarm, one supposes – the reason "why I am you, why we too / never quite seem to escape each other's shadow. / Perhaps drinking has something to do with it / and the colored disc of a beach umbrella, put up long ago against the sun". The beach umbrella is, by way of comical metaphor, the protection against "the heavenly blaze" that is figured in Hölderlin, according to Heidegger, as shade from the sun. In a fragment called *German Song*, the poet "in the deep shade [. . .] sits / And sings, when of the hallowed sober water / Enough he has drunk".[35] In the final words of his essay on Hölderlin's poem *As on a holiday*, Heidegger cites these lines and comments:

> The "deep shade" saves the poetic word from the too great brightness of the "heavenly fire". The "stream that breathes out coolness" protects the poetic word from a too strong blaze of the "heavenly fire". The coolness and shade of sobriety correspond to the holy. This sobriety does not deny inspiration. Sobriety is the sensibility that is always ready for the holy.[36]

Ashbery's "drinking" hardly seems sober, and we wouldn't want to lose the comic deflation of the speaker's allusion to Hölderlin. Nonetheless, even as we retain the sense of defeat that comes from the acknowledgement of drinking too much at a distant beach resort, the sense of sobriety can also guide our sense of Ashbery's tone as his poems come into proximity with the site of the Heideggerian and Hölderlinian "open". Recall that the speaker at the end of the poem feels that "the little house [seems] more sensible" than being exposed out in the open. He thinks this as "a boat passes, acquiescing to / the open, the shore, the listless waves that distract us / out of prurience and melancholy", but that clearly do not bring needed "composure". However, the speaker is not occupying that little house, as appealing as it seems; he is also with the mariners in the boat, persisting steadfastly in "the open", even as he defers to it as "another, someone's, voyage". I understand "the open" to which the boat is "acquiescing" to be the phenomenological site that Ashbery's poetry as "a voyage of discovery" repeatedly encounters. What Ashbery recognised in Hölderlin's work, and at times by way of Heidegger's commentary on that work, may aptly be characterised by the attitude of "acquiescence", which I take to be a name for what Ashbery here affirms as the Hölderlinian and, to be sure, Heideggerian posture before that site.[37] The boat encounters "the open" as a space, which is neither the shore nor the waves, that welcomes the mariners towards itself – outward to the sea on a voyage of discovery, and back towards the source of the brook that plunged into the river. That one needs to acquiesce in order to arrive or to depart suggests that the call is imperative.

NOTES

1. John Ashbery, "Interview" (http://www.benningtonreview.org/john-ashbery), n.p.
2. Martin Heidegger, "Homecoming", in *Existence and Being*, ed. Werner Brock (Washington, DC: Regnery, 1949), 247. In German the line is "*Das Dichten ist ein Finden*" (see Martin Heidegger, *Erläuterungen zu Hölderlins Dichtung* [Frankfurt: Klostermann, 1951], 15), which Hoeller translates as "To compose is to find" (Martin Heidegger, *Elucidations of Hölderlin's Poetry*, trans. Keith Hoeller [Amherst: Humanity Books, 2000], 34). Because of the similarity of Ashbery's formulation to the Douglas Scott translation, which for many years was the only one available in English, I refer to the Brock edition, in which this essay (translated by Scott) appears under its original title, *Remembrance of the Poet* (Heidegger, *Existence* 233–69), rather than its later title, *Homecoming* (see *Elucidations*, 231).
3. John Ashbery, *Selected Prose*, ed. Eugene Richie (Ann Arbor: University of Michigan Press, 2004), 210.
4. As the Paris-based founding editor of *Art & Literature*, Ashbery published an excerpt of French philosopher Gaston Bachelard's *Poetics of Space*; he observed in a November 29 1963 letter to Kenneth Koch that it was "a beautiful thing" (see Kenneth Koch Papers, Henry W. and Albert A. Berg Collection of English and American Literature, The New York Public Library, 196:24); in "Poetical Space", noting that observers of modern painting "have . . . grown accustomed to inhabiting bizarre spaces and finding them sane and comfortable", he cites Bachelard's observation that "We are 'corner dwellers'" (Ashbery, *Prose*, 213). Also, see his discussion of poetry and criticism as, in effect, phenomenological practices of "description" in his long poem "Litany" in John Ashbery, *Collected Poems 1956–1987* (New York: Library of America, 2008), 601.
5. See Richard Sieburth, trans., *Hymns and Fragments by Friedrich Hölderlin* (Princeton: Princeton University Press, 1984). Having lived in Paris from 1955 to 1965, Ashbery would have been aware of the Heideggerian version of Hölderlin by the extensive French translations of Heidegger then underway.
6. My title comes from "The King" in *Hotel Lautréamont* (John Ashbery, *Collected Poems 1991–2000* [New York: Library of America, 2017], 245–46). I have discussed the prominence of Hölderlin in Ashbery's 2005 book *Where Shall I Wander* elsewhere (see Luke Carson, "'Render Unto Caesura': Late Ashbery, Hölderlin, and the Tragic", in *Contemporary Literature* 49, no. 2 [2008]: 180–208). For an excellent discussion of Heidegger's probable presence in Ashbery's poem *Homeless Heart*, see Richard Deming, *Art of the Ordinary: The Everyday Domain of Art, Film, Philosophy, and Poetry* (Ithaca: Cornell University Press, 2018), 85–91.
7. Ashbery, *Poems 1991–2000*, 242–44.
8. Ashbery describes these lines as merely offering "an encouraging sentiment" (Ashbery, *Prose*, 130).
9. Heidegger, *Elucidations*, 122.
10. Ashbery, *Poems 1991–2000*, 262–64.

11. Ashbery, *Poems 1991-2000*, 263.
12. See *Friedrich Hölderlin: Poems and Fragments*, 4th edition, trans. Michael Hamburger (London: Anvil Press, 2004), 331.
13. Martin Heidegger, "The Thinker as Poet", in *Poetry, Language, Thought*, trans. Albert Hofstadter (New York: Harper and Row, 1971), 12.
14. I intend my description to be general enough to suit Ashbery's rhetorical citations of or allusions to philosophical concepts. The concept of "destiny" assumed its first modern philosophical substance in Hegel, and was subject to much modification in German and French existential thinking. For an extended discussion of the concept in Hegel see Jean Hyppolite, *Genesis and Structure of Hegel's Phenomenology of Spirit*, trans. Samuel Cherniak and John Heckman (Evanston: Northwestern University Press, 1974), 352ff; for a powerful example of its use that is contemporaneous with Ashbery's period in France, see Foucault's commentary on Binswanger's phenomenological account of dreams (Michel Foucault and Ludwig Binswanger, *Dream and Existence*, ed. Keith Hoeller [London: Humanities Press, 1993]).
15. Heidegger, "Thinker as Poet", 14.
16. Hamburger, *Hölderlin*, 577.
17. Heidegger, *Elucidations*, 122.
18. See, for example, Heidegger, *Elucidations*, 171.
19. Ashbery, *Poems 1991–2000*, 327–29.
20. "The Open" first appears in Heidegger's Hölderlin essays of the 1940s and in his 1946 essay on Rilke (see Heidegger, *Poetry, Language, Thought*, 106ff.; for his contrast of the two poets on the Open see Heidegger, *Elucidations*, 173 n3).
21. Heidegger, *Existence and Being*, 236.
22. Hamburger, *Hölderlin*, 330.
23. Heidegger, *Existence and Being*, 247.
24. Hamburger, *Hölderlin*, 331, 333.
25. Heidegger, *Elucidations*, 169.
26. Heidegger, *Elucidations* 142–43; cf. 170. *Andenken* was not translated into English until Hoeller's *Elucidations*, but the French translation appeared in *Approche de Hölderlin*, which was first published in 1962 and then again in an augmented edition in 1973, and I assume Ashbery was familiar with it (see Martin Heidegger, *Approche de Hölderlin* [Paris: Gallimard, 1973]).
27. Heidegger, *Existence* and Being, 247–48; cf. Heidegger, *Elucidations*, 35.
28. Heidegger, *Elucidations*, 111.
29. Heidegger, *Elucidations*, 111.
30. Heidegger, *Elucidations*, 118.
31. Heidegger, *Elucidations*, 112–13.
32. Heidegger, *Elucidations*, 113.
33. Heidegger, *Elucidations*, 113.
34. Heidegger, *Elucidations*, 112.
35. Hamburger, *Hölderlin*, 599; cf. Heidegger, *Elucidations*, 98.
36. Heidegger, *Elucidations*, 98.

37. Heideggerian "acquiescence" is *Gelassenheit*, a word central to his work after the mid 1950s; a currently accepted translation is "releasement" (see Bret W. Davis, "Translator's Foreword", in *Martin Heidegger, Country Path Conversations* [Bloomington: Indiana University Press, 2010], xi). Roger Munier translated *Gelassenheit* as "*acquiescement*" in a series of questions submitted to Heidegger in 1966, which were published in *Questions IV* (see Martin Heidegger, *Questions IV* [Paris: Gallimard, 1976], 274) and again – along with Heidegger's commentary on Rimbaud – in the 1983 Heidegger issue of *l'Herne* ("Lettres à Roger Munier", *Cahiers de l'Herne/Heidegger* 46 (1983), 107).

Chapter 11

Heidegger's Mistress?

Meditations on Dasein *in David Markson's* Wittgenstein's Mistress

Tim Personn

In §43 of *Being and Time*, Heidegger attempts to demonstrate that external-world scepticism, that is, doubts about the objective existence of a world outside of human consciousness, is self-defeating. While even Kant, he notes, had made an ill-fated effort to overcome this "scandal of philosophy", Heidegger scoffs at the long line of attempts at refutation, viewing "the fact that such proofs are expected and attempted again and again" as the real 'scandal' here. In turn, the section serves Heidegger as an opportunity to reiterate his key phenomenological claims: that *Dasein* is being-in-the-world [*In-der-Welt-sein*]; that we are always already involved with "external" things; and that the rationalist tradition, as represented by Descartes and his successors, goes wrong in shattering this "primordial phenomenon of being-in-the-world" when it asks, sceptically, how "the isolated subject" can be "joined together with a 'world'".[1] In fact, the entire modern preoccupation with alienation and loneliness, Heidegger insinuates, can be traced back to this 'original sin' of rationalism.

Several decades later, when the writer Ann Beattie read the manuscript of David Markson's 1988 novel *Wittgenstein's Mistress*, she was "floored" by Markson's fictional exploration of precisely this kind of existential solitude, describing the text as "the most intense, really visceral, rendition of loneliness that I've ever encountered".[2] Beattie's report of her reading experience, then, raises the question of Markson's indebtedness to Heidegger. Is the heroine of Markson's book, a solitary woman named Kate, one of Heidegger's "isolated subjects" out of touch with the external world? After all, what *Wittgenstein's Mistress* dramatises is akin to Heidegger's idea that if the "primordial" touch between thinker and world is lost, if indeed the two cannot be "joined together" by a rationalist standard of absolute proof, it might seem to a human subject as if she was confined to the utter solitude of her mind – a conclusion that Kate experiences as the conviction that she is the last person alive on earth.

Given these shared concerns, it is hardly surprising that the author has acknowledged Heidegger as an influence on the composition of *Wittgenstein's Mistress*, telling the critic Joseph Tabbi, "I had a head full of people like Wittgenstein and Heidegger".[3] Owing to the mention of Wittgenstein in the novel's title, much critical attention has been paid to the Austrian philosopher's work as an intertext. However, speaking to Tabbi, Markson also cautioned interpreters that Wittgenstein's philosophy was only *one* influence, "along with several other's".[4] And a few years later, talking to the writer Joey Rubin, Markson referred once again to "all the philosophy buried in [*Wittgenstein's Mistress*]", specifically singling out Heidegger this time, while adding, in a tone of amused incredulity, "though nobody's picked up on him".[5]

In this essay, I will therefore try to 'pick up' on the impact Heidegger's thought had on Markson while writing his masterpiece. In keeping with the spirit of Markson's and Heidegger's own works – one by a novelist who absorbed the history of thought into his novels to recontextualise and thereby interrogate it; the other by a philosopher who frequently turned to poetry to push past the limits of his discipline – this essay confronts philosophy and literature without elevating one over the other. As such, it has a dual purpose: on one hand, I show what we can learn about Markson's novel if we imagine, counterfactually, that the book's title had been "Heidegger's Mistress"; on the other hand, I ask what we can learn about Heidegger's philosophy if we read the novel as dramatising it. The first question will amplify the importance of what the philosopher Hubert Dreyfus, whose work has been significantly influenced by Heidegger's phenomenology, has called the flow experiences of "absorbed coping",[6] in contrast to a strict dualism of mind and world; the second question will indicate why, in spite of the thematic overlap with the thinker's work, the book's title is *not* "Heidegger's Mistress". In fact, as I will show in the following, the reason for why such a title would have misfired informs Markson's literary form of presentation.

Much of this presentation is determined by the author's choice to focalise the novel so closely that it becomes impossible to determine whether Kate is mad or truly the sole survivor of an unexplained catastrophe that has eradicated all humanity. Indeed, Markson's solipsistic premise pushes the idea of unreliable narration to its extremes as we read Kate's account of the decade she has spent crisscrossing the world in search of other souls. After finally giving up on looking for other people, she settles down on a beach to write a novel that could help her make sense of it all. And it is at this point that we meet Kate in the book as published: a woman sitting at a typewriter by a beach house, years after life as we know it has ended for her. In a recursive setup, the story ends with Kate's announcement of her novel project, which has led to the text the reader is holding in her hand and has been reading all along, a first-person narration ostensibly typed by the fictional protagonist herself:

> Because what I am suddenly now thinking about is that it could be an absolutely autobiographical novel that would not start until after I was alone, obviously. [. . .] Certainly that would be an interesting beginning, at any rate. Or at least for a certain type of novel.[7]

Perhaps, the reason for why she finds this "certain type of novel" so "interesting" is that, at some point in her account, Kate realises that her current situation is not unlike her situation a decade earlier. "She had paradoxically", she writes, "been practically as alone before all of this had happened as she was now". An unbridgeable distance, cutting her off from all others, had obtained even *before* the unnamed catastrophe that had left her alone, with "[one] manner of being alone simply being different from another manner of being alone".[8] Slowly, it dawns on Kate that there is something about our expectations of what it means to be close to others, even close to things at large, that keeps us forever locked out.

At some point, Markson must have begun to feel the same way about the premise of his "absolutely autobiographical novel". In fact, Kate's realisation of its possibilities resembles his own process of coming upon his topic. By the account he gave to Tabbi, Markson had started Kate's story in what he called a much more generic, "science-fictiony" way, describing an early draft as "a straight first-person narration of the next eight or ten months of her life [after Kate found herself alone on earth], all the panic, the natural disbelief, the terror over who else might be out there if anyone still was". Then, after revising this draft for eight months, Markson started working on a second part. Now, Kate has become accustomed to dealing with her situation, he explained, "most of [her] fears gone [. . .], simply living with the situation, handling it, psychologically feeding off whatever she was capable of to sustain the balance". Soon Markson realised that this new emphasis was "as extreme a metaphor [. . .] as possible" for "that central concept, the idea of aloneness" which he had meant to dramatise. It was this general dimension of Kate's situation that now persuaded Markson to discard the first part of his manuscript in favour of the second. The new approach at rendering Kate's story, he realised, was suitably more ambiguous and "open-ended", with, as Markson explained,

The woman claiming she was alone, but with nothing in the text to verify it, and all so improbable to the reader – opening things up for all sorts of infinitely more subtle questions of reality than I would have been able to deal with the other way.[9]

KATE'S HEIDEGGERIAN LESSON

This angle makes the novel a valuable intervention into philosophical debates around these "subtle questions of reality". Of course, Heidegger's efforts in *Being and Time* were largely directed at showing such sceptical questions to be an undesirable consequence of Cartesian metaphysics. The term he uses to indicate the solitude that befalls the sceptic upon asking these questions is 'anxiety' [*Angst*]. And in her description of the "certain type of novel" she hopes to write, Kate employs a vocabulary that is strikingly similar to Heidegger's account of anxiety: "Just imagine how the heroine would feel, however, and how full of anxiety she would be. And with every bit of that being real anxiety in this instance, too, as opposed to various illusions. Such as from hormones. Or from age".[10] This passage touches upon a distinction between two types of anxiety – one Kate describes as "the fundamental mood of existence",[11] and the other she dismisses as a pale shadow of this originary experience. For Heidegger, the first kind of anxiety is a mood that both constrains and opens up the possibility of 'achieving' existence authentically: "All things and we ourselves sink into indifference. [. . .] We can get no hold on things. In the slipping away of beings only this 'no hold on things' comes over us and remains. Anxiety reveals the nothing".[12] This anxiety is unlike fear [*Furcht*] of something particular, such as a threat to one's life. It is a condition of such fear; it is objectless, fearing, literally, 'nothing'. And, after recoiling from this fundamental absence at the core of existence, Heidegger claims, we rush back towards our everyday concerns.[13] This condition of self-determination is a recurrent possibility: "Original anxiety can awaken in existence at any moment", Heidegger asserts, "It needs no unusual event to rouse it".[14] The disappearance of all life that leads to Kate's anxiety is certainly an unusual event. But as the book refuses to clarify it, the extraordinary character of Kate's situation fades into the background, making space for Heideggerian overtones.

Readings of the book that amplify these overtones are rare. One exception is Sherril Grace's essay "Messages: Reading *Wittgenstein's Mistress*", which suitably interprets Kate's reflections "on the relationship between physical reality and the representation of it in language or paint" as a variation of

Heidegger's discussion of "the problem of *Dasein*". The answer to Kate's feelings of isolation, Grace suggests, lies in an understanding of this key Heideggerian concept. But while Grace presents existential phenomenology as a possible remedy, she also realises that Kate does not know Heidegger's work: "Her tragedy", Grace argues, "is that she picks up that word [*Dasein*], knows that it is important, but does not know what it means".[15] This is the case in spite of the fact that Kate comes across "no less than seven books by Martin Heidegger" in a box she finds in the basement of her beach house.[16] Written in the original German, which Kate cannot read, Heidegger's works function in the narrative much like the book *Baseball When the Grass Was Real*, which Kate finds in the box, as well, a classic in sporting circles that deals with a time before artificial turf in baseball stadiums. Initially, she does not understand the title. Her comprehension of the book's meaning does not come upon reading it, but when she discovers another box that contains precisely such artificial grass. And Kate's settlement with solitude does not come about through a theoretical grasp of being-in-the-world, either, but through her own lived experience of "original anxiety" [*ursprüngliche Angst*].

As noted at the outset, this key phenomenological notion of the primacy of being over its representations runs like a thread through Heidegger's analytic of *Dasein* in *Being and Time*. It is in particular one aspect of this analytic, namely Heidegger's reflections on spatiality, that I see as a useful hermeneutic for interpreting Kate's monologue. This connection has not yet been addressed in the scholarly debate around *Wittgenstein's Mistress*. To make this point, I focus on two passages that arguably meditate on *Dasein*'s particular spatiality. In the first one, Kate introduces the concept of 'equidistance from each other' for the assumption of a metaphysical distance between the self and the world:

> The more I think about it, the more I seem to remember that Rembrandt rarely went anywhere near strangers.
> Even if he and William Gaddis would have remained equidistant from each other at all times, of course.
> Well, as any other cat and any other person.
> Or even as the cat I saw in the Colosseum and each of those cans of food I put out, also.
> Even though there were as many cans as there must have been Romans watching the Christians, practically.
> In fact, each Christian and each lion would have always remained equidistant from each other, too.
> Except when the lions had eaten the former, naturally.
> Although I can now actually think of another exception to this rule, as well.[17]

We see Kate going deeply into metaphysical reflections here, meditating on the impossibility of overcoming the distance between self and other. Its irreducible otherness, Kate realises, cannot even be reached by absorbing the other, as lions had devoured the early Christians. The fact that Kate thinks up an "exception to [the] rule" that coming close to someone or something is achieved by literally absorbing them indicates that behind her reflections on spatiality is a *nonliteral* concept of absorption. This concept reflects the epistemological desire for a fusion that would guarantee the absence of any illusions in a complete 'possession' of the world. And it is this immodest desire for absolute knowledge that causes scepticism in a detached subject like Kate.

For Heidegger, however, this sceptical yearning for absorption is not an original experience. Rather, it is premised on a mode of being, which in Heideggerian terms is called 'objective presence' or 'presence-at-hand' [*Vorhandenheit*], that is itself secondary when compared with our involvement in everyday affairs. Thus, Heidegger proves to be aware that the 'equidistance' between self and other is predicated on a particular ontology. Our primordial state of being-in-the-world, Heidegger argues, is restored when we cease staring at the world of objects, and re-enter our everyday activities. This is dramatised in a second sequence from the novel. Here, Kate has a similar experience one day, when she takes a stroll in a warm rain:

> [What] I have basically been doing about the rain is ignoring it, to tell the truth.
> How I do that is by walking in it.
> I did not fail to notice that those last two sentences must certainly look like a contradiction, by the way.
> Even if they are no such thing.
> One can very agreeably ignore a rain by walking in it.
> In fact it is when one allows a rain to prevent one from walking in it that one is failing to ignore it.[18]

The rain retreats from Kate's purview here once she stops staring at it as a distinct presence. That one might ignore something by immersing oneself in it, then, is only "a contradiction" in Heidegger's mode of presence-at-hand. In the flowing absorption of everyday activities, while 'taking care' [*besorgen*] of the errands and matters of daily life, it is not a contradiction at all. In this mode of being, which Heidegger calls 'readiness-to-hand' [*Zuhandenheit*], the world has not yet been cast 'out' into the distance of theoretical representation. One's accustomed materials and surroundings do not obtrude yet, but slip under the threshold of consciousness in their very use. In *Being and Time* §23, Heidegger illustrates this through the example of a pair of spectacles, which, while being close in an objectively present way, has "the inconspicuousness of what is initially at hand [*des zunächst Zuhandenen*]".[19] In the same way, the rain becomes inconspicuous in the act of walking in it. Once more it is a simple life event such as walking in the rain, not a theoretical text, which gives Kate a key phenomenological insight. This, then, is Kate's Heideggerian lesson, a lesson she knew, in a way, all along: as acting agent, she has always already been absorbed in the world in a way that seems impossible after the fact, that is, when the rain has become a distinct phenomenon the self can no longer "agreeably ignore" – when she has shifted from the mode of readiness-to-hand to an ontology of objective presence. Scepticism may eventually catch up with her, but for the length of this walk, it has to stay behind.

EQUIDISTANCES AT THE RIJKSMUSEUM

In recent years, this primordial involvement in our life worlds has been at the forefront of a Heidegger renaissance led by the late Hubert Dreyfus and a group of his students, including Sean D. Kelly, Mark Wrathall and Taylor Carman. Drawing on Heidegger's account of spatiality, these philosophers postulate a form of mastery as absorption in the flow of skilful activities such as painting or woodworking – a flow that is broken by "taking a critical distance [that] undermines absorption and so degrades mastery".[20] However, that the "absorbed coper" cannot, in turn, "provide a rational *explanation* of why a certain move worked",[21] indicates Dreyfus's acknowledgement that this key Heideggerian lesson also necessarily silences any thinker trying to approach the preconceptual emptiness of readiness-to-hand. How does the same lesson, then, apply to any literature that sees in such flowing absorption an argument against scepticism? Does it impose the kind of muteness that, as in Heidegger's own account of the "nothing" at the 'bottom' of experience, "robs" a human subject "of all speech"?[22] Notably, questions like these raise doubts about the final fit between Heidegger's phenomenology and *Wittgenstein's Mistress*. For the tone of Markson's novel is different from solemn quietude. In fact, Kate's reflections are shot through with the kind of anxious chatter that expresses a deep longing for an external point of view transcending her claustrophobic existence.

That Kate precisely lacks such a third element outside of the dyad 'Kate-world' is the reason for her repeated sceptical observation that any two entities – houses, cities, human beings and animals, even oneself and one's own mirror image – are equidistant from one another. To be sure, she is acutely aware that in the absence of "a yardstick or a field of comparison",[23] the assumption of equidistance is trivially true. This idea already occurs to her when she first picks up the term 'equidistance' at the abandoned Rijksmuseum while searching for speakers for a phonograph. The two speakers she finds are accompanied by instructions for setup:

> What the directions told me to do was to make certain that the two speakers were equidistant from each other.
> One certainly had to wonder what the person who wrote the instructions should have meant by that.
> Well, or the person who had translated the instructions from the Japanese.
> No matter where one situated them, how could there be any way in which any two objects could be any distance from each other except equidistant?[24]

The recommendation of equidistance between the speakers, Kate implies here, is based on a mistranslation from the original instructions, which seem to have pointed to a third element, the stereo unit perhaps, that could actually function as a yardstick for measuring each speaker's distance to a point outside of their dual relation. Kate's familiarity with the concept of 'equidistance', then, is accompanied from the beginning by an awareness of the desirability of such a third term. That this term is missing, however, must be seen as the source of Kate's anxious longing, the very affect that permeates *Wittgenstein's Mistress*.

WITTGENSTEIN'S HELP WITH *DASEIN*

At this point, the novel brings into play a range of ideas from Wittgenstein's work, where the importance of such a yardstick for determining relations between any given elements in the world is a recurring theme. In *Philosophical Investigations* §50, he addresses it by reference to a standard of measure from the metric rather than the imperial tradition: "the standard metre in Paris", Wittgenstein explains, is a "method of representation" in the "language-game of measuring with a metre-rule".[25] It is this very kind of unimpeachable, external standard that allows for certainty in determining the length the same way a stereo unit might have determined the position of Kate's speakers. But, the later Wittgenstein is at pains to point out that, while there are clearly defined means of representation for specific language games such as 'measuring with a metre-rule', we have no such measure for language at large; that is, there is no transcendent perspective from where to survey the link between language and world – and it is precisely this relation that Kate, like all sceptics, tries to grasp, an attempt which leads her into all kinds of philosophical 'nonsense'.

In light of this connection, it is not surprising that Markson explicitly casts Wittgenstein in the role of a 'third' person who could validate Kate's reflections on *Dasein*: "[What] one might now wish one's self", Kate remarks upon finding Heidegger's books, "is that Wittgenstein had been in the basement with me yesterday, so as to have given me some help with that *Dasein*".[26] Arguably, this imagined dialogue between the two thinkers serves as a description of the novel at large. Heideggerian concepts do not occur in isolation here; rather, they are dramatised with reference to Wittgenstein's style of philosophy. And like Kate, we, too, may need the perspective of another thinker in order to understand Markson's response to scepticism, with Wittgenstein providing some "help" in negotiating Heideggerian concerns.

After all, the book's title sets Kate up as 'mistress' to Wittgenstein's thought, an intellectual intimacy that Markson saw reflected most obviously "in the very way she questions so many of her own 'propositions'".[27] For Wittgenstein, this self-reflexivity migrated from the traditional philosophical preoccupation with propositional arguments into a literary concern with matters of presentation. In his *Tractatus Logico-Philosophicus*, for example, Wittgenstein proposed standards for what can sensibly be asserted, only to breach these standards in the very act of establishing them. The philosopher's way out of self-contradiction was to carry his argument over into the manner of presenting it, namely by *showing* the rules of logic and language that, through this act of showing, need never be *spoken*.[28] Thus, the *Tractatus* ends with the realisation that all its metaphysical talk about the relationship between language and reality was "senseless" – at best the rungs of a "ladder" the philosopher "must throw away [. . .] after he has climbed up on it".[29] The transcendent place a reader reaches through this ascent, Wittgenstein imagined, was one of speechlessness, where one "will see the world aright".[30] "What we cannot speak about", he concluded, "we must pass over in silence".[31] That the argument of *Wittgenstein's Mistress* relies on a similar 'showing' that exceeds all 'telling' is validated by Kate herself, who writes explicitly that her account is "not a scholarly speculation in the manner of Kierkegaard and Martin Heidegger after all.[32]"

Yet like the many misremembered quotations and factoids from western culture jumping about in her head – mistakes that cumulatively show how the 'outside' world is slipping away from her – Kate's disclaimer here also mischaracterises Søren Kierkegaard's works, most of which were published under pseudonyms that allowed for an ironic distance between the writer and the personae he had created. In fact, it is precisely this literary model of indirect communication that has recently inspired a group of philosophers called the 'New Wittgensteinians' to attempt a radical reinterpretation of the *Tractatus* in line with Wittgenstein's later conception of philosophy as 'therapy'.³³ One of them, James Conant, explicitly reads the *Tractarian* play of metaphysical assertion and retraction as a Kierkegaardian exercise in indirect communication: "The method employed in both [Kierkegaard's] *Postscript* and [Wittgenstein's] *Tractatus*", Conant writes, "relies upon the thought that [. . .] the only procedure that will prove genuinely elucidatory is one that attempts to enter into the philosophical illusion of understanding and explode it from within".³⁴ According to this interpretation, the early Wittgenstein advanced conventional philosophical propositions as a form of "deep nonsense" that would allow readers to see the limitations of such propositions "from within".³⁵

DEEP NONSENSE

In a book review that has done more to publicise *Wittgenstein's Mistress* than any public relations campaign, the novelist David Foster Wallace used precisely the concept of 'deep nonsense' to describe Markson's novel as an indirect message that communicates by undermining the distinction between sense and nonsense: "You could call this technique 'Deep Nonsense,'" Wallace writes,

> Meaning I guess a linguistic flow of strings, strands, loops, and quiffs that through the very manner of its formal construction flouts the ordinary cingula of 'sense' and through its defiance of sense's limits manages somehow to 'show' what cannot ordinarily be 'expressed.'³⁶

What cannot be 'expressed' directly here is the significance of everyday experiences of absorbed coping such as Kate's walk in the rain. That the solution to the Kantian 'scandal' of scepticism, then, can be had in the most ordinary of circumstances is an idea that may likely give rise to ironic laughter like Kierkegaard's best parodies. Conant expressly denies the *Tractatus* such "a strategy of parody (with its concomitant devices of irony and humor)".³⁷ The attribution of irony to an utterance, however, varies from individual to individual; and it is notable that a different reader like the psychoanalyst Jonathan Lear, who "began to think about irony" after co-teaching a class on Kierkegaard with Conant in the early 2000s,³⁸ associates an understanding of such deep nonsense with the experience of irony after all.

To be sure, any reading of the self-reflexive turn at the end of the *Tractatus* as ironic has to contend with the long line of interpreters in the analytic tradition who took the propositions of Wittgenstein's book quite seriously. It would be misleading, though, to assume that an ironic view of the *Tractatus* necessarily negates the seriousness of its implications. The seriousness that speaks from the body of the *Tractatus* may even be regarded as a precondition for the 'therapeutic' aim of what Karen Zumhagen-Yekplé has called the book's "Kierkegaardian mirroring strategy",[39] whereby, as she argues in line with the 'New Wittgensteinians', Wittgenstein self-consciously stages "an elaborate mock-doctrine"[40] that readers have to enter imaginatively to fully experience the book's final gesture at self-sublation. It is a short step from an acceptance of this description to the notion that seeing through the staged 'mockery' may create a shift in perception that can be experienced as ironic.[41] One might also turn to none other than Kierkegaard, who dismissed the association of irony with a lack of seriousness in the guise of one of his various personae: "From the fact that irony is present", Johannes Climacus states in the *Postscript* cited by Conant, "it does not follow that earnestness is excluded".[42] At least this is how Markson seems to have viewed the matter. An ironic reading of the *Tractatus* clarifies once more his choice of title and, as such, his commitment to a novelistic version of Wittgensteinian self-reflexivity: like the Tractarian 'mock-doctrine', *Wittgenstein's Mistress* invites its readers into a dramatised illusion of absolute detachment, the affective experience of which is essential for them to 'come out on the other side' with an ironic laugh at their own former attachment to a philosophical 'picture' that seemed to make *Dasein*'s being-in-the-world an impossible achievement.

This ironic note, however, does not seem to be part of Heidegger's repertoire. In fact, while an ironist like Lear makes a forceful case for reclaiming irony as a way of becoming authentically human, in contrast to conventionally accepted standards of human excellence, for Heidegger conventionality is broken open by a different kind of authenticity: individual extinction as the highest reality in anxiety. As Lear notes, Heidegger simply did "not concern himself with the peculiar species of anxiety that is irony",[43] and this is true in spite of obvious similarities between the reflections on anxiety in *Being and Time* and Kierkegaard's 1844 *The Concept of Anxiety* – an affinity Markson acknowledges in *Wittgenstein's Mistress* by letting Kate express confusion over the authorship of the sentence that "inconsequential perplexities now and again [become] the fundamental mood of existence".[44] Was it Heidegger's or Kierkegaard's sentence, she wonders – and it is difficult not to hear Markson chuckle while writing these lines, amused by one of the most famous cases of plagiarism in the history of philosophy.[45]

Many readers seem to have had their own moments of levity while confronting the anxiety of Kate's "absolutely autobiographical novel". In fact, the realisation that insights gained by way of indirect communication are often accompanied by fits of laughter is quite in line with scholarly accounts of the book. Grace, for example, claims that, even though Kate is no stranger to desperation, the novel "finally resists the tragic mythos through its irony, humor".[46] The critic Burton Feldman agrees, stating that

Markson's novel is a "comedy, or at least it isn't tragic".[47] What we might take away from Markson's dramatisation of Heideggerian themes after successful Wittgensteinian 'therapy', then, is the possibility of a kind of irony that allows us to see our philosophical constructs *as* constructs in the very moment of presenting them. The same is true, of course, of the key concepts of Heidegger's analytic of *Dasein*.

That Heidegger would have done well to "concern himself" with the species of anxiety that is irony, to pick up Lear's phrase once more, is also the conclusion of Peter Sloterdijk's engagement with "Heidegger's pathos".[48] In his *Critique of Cynical Reason*, Sloterdijk proposed an authentic irony that would be capable of teaching the lesson of absorbed functioning while at the same time gesturing at the objective absurdity of developing an enormous conceptual apparatus for a very ordinary experience. Arguably, Markson makes the same case when he grants Kate an understanding of Heidegger's idea that *Dasein* is being-in-the-world, without letting her actually read the philosopher's books. And this way of "undercutting Serious Thought", as Ann Beattie remarks of Markson's novelistic method in ironic capital letters, "is funny".[49]

NOTES

1. Martin Heidegger, *Being and Time* (Albany: SUNY Press, 2010), 198–99.
2. Tyler Malone, "A Fonder Admission of Other Small Things: A Conversation with Ann Beattie", *The Scofield* 1, no. 1 (2015), 22–27, here 25.
3. Joseph Tabbi, "An Interview with David Markson", *Review of Contemporary Fiction* 10, no. 2 (1990), 104–17, here 112.
4. Tabbi, "Interview", 113.
5. Joey Rubin, "The Bus has Long Since Pulled Out: A Conversation with David Markson", *The Scofield* 1, no. 1 (2015), 56–62, here 59.
6. Hubert Dreyfus, "The Myth of the Pervasiveness of the Mental", in *Mind, Reason, and Being-in-the-World*, ed. Joseph K. Schear (London: Routledge, 2013), 28.
7. David Markson, *Wittgenstein's Mistress* (Champaign: Dalkey Archive Press, 1988), 230.
8. Markson, *Mistress*, 231.
9. Tabbi, "Interview", 112.
10. Markson, *Mistress*, 230.
11. Markson, *Mistress*, 216.
12. Martin Heidegger, "What is Metaphysics?" in *Basic Writings*, ed. David Farrell Krell (New York: Harper Collins, 1977), 91–113, here 103.
13. To be sure, this is not the only way Heidegger thinks about the "nothing". In texts such as "What Is Metaphysics?" the 'nothing' is also understood in terms of an

"origin" [*Ursprung*]. This terminological vacillation between absence and presence reflects Heidegger's awareness that any way of 'grasping' the "nothing" runs the risk of relapsing into the kind of subject-object metaphysics he tries to avoid by turning to fundamental ontology.

14. Heidegger, "Metaphysics", 108.
15. Sherril E. Grace, "Messages: Reading *Wittgenstein's Mistress*", *Review of Contemporary Fiction* 10, no. 2 (1990), 207–16, here 214.
16. Markson, *Mistress*, 167.
17. Markson, *Mistress*, 144.
18. Markson, *Mistress*, 184.
19. Heidegger, *Being and Time*, 104.
20. Dreyfus, "Myth", 34.
21. Dreyfus, "Myth", 35.
22. Heidegger, "Metaphysics", 102–3.
23. Markson, *Mistress*, 33.
24. Markson, *Mistress*, 91.
25. Ludwig Wittgenstein, *Philosophical Investigations* (Hoboken: Wiley-Blackwell, 2009), 29^e.
26. Markson, *Mistress*, 170.
27. Tabbi, "Interview", 113.
28. This turn to literary means is a consequence of the most rigorous debates in 20th-Century analytical philosophy. Wittgenstein's emphasis on showing in the *Tractatus* was meant to avoid the infinite regress of Bertrand Russell's theory of types, making it a response to Russell's own solution to the antinomy he had discovered in Gottlob Frege's 1879 *Begriffsschrift*.
29. Ludwig Wittgenstein, *Tractatus Logico-Philosophicus* (London: Routledge, 2001), 6.54.
30. Wittgenstein, *Tractatus*, 6.54.
31. Wittgenstein, *Tractatus*, 7.
32. Markson, *Mistress*, 95.
33. Wittgenstein, *Investigations*, 57^e [§133d].
34. James Conant, "Kierkegaard, Wittgenstein, and Nonsense", in *Pursuits of Reason*, ed. Ted Cohen et al. (Lubbock: Texas Tech University Press, 1993), 217–18.
35. Conant, "Nonsense", 215.
36. David Foster Wallace, "The Empty Plenum: David Markson's *Wittgenstein's Mistress*", in *Both Flesh and Not* (Boston: Little, Brown, 2012), 73–121, here 80.
37. Conant, "Nonsense", 224fn86.
38. Jonathan Lear, *A Case for Irony* (Cambridge, MA: Harvard University Press, 2011), xi.
39. Karen Zumhagen-Yekplé, "The Everyday's Fabulous Beyond: Nonsense, Parable, and the Ethics of the Literary in Kafka and Wittgenstein", *Comparative Literature* 64, no. 4 (2012), 429–45, here 442.
40. Zumhagen-Yekplé, "Beyond", 433.
41. For two recent attempts at making this step explicit and reading Wittgenstein's book *sub specie ironiae*, see Stelios Gadris, "Two Cases of Irony: Kant and

Wittgenstein", *Kant-Studien* 107, no. 2 (2016), 343–68, and Shlomy Mualem, "Nonsense and Irony: Wittgenstein's Strategy of Self-Refutation and Kierkegaard's Concept of Indirect Communication", *Tópicos* 53 (2017), 203–27.

42. Søren Kierkegaard, *Concluding Unscientific Postscript to Philosophical Fragments* (Princeton: Princeton UP, 1992), 277n.

43. Lear, *Irony*, 98.

44. Markson, *Mistress*, 216.

45. Markson, *Mistress*, 217.

46. Grace, "Messages", 216.

47. Burton Feldman, "Markson's New Way", *Review of Contemporary Fiction* 10, no. 2 (1990), 157–63, here 162.

48. Peter Sloterdijk, *Critique of Cynical Reason* (Minneapolis: University of Minnesota Press, 1988), 207. In a later essay, entitled "Luhmann, Devil's Advocate" and included in the volume *Not Saved: Essays After Heidegger*, Sloterdijk seems to have modified this position, now entertaining the possibility that Heidegger's refusal of conformity in Chapter 4 of *Being and Time* relies on a subversive and profoundly *ironic* way of inhabiting mainstream culture. This tantalising reading might have resulted from Heidegger's oscillation between positive and negative valences in his account of 'das Man', but it is difficult to see how the irony that Sloterdijk claims to hear is reflected in the literary presentation of Heidegger's argument in *Being and Time*.

49. Malone, "Conversation", 26.

CROSSING THE BOUNDARIES OF THE OTHER

HISTORY, TIME AND SILENCE

Chapter 12

The Impossible Death of Julia de Burgos

Reading "¡Dádme mi número!" at the Limits of Dasein

Ronald Mendoza-de Jesús

ECLIPSED THOUGHT: RETURNING TO HEIDEGGER'S *SPRACHE* TODAY

One could point to any number of aspects within Martin Heidegger's *corpus* that might explain why, after enduring so many eclipses – whether caused by well-deserved scandals, hard-to-predict changes in the intellectual *Zeitgeist*, or simply the passage of time – his thinking continues to find its way into the motley scene of contemporary thought.[1] That said, were I forced to choose which among these aspects represents Heidegger's most decisive contribution to what *today* might still be called "the task of thinking", I would have to go with the *place* that Heidegger grants to *die Sprache* or *language* within his thinking of *Ereignis* or (the event of) appropriation. Furthermore, if asked to explain why I think that it is *this* Heidegger whose return is now most salient, I would first provide a negative answer, insisting on my belief that this return has little to do with the question of whether the so-called linguistic turn still determines the horizon of critical thought within the university and beyond its walls.[2] If pressed for a more positive response, I would wager that the return of and to this Heidegger is, instead, due to the fact that implicit in his thinking of language and *Ereignis* is a rethinking of "the human" which resonates with the renewed sense of urgency with which the question of humanness is being posed today. The causes that might, in turn, explain why "the human" has again become such an urgent problem for thought are too numerous and varied to be adequately summarised here. Still, if pressed any further, I would offer as historical *indicia* two recent phenomena whose *Incubationszeit* – to borrow a metaphor dear to Heidegger[3] – seems to have been programmed so that their symptoms would manifest around the same time: first, the ongoing interdisciplinary debate about the Anthropocene;[4] and, secondly, the increasing emergence of a body of theoretical work that has been labelled "the post-humanist turn".[5] In spite of appearing to be at odds with each other, both phenomena betray a wide-ranging anxiety over the place of the human within the structure of the world and, more precisely, over the political, ethical, environmental and ontological effects of the irreducible anthropocentrism of the modern world-system. Indeed, I would argue that it is Heidegger's longstanding preoccupation with the violent essence of the *Anthropos* that justifies this particular return of and to his thinking.[6] Many of Heidegger's key texts can be read now as attempts to register how the Anthropocene had been prepared all along in and as the metaphysical unfolding of the history of being.

In this essay, I sketch out two different returns to and of *this* Heidegger in order to probe the limits of a conception of the human that, I would argue, remains isomorphic to what Heidegger calls *Dasein*. In the first section, I turn to the work of Giorgio Agamben and Sylvia Wynter to examine how their influential attempts to rethink being human beyond the metaphysical strictures of the *animal rationale* could also be read as returns to Heidegger. My goal, however, is not simply to attest to the survival of the proper name "Heidegger" in the contemporary theoretical landscape. Instead, turning to both Agamben and Wynter allows me to show how Heidegger's *logocentric*[7] understanding of the human as *Dasein* continues to inform the horizon of the postmetaphysical humanisms of Agamben and Wynter, who are taken here as representative of a broader philosophical or theoretical trend characterised by its commitment to retrieving the project of humanism from its violent, and indeed inhuman institution through the imperialistic metaphysics of Western modernity. That said, the logocentrism that I discern in their thinking is not simply limited to a privileging of the *logos* as the dimension in which being essences *as* presencing, thus providing the conditions in which alone the human appropriated to its *proper*, mortal essence by being finally carried beyond the metaphysics of the *Anthropos* and the *animal rationale*. Implicit in this logocentric *closure* of *humanness*, I argue, is also the sedimented metaphysical privilege of the *autos*, the *self* or *das Selbe*, as the paleonymic metaphysical name for the position that human existence would come to occupy in and through the transformative advent of what Heidegger calls *Ereignis*, what Agamben calls *avventura* or *adventure* or what Wynter calls *The Third Event*. My engagement with both Wynter's thinking of *narrativity* and *autopoiesis* as the key components of her thinking of the event and Agamben's thought around chivalric poetry as the lingual medium for the experience that he calls *avventura* or *adventure* suggests that their approaches to the possibility of retrieving the human beyond "Man" not only ratify and reinstantiate the logocentric closures in which Heidegger's thinking is retained, but also reactualise the *ipseitocratic* commitments that structure Heidegger's approach to the thinking of the human.[8]

In the second section of this essay, I explore the limits of Heidegger's thinking concerning the relation between humanness, language and especially poetic language, through a reading of a poem, ¡*Dádme mi número!* (*Give me my number!*), written in the early 1940s by Julia de Burgos, the most celebrated figure in the canon of Puerto Rican letters. My argument is that this poem of de Burgos introduces a split at the very core of that unthought "Wesensverhältnis" or "essential relation" between language and mortality around which Heidegger's thinking of *Ereignis* turns,[9] decoupling each of these possibilities from their essential co-belonging. For lack of space, I can only point to this split by focusing on just two aspects of de Burgos's poem: 1. the status of number in relation to the poet's death, and 2. the problem of address and response, of *Ansprechen* and *Entsprechen*. In presenting a condition of radical *exappropriation* in which names become numbers and in which language, crystalised in its performative force as an address, fails to secure the conditions of its responsibility by a possible addressee, De Burgos's poem allegorically presents a life that is *prior* to *Ereignis* or, to be more precise, a life that has lost the power of appropriation to such an extent that it can no longer encounter *itself* within the humanistic strictures of the properly poetic language and the properly experienced death that constitute *Dasein* at its very ipseitological and logocentric core. By the same token, de Burgos's poem contains the record of an experience whose very possibility undoes the humanising schemas that animate both Wynter and Agamben's post-Heideggerian retrievals of the poetic and the poietic as the transformative medium for the institution of a humanity truly and *properly* human.

By sketching these two different returns to Heidegger's thinking of language and appropriation in its intrinsic relation to the poetic essence of the human – understood, in turn, as *Dasein* – my goal is to pose the following question: If, as de Burgos's poem shows, finite existence is exposed to an infinity of dying that remains in excess of Heidegger's schema of a *proper* death, if existence might be *exappropriated* in such a way that the possibility of returning home remains questionable, then should *Dasein* continue to be upheld as the form that human life should take (and, already, in its essence, *has*) in the wake of our proliferating, all too human catastrophes?

BEING/BECOMING HUMAN AND THE ACTUALITY OF HEIDEGGER'S *SPRACHE*: AGAMBEN'S *AVVENTURA*, WYNTER'S *HOMO NARRANS* AND HEIDEGGER'S *EREIGNIS*

A good place to measure the enduring presence of Heidegger's thinking of language and *Ereignis* in Agamben's recent work can be found in *L'avventura* (2015) – a short text that could be read as recasting the "results" of the *Homo Sacer* series, which reached its end with the publication of *Uso dei corpi* (2014). The philosophical crux of this text lies in Agamben's bold proposal to translate Heidegger's notion of *Ereignis* – perhaps the best candidate for the most important operative term in Heidegger's writings from his so-called middle period onward[10] – within the Modern European lexicon of *adventure*:

> In this sense, adventure is the most correct translation of *Ereignis*. Therefore, it is a genuinely ontological term, which designates being insofar as it occurs— that is to say, in its manifesting itself to man and to language – and language inasmuch as it says and reveals being. For this reason, in chivalric poems it is impossible to distinguish adventure-event from adventure-story; for this reason, the knight, encountering adventure, first of all encounters himself and his most deep-seated being. And if the event in question in adventure is nothing other than anthropogenesis, that is to say, the moment in which, thanks to a transformation of which it is impossible to know its modality, the living has separated – to then rearticulate together – its own life and its own language, this means that, in becoming human, the living has consecrated itself to an adventure which is still in course and whose results are not easily foreseeable.[11]

To be sure, Heidegger himself would have rejected, or at least troubled, Agamben's decision to render his thinking of appropriation or *Ereignis* in terms of both *adventure* and *anthropo-genesis*, two (or three) terms on which Heidegger wrote, critically more often than not.[12] That said, the orthodoxy (or not) of Agamben's engagement with Heidegger matters less for my purposes than the fact that his thinking of anthropogenesis – one of the keystones of his philosophy – amounts to an adaptation of Heidegger's *Ereignis*-motif. Agamben's notion of adventure, understood as the coming-to-being of the human *as* human, is isomorphic to Heidegger's appropriating event: both "movements" name the process through which the human itself undergoes a transformation, but in such a way that, as Agamben puts it, "encountering the adventure", the human "encounters himself first of all and his most deep-seated being".[13] This line is key since it discloses the extent to which the transformative movements of *Ereignis* and *adventure* are not merely processes of change; they are, instead, the *arch-nostic* movements of *return* through which the human, after undergoing the adventurous advent of expropriation, arrives to what had been always already *its own*, appropriating its essence by being appropriated to it. Moreover, for Agamben, *adventure* both necessitates and renders possible a *transformation* of language in a way that is analogous to Heidegger's thinking of *Ereignis*. Recall that in "Der Weg zur Sprache" ("The Way to Language"), Heidegger characterises *Ereignis* as the "saying's way-making towards language" and describes such a *Be-wëgung* (a path-breaking or way-making movement) in terms of a *Wandlung*, a *transformation* that does not so much change *our* understanding of language as it discloses that "in truth the way to language has always already its singular locale in the speaking being itself".[14] The place or the location of language is not in the human, but in a *Sprachwesen* whose speech is the saying of language itself, and to which the human must hark if it is to find itself again.

That being said, it is worth noting that the place of language in Agamben's thinking of adventure deviates from Heidegger's thinking of *Ereignis* in another major way. In keeping with Agamben's commitment to a biopolitical retelling of the history of Western metaphysics as the establishment of a precarious separation between *bios* and *zōē* through the production of what he terms "nuda vita" or "bare life",[15] the transformation of the human in the event of adventure is conceived as necessitating the *rearticulation* of human *life* and its language.[16] This explains why, when placed within the context of the *Homo Sacer* project, *adventure* emerges as the very experiential dimension in and through which the separation at the core of human life that determined the destiny of Western ontology as a sacrificial bio-politics might be overcome, thus interrupting the onto-political machinery of sovereign power and its ever-increasing production of bare life. For this reason, we might say that "adventure", as a name for the event of anthropogenesis, also names the "experience" or, better, the "site" for the emergence of what Agamben already in *Homo Sacer* had called a "forma-di-vita" ("form-of life:")[17] a form of life or a *bios* that, since it is inseparable from its own natural life or *zōē*, would also have to dwell in a language in which the "presuppositional structure" that operates "the inclusive exclusion of the real from the *logos* and in the *logos*" has been deactivated.[18] No doubt Heidegger would have most likely judged Agamben's *biological* emphasis insufficiently fundamental to characterise what is at stake in his thinking of the place of language within *Ereignis*. Still, marking the extent to which Agamben's rethinking of concepts such as "adventure" and "form-of-life" can be read as variations of Heidegger's own *Ereignis*-motif and its account of the place of language in the becoming-human of the human can help us to recognise the survival – or, better, the vitality – of Heidegger's thinking in the landscape of contemporary thought.

A similar Heideggerian legacy can be traced throughout the writings of Jamaican theorist Sylvia Wynter, whose seminal essays have shaped the fields of the postcolonial, Caribbean, gender, and Black studies for the last three decades.[19] A good place to see this is the text titled, *Unparalleled Catastrophe For Our Species? Or, To Give Humanness a Different Future: Conversations*, which reproduces a series of conversations between Wynter and Katherine McKittrick that took place between 2007 and 2014, and where Wynter outlines the main theoretical rudiments of her intellectual trajectory. For our purposes, it is telling that Wynter selects as one of the guiding quotes that will orient her conversations with McKittrick a passage from Heidegger's 1941 summer course, *Grundbegriffe*, in which Heidegger both poses the question concerning the essence of the human and deauthorises, on being-historical grounds, the answers that the science of anthropology has given to this question.[20] Now, Wynter's choice of Heidegger as an ally might seem a bit surprising at first, given not only his well-known involvement with the Nazi party, but also his rabid Eurocentrism. This choice becomes less surprising if we keep in mind that Wynter's project, as McKrittick puts it, "can be identified as that of a *counterhumanism*"[21] that challenges the epochal determination of the human that Wynter calls "Man 2", which is historically bound to its origins in Enlightenment secularisation.[22] Another key component of Wynter's "counterhumanism" is its diagnosis of liberalism's transformation of the *form* of human autonomy that emerges in the Copernican Turn into a "genre of the human" that she conceives under the heading of *homo oeconomicus*.[23] As Wynter argues, Western colonialism has turned this script or "genre" of the human into a global regime in which the economically driven determination of the humanity of the human is buttressed by an "anthropological" determination that understands humanity *biocentrically*, that is, as a biological organism or an animal that is, as it were, *wired* to behave precisely as *homo oeconomicus*:

> The West, over the last five hundred years, has brought the *whole* human species into its *hegemonic*, now purely secular [. . .] mode of being *human*. This is the version in whose terms the human has now been redefined, since the nineteenth century, on the *natural scientific model* of a *natural organism*. [. . .] All the peoples of the world, whatever their religions/cultures, are drawn into the homogenizing global structures that are based on the-model-of-a-natural-organism-world-systemic-order. This is the enacting of a uniquely secular liberal monohumanist *conception* of the human – Man-as-*homo oeconomicus* – as well as of its rhetorical overrepresenting of that member-class conception of being human (as if it is the *class of classes* of being human itself).[24]

We can now see better why Wynter enlists Heidegger as an ally in the struggle to achieve the task that Franz Fanon's outlines in *Peau noire, masques blanques,* namely, "to set man free".[25] The "counterhumanism" of Wynter constitutes a radical attempt to dislodge *this* understanding of the human, which is concomitant with the fact of Western imperial domination, by exposing how such a conception of "liberal monohumanist Man2" remains wedded to an anthropological approach to the human that takes it in primarily "biocentric", that is, phylogenic/ontogenic, terms, understanding it primarily as a "natural organism". Given that Wynter takes such a task to necessitate a radical dismantling of the onto-epistemological framework that not only determines the human in primarily biocentric terms, but also understands the science of biology in exclusively Darwinian, that is, also biocentric, terms, we can see how Heidegger's long-standing critique of the Western metaphysical tradition and its interpretation of humanity in the horizon of animality could serve as a powerful ally to Wynter's project. Wynter's counterhumanism reiterates Heidegger's question in the quote she selects from *Grundbegriffe* – "How then, if we perhaps did not know at all where we are and who we are?"[26] – in order to trouble not only the quantitative and qualitative limits of humanity as it is conceived *today*, but, above all, to interrogate the very historicity of this biocentric conception of human life, which determines even current efforts to challenge the anthropocentrism of our juridical and political frameworks or confront our impending climate catastrophes. Remarking on the minor, but significant, role that Heidegger plays in Wynter's thinking enables us to accentuate even more the ontological stakes of her political wager to set the human free – a task could not be achieved without a radical dismantling of the ontology of humanness that sustains the current global economico-political order.

Still, perhaps the point of closest proximity – and, paradoxically, of widest divergence – between Wynter's thinking of the human and Heidegger's lies precisely in the role that she ascribes to what she calls "languaging" within the structure of a liberated humanity. Bringing together insights from anthropology, neuroscience and biology, Wynter articulates an understanding of "the origin of the human as a hybrid-auto-instituting-languaging-storytelling species: *bios/mythoi*".[27] To the biocentrism of *homo oeconomicus* and its zoo-anthropological understanding of the human, Wynter opposes a conception of the human as *homo narrans*: a structurally hybrid life-form whose biology (phylogeny/ontogeny) is constitutively transformed, from its very beginning as a species, by its lingual – and, more specifically, narratological – sociogeny. "This task – to set the human free – therefore demands that we must begin, for the first time, to track a complete version of our species' history as it had been performatively enacted from its origins"[28] *as* the hybrid intertwining of *biology and storytelling*. Not unlike Heidegger's emphasis on the verbal/adverbial (gerundive) sense of the nouns *das Sein/das Seiende* (being/beings) and *das*

Wesen/ das Wesende (essence/what essences), for Wynter, tracking the history of our species in its originary hybridity as *bios/mythoi* produces a change in our understanding of "humanness", which "is no longer a *noun*:" in the medium of narrativity, "*being human is a praxis*".[29] Humanness thus becomes a verb: to narrate is to humanise. Narration, as it were, *humans* the human, it brings the human into its nonbiocentric, postmetaphysical humanity.

To be sure, Wynter's reliance on neuroscience and biology renders patently obvious the point in which she departs from Heidegger's own assumptions regarding the role that modern science could play in the articulation of the transformability of the human in relation to its own essentially lingual being.[30] Above all, it is Wynter's debt to Humberto Maturana and Francisco Varela's concept of *autopoiesis*,[31] and her insistence on the *agential* nature of the uniquely human (i.e., discursive) processes that override our biology, that seem to be at odds with Heidegger's own insistence on the fact that the human becomes a human only by harking to the languaging of language itself, which is not in and of itself human. I will turn in a moment to the issue of autopoiesis; but before, I want to point out that the radical differences between Wynter and Heidegger do not change the fact that, as was the case also with Agamben, what is at stake in her conception of the human as a *homo narrans* is not the invention of a *new* concept of the human but rather a *return* to what we *always already* have been. And what we always have been is not simply linguistic beings, but rather beings that *poetise*, that is, that *live language* in such a way so as to fashion a *world*. An analogous situation to what we saw with Agamben and Heidegger obtains between Wynter and Heidegger: even her most explicit divergences from the strictures of Heidegger's thinking of appropriation, the event and poetic language reveal a deeper, subterraneous continuity.

Moreover, as the very name "*homo narrans*" suggests, the poetic potency of human language for Wynter becomes concretised primarily in narrative forms. This is why a consideration of the role of narratives in Wynter's conception of the human is not only crucial to understand her postmetaphysical brand of humanism, but also can help us to identify what remains problematic in one of the aspects of Agamben's thinking of *avventura* that we have not yet considered. In *L'avventura*, Agamben privileges one particular genre and epoch within the history of human storytelling – namely, medieval European adventure stories – as somehow granting a privileged access to the anthropogenesis that *Ereignis* is supposed to afford. In other words, the reunification of human life and language, which Agamben claims coincides with the movement of return to our own humanity, seems to have a special affinity to this particular genre of medieval *poiēsis*, so much so that it provides the basis for his translation of *Ereignis* as *avventura*. Wynter's move is radically opposed to this gesture. Rather than singling out any *actual* narrative genres, Wynter first restores narrativity to its status as *the* human *potency par excellence* by pointing to the fact that its *concrete* historical inscription is, on one hand, co-extensive with the very emergence of *homo sapiens sapiens* in Africa, and, on the other hand, has its "privileged" form in the genre of "origin stories", which are attested across different cultures and ethnic groups. The emergence of narrativity is such a transformative event that Wynter refers to it as the "Third Event" – the other two being the origin of the universe and the emergence of biological forms of life – and its scope is such that it contains the very humanness of the whole of humanity within its purview.[32] Hence, to finally know ourselves in our "languaging-cum-storytelling" lives is to rethink humanness in *ecumenical* terms, that is, to recognise that all humans have always had the *possibility* of sharing in the narratological *autopoietic* process through which human life institutes itself in its singularity among other forms of life. That so many have been historically deprived of exercising, this possibility gives a measure of the oppressive nature of the historico-ontological regimes that have produced such inhumanity and then externalised it by ascribing it as an essential property of *other* (radicalised, gendered, less *homo oeconomically*-adapted) humans. Coincidentally, one of the byproducts of reading Wynter with and against Agamben might be a renewed emphasis on the one ecumenical strand in Heidegger's violently Eurocentric thinking of the poetic essence of human language, namely, his claim that "being speaks throughout and continually in the most different ways everywhere through all language".[33]

Finally, though Wynter certainly deviates from Heidegger in that narration remains a human *activity*, her thinking nonetheless retains the humanist strictures of Heidegger's conception of *Dasein* as the sole being whose existence is determined through the possibility of languaging *itself* into existence. In spite of the overwhelming distance that might initially separate Heidegger's account of *Dasein*'s *self*-appropriation of its innermost essence through its lingual appropriation by being's claim from Wynter's account of the narratological autopoietic institution of the human as a *bios/muthos* form of life, I want to suggest that there is a deeper continuity between these two ways of thinking about the transformative becoming-human beyond modernity's epochal determination of the humanity of Man as *animal rationale*. Indeed, the structural continuity between their approaches can be best seen if we pay attention to the recurrence of the lexicon of the "self", the "itself" and the *autos* in Heidegger's talk of "Being it*self*" and of *Dasein* as a form of "*Selbst*heit"[34] as well as in Wynter's reliance on the schema of *auto*poiesis. In spite of their differences, I would argue that these "selves" are isomorphic, at least to the extent that they all refer to a *dynamic* form of ontological *singularity*, to the *autonomous* processes through which Being or *Dasein* or human life bring themselves about *out of their own accord*, constituting themselves in processes of self-institution that *ipso facto* disclose a sense of freedom *other* than the freedom of the liberal-humanist subject. Indeed, since, for Wynter, the singularly human processes of *autopoiesis* find their highest articulation in the narrative language of *homo narrans*, we might say that the language of a humanity that would finally dwell in its essence is a poetics in which what is at stake each time is the *auto*poetic instantiation of the human in its renewed humanity. This *poiesis* would be a doing without a *deed*, a *praxis* without an *ergon*, an open narrativity in excess of any achieved result.

And yet, how truly *other* is this humanising, lingual, narratological or poetological praxis if it retains the deepest sedimented value of Western ontology, namely, the tacit postulation of the *autos* or of *ipseity* as the essence of the human being? This admittedly rhetorical question not only intends the classic deconstructive problematic of the closure or the end of metaphysics, and the status of Heidegger and post-Heideggerian thought therein – in other words, what is at stake in raising this question is not simply whether the nonmetaphysical humanism of Wynter, Agamben and other thinkers is in fact *non*metaphysical. For the (im)position of *ipseity* as the horizon of becoming-human acquires a different, more explicitly political tone as soon as we follow Jacques Derrida's suggestion that *ipseity* constitutes the very essence of sovereign power. The determination of human life or existence as an "I can", as a being to which what is allotted first of all are *possibilities*, including in an eminent sense the possibilities of dying *properly* and of *having* a language, is for Derrida indissociable from mastery and sovereign power. Short of a deconstruction that dissociates the experience of selfhood from the *power to be oneself*, any postulation of the schema of the *self itself* as the mark of a transformed or liberated humanity remains structurally predicated on the very sovereignty that it seeks to displace. This is why, coincidentally, I would argue that any understanding of the humanity of the human that seeks to displace the paradigm of Cartesian subjectivity without interrogating and deconstructing the very sedimented value of ipseity and the attendant structure of autoaffection upon which subjectivity is predicated *cannot actually deliver what it promises*, namely, to let go of the Man-cum-*animal-rationale* in order to release the human into its *proper* lingual-mortal-poetic essence.

INTERPRETATION AND INTERROGATION: POETIC DISPOSSESSION IN DE BURGOS'S POEM

The poetic or poietic language that emerges in the work of Wynter and Agamben echoes in general terms Heidegger's characterisation of poetry as a privileged form of language. As Heidegger puts it in *"dichterisch wohnet der Mensch"*, "poeticizing is the fundamental ability of human dwelling".[35] That said, if *human* dwelling is enabled at its very source by poetising, this is because poetising is the way of being in language that best discloses the "still unthought", "essential relation" that unites finitude and speech as the two Arch-fundamental abilities of human life, understood in its *proper* sense, that is, as a mortal *Dasein*.[36] Moreover, the fact that this "essential relation" remains *unthought* for Heidegger discloses yet another reason why the language of the poets might have an advantage over the language of the thinkers in affording us an experience of the "flash" in and *as* which this essential relation appears. Consider, for instance, how Heidegger, while describing his own idiosyncratic relationship to the poetry of Friedrich Hölderlin in *Über den Anfang*, remarks on this essential difference between the poet and the thinker by stating that the former "poetizes being" through recourse to a name that does not *know* what it names nor *interrogates* it, whereas the latter speaks being "in image-less *knowing word*".[37] The poetic word, that is, the inseparability of name and image, grants out of its own accord the very abode in which the human may properly abide before it can even know itself by coming to terms with its own essential abiding and thus become what it always already has been.

To conclude this essay, I want to turn to a poem by Puerto Rican poet, Julia de Burgos, titled, *¡Dadme mi número!* Written after the poet's exile from Puerto Rico in 1940, the poem is part of her third poetry volume, *El mar y tú*, which the poet finished in Cuba in the years 1940-41, but which only saw the light of day a year after her death in the summer of 1953 in New York City, at the age of 39. To the extent that my reading goes against the grain of both the nationalism that has turned de Burgos into an icon of the island's cultural resistance against US colonisation and of more standard protocols of reading poetry (whether belletristic or literary historical), one might say that the interpretation that I offer here corresponds, in some aspects, to how Heidegger describes the task of carrying out an *Auslegung* of a poet like Hölderlin in *Über den Anfang*.[38] That said, although my *Auslegung* indeed stems from the conviction of a certain "necessity" of a *Zwiesprache* between de Burgos and Heidegger,[39] what emerges from this *dialogue* is not a confirmation of Heidegger's thinking. Instead, I'd like to suggest that de Burgos's poem splits the very core of that unthought "essential relation" between language and mortality around which Heidegger's thinking of *Ereignis* turns, revealing the possibility that these essential possibilities of the human as mortal might be in fact contingent. In that radical splitting of the mysterious bond that binds together the essence of language with the essential finitude of *Dasein*, emerge possibilities that go against the grain of the logocentric and ipseitocratic approach that determines the horizon of Heidegger's thinking, even in its biopolitical or decolonial rearticulations via the work of Agamben and Wynter, among others. The key of these possibilities that my reading of this poem of de Burgos explores is the undoing of the humanist determination of the self-cum-ipseity through the appropriation of mortality. De Burgos's poem consigns an "experience" at the limits of the possible, namely, the experience of a self that is radically *incapable* of dying a *proper* death and thus remains exposed to an infinity of dyings that exponentiate abysmally the measureless impossibility that Heidegger, in *Sein und Zeit*, seems somewhat confident to maintain within the purview of the possible and as the marker of its *ontological authenticity* – as the very *nothing* whose withdrawal *enables* the essence of possibility to remain radically beyond any ontic capture.[40] The situation that is poeticised in this poem is thus more adventurous than Agamben's and it signals, at the same time, an interruption of any belief in narrativity as the medium of the autopoetic self-institution of the human in its restored humanity.

¡Dadme mi número!

¿Qué es lo que esperan? ¿No me llaman?
¿Me han olvidado entre las yerbas
mis camaradas más sencillos,
todos los muertos de la tierra?

¿Por qué no suenan sus campanas?
Ya para el salto estoy dispuesta.
¿Acaso quieren más cadáveres
de sueños muertos de inocencia?
¿Acaso quieren más escombros
de más goteadas primaveras,
más ojos secos en las nubes,
más rostro herido en las tormentas?

¿Quieren el féretro del viento
agazapado entre mis greñas?
¿Quieren el ansia del arroyo,
muerta en mi muerte de poeta?

¿Quieren el sol desmantelado,
ya consumido en mis arterias?
¿Quieren la sombra de mi sombra,
donde no quede ni una estrella?

Casi no puedo con el mundo,
Que azota entero a mi conciencia...

¡Dadme mi número! No quiero
que hasta el amor se me desprenda...

(Unido sueño que me sigue
 como a mis pasos va la huella.)

¡Dadme mi número, porque si no,
me moriré después de muerta![41]

"Give Me My Number!"

What are you waiting for? You don't call me?
Have you forgotten me among the tall grass
my most simple comrades,
all the dead of the earth?

Why don't your bells toll?
I am ready for the leap already.
Perhaps you want more corpses
of dreams dead of innocence?
Perhaps you want more rubble
of more drizzly springs
more dry eyes in the clouds,
more wounded face in the storms?

You want the wind's casket
huddled within my mop of hair?
You want the creek's urge
dead in my poet's death?

You want the sun dismantled
already consumed in my arteries?
You want the shadow of my shadow,
where not even a star is left?

I can barely handle the world,
which whips, entire, my consciousness...

Give me my number! I don't want
even love to detach itself from me...

(United dream that follows me
as footprints go with my steps)

Give me my number, for if not,
I will die after I am dead!

The title of the poem already makes clear why any attempt to read this poem must confront the question of what kind of number is at stake in the speaker's reiterated demand. And indeed, most interpretations of *¡Dadme mi número!* have read this number as indicative of the allegorical nature of the poem, which would represent the poet awaiting the moment of her death as if she was waiting in line to be called for her turn to die.[42] These allegorical interpretations of de Burgos's poem, in turn, imply that the number that the poetic voice demands is an *ordinal*, rather than a *cardinal* number, since this number's function is to grant the speaker–poet *her place* within the line of death. Moreover, this allegorical interpretation presupposes yet another metaphorical exchange, namely, that the *ordinal* number is also a *nominal* number since it functions as a *substitute* for the proper name of the poet. Moreover, since everything hinges on the speaker being called by her dead comrades, the moment in which that call to die is issued would also mark the point in which the poet's number becomes indistinguishably ordinal and nominal, while also ensuring the cardinality of her life's numerical extension. As such, the number here marks her place in the line of death, becomes her name as soon as her number is called, and enables the totality of her life to be counted.

That said, more important than the sense that we might make of this name–number is the fact that it is the thing at the basis of the poet's *demand*, which implies that she does not already *have* it, in spite of being repeatedly invoked as *hers*. But at the heart of this demand lies an *aporia*. Since the entire language of the poem is condensed within its structure of address and its interpellations, our reading arrives at a scene in which we seem to be placed already as *addressees*, which, in this context, means that we might have the power to grant the speaker her number. How can we read or hear this demand without rushing to supply *what* the demand demands, thus filling up and negating the void – the almost nothing – that structures the demanding, exacting language of de Burgos's poem? Given the difficulty of this task, it is not surprising that most readings of *¡Dadme mi número!* have interpreted this poem as an all-too-familiar story in which the poet waits for her turn to die. This reading, though plausible and not at all misguided, does not pay heed to the demanding sense of the poet's petition, which acquires full significance only if we grant that the poetic voice is not in *possession* of her number, that is, *of the possibility of death*. Being deprived of her number/name, the poet is also deprived of the very chance to hear the call of the dead and thus of dying *her own* death, and is therefore not simply waiting for her turn to die but impatiently demanding that such a turn, emblematised in "her number" be granted. This sense of a radical loss is already at work from the very first line of the poem, in which the poetic voice asks the following two questions: "¿Qué es lo que esperan? No me llamán?"

Recall also that these questions are explicitly addressed to the poet's "most simple comrades/all the dead of the earth" ("*camaradas más sencillos / todos los muertos de la tierra*".) Being incapable of hearing their call, the poet is also deprived of the very *possibility* of awaiting the arrival of *her* final death, of the death of her dying. As such, rather than waiting for her turn to die, the poet's incessant demand attests to an impossible facticity, since what is demanded in her demand, that is, her number (of her death) is not simply a demand for the *moment* or the *instant* of death to come but, more radically still, for the sheer *possibility* of death to be granted to her. Indeed, the line "Ya para el salto estoy dispuesta-" could be taken as an indication of the poet's resolute readiness for death in a way that resonates with the kind of "relation" to death that Heidegger calls "*Vorlaufen*" in *Sein und Zeit*: the running ahead or the leap in which *Dasein* understands death as "the possibility of impossibility".[43] Running ahead or *Vorlaufen* names a proper way of understanding death insofar as it discloses death *as* a possibility that *cannot be actualised*. Severing the ties between possibility and actuality, authentic death liberates a notion of "pure" possibility, a possible-in-itself whose infinity can only be delimited by the nonactualisable absoluteness of death *as such*, that is, as an impossibility that "knows no measure".

But, de Burgos's poem overflows Heidegger's schema, which goes to the core of his thinking of *Dasein*. Indeed, the demand of the poetic voice for the number/name of her death betrays an understanding of death that seems to be both *irreducible* and *prior* to Heidegger's disclosure of the existential meaning of death *as* the "*most proper possibility of* Dasein".[44] The poet who petitions for her number in *¡Dadme mi número!* does not comprehend death as *her* possibility, not even as the *possibility* that is hers only insofar she cannot actualise it and thus experience it in its realisation. Dispossessed of *her own* death, the poet in de Burgos's poem is not a *Dasein*. The persistence of her demand for the number of death casts the second verse of the first stanza in its proper, *ironic* light. When the poet states "I am already ready for the leap", she is not attesting to her capacity to liberate the possibility of her own death as the possibility of the impossible; instead, this affirmation is a confession of her incapacity to achieve precisely such liberation. The poet *cannot* take the leap of death *by herself*, in spite of being already ready for it. Hence, the defiant tone that marks the poem in its entirety, and which goes in hand with the performative dimension of its demanding language. The poem does not assent to this condition but rather voices an *exigency*, namely, the speaker's wish to enter into the space in which the impossibility of death will finally become *possible* for her.

From her opening questions – "¿Qué es lo que esperan? ¿No me llaman?" – the poet interpellates her only possible addressee, namely, the dead ones, who are the only ones who could give the poet her number and grant her access to the domain of those who can anticipate their own final death. However, this opening interpellation amounts to an apostrophe in the literal sense of the term: the poet turns to addressees – a plurality of them, constituted in the form of a community or a collective of the dead – who are not there. The apostrophe that traverses this poem in its entirety betrays the poetic's voice enduring and ironic abandonment. Addressing an absence, the poetic voice utters a series of questions whose status remains radically unstable. Neither self-interrogations, nor questions posed to the community of the dead, these questions demand and beg for an end to the eternity of dying, which can only be granted by those who are already gone. The performativity of the poem's initial questions is a weak one; its force is measured by its incapacity to produce the community of the dead comrades through their interpellation. This weakness modulates the language of the poet's demand, depriving it of its imperative valence and turning the poet's demand for her number into a petition or even a prayer. Of this poem, we could say what Werner Hamacher has said regarding the unstable status of the language of prayer:

> Even before any possibility of a concordance with others, this language enounces (*bekundet*) – but it does not express – the mere existence of a separation (*Unterschieds*) from others and even insists on this separation in an attempt to bring it to bear as such. When this language turns itself as a petition to an other, it even goes ahead of the other and is a petition without this other that could fulfill it; a petition before it, which merely opens up a place for the other without being able to decide on whether this place is occupied or remains vacant [. . .]. It is not the speech of a being in command of language but rather of a being without substance that petitions for language, a *zōōn logon euchomenon*.[45]

The questions that constitute the first five stanzas of Burgos's poem unfold in the infinite distance that separates the poet and her comrades. All appearances to the contrary, these questions are neither rhetorical nor interrogative statements that presuppose an answer: their very questionability lies in their immediate modification as a weak address to the other. Following Hamacher, the only plausible function of these questions is to open up a space for the possible arrival of the other, without having the power to decree or to anticipate whether this other will ever come or not. The poetic voice's interrogatory becomes an *inter-rogatory*, her language is a request, a petition, a prayer or a rogation for the *inter* – for being in-between and being-with her dead comrades. The poet's demand is a demand for relationality – a demand that is also a petition for language, for being listened to and for being able to listen to the call of the dead. The desperation that sets the tone of this poem emerges out of the structural insecurity that marks the nonplace from which the poetic voice speaks, which deprives the poet of the possibility of knowing whether her inter-rogations *may* have been answered or not. This uncertainty cannot but generate further petitions – more questions that are always structurally capable of not being heard by those who could only answer them. Questions that interrogate questions, demands that demand the chance of being able to voice a demand – the poetic voice continues to die her poet's death in a desperate attempt to finally stumble upon the dead one who may answer her pleas. In the infinity of this demand/prayer, irrupts the most intense solitude. The failure of the poetic voice to interpellate her dead comrades implies the poet's concomitant failure to interpellate herself *as* someone who truly belongs to the community of "all the dead of the earth".

In order for the poet to interpellate herself as a truly mortal, finite being she must be appropriated by the number of her death. Deprived of *this* number, the self that irrupts in de Burgos's poem is not even able to be-towards-death; it is rather a self *without* ipseity, an impossible self whose voice unfolds within a prayer that is just as impossible. Thus, is this poem written and read – incapable of writing itself and of reading itself, incapable, above all, of decreeing to the other that it ought to respond or even to listen to its plea and deliver the number/name/date of death. Absolved, without responsibility – in the literal sense of being deprived of the possibility of any response – the poem *survives* by entrusting its *self* and entrusting itself upon an other who *may* or *may not* respond to its demand, which is also and always a prayer – to be read. If the poem remains the place *par excellence* in which language emerges as precisely the *Ort* or place in which the human might take residence once more in its essence, this poem of Julia de Burgos exposes the conditions of a life that has not yet been granted the minimal conditions to count as a *Dasein*. A life that speaks without being able to experience death *as* death, without thus being able to configure any world.

And yet, the poem's potency is not only limited to exposing the conditions of a life that has fallen beyond the fallenness that belongs to and, for the most part, coincides with the life of *Dasein*. For the speaker of this poem demands to be granted admission into a world in which death is an unsurpassable limit and language is again endowed with the capacity to disclose and configure this very world in which the human already finds itself. The movement of this poem thus unfolds ambivalently: on one hand, what occurs in this poem points to the internal displacement of the ipseitological structure that constitutes *Dasein* – and which, as my reading of Agamben and Wynter suggests, continues to inform the conceptions of humanness that animate much contemporary thinking that seeks to retrieve the category of the human beyond the so-called posthumanist turn, in response to the challenges posed by the Anthropocene. On the other hand, the speaker of the poem *desires* her address to be corresponded and, with it, a proper end to her enduring dispossession. This ambivalence, however, points to an *aporia*. Can the *same* language and the *same* world that produced this dispossession in the first place become the place and the agent of its removal? Although I won't be able to pursue this question any further in this essay, it is this *aporia* which has animated my own return to Heidegger, Agamben, Wynter and de Burgos. Can "the human" be the answer to its own problem? Can *Dasein* – its proper language, its experience of death *as such*, its worlding movement – continue to function as the form of humanness that harbours the promise of a transformed humanity when its own *homo-logo-thanato-centric* strictures can and indeed often produce the very unworldliness and inhumanity that they are meant to counter? In its ambivalence, de Burgos's poem provides less an answer than a clarification of what is at stake in this question – a question that, to my mind, remains worthy of being asked, beyond any hope of finding a final answer.

NOTES

1. I borrow the figure of the eclipse from the following section from Derrida: "What interests me today is precisely the return of Heidegger and the return to Heidegger [...]. What I would call, without being sure of these words, the force, the necessity, but also the art of a thinking cannot be measured against the duration and permanence of its shining presence, it cannot be measured against the fixedness of a blaze, but against the amount of its eclipses. After each eclipse that this thinking is capable of enduring, it reappears again different as it emerges from the clouds, and the 'same' text, the same legacy is no longer the same, it turns on itself and surprises once again". Jacques Derrida, *Geschlecht III. Sexe, race, nation, humanité*, edited by Geoffrey Bennington, Katie Chenoweth, and Rodrigo Therezo (Paris: Seuil, 2018), 161–62. I am grateful to Ben Brewer for bringing this passage and its figure of the eclipse to my attention. I am also grateful to my colleagues, Natalie Belisle, for her vigilant and enthusiastic feedback on an earlier version of this chapter, and Zakiyyah Iman Jackson, for the many conversations about the intersections of post-humanism, black studies, and post-Heideggerian thought that inform this essay. Although all sources written in languages other than English are directly translated into that language in the body of the essay, I provide page references to the original. All translations are mine unless otherwise noted.

2. For a good overview of the history of the term "the linguistic turn" in philosophy, see Peter S. Hacker, "The Linguistic Turn in Analytic Philosophy", in *The Oxford Handbook of The History of Analytic Philosophy*, edited by Michael Barney (Oxford: Oxford UP, 2013), 926–47.

3. For some examples of Heidegger's use of this metaphor, see Martin Heidegger, *Der Satz vom Grund*, GA 10, edited by Petra Jaeger (Frankfurt am Main: Klostermann, 1997), 80–82.

4. For a helpful summary of debates in science surrounding the Anthropocene as a geological age, see Erle C. Ellis, *Anthropocene: A Very Short Introduction* (Oxford: Oxford UP, 2018).

5. Rosi Braidotti, "Posthuman Critical Theory", in *Journal of Posthuman Studies* 1.1 (2017), 9. For a more compelling take on what constitutes post-humanism, see

Cary Wolfe, "Introduction", in *What is Posthumanism?* (Minneapolis: University of Minnesota Press, 2010), xi–xxxiv.

6. See Martin Heidegger, *Einführung in die Metaphysik*, GA 40, edited by Petra Jaeger (Frankfurt am Main: Klostermann, 1983), 153–73.

7. I am here referring to the notion of *logocentrism* elaborated by Jacques Derrida, see Jacques Derrida, *De la grammatologie* (Paris: Minuit, 1967), 23.

8. On the notion of ipseitocracy at work in this essay, see Derrida, *Voyous: Deux essais sur la raison*, 30–32.

9. Martin Heidegger, *Unterwegs zur Sprache* (Stuttgart: Klett-Cotta, 1959), 215.

10. See the note about *Ereignis* in Heidegger, *Unterwegs zur Sprache*, 260.

11. Giorgio Agamben, *L'avventura* (Rome: nottetempo, 2015), 66–67.

12. For his reservations to the language of adventure, see Martin Heidegger, *Vorträge und Aufsätze* (Stuttgart: Neske, 1954), 64. Concerning anthropo–genesis, see Heidegger, "Der Brief über den Humanismus", in *Wegmarken* (Frankfurt am Main: Klostermann, 1967).

13. Agamben, *L'avventura*, 66.

14. Heidegger, *Unterwegs zur Sprache*, 261.

15. Pertaining the much-debated issue regarding both the sense and the legitimacy of this distinction, see the epilogue to Agamben, *Uso dei corpi* (Vicenza: Neri Pozza, 2014), 333–34.

16. Agamben, *L'avventura*, 66.

17. Agamben, *Homo Sacer. Il potere sovrano e la nuda vita* (Torino: Einaudi, 1995), 211.

18. Agamben, *Uso dei corpi*, 334.

19. In reading together Wynter and Agamben, I follow the steps of Alexander G. Weheliye, who turns to the work of Wynter and other Black feminist theorists in order to, among other things, shed light on the erasure of racialisation—and of blackness, more specifically—within the biopolitical frameworks of Michel Foucault and Agamben. See Alexander G. Weheliye, *Habeas Viscus: Racializing Assemblages, Biopolitics, and Black Feminist Theories of the Human* (Durham: Duke University Press, 2014). Although I agree with Weheliye, his argument does not change the fact that a Heideggerian approach to the irreducible link between language and the essencing of the human is at work in analogous ways in both Agamben and Wynter.

20. Martin Heidegger, *Grundbegriffe*, GA 51, edited by Petra Jaeger (Frankfurt am Main: Klostermann, 1981), 83–84.

21. Sylvia Wynter and Katherine McKittrick, "Unparalleled Catastrophe for Our Species? Or, To Give Humanness a Different Future: Conversations", in *Sylvia Wynter: Being Human as Praxis*, ed. Katherine McKittrick (Durham: Duke UP, 2015), 11.

22. Wynter and McKittrick, "Unparalleled Catastrophe", 22.

23. Wynter and McKittrick, "Unparalleled Catastrophe", 21.

24. Wynter and McKittrick, "Unparalleled Catastrophe", 21.

25. It is worth noting that Wynter quotes Fanon's text in the Charles Lam Markmann translation, which renders the French original "il s'agit de lâcher l'homme"

as "what is to be done is to set man free". Franz Fanon, *Œuvres* (Paris: La découverte, 2011), 64, and Fanon, *Black Skin, White Masks*, trans. Charles Lam Markmann (London: Pluto Press, 1986), 11. The Richard Philcox translation, however, is closer to the French since it renders the verb *lâcher* by "unleashing", translating the whole phrase thus: "the truth is we must unleash the man". Franz Fanon, *Black Skin, White Masks*, trans. Richard Philcox (New York: Grove Press, 1967), xiii. Both translations, however, fail to capture the ambivalence of the French verb *lâcher*, which can certainly mean "to set loose", "to unleash", or "to set free", but also is just as often used in the privative sense to convey the sense of "letting go" of something, of "taking leave" of it. My point is that Fanon could also be read here as insisting that it is "the human" or, more precisely, "Man", which must be abandoned, that it is both the man and the human which must be let go. Rather than freeing humanity, the task might be to free ourselves from the strictures of the human and its onto-political infrastructures. This is a possibility that neither Heidegger, nor Agamben or Wynter (nor Fanon himself for that matter, or at least much of the explicit intentions consigned in his writings), seem to be willing to take to its most extreme consequences. If Heidegger, Agamben, and Wynter have diagnosed the ontological problem that befalls upon human existence from its capture within modernity, these diagnoses are always offered for the sake of retrieving the possibility of being human from such a capture. There is therefore a profoundly humanist strand that subterraneously (or not so subterraneously) circumscribes their own anti-humanism and their radical critiques of Man within the broader task of retrieving the possibility of becoming *truly* human.

26. Heidegger, *Grundbegriffe*, GA 51, 84.
27. Wynter and McKittrick, "Unparalleled Catastrophe", 25.
28. Wynter and McKittrick, "Unparalleled Catastrophe", 63.
29. Wynter and McKittrick, "Unparalleled Catastrophe", 23.
30. For a discussion of what we might call the "double-bind" in which Heidegger puts modern sciences, caught up between the uncircumventability of the beings they must presuppose as their objects and these objects inaccessibility (as beings) for their theoretical methods, see Heidegger, *Vorträge und Aufsätze*, 57–63.
31. Wynter and McKittrick, "Unparalleled Catastrophe", 27–29.
32. Wynter and McKittrick, "Unparalleled Catastrophe", 31.
33. Martin Heidegger, *Holzwege* (Frankfurt am Main: Klostermann, 1950), 366.
34. See, in particular, "197. Dasein – Eigentum – *Selbstheit*" in Heidegger, GA 65: 319–21. I take the liberty of referring the reader to the article, "The Hidden Law of Selfhood: Reading Heidegger's Ipseity After Derrida's Hostipitality", co-authored with Benjamin Brewer and forthcoming in *Oxford Literary Review*, in which we propose a reading of Heidegger's thinking of *Selfhood* circa the 1930s-40s that develops Derrida's inchoate remarks in the first year of his *Hostipitalité* seminar regarding the possibility of translating Heidegger's thinking of *Selbsheit* as *ipseity*.
35. Heidegger, *Vorträge und Aufsätze*, 197.
36. Heidegger, *Unterwegs zur Sprache*, 215.
37. See Heidegger, *Über den Anfang*, GA 70, edited by Paola-Ludovika Coriando (Frankfurt am Main: Klostermann, 2005), 160–61, emphasis mine.

38. Heidegger, *Über den Anfang*, GA 70, 145–68.

39. Heidegger, *Über den Anfang*, GA 70, 162.

40. I am here referring to the key analyses of *Vorlaufen* or "running ahead" as the mode in which proper or authentic death is disclosed to *Dasein* as the possibility of the impossible. I am particularly interested in the question of death's *measurelessness*, its *Maßlos*-character: "In running ahead in this possibility [death] becomes 'always greater', that is to say, it reveals itself as such that no longer knows any measure at all, any more or less, meaning rather the possibility of the measureless impossibility of existence". See Martin Heidegger, *Sein und Zeit* (Tübingen: Niemeyer, 2006), 262. My reference to an exponentiation is meant here to indicate that the infinity of dyings to which the speaker in de Burgos's poem is submitted points to an excess that subtracts the experience of dying from the thinking of withdrawal that finds its support precisely in Heidegger's thinking of death and mortality, according to which the nothing that death harbors can always be taken as the very abyssal *unground* that *grounds* being's radical difference from beings. In the case of the passage quoted above, this appears when the measurelessness of the impossible becomes paired with possibility and indeed emerges as the nothing that vouches for possibility's ontological originarity with regards to actuality and, indeed, any possible realisation. Such a schema, I would argue, is the schema of ipseity, whereby even what knows no measure can secure existence's hold unto itself, unto its innermost proper possibilities. A death whose measurelessness exceeds the measureleness that nonetheless becomes the measure against which *Dasein* will measure itself is precisely what I think speaks in de Burgos's poem.

41. Julia de Burgos, *Obra poética I*, edited by Juan-Varela Portas de Orduña (Madrid: La Discreta, 2008), 196–97.

42. For two brief and illuminating readings of this poem, see Rubén Ríos Ávila, "Julia de Burgos y el instante doloroso del mundo", *Revista Casa de las Américas*, no. 240 (July–September), 93, and Mercedes López-Baralt, "El encuentro de la mujer y el río", in *A Julia de Burgos. Anthologie biligue*, edited by Françoise Morcillo (Paris: Indigo et Côté-Femmes, 2004), 241–42.

43. Heidegger, *Sein und Zeit*, 262.

44. Heidegger, *Sein und Zeit*, 263.

45. Werner Hamacher, "On the Right to Have Rights", trans. Ronald Mendoza-de Jesús, *New Centennial Review* 14, no. 2 (Fall 2014), 201.

Chapter 13

Lezama Lima and the Resurrection of the Image (An Ontological Enigma)

Mauricio González

To Bruno Mazzoldi

The dialogue of thinking and poetry between José Lezama Lima and Martin Heidegger is traversed by all sorts of asymmetric differences. Rough contemporaries (both died in 1976), Heidegger was probably unaware of Lezama's poetic ventures, whereas the Cuban author and co-founder of *Revista Orígenes* (1944–1956), younger by twenty years, was certainly aware of Heidegger's works or paths. Despite the scattered references and explicit or implicit allusions to Heideggerian motifs in his novels, essays and diaries, Lezama's degree of familiarity with the German thinker remains uncertain, though we can surmise that his access to Heidegger was probably mediated by the Spanish translations available at the time. Still, the self-educated erudite of the island of the *Estrella Solitaria* was not only aware of Heidegger's early presence and intensive reception in the Spanish speaking world,[1] he even contributed to this dissemination through his journal *Orígenes*.[2] However, the echoes that reached Latin-America's most progressive literary trends during the 1950's and 60's already involved a mixture of early and late Heideggerian motifs. If the distinction between "early" and "late" phases of an author is problematic, this is even more the case with the "Heidegger" that was stranded at the tropics, in a foreign world and language.

But the space of encounter we are looking for lies beyond the question of reception: it is not a matter of factual "influences", but of *confluences*. Written under the banner of Heidegger's *dictum* "higher than actuality stands *possibility*",[3] this chapter asks the following questions: How does this mixture of Heideggerian echoes resonate within the literary space of Lezama

Lima? How do their textual bodies enter into dialogue, even beyond the author's intentions? And to what extent can Heidegger's "topology of being" (*Topologie des Seins*) be said to encounter in the Cuban writer a radical tropic displacement?

In dialogue with Heidegger and other voices such as Blanchot, Benjamin, Kierkegaard and Schelling, this chapter focuses on the motif of "resurrection" as a key to Lezama's enigmatic ontology of the image.

HISTORY AND ANASTASIS

"Heidegger's affirmation, *man is a being-toward-death*, is overcome by another: *the poet is a causal being-toward-resurrection*".[4] This astonishing statement appears in the drafts of a lecture on *Paradiso* (1966), and it follows "as a consequence" from those "paths of the impossibility" that Lezama admittedly had been traversing in the last decades. This shift from the *ecstatic* mode of finite human existence (*Dasein*) to the *anastatic* mode of poetic existence constitutes a crucial trait of Lezama's poetics of the image. This same affirmation was advanced in his *Preludio a las Eras Imaginarias* (1958), where the reference to Heidegger's "being-toward-death" remains implicit:

> The poet is a causal being-toward-resurrection. The poem is the testimony or image of the causal being toward resurrection, verifiable when the *potens* of poetry, its possibility of creating in the infinitude, acts upon the continuum of the imaginary ages. Poetry makes itself visible, hypostatized in the imaginary ages, where one lives in the image – forerunning in the mirror – the substance of resurrection.[5]

By "imaginary ages", Lezama means the way the image exposes its own historical temporality. Traversing a diversity of registers (historiography, mythology, theology and philosophy), poetry makes itself visible by granting visibility to "the successive in the simultaneous"[6] within a continuum of imaginary ages (which include Egyptian, Greek, Chinese traditions, monarchism and others). In *A partir de la poesía* (1960), Lezama reaches his own historical present and with it a certain end of the world as image:

> The last imaginary age I am alluding to today is the infinite possibility, accompanied among us by José Martí [. . .] The Cuban revolution means that all negative spells [*conjuros*] have been decapitated [. . .] When the people [*pueblo*]

is inhabited by a living image, it gains the overabundance of resurrection. Martí, like the cursed Hernando de Soto, has been buried and unburied, until reaching his peace. Poverty's style, poverty's unheard-of possibilities have reached again, among us, an officiant plenitude.[7]

At the outbreak of the Cuban revolution, the *medium* of this insurrected "resurrection" is the "new spirit of an irradiant poverty". Lezama's discourse on "a most essential poverty" bears perplexing resemblances to Heidegger's remarks on 'the essence of poverty'. Delivered at another critical moment, in June 1945, Heidegger gave a talk where he seeks the 'basic tone' (*Grundton*) of the times in Hölderlin's phrase: "In us everything concentrates on the spiritual, we have become poor in order to become rich".[8] Deviating from Heidegger, Lezama's invocation to the *Ángel de la Jiribilla* discloses in poverty another spiritual richness: "We show the greatest amount of light that a people can show today on earth".[9] Its tone should not hide its underlying ambivalence: Lezama's initial fascination with the revolutionary regime was shadowed by the silent censorship that fell upon him during the next two decades, ending in complete isolation.

Yet, the revolutionary legacy in Lezama merges into another prominent heritage: the age of "catholic concepts: grace, charity, resurrection".[10] This double *ana-stasis* (revolution and resurrection) finds its *medium* of continuity in the *barroco Americano*: "the baroque among us was an *arte de la contraconquista*".[11] Without deepening here into it, Lezama's famous insight intimates in the baroque legacy the utmost emancipatory potential of the image.

But, the baroque imaginary that lurks behind Lezama's motif of resurrection does not prevent him from facing the highest demands of his poetics by writing against the grain of Heidegger's thinking. In his abovementioned lecture drafts, the demand to *overcome* "Heidegger's affirmation" is embedded in a history traversed by other "paths of the impossibility". Among them, Lezama hints at "Tertullian's phrase: it is credible because it is incredible: God's son died", which he immediately reverses into: "it is true because it is impossible: and after death he resurrected".[12] It is perhaps Kierkegaard's reprise of Tertullian's *credo quia absurdum* that gives Lezama the decisive *élan* for extracting an "infinite of possibility" out of the impossible. Resurrection names the experience of the impossible *in* the image: "The human impossibility to justify death enables this impossible to convert resurrection into a possible".[13]

As the site of the impossible, Lezama's resurrection is at once the condition of possibility of history and language. It exposes "an unknown space and an errant time",[14] the verbal time in exile "when writ*ing* the history/story of the resurrected". And it speaks an impossible language of resurrection, whose magnetic field inaugurates a play of decapitations. Thus, his poem *Doce de los Órficos* asks: *Can resurrection arrive in the conjugation of the verb, or, can the magnetic circle decapitate the ellipse?*

A NECROPHILOLOGICAL COMMUNITY
(ON POETIC RESISTANCE)

Always that defenselessness and trembling
when writing the (hi)story of the resurrected.

The pathos that speaks in these lines of another poem, Lezama's *Aguja de Diversos* recalls the lyrical pathos that speaks through Johannes de Silento's *Fear and Trembling*. In a similar way, the pathos of despair that awaits the reader at the entrance of Anti-Climacus' *Sickness unto Death* – "So Lazarus is dead, and yet this sickness is not unto death"[15] – reverberates in the event of resurrection that every act of reading *is*. According to Maurice Blanchot, to read is to say each time: *Lazarus, veni foras!* For him, the "miracle" of reading implies the uncanny experience of wanting to bring back to life a voice that is always already dead, to reawaken those "eyes that are already closed".[16] And it brings along the demand "to read what was never written".[17] There is "resurrection" at the core of legibility: an impossible awakening.

In the spirit of Kierkegaard's address to the mystical society of Συμπαρανεκρώμενοι,[18] let us call this dialogical event of reading a necrophilological community. The philological mode of "being-with" (*Mitsein*) while "being-with-the-without" (*Mit-ohne-Mit*) makes philology not only an eminent expression of what Heidegger calls "being-with the dead [*Mitsein mit dem Toten*]" (SZ §47, 238).[19] It is perhaps the very condition of sociability and of "being-with-the-living", without which these would "become asocial":

> Philology is *nekyia*, descent to the dead, *ad plures ire*. It joins the largest, strangest and always growing collective, and gives some of its language's life to this collective, to bring this underground to speech. She dies – philology, each philologist dies – in order to restore, for a while, the afterlife in language of one or another among this 'many.' Without philology, which socializes with the dead, the living would become asocial.[20]

In this sense, Lezama's "causal being-toward-resurrection" exposes a radical philological gesture. Indeed, he is not alone when considering resurrection as a site for overcoming "Heidegger's affirmation", but stands in prominent company. Let us first evoke Blanchot's testimony, as relayed by Jean-Luc Nancy:

The resurrection in question does not escape death, nor come out of it, nor dialecticise it. On the contrary, it forms the extremity and truth of death. It goes unto death, not to traverse it, but to deepen irremissibly into it, to resurrect *it*. [. . .] To resurrect death differs entirely [*tout à tout*] from resurrecting the dead.[21]

Lezama also moves at the verge of this subtle difference: for him, too, resurrection is the "extremity and truth of death", not its dialectical *Aufhebung*. Lezama also stands here in the company of Walter Benjamin, for whom "the unfinished work of the past" becomes truly graspable in the experience of *Eingedenken*: "What science has 'fixed' remembrance can modify", namely, not by denying the *factum* of death – "the dead are indeed dead"[22] – but by deepening into its mystery. Like Benjamin, Lezama is concerned with "resurrection" *in* the realm of the image.

But, what is meant here by image? Let us borrow for a moment the contrast Benjamin proposed around 1928 between image and expression. Departing from the fact that "language has a body and body has a language",[23] Benjamin takes Ludwig Klages' graphological concept of "expression" (*Ausdruck*) to indicate the body-stratum of language (*das Leibhafte an der Sprache*) – a similar concept might also be in the background of Lezama's *Expresión Americana*.[24] In contrast to "expression", Benjamin argues, the concept of "image" (*Bild*) defines rather the language-stratum of the body (*das Sprechende am Leib*). In this sense, "resurrection" can be considered an essential feature of the image, namely, of *its* body. If we say that the body resurrects (as image) insofar as there is language *in* it, then what we call "resurrection *of* the image" (in the double sense of the genitive) names precisely this astounding event: a body speaks. As an eminent philological event, "resurrection" ought to become one of the highest categories of any necrophilology to come.

Now, does not Lezama's *reino de la imagen* belong to the ontic sphere of (*existentiell*) literary testimonies, without any ontological (*existential*) import? However, as "pre-ontological testimony, whose probatory force is 'only historical'" (SZ §42, 197), his poetics of "resurrection" do not leave the *topos* of Heidegger's fundamental ontology untouched, but rather challenges its most crucial distinctions, beginning with that between *existenziell* and *existenzial*. Lezama's demand that man's "being-toward-death" be *overcome* by the poet's "being-toward-resurrection" proposes a chirurgical intervention on that phenomenological *corpus mysticum* which is the ontic-ontological constitution of existence. Indeed, Lezama's being-toward-resurrection deepens the abyss of existence by giving to read the ecstatic opening of 'being-there' (*Dasein*) *otherwise* than Heidegger does, plunging existence into a wholly different ontic realm of reverberation. This other 'here' (*da*) of readability is the body of the image, its *stasis*.

Decades after the publication of *Being and Time*, Heidegger recognises in the word *stasis* the germ that sprouts within the "*ecstatic* essence of existence":

> As strange as it sounds, the *stasis* of the ecstatic rests on the standing within the 'out' and the 'there' of unconcealment. [. . .] What the name *Existenz* gives to think [. . .] finds its most felicitous denomination in the word *Inständigkeit*. Therefore, we must think at once [. . .] the standing in the openness of being, the endurance of the standing within (care) and the perdurance in extremis (being-toward-death).[25]

In Lezama, this *stasis* germinates otherwise, giving birth to the *ana-stasis* of poetic existence. *Ana-stasis*, the Greek word for "resurrection", names the *stasis* of the image. Another poetic dwelling takes place in it, where things rest and resist out in the Open, enduring 'out' and 'there' (*'Aus' und 'Da'*) in their spectrality. Here, to *overcome* "Heidegger's affirmation" does not mean to oppose being-toward-death, but to linger in its *ecstatic* "perdurance *in* extremis" (*Ausdauern im Äußersten*). Moreover, it means to awaken out of it a resistance (*stasis*) of a wholly different order: a poetic resistance. "The resistance of the mule sows in the abyss, just like poetic duration sows resurging in the stellar. One, resists in the body, the other, resists in time".[26] The resurrection of the image says this two-fold resistance (*ana-stasis*): what properly resists in its body (the mule's endurance) *is* time (poetic duration). Not unlike Levinas' *ethical* resistance of the face, which exposes in the "total nudity of her eyes without defense" an "infinite stronger than death",[27] Lezama's *poetic* resistance refrains from opposing "death" with a greater force. Instead, its resurrecting *anastasis* decapitates "Death" with the *weak* force of language, while its speaking body captivates with Venusian belligerence. The *ana-stasis* of the image says the resistance of the rest, its *restance*.[28]

The opening statement of *A partir de la poesía* (1960) reads: "It is for me the first astonishment of poetry that, submerged in the prelogical world, it is never illogical".[29] Still being nourished by Heidegger's turn towards language in the mid-thirties, Lezama's "prelogical world" of the image virtually distorts the thinker's earlier conceptual distinctions. Opening an undecidable gap among modes of being, it discloses the objectivity of the object as the graceful "being before the eyes" (*ser ante los ojos*, as José Gaos translated in 1951 Heidegger's *Vorhandenheit*) and the tool's being ready-to-hand (*Zuhandenheit*) as the "wait for the other hand". Moreover, it lets the *Als-Struktur* be governed by the poetic laws of the "magnetic as" (*como magnético*) that already operate in language at the bestial and mineral – chthonic, Plutonic – layers of the λόγος σημαντικός. It distorts the "prelogical openness" (*vorlogische Offenheit*) that organises Heidegger's distinctions around 1929/1930, opening an ontological gap between the "world-imaging" (*Weltbilden*) character of the human, the "world-poverty" of the animal and "world-absence" of the stone: all of them find their *restitutio in integrum* in the world of image, as different degrees of plenitude or as different philological strata.[30] As a site of general translatability, such extended *Mitsein* of poetic resistance abides in the 'outside' of the image: it dwells *with* the voice of the animal, where "each word is a little animal that grabs and jumps".[31] It speaks *with* the mute language of the stone, whose speechless *Sprache des S(t)eins* reverberates through Lezama's "diamond-being without walls" (*ente diamante sin murallas*).[32] It gathers a necrophilological community as it speaks *with* the dead.

The realm of the image exhibits such an enormous sea or region of unlikeness (*regio dissimilitudinis*, ἀνομοιότητος τόπος or πόντον), that it turns Heidegger's abyssal ontic-ontological difference into a zone of diff*errance*, of an infinite erring in the "valley of splendor". Resurrection names the threshold of the image.

"BETWEEN DEATH AND DEATH": THE DIFF*ERRANCE*

The image as *medium* of resurrection is the interval "between death and death". It temporises in the mode of the *wait*: "The image extracts a gleam [*vislumbre*] from the enigma, whose lightning [*rayo*] we can penetrate or live at least waiting for resurrection".[33] If Lezama's resurrection comes to intercept Heidegger's mortal paths of existence, it is because for both of them "death" does not merely have the status of an actual (natural or empirical) event, but of its possibility. What he calls "resurrection" touches upon the extreme of death *as* possibility: the enigma that divides its event between the actual and the possible. The last canto of Lezama's poem *Aguja de diversos* touches upon it:

> How will they wait for the second death? That of dying
> his other death, already situated between death
> and the other death after the valley of splendor
> [. . .]
> always that defenselessness and tremor
> when writing the (hi)story of the resurrected.
> Does the resurrected dispose himself for his other death?
> [. . .]
> The resurrected already situated between death and death.[34]

This interstice "between death and death" (*entre la muerte y la muerte*) is the waiting space of the image. The anastatic interval that the poem names "valley of splendor" also gives shelter to the infinite trembling in Lezama's prose. With asthmatic breathing, his writing exposes that subtle difference: between "resurrecting death" and "resurrecting the dead;" between "history" and "story;" in Benjamin's terms, between the novel (the solitude of death) and narration (death as collective experience).[35] Let us recall Blanchot's exploration of this interstice:

> To die means: you are already dead, in an immemorial past, of a death that was never yours, which you therefore have neither known nor lived, but under whose menace you believe yourself to be called to live, waiting for it to come, constructing a future in order to render it finally possible, as something that will take place and belong to experience.[36]

One may locate the encounter between the author of *Paradiso* and Blanchot precisely in this uncanny interval: between the (immemorial) *facticity* of finitude and the *possibility* that detaches from it, Lezama's "wait for a second death". Already in 1967, Julio Cortázar described this distant encounter as prophesy to be fulfilled: "One day, which I suspect distant, this prodigious *Summa* [Lezama's *Paradiso*] will encounter its Maurice Blanchot, because the man who would delve into his fabulous larvae must be of such a kind [*raza, Geschlecht*]".[37] Such prophecy might be already fulfilled, if the virtual conversation between Lezama and Blanchot becomes readable as a response to Heidegger. According to the testimony of Tomás Eloy Martinez, Lezama is alleged to have said in a conversation:

> Heidegger holds that man is a being-toward-death; however, every poet creates resurrection, sings before death a victorious *hurra*. And whoever thinks I am exaggerating would fall prey to disasters, demons and infernal circles.[38]

Like Heidegger's being-toward-death, Lezama's being-toward-resurrection is not an act of recollection, but belongs to the orbit of what Kierkegaard calls "repetition" (*Gjentaelsen*): it recollects forward. However, if here the poet "sings before death a victorious *hurra*", its creation acts against the ground of disaster. In the track of Blanchot's *désastre*, resurrection means a revolt at the core of Heidegger's definition of death: it gives to read death as "the possibility of *its* impossibility" but in reverse, as a *genitivus subjectivus*. Resurrection means that stubborn resistance of "the impossible" at the core of the possibility of death, the repetition of a "past that was never present". It gives to read what was never written, the trace of that "nameless death, without phrase nor concept".[39]

If, for Heidegger, "*death* is uncovered as the *utmost, non-relational, unsurpassable possibility*" (SZ, 250), this utmost property of death (*eigenste*) is beyond all possession (*Besitz*). Due to its radically *irre*lational and *irre*misible character (*unbezüglich*), there is no power and no property rights upon death. Lezama's "resurrection" follows the maniac sign of this *Irre*: the errand-difference "between death and death" – its dif*ferrance*. If, for Heidegger, "death as possibility gives *Dasein* nothing to be 'actualised' [*gibt...nichts zu 'Verwirklichendes'*] and nothing that it could be itself as real [*Wirkliches*]" (SZ §53, 262), Lezama's resurrection of the image unpacks the poetic *gift* of death as "gift of nothing" (*nihil donans*). Opening that zone where "the *Jemeinigkeit* of death withdraws unto its *Jeandersheit*",[40] the image becomes a site of "retrospective causality", where the impossible retroactively creates "a possible act*ing* in the infinitude".

GNOSTIC SPACE OF WAITING

The entanglements of image and possibility, announced by the formula "the poet is a causal being-toward-resurrection", resolve into what Lezama calls *espacio gnóstico*. The end of *La expresión americana* famously depicts "the gnostic space that cognizes through its amplitude of landscape, through its *surplus* gifts [*dones sobrantes*]", while it gives shelter to a "nascent spirit". If its *sympathos* preferred to blossom in the American continent, rather than in Africa or Asia, this is because in these territories "the gnostic space awaited [*esperaba*] a kind of vegetative fecundation, where we find its delicacy allied to extension, and waited [*esperaba*] for grace to provide a suitable temperature for the reception of generative corpuscles".[41] Much has been said about the geo-political dimension of this "vegetative fecundation" and its significance for the Americanist discourse, but less about its underlying ontology. What sustains "the vegetative exigency of this gnostic space" is the remarkably *active*-passivity of its resistance and receptivity (*gestare*), in its most enigmatic feature: the wait.

The enigma of the gnostic space crystallises in *La imagen histórica* (1959), where image and possibility interweave under the sign of resurrection:

> The impossible, as it acts upon the possible, creates a possible acting in the infinitude [*el imposible, al actuar sobre el posible, crea un possible actuando en la infinitud*]. In the fear of that infinitude, the distance becomes creative, the gnostic space emerges, which is not the space that is seen [*el espacio mirado*], but the one that looks for the eyes of man as justification. Man has the nostalgia of a lost measure. The dead children, in the world of resurrection, that is, in that of the plenitude of the image, resuscitate as if they had reached their world

of plenitude. All that man knows is like an enigma, knowledge or ignorance of another hierarchy, of what he will fully acknowledge in death, but has the glimpse [*vislumbre*] that this enigma has a sense. The impossible, the absurd, create their possible, their reason. The impossibility of man to justify death enables this impossible to convert resurrection into a possible.[42]

This passage describes the gnostic space of the image as that "world of resurrection", where "the dead children [. . .] resuscitate *as if* they had reached the world of plenitude". But this "as if" (*como si*) is the index of a poetic *epokhē*: it puts the "world of plenitude" under reserve, the *proviso* of a wait. In its longing for a lost measure, the gnostic space of the image is not "the space that is seen" but an attuned spac*ing* beyond its mere geometric dimension. Noticing how "far we are from the Cartesian space", Lezama's lecture on *Possibility in the American Gnostic Space* (1959) characterises it as an "ultimate dimension":

There is an ultimate dimension in man, where the gnostic space is already granted to him, where the 'other sacredness' is turned favorable, where the invisible, the unreal and the infinite are in the search [*busca*] of their momentary transparency, of the sign in matter, or even of the possibility in the infinitude [. . .] To the extent that man becomes *more* the son of resurrection, he stands the *more* within the circle of the gnostic space.[43]

At the summit of this "more" that indicates an intensified presence, Lezama unfolds that "ultimate dimension in man", which grants the image its sublime measure, as he is confronted once again with the recurrent question: "How does the impossible operate upon the possible, organizing the kingdom of possibility in the infinite?" His oblique answer goes hand in hand with Heidegger and Pascal:

Heidegger's proviso: *neither is space in the subject, nor is the world in space.* Having reached this Heideggerian meditation, it suffices to feel the resonances of the words he uses—the living background of his dialectics—'*paraje*' and '*a la mano*', to notice that we are very far away from the Cartesian space. But let us not reach these extremities without recalling Pascal with tremor: *by space the universe embraces me, by thought I embrace it.*[44]

Lezama's gnostic space opens here an interstice between Pascal and Heidegger. While he seems to improvise a free version of Pascal's famous *Pensée* 113-348 (*Par l'espace l'univers me comprend et m'engloutit comme un point: par la pensée je le comprends*), "Heidegger's proviso" is *verbatim* a citation of *Sein und Zeit* (§24, 111) in José Gaos' Spanish translation.[45] In order to "superpose this negativity in the spatial to the anxious Pascalian situation", Lezama retrieves

Heidegger's gesture of exposing existential spatiality against the background of "the Cartesian 'world' as res extensa" (SZ §§18–21). Heidegger's *Räumlichkeit* is neither the objective space in the Cartesian sense of the *res extensa* as opposed to a world-less subject, the *"weltlose* res cogitans" (SZ, 211), nor is it the subjective space in the Kantian sense of the *a priori* condition of sensibility. If space here is a constituent of *Dasein*'s being-in-the-world, of its being *already* "spatial", this is because existential spatiality exposes a wholly different sense of the *a priori*. In Heidegger's terms:

> Apriority means here: the anteriority of the *encounter* of space (as zone [*Gegend, paraje*]) in the respective *encounter* of the at-hand [*Zuhandenen, a la mano*] in the surrounding world. (SZ, 111)

This could be the passage Lezama has in mind, when he listens to the resounding of the words *'paraje'* and *'a la mano.'* Let us leave here the *hand* that resounds in the *Zuhanden* ('*a la mano*') aside, along with "the enormous role that the hand plays in Heidegger"[46] and in Lezama. Instead, let us focus on Heidegger's *Gegend* ('*paraje*'). *Gegend* is here the zone of a redoubled "encounter within encounter" (. . . *Begegnen* . . . *(als Gegend)* . . .*im Begegnen*. . .). In this track, rather than a space that is merely seen, Lezama's gnostic space of the image retrieves this zone of encounter as *paraje-de-encuentro* (*Begegnen-Gegend, rencontre-contrée*). But, Lezama's *Gegend zumbón*[47] is nearly a step ahead of Heidegger's *Gegend*: it enacts the encounter by letting the distance (*Entfernung*) become creative. In its impassible-passivity, this haunt*ing* space becomes active by elevating a demand of justification: "not the space that is seen, but one that looks for the eyes of man as justification" (*no es el espacio mirado, sino el que busca los ojos del hombre como justificación*). What this gnostic space *seeks for* (*busca*) as justification (of its creation) is not the human mind, but rather its *eyes*: as if its very gaze were already a response to what they encountered. These eyes are themselves "sought" by what they meet, by that gnostic space that looks for them as it seeks to be rescued. Such is Lezama's dialectics of seeing, a return of the gaze as the *instant* (*Augen-Blick*) of resurrection in the world of the image. A passage of his novel *Oppiano Licario* (chap. 5) thus reads:

> Heidegger's expression *salir al encuentro* can only make sense [when] accompanied by another, *nos vienen a buscar*, the coincident instantaneity of both expressions is the *imago*.[48]

Oscillating in Heidegger's Spanish translations between *Entgegenkommen, Begegnen* and the *Begegnenlassen* of beings, the expression *salir al encuentro* belongs to the semantics of the *Gegend* (*paraje*) as sphere of encounter. However, José Gaos' 1951-translation of *Sein und Zeit* introduces an added *find-and-seek* element in the structure of encounter, as he persists in saving the literality of Heidegger's gesture. Challenging any easy readability,[49] Gaos rescues the "find" in the *Befindlichkeit* by translating the structure of mood or attunement in *Dasein* as "*el encontrarse*".[50] In its track, Lezama's gnostic space of the image is the *attuned* spacing, which comes across its paradigm in Pascal: "if the image were refused to man, he would be wholly unaware of resurrection. The image is the unceasing complement of the *entrevisto* and the *entreoído*, the dreadful Pascalian *entredeux* can be fulfilled only by the image".[51] This dreadful *entredeux*, along with Pascal's *attuned* spacing of the infinite as a silent tremor (*Le silence éternel de ces espaces infinis m'effraie*), reverberates in Lezama's passage quoted above: "In the fear of that infinitude, the distance becomes creative, the gnostic space emerges". Such creative distance is the space of the image. It opens up a zone of indistinction between fear and anxiety, where this distinction is *still* to be decided: whether it is "fear" before something *in* the world, or rather "anxiety" before *nothing* but the nude factum of existence (*die nackte 'Dass' im Nichts der Welt*), the uncanny being-in-the-world as "out-of-home" (*Unzuhause*)[52] and its silent call (SZ §40, 189; §57, 276). Lezama must have been attentive to those spaces of mortal dwelling in *Being and Time*, those "zones [*Gegenden*] of life and death [*parajes de vida o muerte*] that determine *Dasein*'s being-in-the-world", whose "premises [*Einrichtungen*], e.g. churches and graves, are laid according to sunrise and sunset" (SZ §22, 104). These refuges and sanctuaries are the index of an image-space that is "splintered" or "shattered into places" (*Der Raum ist die Plätze aufgesplittert*), what Gaos translates as a martyrised body made of membra disjecta and stigmata (*el espacio es hecho astillas en los sitios*).[53]

These attuned spaces of encounter are at once spaces of wait and counter-wait. As suggested by the nexus of *Gegen*, παρα- and *bei*, these *Gegenden* or *parajes* (a *plurale tantum*) surreptitiously let all apparent frontality mutate into laterality. Their lateral, rather than frontal, spacing of vicinity and distant-proximity (*Ent-fernung*) not only distorts the centrality of the "subject", announced by the play of the *bin-bei*.[54] It is "time" that is ultimately stripped of the *frontal* anticipation of a subject, exposed to its *lateral* temporising. The *offene Gegenden* of time are such spacings of a coming-to-presence, where *Gegen-wart* (παρ-όντος) is *An-wesen* (παρ-ουσία).[55] In its ecstatic (anastatic) "temporal root", Lezama's gnostic space exploits the counter-waiting (*Gegen-Warten*) of this coming-to-presence as the wait *for* the unexpectable: the "impossible" that converts "resurrection into a possible". It is the space of a wait without expectation, without an 'object' (*Gegenstand*) to be awaited, if – as we read in Heidegger – "as soon as we represent that which we wait for and bring it to stand [*zum Stehen bringen*] we don't wait anymore".[56] It is a wait whose object needs to be forgotten, if – as Blanchot puts it – "the wait commences when there is nothing more to wait for, not even the end of the wait".[57] Hence, Hamacher concludes, "before expectancy, there was wait" (*Vor der Erwartung war das Warten*), although "we wait in the element of the untimely, of time-withdrawal, of the not-wait".[58] This is also the space of philology, whose present stretches out the counter-wait of its wait at the verge of the word. Counter to all expectation, Lezama's gnostic space exhibits its utmost necrophilological stratum in the poetic *wait* of the unexpectable (resurrection). This zone (*Gegend, contrée, paraje*) of a 'wait' in the element of the untimely, next to the word and counter to all expectation, can be named by a word of the Dionysius Areopagite: παρ'ελπίδα. Here, the παρα- opens a zone counter to all expectation and hope (ἐλπίς): the "world of resurrection" temporises *ex tempore*, all-of-a-sudden (τὸ ἐξαίφνης), in a *súbito*.

GERM AND *REDUCTIO AD ESSENTIAM*

A key to Lezama's enigmatic ontology of the image can be sought in what he calls the "secret relation" between germ and poetic act: the germ-act.

> Germ, act, and then potency [*Germen, acto y después potencia*]. Possibility of the act, the act over a point and a point that resists. [. . .] There is in all of this an infinite possibility that the potency interprets and unfolds. The human act can reproduce the germ in nature and make poetry permanent through a secret relation between the germ and the act. It is a germ-act [*germen acto*] that man can achieve and reproduce [. . .] Through the entanglement of germ, act and potency, what I call imaginary ages and *sobrenaturaleza* forms new and unknown germs, acts and potencies.[59]

What does it mean for the creative act to shelter the *germ* of the possibility? Lezama's apriority of the act as germ of the *potens* (from which its potency blossoms and reproduces) recalls Schelling's ontological reversal (*Umkehrung*) of essence and existence, which crystallises in his late *Philosophy of Revelation* (1841/2).

Let us make a short detour through Schelling. If traditionally "negative philosophy" starts with the *quid* ('*what*,' *essentia, possibilitas*) in order to reach existence, "positive philosophy" now begins with the *quod* ('*that*'): the nude *factum* of "mere existence", whose *actus puro* is an absolute *prius* not preceded by any essence. Schelling calls into question the traditional ontological privilege of the essence over existence (which dominates from Aristotle to Hegel) by departing from the "immemorial being" (*unvordenkliches Sein*). Thus, it is not the possible (essence) what demands its actualisation (existence) – *possibilitas exigat existentiam* (Leibniz) –, but rather the immemorial *actus* of being that first potentialises its possibility and gives birth to its essence.

As it happens, a germ of Schelling's new *Potenzlehre* can be traced back to Caroline's death in 1809. In the wake of this shock, Schelling begins a new inquiry into the world of nature in its "transit to the world of spirits" (*Übergang in der Geisterwelt*). This led him to think of the entanglements of life–death–survival (*Fortdauern*) in parallel to the unfolding of the potencies. So, "we speak of the transit of the human *from* the first potency of his life *to* the second, namely, death".[60] According to its esoteric theological interpretation,[61] the path leading towards "resurrection" (life's third potency) goes through thinking "death" (its second potency) otherwise: not as separation of body and soul, but as *essentification*. However, this means that the immemorial *germ* of an "inner life" is already (intensively) seeded in the body. In *Clara*, a dialogue written under the sign of mourning and impregnated by Caroline's aura, that "spiritual side of the body" (*geistige Seite des Leibes*) is called "germ" (*Keim*): "So, she said, this spiritual form of the body must have already been present in the purely external one, too? / Yes, of course, I answered, but as a germ [*aber als Keim*]", so that "[d]eath, she said, is the liberation of the inner form of life [*Befreiung der inner Lebensgestalt*] from the external one, which keeps it oppressed".[62] In his Stuttgart-lessons (1810), Schelling traces further this intensive direction, arguing that the "death" of the body (at once a mortal *and* moral body) responds to an inborn-principle of spiritual contagion. If "the body [*Leib*] is the soil that hosts that seed [*jeden Samen annimmt*] in which good and evil can be sowed [*gesäetet*]", then it is the body what becomes infected (*inficirt, steckt*) by the spiritual agency of good or evil, not vice-versa. Thus,

> Death is not the separation [*Trennung*] of the spirit from the body, but of the element in the body that contradicts the spirit, thus the separation of the good from the evil and of the evil from the good (therefore, the remains are not called body [*Leib*] but corpse [*Leichnam*]). Hence, not a mere part but rather the whole of the human is immortal [*unsterblich*], according to its true [*wahren*] *Esse*; death is a *reductio ad essentiam*.[63]

Schelling compares this *reductio ad essentiam* to the chemical process of extracting the spirit or essence of a plant. Just like the extracted oil carries along all the force and life of the plant (he has here in mind Oetinger's experiments with the essential oil of Melissa) so that "the whole life of the plant survives [*fortdaure*] in this extract", analogously, in death, the body mutates into a new *essentificated physis*.[64] This does not mean that "natural life" is abandoned, but rather that it is elevated to a higher power by death's "spiritual life" and finally restored into the "natural-spiritual life" (*geistig-natürlichen Leben*) of resurrection. In it resonates once more Schelling's early postulate of an absolute identity between the spiritual *in* us and nature *out* of us; and with it, the insight according to which "nature is the visible spirit and spirit is the invisible nature".[65] (Lezama quotes this early passage in *La expresión americana*, while integrating Schelling's insight into his concept of "landscape" (*paisaje*), as the site where "nature makes friends with man" and with whom "that visible spirit loves to come into dialogue".)[66] In the Schellingian dialogue between nature and the world of spirits, "death" becomes precisely the *medium* of immortality: for immortal is not only a part (the soul) but of the "the whole of the human being". And it is also the *medium* of essentification of *being* as such, of universal restitution and salvation of all of what 'is' (both the good *and* the evil), since – as *Clara* says – the "germ of a higher life ought to be in each thing" (*der Keim eines höheren Lebens. . .in jedem Dinge sein sollte*). Thus, the "end of all things" bears for Schelling (counter to Kant) the germ of universal restitution: "And it is perhaps here where the question of the ἀποκατάστασις πάντων belongs".[67] Hence, what Schelling's eschatology describes as the "sequel of a universal – and at once moral – crisis" culminates in "the coming universal resurrection of the dead as resurrection of the flesh".[68] "Crisis" means here κρίνειν as in Plato's *Gorgias* (523e), 'to separate' – a *reductio ad essentiam*.

Various echoes of Schelling's "resurrection" can be discerned at the backdrop of Walter Benjamin. One of them, Benjamin presents as "a modest methodological proposal": the esoteric theologoumenon of a "historical *apocatastasis*" is a sort of *essentification* of historical life. Its critical moment is to be fulfilled by the gradual separation of the negative element in each epoch ('the vain,' 'retrograde' and 'extinct') from its positive side (the 'fertile,' 'vivid,' 'pregnant with future'), Benjamin adds, "and so on *in infinitum*, until the whole of the past is brought up into the present by a historical *apocatastasis*".[69] Such resurrection, however, crystallises in the "now" of the dialectical image. Allowing the past to reach the "now of its cognoscibility" and become readable by coming into a sudden constellation with the present, the image unfolds the germ of historical life instantly, in a lightning (*blitzhaft*). Not unlike the cinematic moment of his theses on history where "the true image of the past flits by", Benjamin's "historical *apocatastasis*" happens all-of-a-sudden, at an instant of danger.

A key to the ontological enigma of Lezama's resurrection of the image can be intimated, then, by its astonishing kinship to Benjamin and Schelling. Like Benjamin's "historical *apocatastasis*", Lezama's historical image embodies an intensified presence in the poetic act: here too, the germ of resurrection responds to the demand of readability that the past elevates upon the present; Lezama calls this critical instant of readability *el súbito*. Like Schelling's *reductio ad essentiam*, Lezama's poetic act volatilises the germ of its *potens* in the image like an essential oil, where it seeks that "slow evaporation of all what is true", its *aporroia*.[70]

HYPERTELIA: GROUND OF THE IMAGE

Why *causal* being-toward-resurrection? Why does Lezama interpose causality when turning Heidegger's being-toward-death into a *"ser* causal *para-la-resurrección"*? "Resurrection was the only end that could be waited for".[71] This *único final* indicates that Lezama's being-towards-resurrection is "causal" in the sense of a *telos, causa finalis*. At stake is the problem of the "ground" that supports the image. But, this causal ground (αἰτία) is teleological in a special sense. Lezama coins for it the word *hypertelic*.

> In reality, all support of the image is *hypertelic*, it goes beyond its finality, which it disregards [*la desconoce*], and offers the infinite surprise of what I've called the *ecstasy of participation* in the homogenous, an errant point, an image, by extension. [. . .] In some Asian cities, while passing from life to death, the dead body [*el muerto*] is not passed through the door, but a wall is broken, as to prepare him for *a new causality*.[72]

Its *hyper-* is the index of a teleological *excess*. This going "beyond its finality" brings Lezama's *hypertelia* in the proximity to the question Kierkegaard formulates in *Fear and Trembling*: "Is there a teleological suspension of the ethical?" If "by his act [Abraham] transgressed the ethical altogether and had a higher τελος outside it, in relation to which he suspended it",[73] such a transgressive suspension is still *teleo*logical. Retrospectively seen, it is as if Abraham's "wondrous act", by surpassing the *sittliche* finality (the universal) for the sake of higher τελος outside it, were preparing for a new causality. The *ethos* of the image also finds the ultimate ground and support of its *restance* in a teleological excess. This preparing for a new causality defines in *Paradiso* "the exercise of poetry" as "the verbal search of unknown finality, which carried on unfolding in him a strange perception for/through the words".[74]

A certain teleological excess figures already in Heidegger's phenomenological description of death: it "signifies the possibility of the measureless impossibility of existence".[75] The fact that, in "coming closer", death discloses itself as what "knows no measure [*kein Maß*], no more nor less", evokes the tone of Kant's sublime. But, the sublime measure of Heidegger's "measureless death" (*non-comparative magnum*) tends to grow in Lezama into a "cursed magnitude" (*cantidad hechizada*), haunted by "signs that scratched [*que arañaban*] negative quantities", "with what hides behind the moon full of the *less than zero*".[76] Here, the sublime combat between world and earth at the artwork's origin becomes that other "combat between causality and the unconditional".[77] Thus, Hölderlin's verse, *Is there a measure on earth?/No there is none* resonates here otherwise. Responding for the "nostalgia for a lost measure", Lezama's resurrection of the image exhibits the "dignity of poetry" as "the unconditional"[78] of another experience of freedom.

Like Heidegger's *Freiheit-zum-Tode*, Lezama's "*causal* being-toward-resurrection" radicalises Kant's causality-through-freedom. With a hyperbolic gesture that liberates the *telos* from all final constraint, this anastatic causality recalls Benjamin's formula of a "teleology without final purpose". Rather than exhibiting a formal purposiveness without material purpose (as in Kant's judgement upon the beautiful), Lezama's *hypertelia* is akin to the collision between the purposive and the counter-purposive that betrays the artwork's sublime origin (Heidegger's *Stoß ins Offene*).[79]

The "*hypertelic* support of the image" says an excess of life over itself. Its being-toward-resurrection "causes" the momentary suspension of all purposive expectancy of another world, for the sake of an extreme exposure of *this* world. Lezama's "world of resurrection" is, therefore, none other than *this* world in its excessive otherness, insofar as it is *already* other and otherwise than 'is'. Such an *altération du monde*[80] is the anastatic condition of the world of the image.

Let us consider how Lezama reads the nexus between finitude and guilt/debt (*Schuld*) at the ground of the image. Emerging amid a medium that recalls Benjamin's *Nebel der Schuld* and Cortázar's *barro de la culpa*, the ontological swamp of conscience evoked by Heidegger's "being-guilty" not only awakens in Lezama the fascination of the image, but betrays that ground-zero *from* which the image breaks free. Lezama's "resurrection" of the image is, in this sense, disenchantment and conjuration. A diary entry from 1957 gives testimony of this fascination:

> It seems to us very deep, in Heidegger, to join the concept of finitude to that of indebtedness [*culpabilidad = Schuldigsein*]. As soon as the *being feels finite*, it seems to ask: what have I killed? Whom have I destroyed? It lives like tightened, receiving a contradiction without exit wave, without participation in space.[81]

The aphonic call of conscience is here what first awakens the "uncanny fascination" for the image. This reverberates in a passage of *Paradiso* that describes those "Tibetan cities", whose impenetrable landscape names that which "supports the image" and is "the sole reality that comes to us":

Man knows he cannot penetrate those [Tibetan] cities, but there is in him the uncanny fascination for these images, which are the sole reality that comes to us, that bites us, leech that bites without a mouth, which, due to a completive way that supports the image [. . .] hurts us precisely with that of which it lacks. [82]

While this "leech" (*sanguijuela*) relates to blood as symbol of the naked life under the regime of guilt,[83] its "bite without a mouth" may relate to the silent call of conscience (*Gewissenbiss*). The fact that it "hurts us precisely with what it lacks" corresponds to what properly calls *in* Heidegger's call of conscience, namely: *nothing*. As call of nothing, at stake is here a sense of *Schuld* that is prior to all moral evaluation and to all ontic determination; it opens a zone of indistinction between "debt" and "guilt". While carrying the burden of the antique αἰτία in the double sense of "causality" – as *quaestio juris* and as *Ursache* (cause, reason, ground, etc.) – its "thing" (*causa, cosa, Sache*) lies beyond the horizon of ontic disputes (moral, legal and economic). *Schuldig* here means an ontological *being-*in-debt: the "debt" of beings to their be*ing* and ultimately to *No*-thing. If already "the character of the *No* underlies the idea of '*schuldig*'. . "., its formal indication opens in Heidegger the ontological abyss of a "being-ground" (*Grundsein*): "the formal existential idea of '*schuldig*' [is]: being ground for what is determined by its *No* – namely, *being-ground of a nihility*" (SZ §58, 283). A few pages later, he digs deeper into this indebting swamp of nothingness. Redefined as "annihilating *being*-ground of a nihility [*nichtiges Grund*sein *einer Nichtigkeit*]" (SZ §62, 305), Heidegger's *Schuldigsein* inadvertently touches upon another extremity of *this* world: that world-historical event we call "capitalism". According to Walter Benjamin, "capitalism" may designate a religion of its own: perhaps the first case of a "pure cult" not concerned with atonement anymore, but with the intensifying growth of guilt/debt; whose intrinsic tendency towards the universalisation of *Schuld* reaches the extreme point of "cosmic despair", when the only *hope* that remains consists in (its) God's "absolute indebtment" (*völlige Verschuldung Gottes*). Although Benjamin would doubtlessly line up Heidegger within the *Priesterschaft* of this cult (along with Nietzsche, Freud and Marx), Werner Hamacher reads the hyperbolic turn implied by Heidegger's "*being*-ground" as a paradoxical reversal that lays open an ontological precipice, where *Schuldigsein* meets its self-annihilation. For it is at this extreme point of implosion – where *being* is entirely indebted *to* itself – that its "nihility" annihilates all measure of debt/guilt and its ground comes-aground. Such a panic hope of self-implosive *Ent-schuldung* trembles at the ground of the image: *neither* ground/cause *nor* debt/guilt, the "irradiant poverty" (*pobreza irradiante*) that emerges out of it leaves room for a new grace – of what is *sine culpa et causa*.[84]

Lezama's *hypertelia* liberates this self-annihilating ground in the image, as its panic excess awakens attention to the *less than zero*. Herein lies the dignity of poetry: it rescues poetic existence from this abyssal swamp (*Sumpfwelt*) of finitude at the ground of being by bringing it back to life in the *ontic* realm of the image. Sublating "death" *as* penalty in the mythical order of *legal* justice, it allows the gift of death (the finite gift of being) to exceed all punitive dimension and become creative, by responding to the poetic demand of *lingual* justice. "The hypertelic [...] goes beyond its finality: creating, it gives death".[85] Resurrection names the gift of death *in* the image as teleological excess, a *nihil donans*. Here again: *Il faut prendre des leçons d'abîme!*[86]

CODA: ANOTHER HISTORY

However, not only the most progressive side of Heidegger's paths resounds in Lezama's *geo*poetics of the image. Also, the most regressive side does, particularly, his infamous jargon of authenticity and its dangerous political ontology (*Geist, Geschlecht, Geschick, Volk* as being-historical *a prioris*).[87] This constellation virtually reverberates at the end of *La expresión Americana*. The above-mentioned passage reads:

> The *sympathos* of that gnostic space is indebted to its legitimate ancestral world, it is a primitive that acknowledges, that inherits sins and curses, inserted in the forms of an agonizing knowledge, having to justify itself, paradoxically, with a nascent spirit. Why was western spirit not able to extend itself through Asia and Africa, while it indeed did in the Americas in its totality? Because that gnostic space was awaiting a kind of vegetative fecundation.[88]

It is not easy to assess the sympathetic character of notions such as *pueblo, spirit, primitive* and *ancestral world*. Without entering this discussion, once these motifs are framed within a "debt-history" (*Schuldgeschichte*), the question follows: how to grasp the emancipatory potential of Lezama's historical image, without falling prey to its own rhetoric? Lezama's "fables of authenticity and toxicomania" (Mazzoldi) demand further efforts of hypercritical reading, which could follow up on Derrida's project on philosophical nationalisms, by adding a chapter on the myth of "*Nuestr*américa": its rhetorical strategies and geo-philosophical implications, its dislocations and self-deconstructive movements (in Lezama and beyond). If "only the difficult is stimulating", then the critical question to be asked is not just the one that interrupts Heidegger's *Being and Time*: "Does *time* itself reveal itself as the horizon of *being*?" (SZ, 437), but whether the poetic *stimuli* coming from "such a difficult *time* as the tropical, where Saturn always decapitates Chronos", still speaks to us.[89] In other words, whether such a "difficult *time*" that deranges all horizon of *being* with a tropic decapitation, still challenges us to write another (hi)story-of-being – and what does it ultimately mean: being-*at*-the-tropics. Such is "the resistance that defies us".

Lezama's 1957-Americanist manifesto opens with a double difficulty. While a first difficulty concerns the "sense or encounter of a causality bestowed by historicist valuations", the second one is to attain a historic vision (*visión histórica*), namely, "the counterpoint or texture handed over by the *imago*, by the image partaking in history".[90] In its demand for another causality, a sort of formal irony traverses Lezama's historic vision that exerts upon the *topos* of "the proper" a subtle *tropic* displacement. To evoke *Clara*'s clairvoyant words: just like "the soul is surely not where she is, but where she loves",[91] the specter of auto(hetero)chthony that haunts Lezama's *espacio gnóstico americano* finds its conjuration in the resurrection of image. At its ghostly interstice, between the work of art and the work of mourning, this space is "already creative and operating directly upon man".[92] Hence, "if it is true that the ghost excites the unifying desire of rootling autochthony, in order to better let it go astray",[93] a self-deconstructive science of the *fantasmón* already "works through" Lezama's tropology of being.

NOTES

1. Very early, the interest in Heidegger's works spread all over the Spanish-speaking world. When José Gaos' translation of *Sein und Zeit* appeared in Mexico in 1951, translations of minor texts were already circulating – starting with Xubiri's *¿Qué es la metafísica?* (1933). Several other translations appeared during the 1950's and 1960's in Argentina, Chile, Peru, Venezuela, Colombia and elsewhere. See Andrea Cortés-Boussac, *Die Sprache bei Heidegger und die Rezeption seines Werkes in Lateinamerika* (PhD diss., Freie-Universität Berlin, 2005).

2. *Revista Orígenes* #22 hosted the first chapter of Lezama's novel *Paradiso*, accompanied by Humberto Piñera's Spanish version of Heidegger's "Einleitung zu Was ist Metaphysik?", see Martin Heidegger, "El Regreso al Fundamento de la Metafísica", *Orígenes. Revista de Arte y Literatura*, no. 22 (Habana: Verano, 1949), 3–9. For its expanded German version, see Martin Heidegger, *Wegmarken* (Frankfurt: Klostermann, 1976), 365 ff.

3. Martin Heidegger, *Sein und Zeit* (Tübingen: Max Niemeyer Verlag, 1971), 38. All translations from the Spanish, German and French into English are mine, unless otherwise specified.

4. José Lezama Lima, "Dossier: Apuntes para una conferencia sobre Paradiso", in *Paradiso* (Bogotá: Archivos-Unesco, 1988), 710: "Como consecuencia de lo anterior se supera la afirmación de Heidegger: el hombre es un *ser para la muerte*, por otra: el poeta es un *ser causal para la resurrección*".

5. José Lezama Lima, *Las eras imaginarias* (Caracas: Fundamentos, 1971), 30.

6. José Lezama Lima, *Diarios 1939-49/1956-58* (México: Era, 1994), 80.

7. José Lezama Lima, "A partir de la poesía", in *El reino de la imagen* (Caracas: Biblioteca Ayacucho, 2006), 434–35.

8. Martin Heidegger, "Die Armut", *Heidegger Studies* 10 (1994): 5–11.

9. Lezama, "A partir de la poesía", 436.

10. Lezama, "A partir de la poesía", 434.

11. José Lezama Lima, *La expresión americana* (México: FCE, 1993), 80.

12. Lezama, "Dossier", in *Paradiso*, 710.

13. José Lezama Lima, "Imagen histórica", in *Introducción a los vasos órficos* (Barcelona: Barral, 1971), 152. I'll return to this passage.

14. Lezama, "Confluencias", in *Introducción a los vasos órficos*, 258. On gerundive time, see Marcia Sá Cavalcante, *Time in Exile* (New York: University Press, 2020); also, Lezama, "Hai Kai en Gerundio", in *El reino de la imagen*, 168.

15. Søren Kierkegaard, *Sickness unto Death* (Princeton: University Press, 1980), 7.

16. Maurice Blanchot, *L'espace littéraire* (Paris: Gallimard, 1955), 258.

17. Blanchot, *L'espace littéraire*, 259: "Je veut *lire* ce qui n'est pourtant pas écrit". Hofmannsthal's *Was nie geschrieben wurde, lesen* is also a key to Benjamin's theory of readability.

18. Søren Kierkegaard, "Silhouettes", in *Either/Or I* (Princeton: University Press, 1987), 165 ff.

19. See Hans Ruin, *Being with the Dead* (Stanford: University press, 2018); Werner Hamcher, "D'avec: Mutations, Mutismes (ad Nancy)", in *Mit-ohne-Mit* (Berlin: Diaphanes, 2021); Marcia Sá Cavalcante, Jean-Luc Nancy, *Being-with-the-Without* (Stockholm: Axl-Books, 2013); Jacques Lezra, *On the Nature of Marx's Things: Translation as Necrophilology* (Fordham: University Press, 2018).

20. Werner Hamacher, *Was zu Sagen Bleibt* (Schupfart: Engeler Verlag, 2019), 68–69 (thesis '71' on philology).

21. Jean-Luc Nancy, "Résurrection de Blanchot", in *La Déclosion (Déconstruction du Christianisme, 1)* (Paris: Galilée, 2005), 135.

22. Benjamin, "Passagen-Werk", in *Gesammelte Schriften* V.1 (Frankfurt: Suhrkamp, 1991), 589.

23. Benjamin, "Anja und Georg Mendelssohn, *Der Mensch in der Handschrift*", in *GS*-III, 138.

24. Lezama, *Expresión americana*, 60, where Klages is mentioned.

25. Martin Heidegger, "Einleitung zu Was ist Metaphysik?" (1949), in *Wegmarken*, 374.

26. Lezama, "Confluencias", 269: "La resistencia del mulo siembra en el abismo, como la duración poética siembra resurgiendo en lo estelar. Uno, resiste en el cuerpo, otro, resiste en el tiempo…"

27. Emmanuel Lévinas, *Totalité et infini* (Paris: Kluwer Academic, 2006), 217.

28. Jacques Derrida, Bruno Mazzoldi, "Pocketsize Interview [1977]", in *Critical Inquiry* (trans. Tupac Cruz, 33/2, winter-2007), 382–84.

29. Lezama, "A partir de la Poesía", 420.

30. Martin Heidegger, *Grundbegriffe der Metaphysik*, GA 29/30 (Frankfurt: Klostermann, 2004), 498 ff. On the 'magnetic as,' see Lezama, "Confluencias", 259.

31. Lezama, *Paradiso* (Dossier), 729. For an impressive cabalistic reading of Lezama's *Paradiso*, see Einat Davidi, *Paradiso als Pardes* (Stuttgart: Fink, 2012).

32. Lezama, *Paradiso*, 353.

33. Lezama, "Imagen histórica", 157.

34. Lezama, "Aguja de Diversos", in *El reino de la imagen*, 102: "*¿Cómo esperarán la segunda muerte? La de morir / su otra muerte, ya situado entre la muerte / y la otra muerte después del valle del esplendor […] siempre aquella indefensión y temblor / al escribir la historia del resurrecto. / ¿El resurrecto se dispone a su otra muerte? […] El resurrecto situado ya entre la muerte y la muerte*".

For another reading, see Jaime Rodriguez-Matos. *Writing of the Formless* (New York: Fordham University Press, 2017), 82 ff.

35. Benjamin, "Der Erzähler", in *GS*-II.2, 456–58. In contrast to the novel, the fairytale presents another paradigm of resurrection (*Auferstehung*) as disenchantment (*Entzauberung*). Lezama's distant-proximity to Benjamin needs to be explored elsewhere.

36. Maurice Blanchot, *L'écriture du désastre* (Paris: Gallimard, 1980), 108.

37. Julio Cortázar, "Para llegar a Lezama", in *La vuelta al día en ochenta mundos, 2* (México: Siglo-XXI, 1967), 45.

38. José Lezama Lima, *Muerte del narciso. Antología Poética* (México: Era, 2008), 10.

39. Blanchot, *L'écriture du désastre*, 112.

40. Werner Hamacher, *Premises: Essays on Philosophy and Literature from Kant to Celan*, trans. Peter Fenves (Stanford: University Press, 1996), 34.

41. Lezama, *Expresión americana*, 179. See Gerhard Poppenberg, "Espacio gnóstico", in *Creole presence in the Caribbean and Latin-America*, ed. Phaf-Rheinberger (Frankfurt: Vervuert, 1996).

42. Lezama, "Imagen histórica", 152.

43. José Lezama Lima, *Imagen y posibilidad* (Habana: Letras Cubanas, 1981), 102.

44. Lezama Lima, *Imagen y posibilidad*, 102.

45. Martin Heidegger, *El ser y el tiempo,* trans. José Gaos (México: FCE, 1951 [1971]), 127.

46. Jacques Derrida, "La main de Heidegger (Geschlecht II)", in *Heidegger et la question* (Paris: Flammarion, 1990), 175 ff. No less monstrous is Lezama's "situation of the hand in the night": exposing the interplay between encounter and wait (*la espera de la otra mano*), "a weak voice … would tell me: stretch your hand and you will see how she is there, the night and its unknown hand.".. (Lezama, "Confluencias", 255).

47. Bruno Mazzoldi, *Fábulas de autenticidad III*. Bogotá (1994). Video: 24:36 mins. Last modified: 11-13-2011. https://www.youtube.com/watch?v=BFGs7icGjGg (On *Gegend zumbón*: min. 3:45).

48. José Lezama Lima, *Oppiano Licario* (Madrid: Alianza, 1983), 170. For an impressive reading as anastatic series of three resurrections; see Rosario Ferré, "Oppiano Licario o la resurrección por la imagen", in *Escritura: teoría y crítica literarias*, no. 2 (Caracas: jul.-dic.1976), 319–26.

49. In the prologue to his Spanish translation of *Sein und Zeit*, Jorge Rivera calls Gaos' translation "an incomprehensible galimatias". Based on a dubious philological myth, he criticises Gaos for turning "Heidegger's always vivid and eloquent language" into a "hirsute, rigid and somewhat esoteric language", whose phrasing is "convoluted and indecipherable". Lezama surely found in Gaos' baroque style something *more* than a mere "translation defect". See Martin Heidegger, *Ser y tiempo*, trans. Jorge Rivera (Santiago: Ed.Universitaria, 1997), 17.

50. Heidegger, *El ser y el tiempo,* trans. Gaos, 151 (SZ §29, 134).

51. Lezama, "Confluencias", 259.

52. See Mauricio González, *Fuera de casa o de la existencia impropia. Hacia otra lectura de* Ser y Tiempo (Bogotá: Uniandes, 2005).

53. Heidegger, *El ser y el tiempo,* trans. Gaos, 119.
54. "The expression '*bin*' is connected to '*bei*'. 'I am' means 'I dwell, I inhabit by'...the world" (SZ §12, 54).
55. Martin Heidegger, "Der Spruch des Anaximander", in *Holzwege* (Frankfurt: Klostermann, 2003), 346: "The Greeks call *pareónta* what is coming-to-presence [*das gegenwärtig Anwesende*]; παρα- means *bei*, the coming-by in the un-concealment. The '*gegen*' in *gegenwärtig* does not mean the *Gegenüber* of a subject, but the open zone [*offene Gegend*] of un-concealment".
56. Martin Heidegger, *Feldweg-Gespräche*, GA 77 (Frankfurt: Klostermann, 1995), 115–16.
57. Maurice Blanchot, "L'attente", in *Martin Heidegger zum siebzigsten Geburtstag: Festschrift* (Pfullingen: Neske, 1959), 217 (*Urfassung* of Blanchot's *L'attente, l'oubli,* 1962).
58. Hamacher, *Was zu Sagen Bleibt,* 179.
59. Lezama, "Confluencias", 260.
60. F.W. Schelling, *Stuttgarter Privatvorlesungen,* in Historische-Kritische-Ausgabe, Nachlass-8 (Stuttgart: Frommann-Holzboog, 2017), 168.
61. F.W. Schelling, *Philosophie der Offenbarung-II* (Darmstadt: WBG, 1959), 207–11. The 32nd lesson describes the path leading from (A^1) "present life" as free motion of unilateral-natural-life (*Seinkönnende*), through (A^2) "death" as immobility of unilateral-spiritual-life (*Seinmüssende* whose paradigm is Christ's *descensus ad inferos*), unto (A^3) "resurrection" as fulfilled spiritual-natural-life (*Seinsollende* where all unilaterality is overcome in absolute free motion).
62. F.W. Schelling, *Clara or on Nature's Connection to the Spirit World* (New York: State University Press, 2002), 40–41. This dialogue revolves around that "most intimate germ" (*allerinnerste Keim*) which is the "inner germ of life" (*innere Lebenskeim*) or "celestial life-germ" (*himmlische Lebenskeim*). It evokes Paul's germs, grains and seeds; see I. Cor. 15, 35–38.
63. Schelling, *Stuttgarter-Privatvorlesungen,* 172. See David-Farrell Krell, *Contagion. Sexuality, Disease and Death in German Idealism* (Indiana: University Press, 1998), 73–114, whose exploration focuses on Schelling's *Erste Entwurf* (1799).
64. Schelling, *Stuttgarter-Privatvorlesungen,* 172 and *Phil.Offenbarung-II,* 207. See Hartmut Rosenau, "Essentifikation", in *Schellings philosophische Anthropologie*, ed. J. Jantzen (Stuttgart- Bad-Cannstatt: Frommann-Holzboog, 2002), 51ff.
65. F. W. Schelling, *Schriften 1794-98* (Darmstadt: WBG, 1980), 380: "Die Natur soll der sichtbare Geist, der Geist die unsichtbare Natur seyn. *Hier* also, in der absoluten Identität des Geistes *in* uns und der Natur *außer* uns, muß sich das Problem, wie eine Natur außer uns möglich sey, auflösen".
66. Lezama, *Expresión americana,* 167. The *pathos* of a nature that "makes friends" (*amigada*) with man figures already in Schelling, *Clara,* 26: "Nature's... feeling for man is essentially one of friendship [*Freundschaft*] and often of sympathy". In contrast to Lezama's "valley of splendor", the "dialogue between man and the spirit" seeks here in Schelling another extension, the lake (*See*) as tranquil landscape of the soul (*Seele*): "The lake is an image of the past, eternal silence and isolation" (Schelling, *Clara,* 67).

67. Schelling, *Stuttgarter-Privatvorlesungen*, 185. In *Das Ende aller Dinge* (1794), Kant argues against the "unitarist" (Origenes' heretic doctrine), while taking sides (on dubious pragmatic grounds) for the orthodox "dualist" end of all things, according to which not *all* beings, but only a few will be saved.

68. Schelling, *Phil.Offenbarung-II*, 210.
69. Benjamin, *GS*-V.1, 573.
70. Lezama, *Paradiso*, 253.
71. Lezama, *Paradiso*, 331.
72. Lezama, "Confluencias", 260–61.
73. Søren Kierkegaard, *Fear and Trembling / Repetition*, trans. Howard & Edna Hong (New Jersey: Princeton University Press,1983), 56.
74. Lezama, *Paradiso*, 351.
75. Heidegger, *Sein und Zeit* §53, 262.
76. Lezama, "Confluencias", 266.
77. Lezama, *Eras imaginarias*, 21.
78. For another reading of Lezama's "unconditional" and Kant, see Juan-Pablo Lupi, *Reading anew. Lezama-Lima's Rhetorical Investigations* (Madrid: Vervuert, 2012).
79. Heidegger, *Holzwege*, 53. See Mauricio González, "El silencio de lo sublime en el *Origen de la obra de arte*", in *Heidegger. La experiencia del camino* (Barranquilla: Uninorte, 2009), 457 ff.
80. Nancy, *Déclosion*, 151.
81. Lezama, *Diarios*, 107.
82. Lezama, *Paradiso*, 354.
83. On the deep nexus between blood and guilt (*Schuld*), as manifestation of the mythical violence that underlies all governance in the legal world, see Benjamin, "Zur Kritik der Gewalt", in *GS*-II.1, 199–200.
84. Benjamin, *GS*-VI, 100–3; Werner Hamacher, "Schuldgeschichte", in *Kapitalismus als Religion* (Berlin: Kadmos, 2009), 209–10.
85. Lezama, *Paradiso*, 710.
86. Jules Verne, *Voyage au centre de la Terre* (VIII), cited by Cortázar, "Para llegar a Lezama". On *nihil donans*, see Hamacher, *Was zu sagen bleibt*, 65 (thesis '55' on philology). On legal and lingual justice, see Hamacher, *Sprachgerechtigkeit*, passim.
87. Derrida, *Heidegger et la question*, passim.
88. Lezama, *Expresión americana*, 179.
89. Lezama, *Expresión americana*, 49; Lezama, *Paradiso*, 324.
90. Lezama, *Expresión americana*, 49.
91. Schelling. *Clara*, 57.
92. Lezama, *Imagen y posibilidad*, 103.
93. Mazzoldi, *Fábulas de autenticidad III* (min. 12:18).

Chapter 14

The Boundary of Ontological Time and its Crossing

Shūzō Kuki's Analysis of Japanese Poetry as an Unrealised Dialogue with Heidegger

Yohei Kageyama

In his essay, *A Dialogue on Language*, Heidegger looked back on a dialogue with Shūzō Kuki (1888–1941), one of the representatives of modern Japanese philosophy who had studied in Freiburg for a short time. In this text, he discussed the differences between languages as "Houses of Being" and considered the conditions of a dialogue between human beings living through such differences. When he visited Heidegger, Kuki explained his interpretation of *iki*, a traditional understanding of beauty in Japan, in the vocabulary of Western philosophy. Even though profoundly intrigued by Kuki's explanations, Heidegger was concerned about the danger, that, through such a translation, Kuki may ruin the authentic experience of East Asian language and thought; a specific experience that makes its historicity different from that of the Western world. Heidegger asked another of his interlocutors from Japan, Tomio Tezuka, the German language scholar to explain how Japanese people experience their language, *Koto-Ba*.[1] With this explanation, Heidegger hoped to better grasp the difference between "Houses of Being" and bring out the essence (or, rather, the essencing) of the individual languages. As Being is typically considered all-encompassing and therefore bereft of a boundary, it is striking that Heidegger draws a distinction and marks a boundary between "Western" and "Eastern" (or "East Asian") forms of Being in this specific context.

In view of this boundary running through Being, Heidegger characterised human beings as *Grenzgänger*,[2] as border walkers or crossers, that is, as beings who can traverse this boundary by engaging in a dialogue with languages other than their own. The ontological relevance of this capacity lies in the fact that such crossing is understood as that which makes humans aware of their relationship with Being: Crossing this ontologico-linguistic boundary is thus a constitutive moment of human existence. While Being, for much of the history of Western philosophical thought, has been treated like Odysseus' ever-awaiting, readily available homeland, a genuine (home-) coming to Being now only becomes possible when humans transgress their own "house", and thus make visible and explicit its unique silhouette.[3] Against the background of Heidegger's considerations, the question arises how Kuki, standing on the other side of such an East–West boundary, thinks about the possibility and reality of existence as *Grenzgänger*.

Before we address this question in detail, it is necessary to indicate the philosophical constellation in which Kuki stood within Eastern, and especially, Japanese thought. Kuki belonged to the first generation of the so-called *Kyoto School*, the most important philosophical movement in modern Japan. The school was founded by Kitarō Nishida (1870–1945), who was primarily under the influence of Zen Buddhism, although he had intensively studied Western philosophers like Johann Gottlieb Fichte and William James. However, many of Nishida's successors, including Kuki visited Heidegger in Freiburg and Marburg, so that a number of *Kyoto School* philosophers stood amidst the tension between two philosophers with fundamentally different historical (in the sense of *geschichtlich*) horizons.[4] Kuki focused on specific microlevel phenomena of the Japanese life-world. While other thinkers affiliated with the school such as, for example, Tetsurō Watsuji (1889–1960) or Kiyoshi Miki (1897–1945), were more interested in an analysis of the public sphere, Kuki's philosophical investigations revolved around a lifestyle of *iki* and traditional poetry. Yet, all these thinkers relied more or less heavily on Heidegger's phenomenological account of time and space as the foundation of subjective experience.

In this chapter, I focus on Kuki's ontology of poetry to elucidate the way in which the phenomenon of *Grenzgänger* is approached in his philosophy. First, I discuss the problem of plurality as it emerges in his ontological analyses of time as the most fundamental horizon within which *Grenzgänger* can dwell (Section 1). Second, I consider how poetry can be seen as the paradigmatic activity, or rather, active comportment through which the *Grenzgänger* relates to this horizon (Section 2). Like Heidegger, Kuki not only interprets Being in terms of temporality, but also emphasises the significance of poetry as an active relationship that orients humans towards Being. Despite these broad affinities, I argue that Kuki recognisably differs from Heidegger's position while specifying the implications of both these points. Finally, I propose a hypothetical genealogy of *Grenzgänger* in contemporary Japanese thought and literature that has Kuki's analysis of poetry for its point of departure (Section 3). Grasping this point of departure is one of the first tasks at hand, if we hope to adequately explore and further develop the theme of "the poets and Heidegger" in the Japanese and East Asian contexts.

THE BOUNDARY OF ONTOLOGICAL TIME AS THE SITE OF DWELLING FOR *GRENZGÄNGER*

Kuki's philosophy of time encompasses two central dimensions. The first consists in a comparative approach that distinguishes Eastern from Western conceptions of time. When he studied in Paris, Kuki explained his ideas concerning this comparison in *The Notion of Time and Reprise of Time in the East* (1929) and in front of a European audience that included leading intellectual figures of the time, like Vladimir Jankélévitch and Alexandre Koyré. The second characteristic trait of his thinking on time is a systematic approach that provides a detailed critical analysis of both Heidegger's and Henri Bergson's accounts of time, which he exhibited in *The Problem of Time* (1929) and *Metaphysical Time* (1931). Both approaches investigate a fundamental notion of time, which Kuki referred to as "recurrent metaphysical time".[5] Contrary to everyday experience, this kind of time does not flow irreversibly from the past to the future. Rather, it is conceived of as "eternal return". This means that time is reversible insofar as in it, the same present indefinitely repeats itself.[6] Kuki explained this idea by focusing on successive events that take place in the material universe and that are connected according to the law of causality. As these events are causally related, they occur one after another qua cause and effect. According to Kuki, we are subjectively motivated to understand a passage of time that flows from the future to the past in such a successive relation of material universe. In other words, successive relations in the objective nature are ontologically prior to subjective experiences of flowing time.[7] Kuki then shifted his focus to the totality of this material universe. He argued that if the universe in its totality is itself not subject to any causal external influence (like, e.g., God's creation), the universe may partially change, but remain the same as a whole. Thus, at the root of the passage of time that can be experienced in the universe, there must be a temporality of the present that does not move or flow but, as Kuki suggests, rather stands still. This notion of a recurrent, stable present is a crucial alternative to Heidegger's account of time. For Kuki, the ecstatic unity of future, past and present laid out in *Being and Time* must be characterised as "horizontal", while his own idea of the recurrent present is "vertical".[8] Kuki called Heidegger's notion of time "horizontal" insofar as it elucidates the primordial background against which Dasein can exist as Being-in-the-World.[9] In contrast, Kuki focused on the ontic, but ontologically more fundamental materiality into which even the structure of Being-in-the-World is embedded, and tried to clarify how such materiality is given temporally. Such a temporal mode is "vertical", insofar as it essentially precedes Dasein's "horizontal" perspective. In other words, this vertical time is more fundamental than horizontal time as the succession of nature is always there and, in his analysis, is presupposed by all subjective experiences of horizontal time. This is what Kuki's criticism of Heidegger essentially comprises.

Kuki contrasted this primordial present as a crucial feature of Eastern time with Western time.[10] He did so although he knew well that Western philosophy, and in particular, the works of the Stoics, had repeatedly appreciated similar notions of a recurrent present.[11] This shows that he invented a boundary that had not existed before in any historically necessary, let alone natural, way. How can we make sense of and evaluate this invention? In my understanding, there are two major aspects to consider. First, Kuki's invention shows that he recognised the plurality of perspectives on the phenomenon of a primordial present. In contrast to an "occidental" attitude (reflected, e.g., in Heidegger's earlier thought) sceptical, neglectful or openly dismissive of admitting an "oriental" counterpart, Kuki thoroughly considered (or constructed) "the East", its notions of time and Being, in relation with the other, that is, "the West". Second, this construction of "East" and "West" as distinct is also a reflection of modern international politics: at least in part, Kuki's description of plural temporality unfolds in the framework of a historical constellation that is significantly shaped by power in the Foucauldian sense. However, for what precise reasons did Kuki speak of the plurality of a primordial present? As we are always situated in the primordial materiality whose temporal mode is the primordial present, it seems like we have no perspective other than the one from within this present – and this would render all talk of historically plural temporalities phenomenologically meaningless. So how can we justify *drawing the boundary between East and West in the primordial present*?

For Kuki, the crucial point is that perspectives from which we experience the primordial present cannot be homogenous and singular, but must be plural. Insofar as far as alterity, in both the interpersonal and intercultural spheres, is not merely a construct of the self, of *Dasein* in the Heideggerian sense, and the other is aware of and "has" her own existence, the self is always faced with someone else who is also standing in the primordial present, but occupying another vantage point and, consequently, has a perspective different from its own. As the self can never reach the perspective of the other, the present facticity of Being encompassing all reality can be accessed only through an irreducible plurality, however paradoxical this may sound. In his main work, *The Problem of Contingency* (1935), Kuki called this ontological plurality "the encounter of the independent two (*Dokuritsu-naru Nigen no Kaikou*)"[12] and considered it the fundamental element of his metaphysics of contingency.

This amounts to no more than a formal plurality of time that does not involve any substantial distinction between East and West yet. However, the legitimacy of Kuki's assumption concerning a specifically Eastern time can still be recognised. The point is that, as the divergence of the self and the other is founded on the paradoxical plurality of the primordial present, this temporal plurality must also constitute the basis for the various concrete boundaries drawn between "We" and "They" along the lines of gender, class, religion and nation. Insofar as such historical boundaries are gathered (*versammelt* in Heidegger's German) into this plurality, the primordial present may be characterised as the very relationship of the East and West as the encompassing horizon on and within which other boundaries can emerge and become significant. For instance, in *The Structure of "Iki"* (1930), Kuki took up the phenomenon of *Iki* as a sense of beauty peculiar to the Japanese life-world, and analysed it by distinguishing its three typical attitudes towards boundary: *Bitai* (allure) as sexual attraction that keeps distance; *Ikiji* (guts) as defiant self-assertion; and *Akirame* (resignation) as released acceptance of destiny.[13] As each of these attitudes stands for a type of intersubjective interaction between the self and the other, it typifies an existential attitude towards concrete boundaries such as gender or class. For Kuki, these three attitudes crystallise in the phenomenon of *Iki*, which symbolises the freedom of retrieving or reappropriating the historicity of the Japanese horizon.[14] While for Heidegger, such retrieving responses to Being are mainly undertaken by thinker (*Denker*) and poet (*Dichter*), the role of "poet" in Kuki's philosophy deserves further attention.

THE RELATIONSHIP BETWEEN "JAPANHOOD" AND "WORLDHOOD" IN THE PLAY OF RHYME

After returning to Japan, Kuki developed detailed analyses of poetry in works such as *The Rhyme of Japanese Poetry* (1935) and *Metaphysics of Literature* (1940). His guiding idea was rather simple: phonetic similarity of words in poetic rhymes is considered as a medium for responsively relating to the primordial present. Kuki wrote that by repeating the same sound, the rhyme "makes us tarry in the same present place" and "gathers us into an infinite moment of the eternal present".[15] This poetical thesis is supported by Kuki's abovementioned analysis of the plurality of the primordial present. Phonetic coincidence of words materialises, in his eyes, the encounter of plural perspectives on the primordial present. What, then, could be the significance of Kuki's metaphysical poetics with regard to the boundary of the temporality and historicity characterised in terms of the "East" and "West"?

One important thought concerns phonetic similarity in rhyme, that is, the material *Keitai*, the *Gestalt* of language.[16] An example is the following poem by Hōmei Iwano (1873–1920):

Ame ni nurete tachi*machi* / Kawaku ni hayaki ka*tachi* / Namida-moroki mono *niwa* / Sumai-yasuki kono *niwa*.[17]

In the phonetic coincidence of two unrelated words – such as *tachimachi* (moment) which rhymes with *katachi* (shapes), and of *niwa* (someone) with *niwa* (garden) – Kuki saw an "encounter of the two", that is, a responsive relation to the primordial present where beings with entirely different perspectives come in contact with one another: "The play of the rhyme", Kuki writes, "heightens the poetry up to freedom of the free art, gives existentiality of human beings to the language, and brings about the definitive decision for equivocality of disjunctive elements in the moment of the encounter".[18]

The point is to say that the phonetic material or *Gestalt* in the rhyme *subverts* the singularity of each present moment, while at the same time, it is precisely this subversion that enables the retrieval of the primordial present that is singular at each moment. To illustrate this beyond the rhyme *tachimachi/katachi*, there are countless other Japanese words – such as *hatachi* (20-years old), *hankachi* (handkerchief) or *hachi* (bee) – that are acoustically similar. One may also draw on foreign vocabularies and refer to the Korean term *Kkachi* (까치, magpie) or the English term "touch". Thanks to the possibility of arbitrarily establishing connections between phonetic signs and their semantic content, which intensifies the present experience by repetition of the *Gestalt* of a rhyme, the present moment must *a priori* be open to getting connected with completely different situations and contexts that make this moment transform itself. Being mediated by the *Gestalt* of language, the poetic response to the primordial present (or to Being) appropriates one's situation in a way that is always already open to that which is (and to those who are) other.

The equivocality of rhymes introduces the freedom of *playfulness* into our existential stance on the boundary of historicity. Kuki referred to this freedom as "the state of playful open-mindedness (*Kattatsu-Muge no Tenchi*)".[19] The very *Gestalt* of rhyme has an intrinsically playful character and thus draws boundaries where nothing was divided. At the same time, it manifests the contingency of such boundaries that can be redrawn and transformed in endless ways. In this sense, the rhyme can be considered a paradigmatic model of a responsive freedom in relation to historicity. It is therefore reminiscent of Heidegger's reflections on humans in their "free relation" (*freie Beziehung*) to technology, which emphasises an awareness of the contingent coming-into-existence of the late-modern technological world.[20] For both Kuki and

Heidegger, being aware of contingency lets us see the historical world in its openness. Kuki discussed this playful freedom in terms of the relationship between selfhood in the sense of *Nihon-sei* (Japanhood) and *Sekai-sei* (Worldhood). Against the claim made by modern Japanese critics of poetry to discard rhyme, Kuki proposed its rehabilitation and described the task of rehabilitation as follows: "Only when we accomplish this vocation, i.e., when Λόγος awakens as Μέλος, we will be qualified to assert to the world that Japan is 'the nation where the Soul of Words (*Kotodama*) flourishes'. Poetry must have awareness of Japanhood and Worldhood".[21]

According to this passage, on one hand, it is nothing but the rhyme that truly realises the ancient self-description of Japan, as the place where *Kotodama* flourished, by making explicit the historicity at the root of the nation's existence (a historicity that Heidegger typically addressed in terms of "the people", the "*Volk*"). In this sense, it is the rhyme that draws a boundary that demarcates "Japan", and thus, establishes an independent "house" or "home" to dwell in. On the other hand, the rhyme also makes this home of Japan continuous with and opens to outside nations and cultures: for its *Gestalt*, "Μέλος", can *a priori* be shared by any other, foreign language. Accordingly, it is a rhyme that manifests the arbitrariness of the boundary of "Japan" and opens it to the outside, that is, to "the world".[22] This playful and ambivalent freedom – both *for* and *from* the boundary – was also thematised in *The Structure of "Iki"*. There, Kuki described *Iki* as a form of "inconstant love" (*Uwaki-gokoro*) or "detached elegance" (*Tentan Shadatsu*) that expresses an essentially *unbounded* lifestyle within various contexts of the Japanese life-world.

A POSSIBLE GENEALOGY OF *GRENZGÄNGER* AND HIS "HOME" IN MODERN JAPANESE LITERATURE

In the introduction, we cursorily referred to the motif of *Grenzgänger* in philosophical definitions of being human. As we have just seen, this motif finds expression in Kuki's philosophy as the *playful freedom from and to the boundary between home and world*. How can we evaluate the theoretical potential of Kuki's approach, unfolded, among other things, in critical dialogue with Heidegger? In conclusion, I would like to propose the hypothesis that the meaning and appreciation of the figure of *Grenzgänger* in Japanese and East Asian culture and society has undergone dramatic changes since the pre-War period: the playful equilibrium theorised and championed by Kuki has given way to a collapse of the balance between home and world.

In sharp contrast to Aleksandr Dugin and other contemporary "right Heideggerians" who pursue an ontologico-political particularism against globalism,[23] Kuki stressed the importance of finding a balance between Japan and the world. For him, the universality of "the world" is neither substantial nor one that is limited to a specific community (like, e.g., in Hegel's *Sittlichkeit*). Instead, Kuki understood universality in terms of an existential attitude and corresponding actions that incessantly open themselves to the other without giving up their particular historical background and position. While this idea may well be relevant in the context of today's resurgent identity politics, we may still not be satisfied with merely pointing out the two-sided constitution of *Grenzgänger*. One reason for this dissatisfaction is the fact that the conditions in which the boundaries between the self and other, home and world must be (re-)identified, (re-)negotiated and (re-)drawn, are subject to constant change. Owing to such change, the meaning of *Grenzgänger* – as something that is essential to being human – must be reconsidered in concrete historical processes and situations.

In light of this, Kuki's advocacy for a playful equilibrium between Japan and the world (which, on the political level, was represented mainly by the liberal elites in the pre-War era) is, at least in part, the result of such concrete conditions. It reflects or is based on a leisured broad-mindedness that Kuki, a wealthy blue-blooded intellectual who died before Japan's defeat in the Second World War, experienced because of his unique positionality. The ease with which such broad-mindedness can be lost when poverty and military conflict loom, is evidenced by the fact that Kuki ideologically deployed and substantialised the notion of "Japan" in his article *Japanese Character* (1937), which reflected and largely conformed to the rise of nationalism and fascism in the 1930s.[24] Kuki's transformation of his ontological considerations on historicity was motivated by this specific political context – and, therefore, reveals striking similarities to the way in which Heidegger politicised his own philosophical thinking around the same time.

After 1945, ambivalent social tendencies coexisted in Japan: while post-War democracy rejected nationalism, it held on to the symbolic power of Tennoism. Under the impression of this uneasy, fragile balance that notoriously verged on imbalance, representative writers began to break up Kuki's playful equilibrium and committed to either one or the other of its constitutive poles.

For instance, Kōbō Abe (1924–1993) is a representative writer in post-War Japan who had been influenced by Heidegger in his youth and had begun his career after repatriation from the puppet state Manchuria where he had grown up. The central theme of his work was "exile from home". In his first published novel, *At the Guidepost at the End of the Road* (1948), Abe depicted a Japanese man who was taken captive by Chinese guerrillas as a figure of uncompromising rejection of "home" in the Heideggerian sense. The novel's protagonist says: "Humans can leave the home where they grew up. However, they can never be unrelated to it. The same is the case with the home of Being. I thus tried to run away infinitely, just like a road mirage".²⁵ This "I" expresses Abe's perspective on being at home. The metaphor of the road mirage shows that exile from home, Japan, is not equivalent to a move towards some substantial destination. Rather, enduring in Manchuria as the historical boundary of Japan reveals the fictional character of home. Yet, the passage addressing the protagonist's evasion of his origin suggests that he is forever bound by the home from which he tried to escape.

Here, we can recognise a limit situation (*Grenzsituation*) for humans as *Grenzgänger*. While Kuki allowed for "Japan" as the home to have substantial content, which is demarcated by the rhyme, Abe radicalised the reformation of the boundary by spelling it out as "exile from home" so that, ultimately, home became an illusion with no content other than "something to escape from". The style of existence is not defined by living at home, but rather by facing and enduring the world at the boundary of home. In Kuki's terms, this means that the "unbounded" element of playfulness becomes its own end once its substantial content is lost. Abe subsequently developed the same theme further, for example, in the motif of the "city" where strangers gather (see *The Frontier Within*, 1971) or of the "nuclear shelter" where exiles are lodged in the technological age (see *The Arc Sakura*, 1984).

In sharp contrast, Yukio Mishima (1925–1970), another influential writer, who committed traditional Japanese *hara-kiri* after a failed conservative coup he had supported, emphasised the "bounded" element in his literary engagement with the question of home. In *Silk and Insight* (1964), he told the story of the young post-War Japanese businessman Okano who had once been a student of Heidegger and, more generally, had studied the Western intellectual tradition. Okano battled with an old entrepreneur, Komazawa, who represented the traditional patriarchal spirit. In the end, Okano won the battle but, faced with the death of Komazawa, found himself haunted by the shadow of tradition. His attempt to gain independence, that is, at a *Grenzgang*, ironically produced an illusional, yet powerful ideal of "home" – it even resulted in an obsession with this unattainable ideal. The narrative ended with the following account of Okano's thoughts.

> While Komazawa was still alive, he had a distant and trifling personality whom Okano would never take seriously. However, his death suddenly made Komazawa eerily universal, something like a bad scent that seeps into everything in daily life, both inside and outside Okano.²⁶

Mishima's study of Heidegger underlies these descriptions. According to Keiji Shimauchi, Mishima carefully read *Is Heidegger a Nihilist?* (1953) by Masaaki Kosaka, a leading figure in the second generation of the *Kyoto*

School, and underlined the following passage in Heidegger's *Andenken* (1943) translated by Kosaka:[27]

> In order to appropriate what is own (*das Eigene*) ["the flame from heaven"], the Greeks have to go through what is alien (*das Fremde*). That is *the clarity of depiction*. [...] Through what is alien to them, the cool self-restraint, what is own first becomes the property for the Greeks.[28]

Following Heidegger, Kosaka insisted that Japan also needed to appropriate what was truly its own by encountering and experiencing the Occident as the alien.[29] In *Silk and Insight*, Okano as Mishima's alter ego, engaged in an appropriative project of this kind while meditating on Heidegger's philosophy (which, ironically, understands itself in terms of the "destruction" of the Western philosophical tradition). However, as a result, Mishima came to depict an ironic humanity that, by the attempt of *Grenzgang* to establish a free relationship with home, constantly created an illusion of home and made this an obsession despite the awareness of its fictionality. In Kuki's words, there remains only "Japanhood" demarcated by the play that binds humans, though, as the product of the play, it has no objective substance. In my reading, Mishima later elaborated on this imprisonment in an illusion as the central theme of "nothing happens", which was present in his writing until *The Decay of the Angel* (1971), his final literary work.

In my understanding, these two conflicting, yet inseparably entangled existential attitudes, *anonymous exile from home* on the one hand and *obsessive attachment to (the illusion of) home* on the other, continue to exert a strong influence on contemporary Japanese society as a whole. In conclusion, I suggest the possibility of giving an integrated interpretation of today's Japanese society and its specific "humanity" on the ground of this ambiguous, even conflicted style of existence in relation to home. More concretely, one can set out to interpret the experiences of humans who draw and cross the boundaries that define the contours of the Japanese life-world (such as Koreans in Japan, the Ainu or people of Okinawa) as well as phenomena like the history of imperialism and Tennoism or the amendment of a pacifist constitution in light of this profound ambiguity. For such an endeavour, the symbolic power provided by the literary works discussed above can help us better grasp the variety of such experiences and phenomena within this life-world in an integrated manner. Therefore, tracing the genealogy of "the poets and Heidegger" in Japan, that is, the specific literary context in which this influence is prominently addressed and negotiated, would not serve as a guide to attaining the *Heimat* of existence. Rather, such a genealogy would show the uncertainty, confusion and even embarrassment that surround questions of home, exile and the possibility of an existence in the mode of *Grenzgänger*.

Kuki's philosophical texts, some of which have been examined here, provide an indispensable basis for an in-depth theoretical, systematic analysis of this genealogy.

NOTES

1. See Martin Heidegger, *Unterwegs zur Sprache* [1959] (Stuttgart: Klett-Cotta, 1985), 143.

2. Heidegger, *Sprache*, 137.

3. An ambivalent attitude toward the figure of *Grenzgänger* in its relationship to the boundary cannot only be found in Heidegger's speculations but also characterises, albeit in significantly differing and unique registers, Jacques Derrida's ontological account of animals, Judith Butler's analyses of sexual difference, and Seyla Benhabib's considerations on the nation-state under conditions of migration.

4. This tension also resonates in Japan's experience of modernisation since the Meiji restoration in 1868. After the preceding Edo period, in which Japan had shut out diplomatic relations with Western countries, the encounter with Western modern civilisation forced Japanese society to consider the relationship between its own tradition and the West.

5. My translation; see Shūzō Kuki. 1931/2016. "Metaphysical Time" [1931], in Kuki, *Human Beings*
   and Existence (Tokyo: Iwanami, 2016, in Japanese), 208.

6. Kuki, "Metaphysical Time", 213.

7. A strikingly similar argument is made by Paul Ricœur; see Paul Ricœur, *Temps et Récit. Tome III, Le Temps Raconté* (Paris : Seuil, 1985).

8. See Kuki, "Metaphysical Time", 209.

9. See Martin Heidegger, *Sein und Zeit* [1927] (Tübingen: Max Niemeyer, 2006), 365.

10. See Shūzō Kuki, "The Notion of Time and Reprise of Time in the East" [1929], in Kuki, *On Time* (Tokyo: Iwanami, 2016, in Japanese), 9.

11. Kuki, "Notion of Time", 14; Kuki referred to a fragment of Nemesius contained in *The Fragments of the Early Stoics* edited by Hans von Arnim. In this fragment (no. 625), Nemesius described the Stoic notion of periodic return as follows: "Each person such as Socrates and Plato will emerge again with the same friends and fellow people, experience and do the same thing. All the states, the villages and the fields will return likewise". See: Hans von Arnim, *Stoicorum Veterum Fragmenta Vol.II.* [1903] (Stuttgart: Teubner, 1979).

12. My translation; see Shūzō Kuki, *The Problem of Contingency* [1935] (Tokyo: Iwanami, 2015 in Japanese), 277.

13. See Shūzō Kuki, *The Structure of 'Iki'* [1930] (Tokyo: Iwanami, 2016, in Japanese), 32.

14. Kuki, *Structure of 'Iki'*, 106f.

15. My translation; see Shūzō Kuki, "Metaphysics of Literature" [1940], in Kuki, *On Time* (Tokyo: Iwanami, 2016, in Japanese), 164.

16. See Shūzō Kuki, "The Rhyme of Japanese Poetry" [1931], in Kuki, *Collected Works Vol. 4*. (Tokyo: Iwanami, 2011, in Japanese), 444, 448.

17. Translated into English, the poem reads thus: "The moment the rain wets the shapes, / they dry right away. / If you're easily moved to sweep, / this garden makes you feel at ease".

18. Kuki, "Japanese Poetry", 231.

19. Kuki, "Japanese Poetry", 449. My translation.

20. See Martin Heidegger, "Die Frage nach der Technik", in *Gesamtausgabe (GA)* 7, ed. Friedrich von Herrmann (Frankfurt a.M.: Vittorio Klostermann, 2000), 7.

21. My translation; see Kuki, "Japanese Poetry", 449.

22. See Kuki, "Japanese Poetry", 448.

23. See, for example, Aleksandr Dugin, *Die Vierte Politische Theorie* (London: Arktos, 2013).

24. See Shūzō Kuki, "Japanese Character" [1937], in Kuki, *Human Beings and Existence* (Tokyo: Iwanami, 2016, in Japanese).

25. My translation; see Kōbō Abe, *At the Guidepost at the End of the Road* [1948] (Tokyo: Shinchō-sha, 1975, in Japanese), 15.

26. See Yukio Mishima, *Silk and Insight* [1964] (Tokyo: Shinchō-sha, 1987, in Japanese), 358. My translation.

27. See Keiji Shimauchi, "Elucidation of Lights and Shadows of 'Silk and Insight'", in *Bulletin of Denki-Tsūshin University* 18, 1/2 (2006, in Japanese): 127–75, here 171.

28. See Martin Heidegger "'Andenken'" [1943], in Heidegger, *Erläuterungn zu Hölderins Dichtung*, ed. Friedrich von Herrmann (Frankfurt a.M.: Vittorio Klostermann, 1996), 87.

29. Shimauchi, "Elucidation", 172.

Chapter 15

Heidegger and Russian Revolutionary Nonsense

Jeff Love

Nonsense is always revolutionary: it returns us to the origins of sense. As Martin Heidegger noted in one of his more daring lecture courses, "the original and genuine relation to the beginning is the revolutionary".[1] Likewise, the Russian poets who created Russian futurism sought a revolution in language that could return to the beginning, not only of the Russian language, but of all languages. There is no question of influence here: Heidegger became well known only after the futurists had ceased to play any role in the Soviet literary scene, and his work, for obvious political reasons, did not make a deep impression in the Soviet Union.[2] Yet, there is a powerful affinity between Heidegger's thought on language and the most radical experiments of the futurists, an affinity even more intriguing given that the political orientations of the futurists and Heidegger seem to be profoundly opposed.

In this chapter, I want to examine revolution and language within the terms of the poetic experiments of the futurists and important aspects of Heidegger's thought about language. Specifically, Heidegger makes two claims about language that provide the foundation for the chapter: 1) that language originates in silence; 2) that grammar is an interpretation of language and not one of its "inherent" qualities. In this respect, we may speak of a "grammatical" attitude to language that looks to it as a system with a clear purpose and structure. Like Heidegger, the futurists explore silence and put in question the grammatical attitude with arguably the most extreme and philosophically interesting experiments in language of the twentieth century, perhaps exceeding those of the Dadaists and surrealists as well as Gertrude Stein's experiments in prose.[3]

I set out my discussion in three parts. In the first, I give a brief account of Heidegger's two central claims. In the second, I develop these claims with reference to the poetic practice of two Russian poets, Alexei Kruchenykh (1886–1968) and Velimir Khlebnikov (1885–1922). In the third, I ask the question as to how apparently similar approaches to language inform opposed approaches to politics or to the role of poetry in political life.

HEIDEGGER'S SILENCE

In his lecture course on Friedrich Hölderlin's hymns, *Germania* and *The Rhine*, Heidegger makes the following crucial statement:

> If we were to reflect philosophically still further back here regarding the essence and origin of language as originary poetizing, we would have to recognize that language itself has its origin in silence. It is first in silence that something such as "beyng" must have gathered itself, so as then to be spoken out as "world". That silence preceding the world is more powerful than all human powers. No human being alone ever invented language – that is, was alone strong enough to rupture the sway of that silence, unless under the compulsion of the God. We humans are always already thrown into a spoken and enunciated discourse, and can then be silent only in drawing back from such discourse, and even this seldom succeeds.[4]

Heidegger emphasises that language has an origin. Language is not eternal, not a "given" that cannot be altered. To the contrary, a language emerges from what would appear to be utterly other or different from it, a difference recognised only through language itself. The mere act of reflecting on the origin of language is a curious (indeed groundless) one since language cannot reveal or think what is wholly other than it. The reflection on silence in language – and no other reflection is possible – loses its quarry in attempting to gain it. It follows that language cannot adequately express or grasp or understand its own origin. Thus, any construction of the origin must fail or, what is perhaps worse, must turn us away from the origin while attempting to turn to it. In this particular respect, the silence preceding the word must be "more powerful than all human powers": it is infinitely powerful, thus infinitely and absolutely inscrutable.

I want to pause a moment to consider the basic problem Heidegger's claim creates. If turning to the origin is at once necessarily a turning away from it, then all reflection on the origin, as such, is impossible: the origin of language, silence, remains in itself unspeakable and unknowable. Since the origin of language is inaccessible to language, there is no way to give an identity to that origin, to find a foundation in it. The conclusion to draw from this is quite stark: there is no "correct" or fundamental language; there are only languages, none of which can successfully grasp itself fully. For, to grasp itself fully, any language would have to be able to grasp its origin. More sharply put, a language, as a construct, is only that, a construct that has perhaps no other virtue than that of diverting us away from its origin. Language cannot only not speak silence; it conceals silence in a fundamental and irremediable way. If Heidegger suggests that we can only be silent in "drawing back" from discourse, it appears that even such silence is impossible or merely a faint "echo" of that original silence.

This thinking has at least one extremely far-reaching implication: no one account of language or a given language can be adequate. The opacity of the origin points to an implacable opacity. To put the matter in different terms, the incapacity to grasp the act of creation itself, the fact that language is *given* to and not made by us, renders us incapable of understanding language itself or, more precisely, renders any interpretation of language suspect as a way of approaching language that seeks to conceal or "rectify" our fundamental incapacity.

I use the term "rectify" here in reference to another point Heidegger makes in connection with truth. Heidegger famously differentiates truth and "correctness", asserting that what we typically take to be truth is correctness, a standard that conceals its origin in some sort of original disclosure.[5] This original disclosure is the moment of truth; that is, the moment of encounter with what is in the "open" that becomes concealed as soon as the disclosure becomes normative, designating something *as* something.[6] The truth is in this intriguing sense what is necessarily not a "what", not an identity or object, but that which is free of identity or, to return to the thread of our discussion, the origin. When Heidegger states baldly, as he does in *The Essence of Truth*, that "the essence of truth reveals itself as freedom", he alludes to the necessary, fundamental and irremediable inscrutability of truth.[7] Nothing is true: there are only truths which are in the strongest sense clichés concealing their own contingency. They are, like all understanding it would seem, merely ways of making up the furniture of the world. This does not mean these ways are completely arbitrary – on the contrary, they are dictated by what appears to be our need to "humanize" what we encounter, to turn the "earth" into "a world" whose principal purpose is the preservation and extension of life.[8]

Yet, even the world we produce, its grammar remains only a way of approaching the unapproachable, of responding to silence. This is the second claim Heidegger makes regarding language that is relevant for our present purpose. According to Heidegger, grammar is an interpretation of language, the dominant one:

The dominant approach to individual languages and to language in general is passed on to us through what we call grammar. By this we understand the theory of the elements, structures, and rules for structures in a language; separate groups of sentences, individual sentences, and sentence types; analyzed into groups of words, individual words; words into syllables and letters, γράμμα. Hence the name.[9]

But this interpretation can only be inadequate. Its inadequacy stems from the fact that language is unable fully to grasp its origin. At best, grammar can be only a means of concealing the inadequacy of language to grasp or elucidate its own origin. The corollary is that the more the grammatical (and logical) interpretation of language gains ascendance, the farther language wanders from its origin and from the basic problem the origin reveals; namely, the incapacity of language to explain or elucidate itself:

> Grammar dominates the manner in which language is represented. And with this arises the more or less explicit representation of language as if it were primarily and properly the verbal expression of thinking in the sense of the theoretical observation and discussion of things.
>
> One easily sees that this is *a monstrous violation of what language accomplishes*; consider a poem or a living conversation between human beings: the tone of voice, the cadence, the melody of the sentences, the rhythm, and so on.[10]

Here, poetry enters as a kind of language that can reverse or undermine the process of rigidification created by the grammatical interpretation of language. Heidegger insists on this transformation of the grammatical interpretation – he insists on revolution:

> Wherever a more originary relation to language still stirs, one feels how dead these grammatical forms are as mere mechanisms. Language and the study of language have gotten stuck in these rigid forms as if in a net of steel. Beginning with the spiritless and barren language instruction in the schoolroom, these formal concepts and grammar-book labels become empty shells for us, understood and understandable by no one...the first thing we need is a real revolution in our relation to language.[11]

Poetry is one step towards such a revolution – poetry is inherently revolutionary because it estranges. Indeed, one of the most important voices in the early theorisation of the poetic practice of Kruchenykh and

Khlebnikov, Viktor Shklovsky, emphasised the estranging quality of their poetic experiments, their capacity to free language from the deadening "spiritless" everyday or *byt*.[12] By focusing on estrangement, Shklovsky sought to emphasise that the poetic experiments of Kruchenykh and Khlebnikov forced their audience to question not only their understanding of poetry, but also of language itself. Within Heidegger's terms, at least as I have sketched them out thus far, this estrangement is in a sense an act of homecoming as well. It is an act of homecoming, however, in a distinctive sense.

In *On the Essence of Truth*, Heidegger repeatedly refers to the importance of "letting beings be" as an essential condition of possibility for our coming closer to the truth.[13] Truly to come home, truly to come close to the origin, whether understood as truth or silence, is at the same time a way or practice of letting beings be. Yet, how can language allow us to let beings be? As I noted above, normativisation is attached to the preservation of life, our life. We look at things as such largely in terms of their relation to our survival, whether a thing is harmful or beneficial, whether a thing helps us to confront or deter threats to our wellbeing or indeed may do damage to or obliterate it. We are not neutral to things, not indifferent to them, nor can we be completely indifferent since we are not gods: our potential death hangs over us as a goad and threat. In this respect, language often succumbs to utility – it becomes a means of communication, a transparent grammar and logic that facilitates the preservation and enhancement of our being, of our life.[14]

To the extent we can ignore the relation to things that emerges primarily from the needs they satisfy, we begin to see things not as they are for us, as objects to be used or feared, but rather from a much broader perspective as things that should not be interpreted primarily by reference to their relation to the preservation of our life. Language understood not as simply useful, as a tool, is language that brings us much closer to all things and to the original silence that is the highest expression of the freedom from utility – language that proves of no use at all is in fact language that is most likely to change our isolation by opening us up to the risks inherent in letting go of utilitarian considerations. By this, I mean something akin to Kruchenykh's and Khlebnikov's "transense" language that has nothing to do with sense or reference or utility – this is a language equivalent to abstract painting: it represents nothing, it is the pure play of sound, syntax and variability in form itself, creation purified by its freedom from utility. In a complicated sense (to be discussed below), this creation appears as a sort of universal or private language – as madness – as a language that moves beyond sense as the principal attribute of language.

ZAUM' OR TRANSENSE OR BEYONSENSE

Like most aspects of Russian futurism, the term *zaum'* is controversial.[15] The word is itself a neologism formed by combining the preposition "za" with the noun "um". The preposition is highly polysemic: it can mean "for" or "behind" or "at" or "beyond". "Um" is the noun denoting mind or intelligence. The most readily accepted basic translation of the noun "*zaum'*" is "transsense" or "beyonsense", meaning in the specific poetic context a language that is not wholly governed by sense or logic. Kruchenykh writes: "The word (and its components, the sounds) is not simply a truncated thought, not simply logic, it is first of all the transrational (irrational parts, mystical and aesthetic)".[16] But, the notion of being beyond reason or irrational is not helpful in conveying the range of meanings for the term. Suffice it to say for the moment that *zaum'* is a kind of speech that seeks to liberate language from the tyranny of logic or its obligation to "convey" thoughts, to be language only as the language of (useful) thought. Both Kruchenykh and Khlebnikov (as well as others associated with them) sought to liberate language from its tutelage to grammar and logic: for both, the task of poetic art was emancipatory on the most basic level – that of language as such and not merely as useful.[17]

Let me return to Heidegger for a moment to stress an important point that connects linguistic experimentation with a broader questioning of normativity and a narrower questioning of normativity as consisting in the grammatical interpretation of language. It is surely not an overstatement to suggest that the most thoroughgoing normativity to which we are exposed is language itself. I may disobey the laws of the land and be subjected to various kinds of punishments; I may act in a way counter to a given morality and be subjected to various kinds of punishments. Breaking the laws of language is of a wholly different order. For if I choose not to obey the basic patterns of language accepted by a given language community I risk the most radical kind of exclusion. If I refuse to speak as others, to use the same basic patterns as they, I become totally isolated, unable to ask or understand. Even supposing that I can still understand others in my language community, if I refuse to speak following the norms of the given language, I shall remain alone and appear to be mad, to be speaking in tongues or "nonsense".

The poetic experimentation with language is thus a very serious matter because it not only puts in question poetic norms, but moral and political ones. Experimentation in language threatens the language community – or any kind of community – to the extent the experimentation has no objective other than to negate or defy the most basic unifying code in any community, language itself. There is indeed nothing more fundamental and necessary for a community than language as the very basis for its functioning. The political dimension, thus, of Krunchenykh's theoretical stance and poetic practice should be kept in mind as we return to discuss *zaum'*.

Zaum' as a challenge to language took many forms: distortion of phonetic rules, syntax and word-formation (neologisms). Let us take one of the most daring and well-known examples, a poem Kruchenykh published in his collection *Pomada* in 1913. I present both the Russian text and an English version:

Dyr bul shchyl
ubeshchur
skum
vy so bu
r l ez

[Дыр бул щыл
убещур
скум
вы со бу
р л эз]

The poem contains but three readily recognisable standard Russian words, "*vy*", which is the formal or plural "you", and "*dyr*", which can be the genitive plural form of the noun "*dyra*" meaning a "hole", and, finally, "*so*" which can be the preposition "with" before certain consonant combinations. The pronoun is not followed by a recognisable verb, the subject of the genitive is, if anything, a contraction for the Russian word for "boulevard", borrowed from French, and the preposition is not followed by a noun. Several words may echo or parody other Russian words ("*ubeshchur*" may seem to be a distortion of "*abazhur*", a word borrowed from French meaning "lampshade"), but such connections are tenuous. Still others, like "*Shchyl*", have no meaning in Russian, the "word" (for it still follows the typical consonant–vowel–consonant structure of Russian nouns) featuring a combination not allowed by Russian phonetics or spelling rules. The poem also features a progressive dissolution of standard word formation, the final line resembling perhaps nothing so much as the text for an eye examination.

While the poem has given rise to a variety of interpretations or attempts at explanation or elucidation (or even translation) on various levels, it is well to consider what such attempts at interpretation or elucidation seek to do. The obvious problem here is that explanation, interpretation and elucidation all seek to clarify what is obscure or, more precisely, to translate into the language of thought (of the grammatical attitude) what may be poorly, obscurely or cunningly expressed (as thought) such that explanation, interpretation and elucidation become necessary. All these means of approaching a text merely seek to establish a way of translating it into the language of thought so as to master it, so as to eliminate what may seem incapable of being mastered. Yet, in a way that is far more radical than ostensibly "aporetic" or "paradoxical" texts (for both aporias and paradoxes form part of the language of thought), this text brings into question language as thought, as a kind of translation into thought, by means of explanation, interpretation and elucidation, of what is recalcitrant to thought.

There is, however, another aspect to the poem that accentuates its daring. While there exist what may be called translations of the poem, the question that arises here is whether translation, as such, is in fact a possible approach. If, indeed, the poem cannot be translated into the language of thought, then it would seem scarcely possible to translate it into another language without defacing its challenge to the language of thought. One may argue in fact that one of the most interesting aspects of the poem is that it remains equally, or almost equally, devoid of sense (from the point of view of the language of thought) in any language. To be sure, there are Russian letters and sounds that may not exist in other languages, but they do not necessarily render the poem unavailable to anyone from any language group. The point is that, if there is no governing logic to the poem, nothing accessible by translation into the logic of any language, then the poem may indeed be close to universal to the extent its sounds can be imitated. This universality, whether limited or limitable is negative only; it has to do with the relatively simple fact that the resistance of the poem to the language of thought is a kind of silence. I say a "kind" of silence because the poem is obviously not silent in the most basic aural sense, though it is silent in the sense that it offers little or nothing to the language of thought.

Even the notion of indeterminacy that can be connected with the poem is problematic to the degree determinacy means, first and foremost, logical and grammatical clarity and precision. The "dream" of the logician, that the ambiguities of natural language be abolished, runs aground on this poem or results in dismissal of the poem as nonsense or as something trivial, a child's prank.

Khlebnikov's work is in this respect arguably more accessible. Khlebnikov developed an ample theoretical armature with which to justify his experimentation within the language of thought. If Kruchenykh remains, at his most radical, on a fringe, Khlebnikov offers rather more for the adepts of explanation, interpretation and elucidation. Khlebnikov is certainly no Thermidor, but he shrinks back from Kruchenykh's daring. He does so primarily by grounding his experimentation in a search for some sort of

Ursprache, an origin, accessible to all. If Kruchenykh takes us to silence or an origin by way of negation, Khlebnikov takes a *via positiva*.

I start with one of Khlebnikov's most famous poems from 1909:

Incantation by Laughter
Hlaha! Uthlofan, lauflings!
Hlaha! Ufhlofan, lauflings!
Who lawghen with lafe, who hlaehen lewchly,
Hlaha! Ufhlofan hlouly!
Hlaha! Hloufish lauflings lafe uf beloght lauchalorum! Hlaha!
    Loufenish lauflings lafe, hlohan utlaufly! Lawfen, lawfen,
Hloh, hlouh, hlou! Luifekin, luifekin,
Hlofeningum, hlofeningum.
Hlaha! Uthlofan, lauflings!
Hlaha! Ufhlofan, lauflings!

[ЗАКЛЯТИЕ СМЕХОМ
О, рассмейтесь, смехачи!
О, засмейтесь, смехачи!
Что смеются смехами, что смеянствуют смеяльно,
О, засмейтесь усмеяльно!
О, рассмешищ надсмеяльных- смех усмейных смехачей! О, иссмейся рассмеяльно, смех надсмейных смеячей! Смейево, смейево,
Усмей, осмей,
Смешики, смешики,
Смеюнчики, смеюнчики.
О, рассмейтесь, смехачи!
О, засмейтесь, смехачи!]

I offer here a simpler translation:

O laugh it up, laughers!
O laugh away, laughers!
That laugh laughter, that laughalot laughingly
O laugh away, laugherishly
O laughedupness of the onlaugherish – laughter of laughtingly laughers! O laugh
    out laugherishly, laughter
Of onlaughing laughelers! Laughely, laughely,
Laugh at, laugh around
Laughenners, laughenners.
O laugh it up, laughers!
O laugh away, laughers![18]

The two translations, one by Paul Schmidt, the other my own, amply demonstrate the problem. Khlebnikov creates a series of variations on the basic Russian root *smekh-* having to do with laughter. While Khlebnikov maintains many of the standard grammatical features of Russian, his play with the root structure is extensive and unconventional – the elaborate play with the word root and the sound qualities of the root modification outweigh the sense of the poem understood in the manner of the language of thought. To be sure, here the language of thought gives way to aural composition, the pure play of sound, to language more as creating a kind of verbal music where sense is invested more in sound and morphological variation than in the transmission of thought. Exactly what the term "sense" can mean when taken apart from the grammatical attitude to language precisely as the language of thought turns into a pressing question – does not any approach to this kind of sense end up translating it into a conventional logic of some kind?

Khlebnikov was open to this temptation, and his experiments sought ultimately to peel away confusing diversity in favour of a return to a universal language. *Incantation by Laughter* in fact gives a good example *in nuce* of what Khlebnikov in his later theoretical essays would turn into a theory of universal language. Here, the root *smekh-* grounds a striking diversity that is, however, unified by the grounding meaning of the root. Similarly, Khlebnikov in his later theoretical writings tries to give to certain sounds an essential identity that they relate to what we may call conceptual or affective archetypes which may appear in all languages. He writes, characteristically, in the programmatic essay, *Our Fundamentals*:

> Beyonsense language means language situated beyond the boundaries of ordinary reason, just as we say "beyond the river" or "beyond the sea". Beyonsense language is used in charms and incantations, where it dominates and displaces the language of sense, and this shows that it has a special power over human consciousness, a special right to exist alongside the language of reason. But there does in fact exist a way to make beyonsense language intelligible to reason.
>
> If we take any given word, say *chashka* [cup], we have no way of knowing what each separate sound means in terms of the whole word. But if we take every word that begins with the sound *ch* – *chasha, cherep, chan, chulok,* etc. [cup, skull, vat, stocking] – then the common meaning that all these words share will also be the meaning of *ch,* and the remaining letters in each word will cancel each other out. If we compare these words beginning with *ch,* we see that they all mean "one body that encases or envelopes another"; *ch* therefore means case or envelope. Thus does beyonsense language enter the realm of sense. It

constitutes itself a game based on an alphabet that we have postulated – a new art form – and upon its threshold we now stand.

Beyonsense language is based on two premises:

1. The initial consonant of a simple word governs all the rest – it commands the remaining letters.
2. Words that begin with an identical consonant share some identical meaning; it is as if they were drawn from various directions to a single point in the mind.

thus *ch* is not merely a sound, *ch* is a name, an indivisible unit of language. If it turns out that *ch* has an identical meaning in all languages, then the problem of a universal language is solved; all types of footgear will be known as foot-*che,* all types of cups as water-*che.* That is clear and simple.[19]

Hence, Khlebnikov's approach to *zaum'* is quite different from Kruchenykh's. If the former sought ultimately to discover a set of positive universals or archetypes, the latter tends to put the emphasis on the absence of such universals or on silence as the only universal. To put the matter in language used often in reference to Heidegger, Khlebnikov endeavours to bring us closer to the origins of language, not to silence, however, but to certain simple sounds and forms. Kruchenych, to the contrary, is from this perspective perhaps far more radical: where Khlebnikov sees basic forms, Kruchenykh sees the absence of form, an ever recalcitrant silence.

This oscillation appears in Heidegger too. Heidegger's manipulation of German roots is well-known, and it sometimes seems that he, by utilising root variations, is attempting to do something similar to Khlebnikov. There is thus an appearance or nod to basic kinds of experience that are reflected in language in a way that does not necessarily lend itself easily to the grammatical attitude. Yet, if language emerges from a primordial silence, how can these basic kinds of experience be possible? For, if the origin is truly inscrutable, and necessarily so, how can we claim that the language which emerges from it shows definite forms of experience? Of course we may be able to say this in regard to one language, with its inevitably particular history and development, but we cannot declare anything to be a rule across different languages as Khlebnikov seeks to do. There is, in this respect, no universality across different languages – the only universal in the Heideggerian sense would have to be the horizon set by one's own language, and this is a radically different proposition from the one advanced by Khlebnikov.

THE UNIVERSAL

Here, we have two opposing notions of universality that interrogate the notion of universality itself. On the one hand, we have Khlebnikov's notion of a sort of universal *Ursprache*, a collection of basic sonic elements that ground similar structures of sense in different languages. On the other hand, we have the notion that our language is universal in the sense that it prescribes the limits of our world and of the structures that emerge in that world. This universal undermines the other as other because it establishes a basic line of demarcation whereby I can only understand the other in terms that come from my own world. This line of demarcation prohibits the position Khlebnikov takes by definition. Kruchenykh's position seems to take yet another tack, that of the negative universal, that the only universal is silence or absence of a universal.

If we put these positions within a broader political context, we can see how Khlebnikov's universalism supports the kind of universalism largely condemned nowadays for its associations with a tyrannical enlightenment. Yet, the ostensive universalism of a given language community is equally tyrannical, for the other can only exist within the terms set within that language community. Since, in this latter case, there is no third party who can judge as to the accuracy of the representation of one language community in the language of another, all broader universalism is clearly impossible. The final position (Kruchenykh) simply dispenses with the universal other than to consider the universal as absence, the absence of the universal itself, the tyranny of the unknowable and unspeakable.

Perhaps, the most interesting result of these approaches is to bring to light the difference between what we may refer to as a positive universal, having two different forms, one transcendent of any given language community, the other immanent in and relative to that community and a negative universal that performs the role of negating any attempt to establish a positive universal, whether transcendent or immanent. If we may align Khlebnikov with the transcendent view and Kruchenykh with the negative universal, Heidegger appears, once again, as more complicated. Heidegger expresses aspects of all three positions, sometimes appearing to make claims that would seem to apply to all thinking whereas it is more consistent of him to restrict his comments to Western thinking. Moreover, the "essential" inscrutability of Being as such also tends to affirm the negative universal – thus, no matter what Heidegger claims, that claim cannot take on universal force or authority. In this respect, Heidegger wavers and changes, joining forces with the poet as *vates*, or seer of what lies beyond common appearances, and with the poet who mocks the seer – who knows more because she recognises the failure of knowing. In his own words, "every philosophy, as a human thing, intrinsically fails".[20]

NOTES

1. Martin Heidegger, *Basic Questions of Philosophy: Selected "Problems" of "Logic"*, trans. Richard Rojcewicz and André Schuwer (Bloomington: Indiana University Press, 1994), 35.

2. This is not to say, however, that Heidegger went unnoticed. The influential symbolist poet Vyacheslav Ivanov was quite aware of Heidegger and very suspicious of his thought. But Ivanov, like others (Nikolai Berdyaev, Simyon Frank), were outside of the Soviet Union and enjoyed access to Heidegger that others did not. For a fine account of this encounter (and Heidegger's interest in Russia), see Robert Bird, "Martin Heidegger and Russian Symbolist Philosophy", *Studies in East European Thought* 51 (1999): 85–108. See, also, Jeff Love, ed. *Heidegger in Russia and Eastern Europe* (London: Rowman & Littlefield, 2017), ix–xvi. Heidegger also met famously with the Russian poet Andrei Voznesensky in 1967 but this meeting was not substantial. See Heinrich Wiegand Petzet, *Encounters and Dialogues with Martin Heidegger, 1929-1976* (Chicago: The University of Chicago Press, 1993), 120–23. Voznesensky published a text roughly 25 years later, "The Tooth of Reason" ("Зуб разума") on this encounter.

3. See Marjorie Perloff, *The Futurist Moment: Avant-Garde, Avant Guerre, and the Language of Rupture* (Chicago: The University of Chicago Press, 1987).

4. Martin Heidegger, *Hölderlin's Hymns "Germania" and "The Rhine"*, trans. William McNeill and Julia Ireland (Bloomington: Indiana University Press, 2014), 199.

5. Martin Heidegger, "On the Essence of Truth", in *Basic Writings*, ed. David Farrell Krell (New York: Harper & Row Publishers, 1977), 124–25.

6. Heidegger, "Essence of Truth", 123–24.

7. Heidegger, "Essence of Truth", 130.

8. Heidegger, "Essence of Truth", 126. Heidegger uses the terminology of "earth" and "world" not only in his lectures on art published in *Off the Beaten Track* (*Holzwege*) but also in his unpublished work from the 1930s. See, for example, Martin Heidegger, *Mindfulness*, trans. Parvis Emad and Thomas Kalary (London: Continuum, 2006), 11. That correctness has to do with self-preservation is perhaps a more daring interpretation, but it is consistent with Heidegger's identification of metaphysics with will to power or the occlusion of Being.

9. Martin Heidegger, *Being and Truth*, trans. Gregory Fried and Richard Polt (Bloomington: Indiana University Press, 2010), 80–81.

10. Heidegger, *Being and Truth*, 82.

11. Martin Heidegger, *Introduction to Metaphysics*, trans. Gregory Fried and Richard Polt (New Haven: Yale University Press, 2000), 56.

12. See Viktor Shklovsky, "On Poetry and Trans-Sense Language", trans. Gerald Janecek and Peter Mayer *October* 34 (Autumn 1985): 3–24. See, also,

Vladimir Mayakovsky's famous poem, "She loves me, she loves me not" in Vladimir Mayakovsky, *Selected Poems*, trans. James H. McGavran III (Evanston: Northwestern University Press, 2013), 154.

13. Martin Heidegger, "On the Essence of Truth", in *Basic Writings*, ed. David Farrell Krell (New York: Harper & Row Publishers, 1977), 113–43.

14. Martin Heidegger, *The Principle of Reason*, trans. Reginald Lilly (Bloomington: Indiana University Press, 1996), 124.

15. The most comprehensive treatment of *zaum'* is: Gerald Janecek, *Zaum: The Transrational Poetry of Russian Futurism* (San Diego: San Diego State University Press, 1996).

16. Aleksei Kruchenykh, "New Ways of the Word", in *Russian Futurism through its Manifestoes, 1912-1928*, ed. Anna Lawton (Ithaca: Cornell University Press, 1988), 71.

17. It is no accident that two programmatic statements of both are "The Word as Such" and "The Letter as Such".

18. Velimir Khlebnikov, *Collected Works 3: Selected Poems*, trans. Paul Schmidt (Cambridge, MA: Harvard University Press, 1997), 30. The poem is one of the most famous in modern Russian poetry and was examined closely by Khlebnikov's friend, Roman Jakobson, in a celebrated article. See Roman Jakobson, *Selected Writings*, eds. Stephen Rudy and Martha Taylor (The Hague: Mouton, 1979), 330.

19. Velimir Khlebnikov, *Collected Works 1: Letters and Theoretical Writings*, trans. Paul Schmidt (Cambridge, MA: Harvard University Press, 1987), 383–84.

20. Martin Heidegger, *The Metaphysical Foundations of Logic*, trans. Michael Henry Heim (Bloomington: University of Indiana Press, 1984), 76.

Bibliography

I. POETIC AND LITERARY WORKS

Abe, Kōbō. *At the Guidepost at the End of the Road*. Tokyo: Shinchō-sha, 1975.

Ashbery, John. *Collected Poems 1956–1987*. Edited by Mark Ford. New York: Library of America, 2008.

Ashbery, John. *Collected Poems 1991-2000*. Edited by Mark Ford. New York: Library of America, 2017.

Ashbery, John. "John Ashbery in Conversation with David Remnick." In *Bennington Review* no. 8 (Fall 1980), http://www.benningtonreview.org/john-ashbery.

Ashbery, John. *Selected Prose*. Edited by Eugene Richie. Ann Arbor: University of Michigan Press, 2004.

Bachmann, Ingeborg. *Malina*. Frankfurt: Suhrkamp, 1971.

Bellow, Saul. *Herzog*. New York: Viking Press, 1964.

Bernhard, Thomas. *Old Masters: A Comedy*. Translated by Ewald Osers. London: Penguin, 2010.

Celan, Paul. "Ansprache anlässlich der Entgegennahme des Literaturpreises der Freien Hansestadt Bremen." In *Gesammelte Werke*, vol. 3. Edited by Beda Allemann, Stefan Reichert et al., 185–186. Frankfurt: Suhrkamp, 2000.

Celan, Paul. *Der Meridian: Endfassung, Entwürfe, Materialien*. Frankfurt: Suhrkamp, 1999.

Celan, Paul. *Die Gedichte: Kommentierte Gesamtausgabe*. Edited by Barbara Wiedemann. Frankfurt: Suhrkamp, 2005.

Celan, Paul. *"etwas ganz und gar Persönliches." Briefe 1934-1970*. Edited by Barbara Wiedmann. Berlin: Suhrkamp, 2019.

Celan, Paul. *Paul Celan: Poems. A Bilingual Edition*. Translated by Michael Hamburger. New York: Persea, 1980.

Celan, Paul. *The Meridian: Final Version-Drafts-Materials*. Translated by Pierre Joris. Stanford: Stanford University Press, 2011.

Celan, Paul. "Speech on the Occasion of Receiving the Literature Prize of the Free Hanseatic City of Bremen." In *Selected Poems and Prose of Paul Celan*. Translated by John Felstiner, 395–396. New York and London: W.W. Norton, 2001.
de Burgos, Julia. *Obra poética I*. Edited by Juan-Varela Portas de Orduña. Madrid: La Discreta, 2008.
Faulkner, William. *Absalom, Absalom!*. In *William Faulkner: Novels 1936-1940*. Edited by Joseph Blotner and Noel Polk, 1–315. New York: Library of America, 1990.
Faulkner, William. *The Sound and the Fury*. In *William Faulkner: Novels 1926-1929*. Edited by Joseph Blotner and Noel Polk. New York: Library of America, 2006.
Graf, Oskar Maria. "Unser Dialekt und der Existenzialismus." In *An manchen Tagen: Reden, Gedanken und Zeitbetrachtungen*, 97–127. Frankfurt: Nest Verlag, 1961.
Grass, Günter. *Dog Years*. Translated by Ralph Manheim. London: Minerva, 1997.
Handke, Peter. "Nobel Lecture by Peter Handke. Nobel Laureate in Literature 2019." https://www.nobelprize.org/prizes/literature/2019/handke/lecture/.
Handke, Peter. *Slow Homecoming*. Translated by Ralph Manheim. New York: New York Review Books, 2009.
Hölderlin, Friedrich. "In lieblicher Bläue." In *Sämtliche Werke (Große Stuttgarter Ausgabe)*, vol. 2. Edited by Friedrich Beissner, 372–374. Stuttgart: Kohlhammer 1951.
Hölderlin, Friedrich. *Sämtliche Werke*. Edited by Friedrich Beissner and Adolf Beck. 6 Vols. Stuttgart: W. Kohlhammer, 1954.
Jelinek, Elfriede. *Totenauberg*. Reinbek: Rowohlt, 1991.
Khlebnikov, Velimir. *Collected Works 1: Letters and Theoretical Writings*. Translated by Paul Schmidt. Cambridge, MA: Harvard University Press, 1987.
Khlebnikov, Velimir. *Collected Works 3: Selected Poems*. Translated by Paul Schmidt. Cambridge, MA: Harvard University Press, 1997.
Kozinski, Jerzy. *Being There*. New York: Harcourt Brace Jovanovich, 1970.
Kruchenykh, Aleksei. "New Ways of the Word." In *Russian Futurism through its Manifestoes, 1912-1928*. Edited by Anna Lawton, 69–77. Ithaca: Cornell University Press, 1988.
Kunkel, Benjamin. *Indecision*. New York: Random House, 2005.
Lezama Lima, José. *Diarios 1939-49 /1956-58*. México: Era, 1994.
Lezama Lima, José. *Imagen y Posibilidad*. Habana: Editorial Letras Cubanas, 1981.
Lezama Lima, José. *La Expresión Americana*. México: Fondo de Cultura Económica, 1993.
Lezama Lima, José. *Las Eras Imaginarias*. Caracas: Fundamentos, 1971.
Lezama Lima, José. *Los Vasos Órficos*. Barcelona: Barral Editores, 1971.
Lezama Lima, José. *Muerte del narciso. Antología Poética*. México: Era, 2008.
Lezama Lima, José. *Oppiano Licario*. Madrid: Alianza, 1983.
Lezama Lima, José. *Paradiso*. Bogotá: Archivos Unesco, 1988.
Lezama Lima, José. *Reino de la Imagen*. Caracas: Biblioteca Ayacucho, 2006.
Marcel, Gabriel. *La Dimension Florestan*. Paris: Plon, 1958.
Markson, David. *Wittgenstein's Mistress*. Champaign: Dalkey Archive Press, 1988.

Mayakovsky, Vladimir. "She loves me, she loves me not." In *Selected Poems*. Translated by James H. McGavran III, 154. Evanston: Northwestern University Press, 2013.
McCarthy, Cormac. *The Border Trilogy (All the Pretty Horses, The Crossing, Cities of the Plain)*. New York et al.: Alfred A. Knopf, 1999.
Mishima, Yukio. *Silk and Insight*. Tokyo: Shinchō-sha, 1987.
O'Connor, Mary Flannery. "Good Country People." In *The Complete Stories*, 271–291. New York: Farrar, Straus and Giroux, 1971.
Schiller, Friedrich. "Das verschleiert Bild zu Sais." In *Gedichte und Dramen I, Sämtliche Werke*, vol. 1. Edited by Gerhard Fricke and Herbert G. Göpfert, 224–226. Darmstadt: Wissenschaftliche Buchgesellschaft, 1984.
Schiller, Friedrich. "The Veiled Image of Sais." In *The Poems and Ballads of Schiller*. Translated by Sir Edward Bulwer Lytton, 88–91. New York: Thomas Y. Crowell & Co, ca. 1880.
Stadler, Arnold. "Letzte Heiterkeit: Gehversuche auf Heideggers Feldweg." In *Erbarmen mit dem Seziermesser: Über Literatur, Menschen und Orte*, 88–101. Cologne: Kiepenheuer & Witsch, 2000.
Stadler, Arnold. *Mein Hund, meine Sau, mein Leben*. Frankfurt: Suhrkamp, 1996.
Stevens, Wallace. *Wallace Stevens: Collected Poetry and Prose*. Edited by Frank Kermode and Joan Richardson. New York: Library of America, 1997.
Stevens, Wallace. *Letters of Wallace Stevens*. Edited by Holly Stevens. Berkeley: University of California Press, 1996.
Waiblinger, Friedrich Wilhelm. *Phaeton*, Zweiter Theil. Stuttgart: Friedrich Franck, 1823.
Wallace, David Foster. "The Empty Plenum: David Markson's *Wittgenstein's Mistress*." In *Both Flesh and Not*, 73–121. Boston: Little, Brown, 2012.

II. WORKS BY HEIDEGGER

Heidegger, Martin. "Andenken." In *Erläuterungn zu Hölderlins Dichtung* (GA 4). Edited by Friedrich-Wilhelm von Herrmann, 79–151. Frankfurt: Klostermann, 1996.
Heidegger, Martin. *Approche de Hölderlin*. Translated by Henry Corbin. Paris: Gallimard, 1973.
Heidegger, Martin. "Art and Space." Translated by Charles H. Seibert. In *Man and World*, 6 (1973): 3–8.
Heidegger, Martin. "Aus der Erfahrung des Denkens." In *Aus der Erfahrung des Denkens: 1910-1979* (GA 13). Edited by Hermann Heidegger, 75–86. Frankfurt: Klostermann, 1983.
Heidegger, Martin. *Basic Questions of Philosophy: Selected "Problems" of "Logic."* Translated by Richard Rojcewicz and André Schuwer. Bloomington: Indiana University Press, 1994.

Heidegger, Martin. *Being and Time*. Translated by John Macquarrie and Edward Robinson. New York: Harper & Row, 1962.
Heidegger, Martin. *Beiträge zur Philosophie. Vom Ereignis* (GA 65). Edited by Friedrich-Wilhelm von Herrmann, Frankfurt: Klostermann, 1989.
Heidegger, Martin. "Brief über den Humanismus." In *Wegmarken*. Frankfurt: Klostermann, 1967.
Heidegger, Martin. "Building Dwelling Thinking." In *Poetry, Language, Thought*, translated by Albert Hofstadter, 143–159. New York: Harper & Row, 1971.
Heidegger, Martin. "Das Ende der Philosophie und der Anfang des Denkens." In *Zur Sache des Denkens* (GA 14). Edited by Friedrich Wilhelm v. Herrmann, 67–90. Frankfurt: Klostermann, 2007.
Heidegger, Martin. *Das Ereignis* (GA 71). Frankfurt: Klostermann, 2009.
Heidegger, Martin. "Declaration of Support for Adolf Hitler and the National Socialist State (November 11, 1933)." In *The Heidegger Controversy: A Critical Reader*, edited by Richard Wolin, 49–52. New York: Columbia University Press, 1991.
Heidegger, Martin. *Der Satz vom Grund* (GA 10). Edited by Petra Jaeger, Frankfurt: Klostermann, 1997.
Heidegger, Martin. "Der Ursprung des Kunstwerks." In *Holzwege* (GA 5). Edited by Friedrich Wilhelm v. Herrmann, 1–74. Frankfurt: Klostermann, 1977.
Heidegger, Martin. "'…dichterisch wohnet der Mensch…'." In *Vorträge und Aufsätze* (GA 7). Edited by Friedrich Wilhelm v. Herrmann, 189–210. Frankfurt: Klostermann, 2000.
Heidegger, Martin. "Die Frage nach der Technik". In *Vorträge und Aufsätze* (GA 7). Edited by Friedrich-Wilhelm von Herrmann, 7–36. Frankfurt: Klostermann, 2000.
Heidegger, Martin. "Die Kunst und der Raum." In *Aus der Erfahrung des Denkens (1910-1976)* (GA 13). Edited by Hermann Heidegger, 203–210.
Heidegger, Martin. *Discourse on Thinking*. Translated by John M. Anderson and E. Hans Freund. New York: Harper, 1969.
Heidegger, Martin. *Einführung in die Metaphysik* (GA 40). Edited by Petra Jaeger. Frankfurt: Klostermann, 1983.
Heidegger, Martin. *Elucidations of Hölderlin's Poetry*. Translated by Keith Hoeller. Amherst: Humanity Books, 2000.
Heidegger, Martin. *Erlaüterungen zu Hölderlins Dichtung*. Edited by Friedrich-Wilhelm von Herrmann. Frankfurt: Klostermann 1996.
Heidegger, Martin. *Existence and Being*. Edited by Werner Brock, Washington, DC: Regnery, 1949.
Heidegger, Martin. *Grundbegriffe* (GA 51). Edited by Petra Jaeger. Frankfurt: Klostermann, 1981.
Heidegger, Martin. *Hölderlins Hymnen "Germanien" und "Der Rhein"* (GA 39). Edited by Susanne Ziegler. Frankfurt: Klostermann, 1980.
Heidegger, Martin. *Hölderlin's Hymns "Germania" and "The Rhine."* Translated by William McNeill and Julia Ireland. Bloomington: Indiana University Press, 2014.
Heidegger, Martin. *Holzwege*. Frankfurt: Klostermann, 1950.

Heidegger, Martin. *Introduction to Metaphysics*. Translated by Gregory Fried and Richard Polt. New Haven: Yale University Press, 2014.

Heidegger, Martin. *Kant und das Problem der Metaphysik*. Frankfurt: Klostermann, 1991.

Heidegger, Martin. "Language." In *Poetry, Language, Thought*, translated by Albert Hofstadter, 187–208. New York: Harper & Row, 1971.

Heidegger, Martin. "Language in the Poem." In *On the Way to Language*, translated by Peter Demetz, 159–198. New York: Harper & Row, 1971.

Heidegger, Martin. "Letter on 'Humanism'." In *Pathmarks*, edited and translated by William McNeill, 239–276. Cambridge: Cambridge University Press, 2006.

Heidegger, Martin. "Lettres à Roger Munier." *Cahier de l'Herne/Heidegger* 46 (1983): 106–118.

Heidegger, Martin. *Logic as the Question Concerning the Essence of Language*. Translated by Wanda Torres Gregory and Yvonne Unnab. Albany: SUNY Press, 2009.

Heidegger, Martin. "Logos (Heraclitus Fragment B 50)." In *Early Greek Thinking*, translated by David Farell Krell and Frank A. Capuzzi, 59–78. New York: Harper & Row, 1975.

Heidegger, Martin. *Mindfulness*. Translated by Parvis Emad and Thomas Kalary. London: Continuum, 2006.

Heidegger, Martin. "Nachwort zu: *Was ist Metaphysik?*" In *Wegmarken* (GA 9). Edited by Friedrich Wilhelm v. Herrmann, 303–312. Frankfurt: Klostermann, 2004.

Heidegger, Martin. "Notizen zu Klee/Notes on Klee." Compiled and translated by María del Rosario Acosta López, Tobias Keiling, Ian Alexander Moore, and Yuliya Aleksandrovna Tsutserova. *Philosophy Today* 61, no. 1 (Winter 2017): 7–17.

Heidegger, Martin. "Only a God Can Save Us: The *Spiegel* Interview (1966)." In *Heidegger: The Man and the Thinker*, edited by Thomas Sheehan, 45–68. Precedent Publishing, 1966.

Heidegger, Martin. "On the Essence of Truth." In *Basic Writings*, edited and translated by David Farrell Krell, 113–143. New York: Harper & Row, 1977.

Heidegger, Martin. "On the Essence of Truth." In *Pathmarks*. Edited by William McNeill, 136–154. Cambridge: Cambridge University Press, 1998.

Heidegger, Martin. "'…poetically men dwells…'." In *Poetry, Language, Thought*, translated by Alfred Hofstadter 209–227. New York: Harper Collins, 2001.

Heidegger, Martin. *Poetry, Language, Thought*. Translated by Albert Hofstadter. New York: Harper & Row, 1971.

Heidegger, Martin. *Ponderings II-VI: Black Notebooks 1931-1938*. Translated by Richard Rojcewicz. Bloomington: Indiana University Press, 2016.

Heidegger, Martin. *Reden und andere Zeugnisse eines Lebensweges* (GA 16). Frankfurt: Klostermann, 2000.

Heidegger, Martin. *Sein und Zeit* (GA 2). Edited by Friedrich-Wilhelm von Herrmann. Frankfurt: Klostermann, 1977.

Heidegger, Martin. "Seminar in Le Thor 1969." In *Seminare (1951-1973)* (GA 15). Edited by Curd Ochwadt, 326–371. Frankfurt: Klostermann, 1986.

Heidegger, Martin. "The End of Philosophy and the Task of thinking." Translated by Joan Stambaugh. Reprint in *Martin Heidegger. Basic Writings: from 'Being and Time' (1927) to 'The Task of Thinking' (1964)*, edited by David Krell, 427–449. New York: Harper Collins, 1977.

Heidegger, Martin. *The Metaphysical Foundations of Logic*. Translated by Michael Henry Heim. Bloomington: University of Indiana Press, 1984.

Heidegger, Martin. "The Nature of Language." In *On the Way to Language*, translated by Peter Demetz, 57–108. New York: Harper & Row, 1971.

Heidegger, Martin. "The Origin of the Work of Art." In *Basic Writings*, edited and translated by David Farrell Krell, 139–212. New York: Harper & Row, 1977.

Heidegger, Martin. *The Principle of Reason*. Translated by Reginald Lilly. Bloomington: Indiana University Press, 1996.

Heidegger, Martin. "The Question Concerning Technology." In *The Question Concerning Technology and Other Essays*, translated by William Lovitt, 3–35. New York/London: Garland, 1977.

Heidegger, Martin. "The Thing." In *Poetry, Language, Thought*, translated by Albert Hofstadter, 163–180. New York: Harper & Row, 1971.

Heidegger, Martin. *Über den Anfang* (GA 70). Edited by Paola-Ludovika Coriando. Frankfurt: Klostermann, 2005.

Heidegger, Martin. *Überlegungen II-VI (Schwarze Hefte 1931-1938)* (GA 94). Edited by Peter Trawny. Frankfurt: Klostermann, 2014.

Heidegger, Martin. *Überlegungen VII-XI (Schwarze Hefte 1938-1939)* (GA 95). Edited by Peter Trawny. Frankfurt: Klostermann, 2014.

Heidegger, Martin. *Überlegungen XII-XV (Schwarze Hefte 1939-1941)* (GA 96). Edited by Peter Trawny. Frankfurt: Klostermann, 2014.

Heidegger, Martin. *Unterwegs zur Sprache*. Stuttgart: Klett-Cotta, 1959.

Heidegger, Martin. "Vom Wesen der Wahrheit." In *Wegmarken* (GA 9). Edited by Friedrich Willhelm v. Herrmann, 177–202. Frankfurt: Klostermann, 2004.

Heidegger, Martin. *Vorträge und Aufsätze* (GA 7). Edited by Friedrich-Wilhelm von Herrmann. Frankfurt: Klostermann, 2000.

Heidegger, Martin. "What is Metaphysics?" In *Basic Writings*, edited and translated by David Farrell Krell, 91–113. New York: Harper & Row, 1977.

III. SECONDARY WORKS

Agamben, Giorgio. *Homo Sacer: Il potere sovrano e la nuda vita*. Turin: Einaudi, 1995.

Agamben, Giorgio. *L'avventura*. Rome: nottetempo, 2015.

Agamben, Giorgio. *Uso dei corpi*. Vicenza: Neri Pozza, 2014.

Agamben, Giorgio. *What Is Philosophy?* Translated by Lorenzo Chiesa. Stanford: Stanford University Press, 2017.

Arendt, Hannah. "Heidegger, the Fox." In *Essays in Understanding 1930-1954*, edited by Jerome Kohn, 361–362. New York: Harcourt Brace & Company, 1994.

Aristotle. *Aristotle's Physics. A Revised Text with Introduction and Commentary.* Translated by W. D. Ross. Oxford: Oxford University Press, 1936.
Auerbach, Erich. *Mimesis: Dargestellte Wirklichkeit in der abendländischen Literatur.* Berne: Francke, 1994.
Auerbach, Erich. *Mimesis: The Representation of Reality in Western Literature.* Translated by Willard Trask. Princeton: Princeton University Press, 2003.
Bachmann, Ingeborg. *Die kritische Aufnahme der Existentialphilosophie Martin Heideggers.* Edited by Robert Pichl. Munich: Piper, 1985.
Badiou, Alain. *Being and Event,* New York: Continuum, 2005.
Badiou, Alain. *Briefings on Existence: A Short Treatise on Transitory Ontology,* Albany: State University of New York Press, 2006 [French original: *Court traité d'ontologie transitoire,* Paris: Éditions du Seuil, 1998].
Badiou, Alain. "L'hypothèse communiste – interview d'Alain Badiou par Pierre Gaultier." *Newsnet.fr,* August 7, 2009. http://newsnet.fr/29896.
Badiou, Alain. *Manifesto for Philosophy,* Albany: State University of New York Press, 1999.
Bakewell, Sarah. *At the Existentialist Café: Freedom, Being, and Apricot Cocktails.* New York: Other Press, 2016.
Benjamin, Andrew. "Prologue. Placing Heidegger's Hut." In *Heidegger's Hut,* Adam Sharr, xv–xx. Cambridge, MA: MIT Press, 2006.
Benjamin, Walter. *Gesammelte Briefe.* Edited by Christoph Gödde and Henri Lonitz. Frankfurt/Berlin: Suhrkamp, 2008.
Benjamin, Walter. *Gesammelte Schriften,* V.1. Edited by Rolf Tiedemann and Hermann Schweppenhäuser. Frankfurt: Suhrkamp, 1991.
Benjamin, Walter. "Über die Sprache überhaupt und über die Sprache des Menschen." In *Gesammelte Schriften II.1,* edited by Rolf Tiedemann and Hermann Schweppenhäuser, 140–157. Frankfurt: Suhrkamp, 2002.
Benjamin, Walter. "Zwei Gedichte von Friedrich Hölderlin: *Dichtermut—Blödigkeit.*" In *GS II.1,* edited by Rolf Tiedemann and Hermann Schweppenhäuser, 105–126. Frankfurt: Suhrkamp, 2002.
Bird, Robert. "Martin Heidegger and Russian Symbolist Philosophy." *Studies in East European Thought* 51 (1999): 85–108.
Björk, Mårten, and Jayne Svenungsson, eds. *Heidegger's Black Notebooks and the Future of Theology.* London: Palgrave Macmillan, 2017.
Blanchot, Maurice. *L'attente, L'oubli.* Paris: Gallimard, 1962.
Blanchot, Maurice. *L'Écriture du Désastre.* Paris: Gallimard, 1980.
Blanchot, Maurice. *L'Espace Littéraire.* Paris: Gallimard, 1955.
Blumenberg, Hans. *Ästhetische und metaphorische Schriften.* Edited by Anselm Haverkamp, 139–171. Frankfurt: Suhrkamp, 2008.
Braidotti, Rosi. "Posthuman Critical Theory." *Journal of Posthuman Studies* 1, no. 1 (2017): 9–25.
Bové, Paul. *Destructive Poetics: Heidegger and Modern American Poetry.* New York: Columbia University Press, 1980.
Boyarin, Daniel. *A Traveling Homeland: The Babylonian Talmud as Diaspora.* Philadelphia: University of Pennsylvania Press, 2015.

Boyarin, Daniel. *Socrates & the Fat Rabbis*. Chicago/London: The University of Chicago Press, 2009.

Braun, Luzia. "Da-Da-Da-Sein: Fritz Heidegger: Holzwege zur Sprache. Quasi una Philosophia." *Die Zeit*, September 22 (1989): 58.

Cameron, Esther. *Western Art and Jewish Presence in the Work of Paul Celan: Roots and Ramifications of the Meridian-Speech*. Lanham, MD: Lexington/Roman & Littlefield, 2014.

Caputo, John. "People of God, People of Being: The Theological Presuppositions of Heidegger's Path of Thought." In *Appropriating Heidegger*, edited by James E. Falconer and Mark A. Wrathall, 85–100. Cambridge: Cambridge University Press, 2000.

Carson, Luke. "'Render Unto Caesura': Late Ashbery, Hölderlin, and the Tragic." *Contemporary Literature* 49, no. 2 (2008): 180–208.

Conant, James. "Kierkegaard, Wittgenstein, and Nonsense." In *Pursuits of Reason*, edited by Ted Cohen et al., 195–224. Lubbock: Texas Tech University Press, 1993.

Danto, Arthur. "Wakeful Dreams." In *What Art Is*, 1–52. New Haven/London: Yale University Press, 2013.

Dastur, Françoise. "Y a-t-il une 'essence' de l'antisémitisme?" In *Heidegger, die Juden, noch einmal*, edited by Peter Trawny and Andrew J. Mitchell, 75–96. Frankfurt: Klostermann, 2015.

Davis, Bret W. "Translator's Foreword." In *Martin Heidegger: Country Path Conversations*, translated by Bret W. Davis, vii–xxii. Bloomington: Indiana University Press, 2010.

Deming, Richard. *Art of the Ordinary: The Everyday Domain of Art, Film, Philosophy, and Poetry*. Ithaca: Cornell University Press, 2018.

Derrida, Jacques. *Geschlecht III: Sexe, race, nation, humanité*. Edited by Geoff Bennington, Katie Chenoweth, and Rodrigo Therezo. Paris: Seuil, 2018.

Derrida, Jacques. *Heidegger et la Question: De l'Esprit et Autres Essais*. Paris: Flammarion, 1990.

Derrida, Jacques. "La mythologie blanche. La métaphore dans le texte philosophique." In *Marges de la philosophie*. 247–324. Paris: Edition de Minuit, 1972.

Derrida, Jacques. *Sovereignties in Question: The Poetics of Paul Celan*. Edited by Thomas Dutoit and Outi Pasanen. New York: Fordham University Press, 2005.

Derrida, Jacques. "White Mythology. Metaphor in the Text of Philosophy." Translated by F. C. T. Moore. In *New Literary History*, vol 6/1, "On Metaphor", 5–74. Baltimore: Johns Hopkins University Press, 1974.

Di Blasi, Luca. "Less than Nihilism." In *Nihilism and the State of Israel: New Critical Perspectives*, edited by Nitzan Lebovic and Roy Ben Shai, 35–49. London et al.: Bloomsbury, 2014.

Di Cesare, Donatella. "Being and the Jew: Between Heidegger and Levinas." In *Heidegger and Jewish Thought. Difficult Others*, edited by Elad Lapidot and Micha Brumlik, 75–86. London/New York: Rowman & Littlefield, 2018.

Dolgopolski, Sergey. *Other Others. The Political After the Talmud*. New York: Fordham University Press, 2018.

Dolgopolski, Sergey. *What Is Talmud? The Art of Disagreement*. New York: Fordham University Press, 2009.
Dretske, Fred. "Entitlement: Epistemic Rights without Epistemic Duties?" *Philosophy and Phenomenological Research* 60, no. 3 (2000): 591–606.
Dreyfus, Hubert and Sean D. Kelly. *All Things Shining: Reading the Western Classics to Find Meaning in a Secular Age*. New York: Free Press, 2011.
Dreyfus, Hubert. "The Myth of the Pervasiveness of the Mental." In *Mind, Reason, and Being-in-the-World*, edited by Joseph K. Schear, 15–40. London: Routledge, 2013.
Dugin, Aleksandr. *Die vierte politische Theorie*. London: Arktos, 2013.
Dworkin, Ronald. *Religion Without God*. Cambridge, MA: Harvard University Press, 2013.
Eisenmenger, Johann Andreas. *Entdecktes Judentum*. Dresden: Otto Brander, 1700/1893.
Ellis, Erle C. *Anthropocene: A Very Short Introduction*. Oxford: Oxford UP, 2018.
Eshel, Amir. "Paul Celan's Other: History, Poetics, and Ethics." *New German Critique* 91 (Winter 2004): 57–77.
Fagenblat, Michael. "Levinas and Heidegger: The Elemental Confrontation." In *The Oxford Handbook of Levinas*, edited by Michael L. Morgan, 103–133. Oxford: Oxford University Press, 2019.
Fagenblat, Michael. "On Dwelling Prophetically: On Heidegger and Jewish Political Theology." In *Heidegger and Jewish Thought: Difficult Others*, edited by Elad Lapidot and Micha Brumlik, 245–268. London/New York: Rowman & Littlefield, 2017.
Fanon, Franz. *Black Skin, White Masks*. Translated by Charles Lam Markmann. London: Pluto Press, 1986.
Fanon, Franz *Black Skin, White Masks*. Translated by Richard Philcox. New York: Grove Press, 1967.
Fanon, Franz. *Œuvres*. Paris: La découverte, 2011.
Figal, Günter, and Ulrich Raulff, eds. *Heidegger und die Literatur*. Frankfurt: Klostermann, 2012.
Filreis, Alan. *Wallace Stevens and the Actual World*. Princeton: Princeton University Press, 1991.
Feldman, Burton. "Markson's New Way." *Review of Contemporary Fiction* 10, no. 2 (1990): 157–163.
Felstiner, John. *Paul Celan: Poet, Survivor, Jew*. New Haven: Yale University Press, 2001.
Firges, Jean. "Sprache und Sein in der Dichtung Paul Celans." In *Muttersprache* 72, no. 9 (1962): 261–269.
Fitzgerald, William. *Agonistic Poetry: The Pindaric Mode in Pindar, Horace, Hölderlin, and the English Ode*. Berkeley: University of California Press, 1987.
Fóti, Véronique. *Heidegger and the Poets: Poēsis/Sophia/Technē*. New York: Humanity Books, 1992.
Frey, Hans-Jost. "Hölderlin's Marginalization of Language." In *The Solid Letter: Readings of Friedrich Hölderlin*, edited by Aris Fioretos, 356–374. Palo Alto: Stanford University Press, 2000.

Frisch, Max. "Vom Ursprung der Kunst: Vortrag von Martin Heidegger." *Tagesanzeiger* no. 21, January 25 (1936): n.p.

Gabbay, Dov M., C.J. Hogger, and J.A. Robinson, eds. *Handbook of Logic in Artificial Intelligence and Logic Programming: Nonmonotonic Reasoning and Uncertain Reasoning.* Oxford: Oxford University Press, 1994.

Gadamer, Hans-Georg. *Heidegger's Ways.* Albany: State University of New York Press, 1994.

Gadris, Stelios. "Two Cases of Irony: Kant and Wittgenstein." *Kant-Studien* 107, no. 2 (2016): 343–368.

Glick, Jeffrey. "Justification and the Right to Believe." *Philosophical Quarterly* 60, no. 240 (2010): 532–544.

Glissant, Edouard. *Faulkner, Mississippi.* Translated by Barbara Lewis and Thomas C. Spear. New York: Strauss & Giroux, 1996.

González, Mauricio. "El Silencio de lo Sublime en el *Origen de la Obra de Arte* de Heidegger." In *Martin Heidegger: La Experiencia del Camino*, edited by Alfredo Rocha, 457–485. Barranquilla: Ediciones Uninorte, 2009.

Gordon, Peter E. *Continental Divide: Heidegger, Cassirer, Davos.* Cambridge, MA: Harvard University Press, 2012.

Grace, Sherril E. "Messages: Reading *Wittgenstein's Mistress*." *Review of Contemporary Fiction* 10, no. 2 (1990): 207–216.

Greisch, Jean. "Paul Celan. Das 'befremdete Ich' und die Sprache des Seins." In *Heidegger Handbuch: Leben-Werk-Wirkung*, edited by Dieter Thomä, 2nd ed., 523–529. Stuttgart: J.B. Metzler, 2013.

Grosser, Florian. "Selbstheit, Andersheit und die 'Möglichkeit des elementalen Bösen': Levinas' Heidegger-Kritik im Licht der *Schwarzen Hefte*. " In *Heidegger, die Juden, noch einmal*, edited by Peter Trawny and Andrew J. Mitchell, 191–214. Frankfurt: Klostermann, 2015.

Hacker, Peter M.S. "The Linguistic Turn in Analytic Philosophy." In *The Oxford Handbook of The History of Analytic Philosophy*, edited by Michael Barney, 926–47. Oxford: Oxford UP, 2013.

Hadot, Pierre. *The Veil of Isis. An Essay on the History of the Idea of Nature.* Translated by Michael Chase. Cambridge, MA/London: The Belknap Press of Harvard University Press, 2006.

Hamacher, Werner. "On the Right to Have Rights: Human Rights; Marx and Arendt." Translated by Ronald Mendoza-de Jesús. *New Centennial Review* 14, no. 2 (June): 169–214.

Hamacher, Werner. *Premises.* Translated by Peter Fenves. Stanford: Stanford University Press, 1999.

Hamacher, Werner. *Sprachgerechtigkeit.* Frankfurt: S. Fischer, 2018.

Hamacher, Werner. "The Second of Inversion—Movements of a Figure through Celan's Poetry." Translated by William D. Jewett, in *Word-Traces: On Paul Celan's Poetry*, edited by Aris Fioretos, 214–263. Baltimore: The Johns Hopkins University Press, 1994.

Hamacher, Werner. *Was zu sagen bleibt.* Schupfart: Engeler Verlag, 2019.

Hamacher, Werner. "Wasen: On Celan's *Todtnauberg*." Translated by Heidi Hart. In *The Yearbook of Comparative Literature* 57 (2011): 15–54.
Hamacher, Werner. "WASEN. Um Celans Todtnauberg." In *Das Robert Altmann Projekt. Quaderno III: "Paul Celan in Vaduz,"* edited by Norbert Haas, Vreni Haas, Hansjörg Quaderer, 35–84. Vaduz: edition eupalinos, 2012.
Hamburger, Michael, trans. *Friedrich Hölderlin: Poems and Fragments*. Vancouver: Anvil Press, 2004.
Handelman, Sarah. *The Slayers of Moses: The Emergence of Rabbinic Interpretation in Modern Literary Theory*. Albany: State University of New York Press, 1982.
Harries, Karsten. "The Root of All Evil: Lessons of an Epigram." *International Journal of Philosophical Studies* 1, no. 1 (1993): 1–20.
Hayes, Josh Michael. "Being-at-Home: Gary Snyder and the Poetics of Place." In *The Philosophy of the Beats*, edited by Sharin N. Elkholy, 47–61. Lexington: University of Kentucky Press, 2012.
Hemming, Laurence Paul. "Heidegger's God." In *Heidegger Reexamined. Vol. 3: Art, Poetry, Technology*, edited by Hubert Dreyfus and Mark Wrathall, 249–294. New York/London: Routledge, 2002.
Hennig, Thomas. *Intertextualität als ethische Dimension: Peter Handkes Ästhetik 'nach Auschwitz'*. Würzburg: Königshausen & Neumann, 1996.
Hines, Thomas J. *The Later Poetry of Wallace Stevens: Phenomenological Parallels to Husserl and Heidegger*. Lewisburg: Bucknell University Press, 1976.
Hoeller, Keith, ed. *Dream and Existence: Michel Foucault and Ludwig Binswanger*. London: Humanities Press, 1993.
Hoffman, Joel. *In the Beginning: A Short History of the Hebrew Language*. New York/London: New York University Press, 2004.
Homolka, Walter and Arnulf Heidegger eds. *Heidegger und der Antisemitismus: Positionen im Widerstreit*. Freiburg: Herder Verlag, 2016.
Idel, Moshe. "Reification of Language in Jewish Mysticism." In *Mysticism and Language*, edited by Steven T. Katz, 42–79. New York/Oxford: Oxford University Press, 1992.
Jakobson, Roman. *Selected Writings*. Edited by Stephen Rudy and Martha Taylor. The Hague: Mouton, 1979.
Janecek, Gerald. *Zaum: The Transrational Poetry of Russian Futurism*. San Diego: San Diego State University Press, 1996.
Jay, Gregory S. *America, The Scrivener: Deconstruction and the Subject of Literary History*. Ithaca: Cornell University Press, 1990.
Jean Paul. *Vorschule der Ästhetik: Werke in zwölf Bänden, Vol. 9*. Edited by Norbert Miller. Munich/Vienna: Hanser, 1975.
Kaiser, Katharina. "Gespräch mit Hölderlin I: 'Eigenes' und 'Fremdes'." In *Heidegger-Handbuch: Leben-Werk- Wirkung*, edited by Dieter Thomä, 2nd ed., 184–188. Stuttgart: J.B. Metzler, 2013.
Kant, Immanuel. *Critique of the Power of Judgment*. Edited by Paul Guyer, translated by Paul Guyer and Eric Matthews. Cambridge: Cambridge University Press, 2000.

Kermode, Frank. "Dwelling Poetically in Connecticut." In *Wallace Stevens: A Celebration*, edited by Robert Buttel and Frank Doggett, 256–273. Princeton: Princeton University Press, 1980.

Kierkegaard, Søren. *Concluding Unscientific Postscript to Philosophical Fragments*. Translated by Walter Lowrie and Joseph Campbell. Princeton: Princeton University Press, 1992.

Kierkegaard, Søren. *Fear and Trembling / Repetition*. Translated by Howard & Edna Hong. Princeton: Princeton University Press, 1983.

Kierkegaard, Søren. *Sickness unto Death*. Translated by Howard & Edna Hong. Princeton: Princeton University Press.

Kinder, Anna, ed. *Peter Handke: Stationen, Orte, Positionen*. Berlin/Boston: De Gruyter, 2014.

Kleinberg, Ethan. "Levinas as a Reader of Jewish Texts: The Talmudic Commentaries." In *Handbook of Levinas*, edited by Michael L. Morgan, 300–317. Oxford: Oxford University Press, 2019.

Kommerell, Max. *Max Kommerell: Briefe und Aufzeichnungen 1919-1944*. Edited by Inge Jens. Olten/Freiburg im Breisgau: Walter Verlag, 1967.

Kuki, Shūzō. "The Notion of Time and Reprise of Time in the East". In *On Time*. Tokyo: Iwanami, 2016.

Kuki, Shūzō. *The Structure of 'Iki'*. Tokyo: Iwanami, 2016.

Kuki, Shūzō. "The Rhyme of Japanese Poetry." In *Collected Works Vol.4*. Tokyo: Iwanami, 2011.

Kuki, Shūzō. "Metaphysical Time." In *Human Beings and Existence*. Tokyo: Iwanami, 2016.

Kuki, Shūzō. *The Problem of Contingency*. Tokyo: Iwanami, 2015.

Kuki, Shūzō. "Japanese Character." In *Human Beings and Existence*. Tokyo: Iwanami, 2016.

Kuki, Shūzō. "Metaphysics of Literature." In *On Time*. Tokyo: Iwanami, 2016.

Kunkel, Benjamin. "Introduction." In Peter Handke, *Slow Homecoming*, vii–xiv. New York: New York Review Books, 2009.

Lachmann, Eduard. "Hölderlins erste Hymne." *Deutsche Vierteljahresschrift für Literaturwissenschaft und Geistesgeschichte* 17 (1939): 221–251.

Lacoue-Labarthe, Philippe. *Heidegger and the Politics of Poetry*. Translated by Jeff Fort. Urbana/Chicago: University of Illinois Press, 2007.

Lacoue-Labarthe, Philippe. *Heidegger, Art and Politics. The Fiction of the Political*. Translated by Chris Turner. Oxford: Blackwell, 1990.

Philippe Lacoue-Labarthe, *Heidegger: La politique du poème*. Paris: Galilée, 2002.

Lacoue-Labarthe, Philippe. *La Fiction du politique: Heidegger, l'art et la politique*. Paris: Christian Bourgois Editeur, 1998.

Lacoue-Labarthe, Phillipe and Jean-Luc Nancy. *Le mythe nazi*. La Tour d'Aigues: Editions de l'Aube, 1991.

Lapidot, Elad and Micha Brumlik, eds. *Heidegger and Jewish Though: Difficult Others*. London/New York: Rowman & Littlefield, 2018.

Lapidot, Elad. *Jews Out of the Question: A Critique of Anti-Anti-Semitism*. Albany: SUNY Press, 2020.

Lear, Jonathan. *A Case for Irony*. Cambridge, MA: Harvard University Press, 2011.
Leggett, B.J. *Late Stevens: The Final Fiction*. Baton Rouge: Louisiana State University Press, 2005.
Lemke, Anja. *Konstellation ohne Sterne. Zur poetischen und geschichtlichen Zäsur bei Martin Heidegger und Paul Celan*. Munich: Wilhelm Fink, 2002.
Leonard, James S. and Christine E. Wharton. "Wallace Stevens as Phenomenologist." *Texas Studies in Literature and Language* 26, no. 3 (Fall 1984): 331–361.
Levinas, Emmanuel. *Totalité et Infini: Essai sur l'extériorité*. Paris: Kluwer Academic, 1991.
Levinas, Emmanuel. *Totality and Infinity: An Essay on Exteriority*. Translated by Alphonso Lingis. The Hague/Boston/London: Martinus Nijhoff Publishers, 1979.
Levine, Michael G. "Pendant: Büchner, Celan, and the Terrible Voice of the Meridian." In ibid., *A Weak Messianic Power: Figures of Time to Come in Benjamin, Derrida, and Celan*, 37–62. New York: Fordham University Press, 2014.
Liska, Vivian. "'Roots again st Heaven.' An Aporetic Inversion in Paul Celan." *New German Critique* 91 (Winter 2004): 41–56.
López-Baralt, Mercedes. "El encuentro de la mujer y el río: sobre la poesía de Julia de Burgos." In *A Julia de Burgos : Anthologie bilingue*, edited by Françoise Morcillo, 225–47. Paris: Indigo et Côté-Femmes, 2004.
Love, Jeff, ed. *Heidegger in Russia and Eastern Europe*. London/New York: Rowman & Littlefield, 2017.
Luckscheiter, Christian. "Flüchtlinge in der Literatur Peter Handkes." In *Niemandsbuchten und Schutzbefohlene*, edited by Thomas Hardke et al., 85–95. Göttingen: V&R unipress, 2017.
Lupi, Juan Pablo. *Reading Anew: Lezama Lima's Rhetorical Investigations*. Madrid: Interamericana-Vervuert, 2012.
Lyon, James K. *Paul Celan and Martin Heidegger: An Unresolved Conversation, 1951–1970*. Baltimore: Johns Hopkins University Press, 2006.
Lyotard, Jean-François. "Argumentation and Presentation: The Foundation Crisis." Translated by Chris Turner. *Cultural Politics* 9, no. 2 (2013), 117–143.
Lyotard, Jean-François. "Philosophy and Painting in the Age of Their Experimentation: Contribution to an Idea of Postmodernity." Translated by Mária Minich Brewer and Daniel Brewer. In *The Merleau-Ponty Aesthetics Reader: Philosophy and Painting*, edited by Galen A. Johnson, 323–335. Evanston: Northwestern University Press, 1993.
Lyotard, Jean-François. *The Inhuman: Reflections on Time*. Translated by Geoffrey Bennington and Rachel Bowlby. Stanford: Stanford University Press, 1991.
Lyotard Jean-François. "The Sublime and the Avant-Garde." In *The Bloomsbury Anthology of Aesthetics*, edited by Joseph Tanke and Colin McQuillan, 531–542. New York: Bloomsbury, 2012.
Malone, Tyler. "A Fonder Admission of Other Small Things: A Conversation with Ann Beattie." *The Scofield* 1, no. 1 (2015): 22–27.
Malpas, Jeff. *Heidegger's Topology: Being, Place, World*. Cambridge, MA/London: The MIT Press, 2006.

Mann, Thomas. "Das Deutscheste: Thomas Mann an Paul Tillich, 13. April 1944." *Frankfurter Allgemeine Zeitung*, June 20 (2002): 45.
Mann, Thomas. *Reflections of a Nonpolitical Man*. Translated by Walter D. Morris. New York: Ungar, 1987.
Matos, Jaime Rodriguez. *Writing of the Formless. Jose Lezama Lima and the End of Time*. New York: Fordham University Press, 2017.
Mehring, Reinhard. "Heidegger und Carl Schmitt: Verschärfer und Neutralisierer des Nationalsozialismus." In *Heidegger-Handbuch: Leben-Werk- Wirkung*, edited by Dieter Thomä, 2nd ed., 352–355. Stuttgart: J.B. Metzler, 2013.
Merleau-Ponty, Maurice. "Cézanne's Doubt." In *The Merleau-Ponty Aesthetics Reader: Philosophy and Painting*, edited by Galen A. Johnson, 59–75. Evanston: Northwestern University Press, 1993.
Merleau-Ponty, Maurice. "Eye and Mind." In *The Merleau-Ponty Aesthetics Reader: Philosophy and Painting*, edited by Galen A. Johnson, 121–149. Evanston: Northwestern University Press, 1993.
Metz, Christian. "Unausgesprochen bleibt das Gedicht nur bei Heidegger." *Frankfurter Allgemeine Zeitung*, no. 88, April 13 (2017): 12.
Most, Glenn W. "Heidegger's Greeks." *Arion: A Journal of Humanities and the Classics* 10, no. 1 (2002): 83–98.
Mualem, Shlomy. "Nonsense and Irony: Wittgenstein's Strategy of Self-Refutation and Kierkegaard's Concept of Indirect Communication." *Tópicos* 53 (2017): 203–227.
Mugerauer, Robert. *Responding to Loss: Heideggerian Reflections on Literature, Architecture, and Film*. New York: Fordham University Press, 2015.
Nägele, Rainer. *Reading After Freud: Essays on Goethe, Hölderlin, Habermas, Nietzsche, Brecht, Celan, and Freud*. New York: Columbia University Press, 1987.
Nancy, Jean-Luc. *La communauté désoeuvrée*. Paris: Christian Bourgois Editeur, 1986.
Nietzsche, Friedrich. *Ecce Homo*. Translated by R.J. Hollingdale. New York: Penguin Books, 1988.
O'Brien, William Arctander. "Getting blasted: Hölderlin's 'Wie Wenn am Feiertage…'." *MLN* 94, no. 3 (April 1979): 596–586.
Petzet, Heinrich Wiegand. *Encounters and Dialogues with Martin Heidegger, 1929-1976*. Chicago: The University of Chicago Press, 1993.
Perloff, Marjorie. *The Futurist Moment: Avant-Garde, Avant Guerre, and the Language of Rupture*. Chicago: The University of Chicago Press, 1987.
Plimpton, George A. and Rocco Landesman. "The Art of Fiction XLVI." In *Conversations with Jerzy Kosinski*, edited by Tom Teicholz, 20–36. Jackson: University Press of Mississippi, 1993.
Plutarch. "Isis and Osiris." In *Moralia*, vol. V. Translated by Frank Cole Babbitt. London/Cambridge: Loeb Classical Library, 1936.
Pöggeler, Otto. *Der Denkweg Martin Heideggers*. Pfullingen: Neske, 1963.
Pöggeler, Otto. "Todtnauberg." In *Martin Heidegger and the Holocaust*, edited by Alan Milchman and Alan Rosenberg, 102–112. New Jersey: Humanities Press, 1996.

Pöggeler, Otto. "Heideggers Begegnung mit Paul Celan." In *Disputatio Philosophica* 1 (1999): 38–49.
Pollock, John L. "Defeasible Reasoning." *Cognitive Science* 11, no. 4 (1987): 481–518.
Presner, Todd S. *Mobile Modernity: Germans, Jews, Trains*. New York: Columbia University Press, 2007.
Ricœur, Paul. *Temps et Récit, tome III: Le Temps Raconté*. Paris: Seuil, 1985.
Ríos Ávila, Rubén. "Julia de Burgos y el instante doloroso del mundo." *Revista Casa de las Américas* 240 (July-September 2005): 89–95.
Rohling, August. *Der Talmudjude*. Münster: Adolph Russells Verlag, 1871.
Rubin, Joey. "The Bus Has Long Since Pulled Out: A Conversation with David Markson." *The Scofield* 1, no. 1 (2015): 56–62.
Sahraoui, Nassima. *Dynamis: Eine materialistische Philosophie der Differenz*. Bielefeld: Transcript, 2021.
Sahraoui, Nassima. "Martin Heidegger: Wendungen. Zur Destruktion der Destruktion der Philosophie." In *Entwendungen: Walter Benjamin und seine Quellen*, edited by Jessica Nitsche and Nadine Werner, 149–168. Paderborn: Wilhelm Fink, 2019.
Sartre, Jean-Paul. "A propos de 'Le Bruit et la fureur:' La Temporalité chez Faulkner." In *Situations, I: Essais Critiques*, 64–75. Paris: Gallimard, 1947.
Scanlon, T.M. *What We Owe to Each Other*. Cambridge, MA: Harvard University Press, 1998.
Sharkey, Rodney. "Beaufret, Beckett, and Heidegger: The Question(s) of Influence." *Samuel Beckett Today/Aujourd'hui* 22 (2010): 409–422.
Sharr, Adam. *Heidegger's Hut*. Cambridge, MA: MIT Press, 2006.
Shemtov, Vered Karti. "Poetry and Dwelling: From Martin Heidegger to the Songbook of the Tent Revolution in Israel." *Prooftexts* 35, no. 2–3 (Spring-Fall 2015): 271–290.
Shimauchi, Keiji. "Elucidation of Lights and Shadows of 'Silk and Insight." *Bulletin of Denki-Tsūshin University* 18, no. 1–2 (2006): 127–175.
Shklovsky, Viktor. "On Poetry and Trans-Sense Language," translated by Gerald Janecek and Peter Mayer. *October* 34 (Autumn 1985): 3–24.
Sieburth, Richard, trans. *Hymns and Fragments by Friedrich Hölderlin*. Princeton: Princeton University Press, 1984.
Sloterdijk, Peter. *Critique of Cynical Reason*. Translated by Michael Eldred. Minneapolis: University of Minnesota Press, 1988.
Spillers, Hortense. "Faulkner Adds Up: Reading *Absalom, Absalom!* and *The Sound and the Fury*." In *Black, White, and in Color: Essays on American Literature and Culture*, 336–375. Chicago: University of Chicago Press, 2003.
Storck, Joachim W. "'Zwiesprache von Dichten und Denken': Hölderlin bei Martin Heidegger und Max Kommerell." In *Klassiker in finsteren Zeiten 1933-1945 Vol. I*, 352–357, edited by Bernhard Zeller. Marbach: Deutsche Schillergesellschaft, 1983.
Szondi, Peter. "Die Überwindung des Klassizismus." In *Hölderlin-Studien – Mit einem Traktat über philologische Erkenntnis*, 95–118. Frankfurt: Suhrkamp, 1970.

Szondi, Peter. "The Other Arrow: On the Genesis of the Late Hymnic Style." In *On Textual Understanding and Other Essays*, translated by Harvey Mendelsohn, 23–42. Minneapolis: University of Minnesota Press, 1986.

Tabbi, Joseph. "An Interview with David Markson." *Review of Contemporary Fiction* 10, no. 2 (1990): 104–117.

Thomä, Dieter, "Am Ab-Ort des Seins: Lächerliches und Erhabenes in Heideggers Philosophie." In *Verwindungen: Arbeit an Heidegger*, edited by Wolfgang Ullrich, 89–109. Frankfurt: Fischer, 2003.

Thomä, Dieter. "Groundlessness and Worldlessness: Heidegger's Anti-Semitism and Jewish Thought." In *Heidegger and Jewish Thought: Difficult Others*, edited by Elad Lapidot and Micha Brumlik, 109–134. London/New York: Rowman & Littlefield, 2018.

Thomä, Dieter, ed. *Heidegger-Handbuch: Leben-Werk- Wirkung*, in collaboration with Florian Grosser, Katrin Meyer, and Hans Bernhard Schmid, 2nd ed. Stuttgart: J.B. Metzler, 2013.

Thomä, Dieter. "Heidegger in der Satire: Das Herrchen des Seins." In *Heidegger-Handbuch: Leben-Werk- Wirkung*, edited by Dieter Thomä, 2nd ed., 536–539. Stuttgart: J.B. Metzler, 2013.

Thomä, Dieter "The Imperative Mode of Heidegger's Thought, National Socialism, and Anti-Semitism." In *Confronting Heidegger: A Critical Dialogue on Politics and Philosophy*, edited by Gregory Fried, chapter 6. London/New York: Rowman & Littlefield, 2019.

Thomson, Iain. *Heidegger, Art, and Postmodernity*. Cambridge: Cambridge University Press, 2011.

Thomson, Iain. "Technology, Ontotheology." In *Heidegger on Technology*, edited by Aaron James Wendland et al., 174–193, New York: Taylor & Francis, 2018.

Tobias, Rochelle. *The Discourse of Nature in the Poetry of Paul Celan*. Baltimore: Johns Hopkins University Press, 2006.

Tomšič, Samo. "Matheme." In *The Badiou Dictionary*, edited by Steven Corcoran, 196–199. Edinburgh: Edinburgh University Press, 2015.

von Bülow, Ulrich. "Raum Zeit Sprache: Peter Handke liest Martin Heidegger." In *Peter Handke: Stationen, Orte, Positionen*, edited by Anna Kinder, 111–140. Berlin/Boston: De Gruyter, 2014.

Weheliye, Alexander G. *Habeas Viscus: Racializing Assemblages, Biopolitics, and Black Feminist Theories of the Human*. Durham: Duke University Press, 2014.

Wenar, Leif. "Epistemic Rights and Legal Rights." *Analysis* 63, no. 2 (2003): 142–146.

Wimpfheimer, Barry. *The Talmud: A Biography*. Princeton; Oxford: Princeton University Press, 2018.

Wittgenstein, Ludwig. *Tractatus Logico-Philosophicus*. London: Routledge, 2001.

Wittgenstein, Ludwig. *Philosophical Investigations*. Hoboken: Wiley-Blackwell, 2009.

Woessner, Martin. *Heidegger in America*. Cambridge: Cambridge University Press, 2011.

Wolfe, Cary. "Introduction." In *What is Posthumanism?*, xi–xxxiv. Minneapolis: University of Minnesota Press, 2010.

Wolfson, Elliot. *Alef, Mem, Tau: Kabbalistic Musings on Time, Truth, and Death*. Berkeley et al.: University of California Press, 2006.
Wolfson Elliot. *Giving Beyond the Gift: Apophasis and Overcoming Theomania*. New York: Fordham University Press, 2014.
Wolfson, Elliot. *Heidegger and Kabbalah: Hidden Gnosis and the Path of Poiēsis*. Bloomington: Indiana University Press, 2019.
Wolfson, Elliot. *Language, Eros, and Being: Kabbalistic Hermeneutics and the Poetic Imagination*. New York: Fordham University Press, 2005.
Wolfson, Elliot. *The Duplicity of Philosophy's Shadow: Heidegger, Nazism, and the Jewish Other*. New York: Columbia University Press, 2018.
Wright, Kathleen. "Gespräch mit Hölderlin II. Die Heroisierung Hölderlins um 1933." In *Heidegger Handbuch: Leben-Werk- Wirkung*, edited by Dieter Thomä, 2nd ed., 188–200. Stuttgart: J.B. Metzler, 2013.
Wynter, Sylvia, and Katherine McKittrick. "Unparalleled Catastrophe For Our Species? Or, To Give Humanness a Different Future: Conversations." In *Sylvia Wynter: Being Human as Praxis*, edited by Katherine McKittrick, 9–89. Durham: Duke University Press, 2015.
Zarader, Marlène. *La Dette impensée: Heidegger et l'héritage hébraïque*. Paris: Seuil, 1990. Zarader, Marlène. *The Unthought Debt: Heidegger and the Hebraic Heritage*. Translated by Bettina Bergo. Stanford: Stanford University Press, 2006.
Ziarek, Krystof. "The Reception of Heidegger's Thought in American Literary Criticism." *Diacritics* 19 (1989): 124–126.
Ziarek, Krysztof. "Semiosis of Listening: The Other in Heidegger's Writings on Hölderlin and Celan's *Meridian*." *Research in Phenomenology* 24 (1994): 113–132.
Zimmermann, Hans Dieter. *Martin und Fritz Heidegger: Philosophie und Fastnacht*. Munich: C.H. Beck, 2005.
Zumhagen-Yekplé, Karen. "The Everyday's Fabulous Beyond: Nonsense, Parable, and the Ethics of the Literary in Kafka and Wittgenstein." *Comparative Literature* 64, no. 4 (2012): 429–445.

Index

Abe, Kōbō, xix, 236
absence (*Abwesenheit*), 12, 17, 22, 27–29, 83, 162, 172, 181n13, 199, 211, 251–52
activity/active, 59, 90, 129, 132, 193, 213, 230
Adorno, Theodor W., 5, 16, 103
adventure (*avventura*), 186–89, 192, 202n12
Agamben, Giorgio, 45n37, 186, 188–89, 192–95, 200–201, 202n19, 203n25
alienation, 109–10, 119n38, 169
America/American, x, xxn2, 54, 109, 147, 214
anastasis/ana-stasis, 206–7, 210. *See also stasis*
the Anthropocene, xviii, 186, 200, 201n4
anthropos/anthropology/anthropological/anthropogenesis, 186, 188–92
anti-Judaism, 22–24, 34n4
anti-Semitism/anti-Semitic, xiii, 21–24, 34n1, 34n4, 63n36, 79n37
anxiety (*Angst*), 108, 172–73
Arendt, Hannah, 48–49, 55, 57
Aristotle, 96n8, 217
art/artwork, ix–x, 30–31, 41, 86–90, 93, 97nn18–19, 112–13, 120n54, 136, 144, 164, 221, 224, 234, 246, 251

Ashbery, John, xx, xvi–xvii, 157–68
Auschwitz, 31–32, 119n36
authenticity/authentic (*Eigentlichkeit, eigentlich*), 40, 54–55, 57, 106, 118n14, 143–44, 148, 152, 179, 196, 198, 204n40, 223, 229
autopoiesis/autopoetic, 186, 192–94

Bachmann, Ingeborg, xi, xxin5, 56, 62n30, 101n46
Badiou, Alain, xiii–xiv, 37–45
Baudelaire, Charles, 158
Beat Generation, x
Beattie, Anne, 169, 180
Beckett, Samuel, x
Being (*Sein*), xiv–xv, xvii, 13, 22–23, 26, 28, 34n5, 40–41, 47, 49–52, 57, 60, 67–69, 74, 76, 77n5, 81–88, 90–91, 94–95, 106, 109, 127–28, 130–31, 133–34, 136–37, 145–46, 160–61, 163, 174, 186, 188–89, 191, 193, 195, 206, 210, 217, 219, 222–24, 229–30, 232–34, 237, 252, 253n8; forgetfulness of Being (*Seinsvergessenheit*), 40–41, 53, 84
Being and Time (*Sein und Zeit*), ix, 15, 85, 106, 118, 127, 133, 136, 143, 169, 172–74, 179, 182n48, 210, 216, 223, 231

being-in-the-world (*in-der-Welt-sein*), 130, 169, 173–74, 180, 215–16, 231–32
being-there (*Dasein*), xii, xviii, 13, 52–54, 74, 84, 88, 90–91, 118n19, 132, 145, 169, 173, 176–77, 179–80, 185–87, 193, 195, 198, 200–201, 204n40, 206, 209, 213, 215–16, 231–32
being-toward-death (*Sein-zum-Tode*), 206, 209–10, 212, 220
being-with (*Mitsein*), 199, 208, 211
Beißner, Friedrich, 10, 14, 17, 19n2
Bellow, Saul, x, 48, 53
Benjamin, Andrew, 67, 69, 83
Benjamin, Walter, xviii, 31–32, 82, 98n24, 206, 209, 212, 219, 221–22, 226n35
Bergson, Henri, 231
Bernhard, Thomas, 48, 55–57
Beyng (*Seyn*), 82, 85, 93, 242
Bible, 22–28, 30, 32–33, 34n2, 50
biopolitics/biopolitical, 189, 195, 202n19
Black Notebooks (*Schwarze Hefte*), xiii, 21–23, 28, 119n47
Black studies, 190, 201n1
Blanchot, Maurice, xviii, 32, 206, 208, 212, 216, 225n17
body, 108, 114, 147–48, 150–51, 209–10, 218, 220
Buber, Martin, 53
Bülow, Ulrich von, 103, 117n3, 117n5, 119n48, 121n72

care (*Sorge*), 51, 53, 87, 104–7, 110, 118n14, 174, 210
Carman, Taylor, 175
Cassirer, Ernst, 81
Celan, Paul, x, xv, 39–40, 56, 67–79, 81–84, 89, 91, 94–101
Cézanne, Paul, 104–5, 111–13, 116, 120n54, 121n73
Chagall, Marc, 71, 78n16
Christianity/Christian, 22–26, 28–30, 32–33, 34n4, 130, 135, 173–74
clearing (*Lichtung*), xv, 41, 81, 83, 85–88, 98n21, 121n29, 131

the comical, xiii, 47–50, 55–56, 58–60
community/communality/communal, x, 17, 108–10, 113, 115, 118n27, 143, 199–200, 208, 211, 236, 246–47, 252
concealment/concealed, 49, 60, 83–84, 91, 95, 243
confluences (*confluencias*), xviii, 205
constellation/constellatory, xi, xvi, xviii, 68–70, 72, 74, 82, 86, 90, 106, 109, 112, 135, 219, 223, 230, 232
conversation (*Gespräch*), xii, 15, 67–69, 103, 108, 141, 145–46, 148, 212, 244
counterhumanism, 190–91. *See also* humanism
creators/creating (*Schaffende*, *Schaffen*), xiv, 69, 90–91, 130, 137, 212–13, 243, 245
criticism/critics, xiii, xvi, 5–20, 37, 40, 47, 77n5, 134, 142, 166n4, 235

danger (*Gefahr*), xi, xiii, 6, 8, 10–18, 60, 153, 219, 229
Dastur, Françoise, 23, 34n8
Davos, 81, 95n2
death, xii, xviii, 38, 51–52, 54, 57, 67, 71, 81, 108, 130, 135, 147, 162, 185, 187, 196–98, 200–201, 204n40, 207–14, 216, 218–20, 223, 237, 245
debt (*Schuld*), 33, 221–23. *See also* guilt
de Burgos, Julia, xvii–xviii, 185–204
deconstruction/deconstructive, xi, 38, 82, 93, 97n19, 109, 111, 116, 194, 223–24
de Man, Paul, 5, 7–8, 13–14, 16
Derrida, Jacques, xii, 33, 86, 194, 201n1, 202n7, 203n34, 223, 239n3
Der Spiegel (interview), 37, 55–56, 117n5, 137n4
Descartes, René, Cartesian, 134, 169, 172, 194, 214–15
destiny, xvi–xvii, 15, 60, 106, 109, 118n18, 143–48, 151–53, 160, 167n14, 233
destruction (of metaphysics), ix, xiv, 38, 110, 238

Index

disclosure/disclosing (*Entbergung, entbergen*), 12–13, 15–17, 47, 49, 86, 108, 128, 130, 132, 143, 145, 193, 198, 243
discourse (*Rede*), 15, 24, 27, 158, 192, 242–43
disfiguration, xi, 31–32. *See also* figuration
the divine/divinities, xiii, 8–14, 16–17, 30, 68, 74, 137
Dostoevsky, Fyodor, x
Dreyfus, Hubert, xxn2, 170, 175
Dugin, Aleksandr, 235
dwelling (*Wohnen*), xii, xiv–xvi, 24–25, 27, 29–30, 67–79, 89–90, 106, 109, 114–15, 127–28, 131, 160–61, 189, 194, 216, 227n54, 230–31, 235; poetic dwelling (*dichterisch wohnen*), 24–25, 68–69, 74, 89, 194, 210
Dworkin, Ronald, 129

earth/earthly, xiv, 8–14, 16, 27, 41–43, 45n34, 70–71, 74–76, 82–83, 86, 88–91, 93–95, 98n20, 111, 114, 136, 221, 243, 253n8
the East/Eastern, xii, xix, 69, 71, 75, 99n27, 164, 229–33
eclipse, 185, 201n1
ecology/ecological, 40, 43, 51
ecstasy/ecstatic, 108, 206, 209–10, 216, 220, 231
Eliot, T.S., 133
ellipse/ellipsis, xvi, 83, 89, 91, 94–95, 99n27, 205, 208
enframing (*Gestell*), 127
epos/epic, xvi, 116, 117n4, 120n54, 129
essence/essencing/essential (*Wesen, wesentlich*), ix, 7, 15, 25, 31, 52, 76, 86–88, 90, 100n38, 106, 130, 135, 143–46, 158, 161, 164, 187, 189–90, 192–96, 207, 210, 217, 229, 236, 242–43, 245, 250, 252
ethics/(the) ethical, xii, xviii, 32, 93, 109, 119n36, 186, 210, 220

event/event of appropriation (*Ereignis*), xviii, 7, 10, 12–17, 22, 31, 40, 59, 67, 82, 86, 97n19, 106, 112, 185–89, 192, 195, 208–9
everydayness (*Alltäglichkeit*)/(the) everyday, 53–55, 105, 128, 172, 174, 178, 231, 245
exile, 26, 71, 73–74, 133, 195, 208, 236–38
experience (*Erfahrung*), xv, 11, 57, 60, 71, 77, 108–9, 111–12, 114–16, 119n45, 132, 145–46, 163, 172–75, 179, 187, 189, 194–96, 200–201, 207, 212, 229, 232, 234, 251
expression (*Ausdruck*), 11, 13–14, 38, 112, 209, 215, 244

facticity, 52, 198, 212, 232
falling (*Verfallen*), 30, 53–54, 60, 106, 161, 200
Fanon, Frantz, 191, 202n25
Faulkner, William, xvi, 141–55
Fichte, Johann Gottlieb, 230
figuration, 31–32, 72, 75, 144. *See also* disfiguration
finitude/finite, xviii, 8, 10, 14–15, 17, 38, 41–43, 187, 195, 200, 206, 212, 221–23
Fitzgerald, William, 6, 14, 20n6
Flannery O'Connor, Mary, 48, 50–51, 61n10
Flaubert, Gustave, 54
foreign (*fremd*), xi, xvi, 26, 104–7, 109–10, 115, 119n43, 119n45, 119n47, 144–46, 152–53, 155n34, 163–64, 205, 234–35
foundation/foundational/founding (*stiften, gründen*), 12, 24–27, 29–30, 42, 90, 106, 108, 143, 145, 153, 163–64, 242
fourfold (*Geviert*), ix, 74–75, 115
freedom/free, 32, 54, 113, 121n73, 128, 130–31, 133–34, 144, 162, 191, 193, 202n25, 221, 233–35, 238, 243, 245; free relation (*freies Verhältnis*), 114, 234

Frisch, Max, x

Gadamer, Hans-Georg, 41
Gaos, José, 210, 214–16, 224n1, 226n49
gather/gathering (*Versammeln, Versammlung*), 71, 73, 75, 115, 161, 233, 237
genealogy, xix, 91, 119n38, 134, 230, 235, 238–39
geography/geographies/geopolitical, xii, xv, xvii–xviii, 72–73, 81, 83, 86–87, 94, 111
George, Stefan, 106
Germany/(the) German/Germans, 8, 16–17, 26, 54–56, 74, 76, 106, 109, 118n19, 143–46, 163–65; German language, literature, and philosophical tradition, 34n4, 55, 75–76, 144
God/gods, xiii–xiv, xvi, 10, 11–13, 16–17, 23–30, 32, 37–39, 43, 45n36, 54, 72, 83, 88, 95, 127–31, 134, 136, 157–58, 160, 162, 164, 207, 222, 231, 242, 245; Goddess, xiii, 84; God of poets, 37–40, 42–43, 44n12
Goethe, Johann Wolfgang von, 104
Graf, Oskar Maria, 48, 51–52, 57
grammar/grammatical, xix, 6–7, 9–10, 17, 161, 241, 243–46, 248, 250–51
Grass, Günter, x, 48, 52–53, 56–57
Greece/(the) Greek/Greeks, xiii, 16, 22–24, 26, 40–41, 75–76, 83, 89, 98n22, 104, 109, 131, 143–46, 154n6, 154n9, 163–64, 206, 210, 238
ground (*Grund*)/groundlessness/groundless, xi, xv, 13, 24, 52, 70–71, 73, 89–91, 93, 108, 220–22, 238, 242
guilt (*Schuld*), 11, 221–22, 228n83. *See also* debt

Hamacher, Werner, 83, 95n4, 100n41, 100n43, 101n45, 199, 217, 222
Hamsun, Knut, x
Handke, Peter, x, xv, 61n1, 103–21
heart (*Herz*), 5, 9, 11, 14, 18, 69, 92–94

heaven/heavenly, 8, 11, 74, 82, 89–90, 93, 95, 109, 114, 160, 163–65, 238
Hebrew language and literature, xv, 34n4, 67–68, 72–73, 75–76, 77n5
Hegel, G.W.F., 6, 8, 14, 119n43, 167n14, 217, 236
Heidegger, Fritz, 49, 61n8
Heine, Heinrich, 73
Hellingrath, Norbert von, 5–9, 17
Heraclitus, 12, 34n5, 110
hermeneutics/hermeneutic, xii, 6–8, 15–16, 33, 54, 173
Herzl, Theodor, 71
historicity/historical (*geschichtlich*), xii–xiii, 7, 15, 17, 25, 27, 29–30, 74, 84, 88–91, 104, 106, 141, 144–45, 190–91, 209, 223, 229–30, 233–36; history of Being (*Seinsgeschichte*), xxn2, 186, 190, 223
Hitler, Adolf, 42, 51, 74, 144
Hölderlin, Friedrich, ix, xiii, xvi–xvii, 5–12, 14–17, 20n12, 24–32, 38–39, 41–42, 45n36, 69, 74, 84, 89, 98n22, 98n24, 104, 106–8, 110–11, 118n19, 119n44, 127, 141–46, 148–49, 152–53, 154n6, 154n9, 155n34, 157–65, 166nn5–6, 167n20, 167n26, 195, 207, 221, 242
holiday (*Feiertag*), xiii, 5–9, 11, 13, 16–17, 19n2, 20n12, 71, 165
Holocaust, 21–22
(the) holy, 9–11, 13, 16, 27–31, 58, 84, 87, 90, 160, 164–65
homecoming (*Heimkehr*), xv, xvii, 103–4, 106–9, 111–14, 116, 117n2, 120n57, 145, 150, 157, 159–63, 245
home/homeland (*Heimat*), xi, 25–26, 29, 57, 73, 106, 112, 132, 145, 152, 159, 230
homelessness (*Heimatlosigkeit*), xvi, 26, 28–29, 115, 133
homo oeconomicus, 190–91
horizon/horizontal, 29, 31, 114, 135, 186, 191, 194, 222–23, 230–33, 251

house of Being (*Haus des Seins*), xiv–xv, 49, 67–69, 76, 77n5, 83, 94–95
the human, 15, 185–96, 200–201, 202n19, 202n25, 211, 218
humanism, xiv, 49, 69, 76, 186, 192, 194. *See also* counterhumanism
Husserl, Edmund, 53
hut (*Hütte*), xv, 56–57, 67–69, 71, 73, 76, 81, 91–92
hymn/the hymnic (*das Hymnische*), xiii, 5–14, 16–17, 19n2, 106, 108
hypertelia/hypertelic, 220–23

iki (beauty), 229–30, 233, 235
image, xviii, 29, 32, 68–69, 71, 73–76, 77n5, 82, 84, 91, 112, 120n61, 158, 195, 205–27
immediacy/immediate, 8, 10, 12–14, 16, 26–28, 89–90, 99n27, 106, 131, 134
(the) impossible, 39, 142, 185, 188, 198, 200, 204n40, 207, 212–14, 216
in-between (*zwischen, das Zwischen*), xii–xiv, 10, 84, 90, 93–94, 199
interpretation/interpretive, ix, xi–xiii, xix, 6–9, 11, 14, 16–17, 19n1, 43, 106, 112, 141, 143, 191, 194–95, 197, 218, 229, 241, 243–44, 246–48, 253n8; interpretive violence, 7, 9, 17
ipseity/ipseitological/ipseitocratic, xviii, 187, 194–96, 200, 203n34, 204n40
irony/ironic, xvii, 8, 17, 50, 57, 137n1, 141–42, 153, 177–80, 182n48, 198–99, 224, 237–38

James, William, 230
Jankélévitch, Vladimir, 231
Japan, Japanese thought and literature, xix, 229–30, 235–38
"Japanhood" (*Nihon-sei*), 233, 235, 238
Jean Paul, 58
Jelinek, Elfriede, x, 48, 56–57
"the Jewish", xiii, 21–24, 33
Jews, Jewish life and thought, 23, 29, 31–32, 34n4, 69, 71, 75–76, 119n47
Joyce, James, 133

joy/joyous, 162–63
Judaism, 28
Jünger, Ernst, x

Kabbalah/kabbalistic, 22, 33, 36n29, 72, 77n4
Kafka, Franz, 49
Kant, Immanuel, Kantian, 59–60, 169, 178, 215, 219–21, 228n67
Kelly, Sean D., xxn2, 175
Kermode, Frank, 127, 137n1
Khlebnikov, Velimir, xviii–xix, 242, 245–46, 248–52, 254n18
Kierkegaard, Søren, 53, 177–79, 206–8, 212, 220
Klee, Paul, 112, 121n74
knowledge, 21, 28, 33, 40, 68, 134–36, 174, 214, 223
Kommerell, Max, 19n1, 19n3
Kosinski, Jerzy, 48, 54, 62n26
Koyré, Alexandre, 231
Kruchenykh, Alexei, xviii–xix, 242, 244–49, 251–52
Kuki, Shūzō, xviii–xix, 229–40
Kunkel, Benjamin, x
Kyoto School, 230, 237

Lachmann, Eduard, xiii, 5–11, 13–14, 16–17, 19n1
Lacoue-Labarthe, Philippe, 29–32, 33, 35n14, 45n38
language (*Sprache*), x–xi, xiv–xv, xviii, xix, 6–8, 10–17, 22, 24, 26–27, 30–33, 38–39, 48–49, 51–53, 56, 60, 67–69, 71–77, 77n5, 78n8, 81–83, 86–90, 93–94, 98n24, 100n38, 100n43, 104–5, 107, 113, 116, 120n56, 128, 131–32, 136, 141, 143, 148, 172, 176, 177, 185, 187–89, 192–99, 200–201, 202n19, 205, 207–11, 226n49, 229, 234–35, 241–48, 250–52; address (*Ansprechen*), 100n38, 187, 197–200; origin of language, xi, 23, 25, 242; response (*Entsprechen*), 187, 200

law of historicity, 104–7, 110–11
Lear, Jonathan, 178–80
Lemke, Anja, 68, 95n4
Lestrange, Gisèle, 83, 91
letting be (*Gelassenheit*), 42, 130–31, 168n37, 245
Levinas, Emmanuel, 22, 33, 34n5, 36n31, 78n23, 99n27, 210
Lezama Lima, José, xviii, 205–17, 219–24, 226n49, 227n66
literature/literary, x–xix, 15, 17, 21, 23, 29, 30–33, 34n4, 48, 55, 77n6, 82, 84, 103–4, 113, 115, 129, 132, 141–42, 159, 170, 175, 177, 181, 182, 195, 205–6, 209, 230, 233, 235, 237–38, 241
Littell, Jonathan, 115
logocentrism/logocentric, xviii, 186–87, 195, 202n7
logos, xii–xiii, xv, 15, 27, 29–30, 33, 83, 89, 100n41, 186, 189
Lucretius, 103, 118n22
Lukács, Georg, 48
Lyotard, Jean-François, 59

Mann, Thomas, 48, 55, 57, 60
Marcel, Gabriel, 8, 51, 61n14
Markson, David, xvi–xvii, 169–71, 175, 177–80
Matisse, Henri, 112
McCarthy, Cormac, x, xxn4
mediacy, 8, 10
melancholy/melancholic, xiv, 37–38, 41, 43, 45n36, 147, 162, 165
meridian, 15, 68, 74, 78n8, 68, 81, 83, 85, 87, 89, 91, 93–95, 95n3, 99n27
Merleau-Ponty, Maurice, 112, 120n61
metaphysics/metaphysical, ix, xiv, xiii, xvi, xviii, 7–8, 12–14, 23–24, 37–38, 40, 50, 85–87, 90, 110, 127, 131, 136, 141–42, 146, 172–74, 177–78, 186, 189, 191, 194, 231–33, 253n8
Miki, Kiyoshi, 230
Mishima, Yukio, xix, 237–38
moment of vision (*Augenblick*), 13, 105–6

mood (*Stimmung*), xi, 105, 132, 136, 172, 179, 216
mortality/mortal, xviii, 8, 10, 12, 14, 38, 83–84, 136, 163, 186–87, 194–96, 200, 204n40, 211, 216, 218; mortals (*Sterbliche*), 74, 114, 163
mountain (*Berg, Gebirge*), 48, 81–82, 86, 95, 95n1, 111, 132, 160–61
Muschg, Walter, 5
music/musical, 60, 108, 129, 135, 158–59, 250
myth/mythos/mythology/mythological, xv, 10, 23, 25, 30, 31, 32, 73–74, 83–84, 86, 91, 96n13, 98n24, 127, 130, 133, 179, 191–92, 206, 223, 226n49, 228n83

the name, 11, 24, 26, 31, 33, 70–72, 81, 85, 87, 90, 92, 94, 98n24, 101n46, 105, 117n11, 128, 147–49, 151, 158, 162–63, 186–89, 192, 195, 197–98, 200, 207, 209–12, 217, 221, 223, 244, 251; naming, x, 24, 87–88, 90, 93–94, 98n24, 104–5, 110, 113, 116, 117n11
Nancy, Jean-Luc, 35n14, 208
narràns, 188, 191–92, 194
narrative/narrativity, xii, 31, 71, 73, 76, 119n38, 173, 186, 192–94, 196, 237
nation/(the) national/nationalism/ nationalist, 5, 7, 23, 26, 30, 51, 73–74, 79n25, 110, 115–16, 119n44, 144, 159, 195, 223, 233, 235–36, 239n3
National Socialism/National Socialist/ Nazism/Nazi, ix, xv, 8, 11, 15, 22–26, 28–31, 48, 52–53, 55, 71, 75, 79n37, 82, 86, 92–93, 107, 115, 190
necrophiloloy/necrophilological, 208–9, 211, 217
"New People" (*Neue Leute*), x
Nietzsche, Friedrich, xvi, 13, 24, 106, 111, 117n5, 120n49, 128, 130, 136, 222
nihilism/nihilist, xi, 41–42, 44n12, 51, 128, 237

Nishida, Kitarō, 230
nostalgia/nostalgic, xiv, 37–40, 42–43, 54, 213, 221
nothing/(the) nothing/nothingness, 39, 50–53, 57, 88, 90, 99n25, 104, 113–14, 149, 172, 175, 189n13, 196–97, 204n40, 213, 216, 222
Novalis, x, 104

O'Brien, William Arctander, 7–8, 10, 14
Odyssey/Odysseus, 34n2, 119n38, 230
Old Testament, 23–24, 25, 30, 32–33
ontic/ontic-ontological, 53, 196, 209–11, 222, 231
ontology/ontological, xvi, 7, 15, 17, 38, 51, 59, 85, 88, 111, 115, 118n19, 136, 147, 174–75, 181n13, 186, 188–89, 191, 193–94, 196, 203n25, 204n40, 205–6, 209, 211, 213, 217, 219, 221–23, 229–32, 236, 239n3
onto-theology/onto-theological, 13, 28
the open/the opening/openness, xx, 38, 88, 91, 113, 162, 165, 167n20, 210
(the) origin (*Ursprung*), xi, xvi, 23, 28–29, 32, 106, 149, 191, 193, 242
The Origin of the Work of Art, x, 45n34, 86, 88–90, 93, 97n18–19, 97–98, 136
origin/original (*Ursprung, ursprünglich*), x–xi, xvi, 13–15, 22–23, 25, 28–29, 32, 40, 42, 53, 59, 75, 84–86, 89–90, 97n18, 98n21, 106–7, 111, 116, 136, 143–44, 146, 169, 172–74, 181n13, 191–93, 204n40, 221, 241–45, 249, 251
own (*eigen*)/ownmost (*eigenst*), 104, 106, 109–10, 115, 119n45, 143–44, 148, 155n34, 213, 238. *See also* proper

Pascal, Blaise, Pascalian, 214, 216
the people (*das Volk*), xvii, 8, 11–12, 14–17, 18, 23, 25–26, 30–32, 43, 69, 71–72, 88–91, 93, 97, 106, 108, 110, 116, 143–48, 155n34, 190, 207, 223, 235

phenomenology/phenomenological, xvi–xvii, 51, 157, 159–61, 165, 166n4, 167n14, 169–70, 173, 175, 209, 220, 230, 232
Pindar, x, 10, 137
place (*Ort*), xiv, 22, 27, 51, 67, 69, 72, 76, 81–82, 84, 86, 88, 93, 99n27, 100n41, 105, 107, 110–12, 117n11, 120n57, 131, 133, 136–37, 157, 160, 163–64, 177, 185–86, 189, 197, 199–200, 210, 216, 233, 235. *See also* spatiality, space
Plato/Platonic, 29–31, 40, 42, 83, 136, 142, 219
play (*Spiel*)/playfulness/playful, xi, xii, xvi, 8, 10, 12, 15–16, 40, 47–49, 51, 54, 56, 59–60, 115, 128, 132, 160, 178, 208, 216, 233–38, 241, 245, 250
plurality, 16, 115, 199, 230, 232–33
Plutarch, 83, 94, 96n13
poem (*Gedicht*), xi–xiii, xv–xvi, xviii, 5–6, 9, 11–13, 17, 19n2, 25, 30, 38–40, 67–69, 71–76, 77nn4–6, 78n8, 83–84, 89–93, 98n24, 99n28, 100n38, 101n46, 131, 133–34, 137, 155n34, 157–63, 165, 187–88, 194–201, 204n40, 206, 208, 211–12, 234, 244, 247–50
poet (*Dichter*), ix–xi, xiii–xx, 6–17, 24, 26, 29, 37–43, 44n12, 58, 67–68, 77n6, 81–83, 87, 89–90, 93, 106–7, 117n11, 119n44, 127–29, 131–32, 136–37, 141, 145–46, 157–58, 160–65, 187, 195–200, 206, 209, 212–13, 231, 233, 238, 241–42, 252, 253n2; poet's vocation, xiii, 6, 8, 10–11
poetically, xvi, xx, 24, 67, 69, 73, 76, 89, 108, 113, 117n11, 127
poeticise, xiii, 91, 93, 110, 118n19, 194, 196
poetics, ix, xvi, 31, 42, 103, 111, 194, 206–7, 209, 233
poetise (*dichten*), ix, 106, 113, 128, 145, 192
poetology/poetological, 29, 104, 110–11, 194

poetry (*Dichtung*), x–xvi, xviii–xix, 5, 7, 11–12, 14–17, 20n12, 22, 24–26, 30–31, 37, 39, 41–42, 68–69, 76–77, 77n4, 77n6, 81–84, 86–90, 93, 98n22, 100n43, 104, 112, 128–32, 134–37, 138n16, 141–46, 157–59, 161–65, 166n4, 170, 187, 194–95, 205–6, 210, 217, 220–22, 229–30, 233–35, 242, 244–45, 254n18; poetics, ix, xvi, 31, 42, 103, 111, 194, 206–7, 209, 233; poetic thinking, ix–xi, xix–xx, 113, 116–17, 128, 132
Pöggeler, Otto, 73, 96n6
poiēsis, 24, 88, 90, 98n24, 130, 192, 194
polemos (*Auseinandersetzung, Kampf*), 110, 119n45, 119n47
politics/(the) political, ix, xi–xiii, xv–xvii, xix, 7, 22–27, 29–31, 33, 42, 47, 57–58, 74, 81–82, 86, 97n19, 101n46, 104, 106, 108, 111, 115–16, 118n19, 127, 131, 134, 146–47, 186, 189, 191, 194, 213, 223, 232, 235–36, 241–42, 246–47, 252
postmodernity/postmodern, 41, 44n12, 59–60
potency/potentiality, 52, 192–93, 200, 217–18
Pound, Ezra, 133
presence/presencing (*Anwesenheit*), xix, 13–16, 22–24, 27–33, 40, 68, 72, 75, 110, 130–33, 158, 162, 164, 174–75, 181n13, 186, 188, 201n1, 214, 216, 219, 227n55
present-at-hand/presence-at-hand (*vorhanden, Vorhandenheit*), 11, 15–16, 144, 174, 210
preserving (*bewahren*), 14–15, 17, 131
pre-Socratic, 23, 53
primordial, 74, 107, 130, 133, 169, 174–75, 231–34, 251
projection (*Entwerfen*), 88, 91, 93, 99n25

proper (*eigen*), 106, 108, 110, 114, 119n43, 141–53, 154n9, 155n34, 163–64, 186–87, 194–98, 201, 204n40, 224. See also own
property (*Eigentum*), 143, 193, 213, 238
prophet/prophecy/prophetic, 22, 25–28, 30, 33, 38

Rabbi/rabbinic, xiii, 21, 32–33, 34n4, 72
rational/rationalism/rationalist/ rationality, xvii, 59, 169–70, 175
reactionary, 37, 42–43
ready-to-hand/readiness-to-hand (*zuhanden, Zuhandenheit*), xvii, 15, 174–75, 210, 215
Rectoral address (*Rektoratsrede*), 82, 86
region (*Gegend*), 82, 105, 115, 211, 215–17, 227n55
religion, 23, 30, 37–38, 129, 190, 222, 233
remembrance (*Andenken*), xvi–xvii, 26, 106, 143–49, 153, 159, 161–62, 209
Remnick, David, 157
repetition/retrieval (*Wiederholung*), 72, 115, 141, 147, 212, 234
resurrection, 205–21, 223–24, 226n48, 227n61
return/returning, xvi, xvii–xix, 15, 26, 38–40, 45n36, 75, 94, 103–7, 109–11, 114–15, 119n38, 120n57, 144, 146–47, 150–53, 157, 161–63, 185–87, 189, 192, 201, 201n1, 215, 231, 239n11, 241, 243, 246–47, 250
revolution/revolutionary, xi–xii, xix, 207, 241, 244
rhyme, xix, 233–35, 237
Ricœur, Paul, 23
Rilke, Rainer Maria, x
romanticism, 38, 45n36, 84, 158
rootedness, 67, 73, 108
rootlessness, 73. See also uprootedness
Rubin, Joey, 170
Rushdie, Salman, 115
Russian futurism/futurists, xviii–xix, 241, 246

Sachsen-Meiningen, Margot von, 48–49, 55, 57
Sartre, Jean-Paul, 52, 141–42, 146–47, 152
satire/satirical, xiii–xiv, 47–52, 55, 58–60
saving power (*das Rettende*), 153
saying (*Sagen*), 16, 24, 27–28, 75, 87–88, 90, 94, 141, 189
scepticism, xvii, 169, 174–75, 177–78
Schelling, Friedrich Wilhelm Joseph, 206, 217–20, 227n66
Schiller, Friedrich, 206, 217–20, 227n66
Schmitt, Carl, 48, 51, 55–56
Scott, Douglas, 162, 166n2
self-alienation, 109, 119n38
self-assertion (*Selbstbehauptung*), 59, 86, 118n19, 233
selfhood/self, xvi, 7, 9, 12, 14–16, 22–23, 30–31, 41, 45n34, 50, 54, 57, 59–60, 91, 104, 107–10, 112–13, 116, 119n45, 120n54, 121n73, 131–34, 141, 152, 155n34, 157, 160, 162, 164, 169, 172–75, 177–79, 186, 193–96, 199–200, 203n34, 205, 222–24, 232–33, 235–36, 238
sense, ix, 7, 12, 39, 67, 74, 84–85, 87, 90, 104–5, 108–9, 112–13, 129, 130, 132, 134, 137, 143, 147, 159, 165, 177–78, 185, 191, 193–95, 197, 199–200, 203n25, 209, 214–15, 220, 222–23, 230, 232–33, 235–36, 241, 243–46, 248–53; beyonsense, transense (*zaum'*), 245–47, 250–51; nonsense, 176, 178, 241, 246, 248
sheltering (*Bergen*), xv, 45n34, 85–86, 95
Sieburth, Richard, 158
silence, xi–xii, xv, xvii, xix, 22, 75, 82, 92–94, 100n43, 101n46, 104, 107, 116, 148, 161, 175, 177, 183, 216, 227n66, 241–43, 245, 248–49, 251–52
site (*Stätte*), ix, xiv–xv, xvii, 12, 22–27, 29, 51, 71–72, 75–76, 81, 88–91, 112, 114, 152, 157–59, 161–62, 165, 189, 207–8, 211, 213, 219, 231
sky, 71, 74, 76, 89, 136
Sloterdijk, Peter, 180, 182n48
solipsism/solipsist, xvii, 116, 170
solitude, 169–70, 172–73, 200, 212
song, 8, 11, 12, 51, 62n15, 158–61, 165
spatiality, space (*Räumlichkeit, Raum*), xi, xvi–xviii, xx, 6, 22, 27, 52, 68–69, 72, 76–77, 93, 104–5, 111, 113–15, 145, 160–61, 163, 165, 166n4, 172–75, 187, 198–99, 206–7, 212–17, 221, 223–24, 230; spatio-temparal/space-time/time-space, 13, 27, 29
species, 43, 179–80, 190–92
Spengler, Oswald, 53
Spinoza, Baruch, 103, 109, 118n22
Stadler, Arnold, 48, 57–58
stasis, 210. *See also anastasis/ana-stasis*
Stein, Gertrude, 241
Stevens, Wallace, xvi, 127–37, 137n1
Stifter, Adalbert, 55, 57, 145
style, xi, xvii, 5, 16–17, 117, 207, 226n49, 237–38
subject, ix, 30–31, 39–40, 59, 73, 121n69, 128, 130, 134, 169–70, 174–75, 181, 193–94, 212, 214–16, 227n55, 231, 236, 247; intersubjective, 108, 233; subjectivation, 60; subjectivism/subjectivist/subjective/subjectivity, xvii, 9, 14, 103, 113, 230, 231–32
the sublime, xiii–xiv, 47, 58–60, 82, 129, 214, 220–21
Szondi, Peter, 5–10, 14, 16

Tabbi, Joseph, 170–71
Talmud, Talmudic, xi, xiii, 21–23, 29, 32–33, 34n4, 36n31
technology/technological, 25, 28, 41–43, 112, 127–28, 234, 237
teleology/teleological, 220–21, 223
temporality/temporal/time (*Zeitlichkeit, Zeit*), ix, xi–xiv, xvi–xix, 7–8, 10–12,

14–17, 22, 25, 27–29, 31, 52, 74, 85, 105–6, 114, 127, 133, 136, 141–43, 145–47, 149, 151–52, 158–59, 161–62, 169, 172–74, 179, 185, 206, 208, 210, 216–17, 223, 229–34, 236
terrestrial, xv, 82, 89–90, 94–95
territory/territoriality/territorial, 71, 73, 77, 119n38, 160
Tezuka, Tomio, 229
thing/thinging (*Ding, Dingen*), 15, 49, 51, 59–60, 75, 111–12, 114, 117, 121n73, 129–32, 135–36, 157–58, 161, 163, 169, 171–72, 174, 210, 219, 222, 244–45
thinker (*Denker*), xvi, 27, 29, 31, 87, 49, 53, 55–60, 67–68, 87–88, 90, 93, 128–29, 135, 144, 160–61, 169–70, 175, 177, 194–95, 205, 210, 230, 233
Thomä, Dieter, xix, 74–75
Tobias, Rochelle, 68, 72
Todtnauberg, xv, 5, 56, 67, 81, 83, 91–94, 95n1, 101n46
topology/topological, xv, 51, 81–83, 86, 93–94, 100n41, 160–61, 206; topology of Being, 82, 160–61, 206
topos, xv, 31–32, 51, 81–83, 93–94, 209, 224
Torah, 72–73
Trakl, Georg, x, 52
transition, 10, 104, 111–12, 115, 120n50, 133
translation, xviii, 10, 19n1, 32, 34n4, 48, 68, 73, 75, 158, 160, 162, 166n2, 166n5, 167n26, 168n37, 176, 188, 192, 201n1, 202n25, 203n25, 205, 214–15, 224n1, 226n49, 229, 246–50
truth (*alētheia, Unverborgenheit, Wahrheit*), ix, xv, 26, 30, 40–41, 49, 81–88, 90, 95, 97n14, 98n21, 113, 130–31, 133–34, 136–37, 142, 145–46, 150, 152–53, 159–60, 174, 189, 203n25, 209, 243, 245

uncanny (*unheimlich*), 26, 60, 83, 104, 143, 153, 208, 212, 216, 221–22
unconcealment/unconcealed (*Unverborgenheit, unverborgen*), 29, 52, 60, 84–86, 88, 91, 210
universalism/universal/universality, 10, 23, 219–20, 222, 236–37, 245, 248, 250–52
unveil/unveiling, 13–16, 81, 83–85, 91, 94, 112
uprootedness, 73, 74. *See also* rootlessness

veil/veiled, 12–16, 81, 83–84, 91, 94–95, 112. *See also* unveil
violence, xii, 7, 9, 17, 48, 74, 97, 100n43, 107, 116, 129, 131–32, 136
voyage, xvii, 105, 145, 157–59, 161–65

Wallace, David Foster, 178
Watsuji, Tetsurō, 230
"the West", 232
Wittgenstein, Ludwig, xvii, 128, 169–70, 172–73, 175–80
worldlessness/worldless (*weltlos*), 53, 119n47, 215
world/worlding, ix–x, xii, xiv–xviii, 22, 24, 28, 37–39, 41, 45n34, 48–49, 53–54, 58–60, 68–69, 71, 73, 75, 83, 86–91, 95, 104–5, 111–13, 115–16, 127–28, 130–33, 135–37, 158, 161, 163, 169–70, 173–77, 179–80, 186, 190, 192, 196, 200–201, 205–6, 210–11, 213–19, 221–23, 229–38, 242–43, 252, 253n8
Wrathall, Mark, 175
Wynter, Sylvia, xviii, 186–88, 190–95, 200–201, 202n19, 203n25

Zarader, Marlène, 22–23, 27, 33
Zen Buddhism, 230
Zinkernagel, Franz, 5–6, 17

About the Contributors

Benjamin Brewer is a doctoral candidate in philosophy at Emory University. His work interrogates the aesthetic and political implications of ontological relationality, focusing primarily on 19th- and 20th-century European thought and literature. His dissertation investigates Walter Benjamin and Martin Heidegger's attempts to rethink memory in light of the changes in the structure of experience wrought by technological modernity. Focusing on their respective readings of Charles Baudelaire and Friedrich Hölderlin, he argues that their differing concepts of memory in the age of technology should be understood as entangled in their differing ontological and political commitments. He has published essays on Heidegger, Benjamin, Stanley Cavell, F.W.J. Schelling and Jacques Derrida. He is currently working on a book on Heidegger's nationalism and two translation projects – a volume of Heidegger's *Gesamtausgabe* and a selection of Oskar Becker's phenomenological writings.

Luke Carson is an associate professor of English at the University of Victoria, British Columbia. His main area of research is modern and contemporary American poetry. His publications include "'La Plénitude du grand songe': John Ashbery, Rimbaud et l'Inconnu". (in *Parade sauvage: revue d'études rimbaldiennes* 32, 2021); "'The Malady of Ideality': Mallarmé's *Igitur* in John Ashbery's 'Fragment'" (in *Texas Studies in Literature and Language* 59.1, 2017); and "'Render Unto Caesura': Late Ashbery, Hölderlin, and the Tragic" (in *Contemporary Literature* 49.2, 2008).

Luca Di Blasi is a professor of philosophy at the Theological Faculty of the University of Bern, Switzerland and an associate member of the Institute for Cultural Inquiry, Berlin where he leads the project "Disagreement

Between Religions: Epistemology of Religious Conflicts". His main theoretical interests include philosophy of religion, modern continental philosophy, political theology and cultural theory. Major publications include *Dezentrierungen. Beiträge zur Religion der Philosophie im 20. Jahrhundert* (Vienna: Turia+Kant, 2018); *Der weiße Mann. Ein Anti-Manifest* (Bielefeld: transcript, 2013); and *Der Geist in der Revolte. Der Gnostizismus und seine Wiederkehr in der Postmoderne* (Munich: Fink, 2002).

Frederick M. Dolan is a professor of rhetoric, emeritus, at the University of California, Berkeley. His research interests lie in political and moral philosophy, American politics and culture and philosophy of art. His publications include *Allegories of America: Narratives, Metaphysics, Politics* (Ithaca: Cornell University Press, 1994), and some of his other work can be found at https://berkeley.academia.edu/FrederickDolan.

Mauricio González is a research editor at the Max Planck Institute for Legal History and Legal Theory in Frankfurt, Germany. He holds a PhD in comparative literature from Goethe University, Frankfurt and has taught at Los Andes University and the National University in Bogotá. His research interests include the crossroads of critical theory, deconstruction and aesthetics (with an interest in contemporary Latin American literature). He has published a book on improper existence (in Heidegger) and articles on a variety of topics (e.g., theories of the image, the sublime, violence and ethical resistance). Currently, he is preparing a book on time and language in the late Schelling and Kierkegaard. He has translated works of Walter Benjamin, Friedrich Kittler and Werner Hamacher into Spanish.

Florian Grosser teaches in the Visual & Critical Studies Program at California College of the Arts, San Francisco and in the Department of Philosophy at the University of California, Berkeley. His research interests lie in 20th century continental philosophy, political and social philosophy and aesthetics. He is the author of the monographs *Revolution denken. Heidegger und das Politische 1919-1969* (Munich: C.H. Beck, 2011; 2nd edition 2020) and *Theorien der Revolution* (Hamburg: Junius, 2013; revised 2nd edition 2018). His articles have appeared in journals such as *European Journal of Philosophy*, *Philosophisches Jahrbuch* and *Social Philosophy Today*. His research has been supported by inter alia, the Alexander von Humboldt Foundation and the Ludwig Maximilian University-UC Berkeley Research in the Humanities Program.

Julia A. Ireland is an associate professor of philosophy at Whitman College in Walla Walla, Washington. She specialises in European philosophy, with an emphasis on 19th- and 20th-century German philosophy, comparative literature and ancient Greek philosophy. She has published numerous articles on Heidegger and Hölderlin and on Heidegger's politics. Together with William McNeill, she is co-translator of Heidegger's three Hölderlin lecture courses. Currently, she is completing two books on Heidegger – one on Heidegger's relationship to Hölderlin, and the other on Heidegger's politics during National Socialism. Her research has been supported by grants from the National Endowment for the Humanities, the Alexander von Humboldt Foundation and the Fulbright Foundation.

Yohei Kageyama is an associate professor of philosophy at Kwansei Gakuin University, Japan. He specialises in phenomenology, especially Heidegger, and modern Japanese philosophy, especially the Kyoto School. He is also interested in comparative philosophy and works on bringing Spanish thinkers (Ortega and Unamuno) into conversation with German and Japanese philosophers. Currently, his work aims at reconceiving the concept of humanity after the challenge of post-modernism in a way that responds to contemporary "border studies". He received a scholarship of the German Academic Exchange Service and an award by the Japanese Society for Phenomenology in 2012. He has published the monograph *Event and Self-Transformation: The Problem of Selfhood in the Structure and Genesis of Heidegger's Philosophy* (Tokyo: Sobunsha, 2015, in Japanese). His main articles include "The Problem of the World in Kitaro Nishida and his Relation to Phenomenology" (Tübingen: Mohr Siebeck, 2020, in German) and "Language as Phenomenon in Heidegger and Henry" (*Michel Henry Studies*, 2016, in Japanese).

Elad Lapidot is a professor for philosophy and Talmud at the University of Bern, Switzerland. He is regularly teaching at the Humboldt Universität, Freie Univeristät, Universität der Künste, Selma Stern Center for Jewish Studies, Touro College, and Zacharias Frankel College in Berlin. His work is focused on contemporary, mainly continental philosophy and rabbinic thought; it is guided by questions concerning the relation between epistemology and politics. Among his publications are *Heidegger and Jewish Thought: Difficult Others,* edited with M. Brumlik (London/New York: Rowman & Littlefield, 2018); a translation into Hebrew, with introduction and commentary (with R. Bar), of G.W.F. Hegel, *Phänomenologie des Geistes*, Vol. 1 (Tel Aviv: Resling Publishing, 2020); *Jews Out of the Question: A Critique of Anti-Anti-Semitism* (Albany: SUNY Press, 2020); and *Être sans mot dire: La logique de 'Sein und Zeit'* (Bucarest: Zeta Books, 2010).

Jeff Love is a research professor of German and Russian at Clemson University. He is the author of *The Black Circle: A Life of Alexandre Kojève*

(New York: Columbia University Press, 2018), *Tolstoy: A Guide for the Perplexed* (London/New York: Continuum, 2008), and *The Overcoming of History in* War and Peace (Leiden: Brill, 2004). He has also published a translation of Alexandre Kojève's *Atheism* (New York: Columbia University Press, 2018), an annotated translation (with Johannes Schmidt) of F.W.J. Schelling's *Philosophical Investigations into the Essence of Human Freedom* (Albany: SUNY Press, 2006), a co-edited volume, *Nietzsche and Dostoevsky: Philosophy, Morality, Tragedy* (Evanston: Northwestern University Press, 2016), and an edited volume, *Heidegger in Russia and Eastern Europe* (London/New York: Rowman & Littlefield International, 2017). His most recent work is a translation of António Lobo Antunes's novel *Until Stones Become Lighter than Water* (New Haven: Yale University Press, 2019).

Ronald Mendoza-de Jesús is an assistant professor in the Departments of Latin American and Iberian Cultures and Comparative Literature at the University of Southern California. He is currently working on two book projects. The first one, *Reading Danger: The Catastrophic Modernity of Julia de Burgos*, turns to deconstruction and critical theory to develop a notion of literary events that amplifies the danger they pose to any reader seeking to turn the (literary) past into the medium for the constitution of their ipseity. The book centers the figure of Julia de Burgos – Puerto Rico's most iconic modern author – with the goal of removing her from the monumental and mythologising reading protocols that have determined her reception so as to be able to read her historical inscription within the constellation of Puerto Rican modernity. His second book project, *Unworldly Islands: Poetics of Dispossession and the Afterlife of Sovereignty in Caribbean Life*, explores a Caribbean literary and philosophical archive in order to show how the desire for sovereignty is paradoxically at the source of the forms of un-freedom and abjection that still mire the postcolonial Caribbean. His essays on deconstruction and Caribbean literature have appeared in *Diacritics*, *New Centennial Review*, *CENTRO Journal*, *Oxford Literary Review*, *Mosaic*, *Política común*, and *Revista Pléyade*.

Tim Personn teaches contemporary literature, American fiction and rhetoric and composition at the University of Victoria, British Columbia. He is a Vanier scholar, a Fulbright alumnus, and a former fellow at the Centre for the Study of Religion and Society in Victoria. He holds a PhD in English-CSPT (Cultural, Social and Political Thought) from the University of Victoria. His dissertation focused on the intersection of philosophy and literature in a group of contemporary Anglo-American novelists around David Foster Wallace. He is the translator of Harald R. Wohlrapp's *The Concept of Argument: A*

Philosophical Foundation (New York: Springer, 2014). His research interests include aesthetics, postmodernism (theory & fiction), neoliberalism and the relationship of contemporary fiction to philosophy of language and religion.

Nassima Sahraoui is a researcher based in Germany. Her areas of research are in political theory, history of philosophy and philosophy of history, intersections between literature and philosophy, materialism and metaphysics, critical theory and deconstruction. Currently, she is publishing a book, *Dynamis. Eine materialistische Philosophie der Differenz* (Bielefeld: Transcript, forthcoming). She is also completing a book project entitled *Forms of Resistance*. Her publications include essays on Derrida, Benjamin, Heidegger, democracy, messianism, labour and otium, and the relation between philology and philosophy. She co-edited an anthology on the concept of idleness *Kleine Philosopie der Faulheit* (Frankfurt: FTB, 2012), a special edition of the *Oxford Literary Review*, "The Present of Deconstruction" (Edinburgh: Edinburgh UP, 2014), as well as the volume *Thinking in Constellations: Walter Benjamin in the Humanities* (Newcastle upon Tyne: Cambridge Scholars Publishing, 2018). She is co-organiser of two international workshop series: one on Walter Benjamin's philosophy and the other on the notion of violence. In 2019, she joined the newly founded "Women in Theory" network and since 2021 she is a member of the network "New Voices on Women in the History of Philosophy" at the Center for the History of Women Philosophers and Scientists. Apart from her work as an academic scholar, she also works as translator, editor, teacher and moderator.

Simone Stirner is an assistant professor of German Studies at Vanderbilt University. Her research focuses on modern and contemporary German literature in dialogue with Hebrew and French language traditions, with particular interests in poetry and poetics, memory studies and critical theory. Her writing has been published in *New Literary History* and *Qui Parle*.

Dieter Thomä is professor of philosophy at the University of St. Gallen. His research interests are in social philosophy, ethics, cultural philosophy, political philosophy and phenomenology. His main publications include *Troublemakers: A Philosophy of Puer Robustus* (New York: Polity, 2019) and *Heidegger-Handbuch* (editor; Stuttgart: Metzler, 2003, revised 2nd edition 2013). He was a fellow at the Getty Research Institute in Los Angeles (2002–03), the Max Weber Center in Erfurt (2007–08), the Wissenschaftskolleg in Berlin (2009–10), and the Institute for Advanced Study in Princeton (2018–19). In 1996, he won the Prize for Essayism at the international Joseph-Roth competition.

www.ingramcontent.com/pod-product-compliance
Lightning Source LLC
Chambersburg PA
CBHW021847300426
44115CB00005B/44